Limiting Oil Imports

An Economic History and Analysis

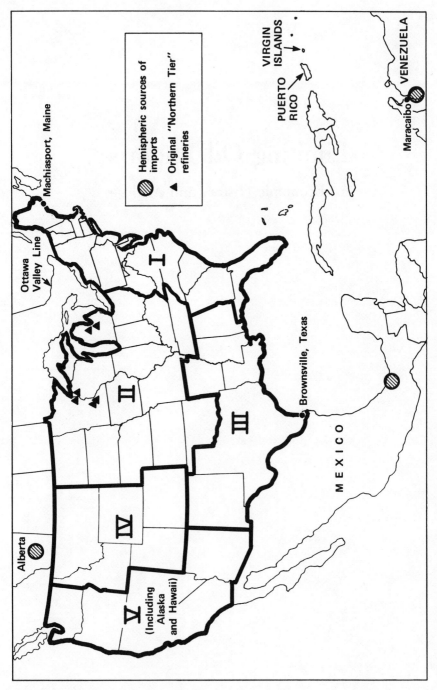

Petroleum Administration for Defense Districts

Limiting Oil Imports

An Economic History and Analysis

Douglas R. Bohi and Milton Russell

Published for Resources for the Future
by The Johns Hopkins University Press
Baltimore and London

Library of Congress Catalog Card Number 77-18881

ISBN 0-8018-2106-1

Library of Congress Cataloging in Publication Data will be found
on the last printed page of this book.

Contents

Tables

Figures

Foreword

It has long been a convention at RFF that division directors have the privilege of prefacing publications emanating from their program with a few words that set the study in context.

In the case at hand, this responsibility is discharged easily and with pleasure. With one exception. Releasing the study brings back memories of the first set of investigators, Paul Homan and Wallace Lovejoy, who died in 1969 and 1970, respectively: Paul at the end of a long and rewarding professional life that included the vice presidency of the American Economic Association and Wally in the midst of a highly promising career as an energy economist, when that designation was still a relative rarity. Both combined an uncommon sense of the intricacies of energy economics with a flair for clear prose.

Initiated in 1964, the project was temporarily abandoned, until two professors at Southern Illinois University, Douglas R. Bohi and Milton Russell, resumed the research. They bring to the subject a special expertise. Bohi has served as a consultant on international economic policy for the Office of Management and Budget as well as congressional committees. Russell was senior staff economist for energy with the Council of Economic Advisers from 1974 to 1976—years of intense debate on energy policy.

The study, as its title suggests, is both a history of U.S. oil import regulations and an analysis of their economic implications. It contains the more important regulations, from the earliest attempts of the Eisenhower administration to the present, and examines both their rationale and their effects. It will stand as a reference book for those who wish to inform themselves of the past attempts to manage oil imports. In addition, it examines policies that were not tried and attempts to judge their relative effects and merits. Thus the book also will serve those who look ahead rather than backward. By combining history with economic analysis, the authors have put theoretical muscle on historical bones, or, from a reverse point of view, illuminated theoretical analysis with statistics, legislative events, and politics. In the process they have produced a long book. Fortunately, its structure is sufficiently crisp to enable readers with different interests to go to those segments that interest them most. Among the increasing flood of energy books, it is my guess that this one will constitute one of those volumes that reviewers suggest be on everyone's shelf as a basic source, not necessarily to be read from first to last page, as a novel, but selectively, as issues arise.

Thanks are due not only to the authors but also to my friend and colleague, Sam Schurr, who initiated the project when he headed the Energy and Minerals Division of RFF and with whom I now jointly direct work in energy and materials. The bulk of the funds came from RFF, but beginning in 1974 the National Science Foundation allowed us to use funds granted for energy research at RFF to sharpen the forward-looking aspect of the study. It was, above all, the lively interest taken by Paul Craig, then at NSF and now at the University of California, which made this possible. His contribution and that of NSF are gratefully acknowledged. It remains only to be said that Milton Russell has since joined the staff of RFF, and to the extent that the book has been a factor in this event it is a particular pleasure to send it on its way.

April 1978   Hans H. Landsberg
                                        Co-Director
                                        Center for Energy Policy Research

Preface
and Acknowledgments

This book presents the results of the third phase of our analysis of U.S. oil imports in relation to U.S. energy policy. Our research began with a grant from Resources for the Future in early 1973. Shortly after the effort started, the quota program was eliminated in favor of a system of import fees; a few months later the petroleum world was turned upside down by the Arab embargo and the subsequent dramatic rise in the price of oil.

As it evolved in response to these events, our research considered three overlapping questions. The first was how the U.S. energy situation, especially energy security, was affected by what was going on in the rest of the world. The second was the more narrow issue of what energy security options appeared available to the United States from the perspective of the special conditions which existed during 1974–75. The third question, the subject of this book, and the one with which we initially began, was what lessons might be learned from earlier efforts to limit imports, especially through the Mandatory Oil Import Program.

Much of our work on the first question was presented in 1974 in a report entitled "Oil Imports and Energy Security: An Analysis of the Current Situation and Future Prospects," prepared for the Ad Hoc Subcommittee on Domestic and International Monetary Aspects of Energy and Natural Resource Pricing of the House Committee on Banking, Currency and Housing. This subcommittee, under the chairmanship of Congressman Thomas M. Rees, provided financial support for that study. Nancy McCarthy Snyder joined the authors in preparing this report. It traced the development of the international and domestic energy markets, examined the effects of the 1973–74 shortage, analyzed the prospects for energy prices and further supply interruptions, and suggested some implications for U.S. policy.

Building further on this analysis, we completed *U.S. Energy Policy: Alternatives for Security* in 1975. It was published by RFF. This book addressed directly the question of what the United States might do to lessen the risks to prosperity and peace brought by the 1973–74 change in the world oil situation. While the writing of this volume was supported by RFF, the National Science Foundation joined with RFF to sponsor a seminar to discuss its findings, and provided funds to assist the authors with revisions and in integrating the discussions of that seminar into our overall study of oil import policy.

The present volume examines in detail the oil import control experience and its implications for energy policy development; like the earlier two works, it stands on its own. Taken together, these companion volumes cover our history and analysis of U.S. oil security policy in an international context, especially as it relates to import controls.

We had three purposes in writing this volume. First, we sought to provide a history of U.S. efforts to limit oil imports so that the reader could see the main thrusts of policy. Second, we wanted to analyze the mandatory quota program and alternatives to it so that the reader could understand the costs and benefits associated with past efforts to limit oil imports. And, finally, we wanted to improve future choices regarding oil import policy.

There are several important studies of the Mandatory Oil Import Program—particularly those by Burrows and Domenich, Dam, and the Cabinet Task Force on Oil Import Control. Unlike those works, however, this book covers the entire period of controls, both voluntary and mandatory, and carries the record beyond the formal import control period to examine the way other policies affected imports. The emphasis here is on analysis, and in this analytical effort we consider the effect of government policies and decisions on developments in the energy industries, and how these developments affect policy and the broader economy. We therefore concentrate on the public record that reflects the flow of these events—the ones important to our concerns.

The story we tell here begins in the early 1950s, when the volume of imports began to attract concern, and concludes with the passage of the Energy Policy and Conservation Act (EPCA) of December 1975. EPCA did not resolve the oil import issue—indeed we believe oil import control will be a continuing national preoccupation—but it was the climax of energy policy action within the Nixon–Ford administrations. As such, its acceptance serves as a convenient point from which to view the prospects for energy policy under succeeding administrations and congresses.

The mandatory quota program affected all segments of the energy sector, changed the allocation of resources and the distribution of income, and altered the way the petroleum industry developed. Our second major purpose in this book is to show what these effects were, to demonstrate how they were transmitted through the economy, and to evaluate the consequences of the program. In doing the latter, we compared the results of the mandatory quota program with those of alternative policies which might have been chosen to achieve the same energy security results.

While the history and analysis of import controls are of interest and importance in themselves, they also provide insight into policy choices for the future. The quantity of oil imports has been and will probably continue to be the focus of policy attention. The debate over the Carter energy program is progressing as this book is completed. That program emphasizes domestic policies and leaves import levels to be determined as a residual, even though limiting import dependence is a major objective of the program. Should indirect policies not lower imports to the desired level, the question of direct import controls will certainly arise. We believe that our analysis of past experience will be useful in any future debate over the wisdom of limiting imports; it also may illuminate the choice among different instruments in accomplishing that end.

This book has benefited from work done by Paul T. Homan and Wallace F. Lovejoy, who had gathered materials and prepared drafts on some aspects of the quota program before their respective deaths in 1969 and 1970. Their fruitful insights are reflected in the early chapters on the history of the quota program. We wish to acknowledge here the preparatory work they did on this subject.

Financial support for different phases of our study has been provided by Southern Illinois University, the House Committee on Banking, Currency and Housing, the National Science Foundation, and Resources for the Future.

The intellectual content of this book has benefited, of course, from numerous conversations with and comments from our colleagues at Southern Illinois University, the Council of Economic Advisers, Resources for the Future, and the Institute of Economic Geography, Erasmus University, Rotterdam. We wish to express our special appreciation to Robert S. Stillman and Bryan D. Wright who read this manuscript in an early draft and supplied suggestions which resulted in clarification and improvement of the work. M. A. Adelman, James L. Cochrane, Mariano Gurfinkel, William A. Johnson, James W. McKie, and Walter J. Mead reviewed this book in its near-final form; their special knowledge of the energy industry and of some of the developments we examine made their comments especially valuable.

We are grateful for the help of Sally Nishiyama in checking facts and references. Ruth Haas edited this book, as she did our *U.S. Energy Policy,* with unusual care, patience, and efficiency. While many have contributed to this book, the authors bear full responsibility for the evidence we offer, for the conclusions we reach, and for the way in which the results of this work are presented.

The long gestation of this book was matched by the varied institutional settings in which it was written. Consequently, the authors are indebted to numerous persons for clerical, research, and library support. We hope that our appreciation for their help and thoughtfulness was adequately expressed, as we intended it would be, as we went along. At this time we offer a collective "thank you" for the efforts by them that made this book possible.

Finally, we wish to express our appreciation to Sam H. Schurr under whose direction this research began, to Hans H. Landsberg, who provided encouragement through some of its difficult phases and to them both for the support they jointly gave at its completion as Co-Directors of the Center for Energy Policy Research at RFF.

February 1978   Douglas R. Bohi
                                                 Milton Russell

Limiting Oil Imports

An Economic History and Analysis

1

Introduction

Oil import policy over the past quarter century has been subject to a changing world oil market and a shifting role for the United States within it. Through all these changes two policy issues regarding oil imports have been debated: what costs should U.S. consumers and taxpayers be asked to pay for uncertain future benefits from greater energy security, and how are these costs to be distributed. As we demonstrate in the work that follows, the resolution of these issues has taken different forms at different times, but one characteristic is predominant: each decision has been heavily influenced by broad political factors. The evaluation of oil import policy has been an experience in political economy and, as such, cannot be contained within the narrow confines of economic analysis. Neither, of course, can it be viewed solely as a matter of ideology or political power groupings; frequent reference must be made to its impact on resource allocation, income distribution, and market structure.

There was no formal U.S. position on controlling oil imports until 1957, when a voluntary control program was implemented to hold back an anticipated surge in imports. Predictably, the voluntary program foundered as soon as it seriously affected private interests, and the Mandatory Oil Import Program was implemented in 1959. That program came to limit crude oil and petroleum product imports to approximately 12.2 percent of domestic production. It was designed in such a way that its costs were somewhat camouflaged, and its effects could be shifted among interest groups. It was administered with flexibility and political skill.

1

Consequently, the basic elements and structure of this program survived great changes in its economic effects, rationale, and political impact. During its life the quota brought about substantial changes in the structure of petroleum production, refining, and consumption; effects that will far outlive its formal abandonment in 1973.

The mandatory quota program came under increasing attack in the late 1960s on two fronts: it was regarded by oil producers as badly administered because of an increasing number of special quota allocations, both inside and outside the 12.2 percent rule; it was offensive to consumer groups because its cost had become higher, more obvious, and the inefficiences of its discriminatory application were better recognized. A Cabinet Task Force on Oil Import Control was formed in 1969 to study oil import policy and make appropriate recommendations for changes. The task force recommended in 1970 that the quota program be abolished in favor of a less restrictive and more neutral import tariff.

The quota instrument was not abandoned, but quantitative restrictions were eased to allow more imports during the period from 1970 to 1973. Relaxation of controls owed less to a change in import policy than it did to the Nixon administration's willingness to abandon restraint in order to relieve the upward pressure on prices. On April 18, 1973, the mandatory quota program was suspended and a license-fee system was imposed—but at rates which actually lowered the total levy below the previous tariff. Oil imports returned to the formally uncontrolled status that they had known before 1957.

The Arab oil embargo of October 1973 revived general support for a policy of limiting U.S. dependence on imports—or in any event, for a policy which would avoid the vulnerability which had so forcefully been exposed. President Nixon responded with the Project Independence Program, promoted initially as a series of actions which would eliminate U.S. dependence on foreign energy supplies by 1980. It was soon clear that the cost of any such program would be far higher than the public would tolerate, and, moreover, far higher than the present expected value of any benefits it might yield.

Denied easy solutions, the nation agonized over how much energy security it was worth buying, how efficiently it was to be provided, who was going to pay for it, and in what way. The issues were not posed in this way, of course, but in such terms as: demand reduction versus supply enhancement; market decision making versus government allocation; strategic storage and standby emergency preparedness versus "drain America first" or "strength through exhaustion"; and unjust enrichment of energy companies through exploitation of the poor versus subsidization of wasteful energy consumption. While laws were passed, research budgets increased, slogans adopted, international conferences called, solemn declarations signed, and developments in the oil market closely watched, the level of oil imports rose, the ratio of imported oil to domestic oil grew, the proportion of imported oil used in total energy consumption increased, and dependence on those nations which had sought to restrict oil supplies in 1973 was escalated.

The debate regarding energy security is likely to continue for some time. As it progresses, however, inaction means that the course chosen, in effect, is one of increased imports of Arab oil. Oil consumption is rising relative to domestic oil production, a process that will not be reversed until the long-term world transition away from oil and gas is well under way. The debate, in the meantime, will return over and over again to the basic issues of the amount of security that should be purchased, how it is to be acquired, and who is to pay for it.

It is hoped that this volume will improve the quality of that debate and indicate the implications of some of the choices available. It supplies a history and analysis of past oil import policy, including recent attempts to formulate changes in that policy. The bulk of the discussion is directed to the mandatory quota program, which constitutes the only U.S. experience of sufficient duration and effectiveness to be informative. The rationale for the program, its administration and special provisions, and the associated political responses by vested interest groups remain of interest because they are all present in or lie behind current energy policy discussions. Indeed, to some degree the roots of the current energy dilemma can be traced to the program and to the reactions to it. To a remarkable degree, despite the changes in the world oil market, the current situation is the predictable outcome of actions taken and rejected over the twenty or so years before 1973.

Our investigation of U.S. import policy proceeds on two levels: institutional and theoretical. Chapters 2 through 6 provide a detailed institutional history of the mandatory quota program to give readers an idea of how the program evolved and was implemented. The discussion extends beyond the program's end and through the reformulation of energy policy, culminating with the Energy Policy and Conservation Act of December 1975. The theoretical analysis in chapters 7 through 9 identifies and measures the effects of the program on consumers, the domestic industry, and on imports. These measures are used in comparisons with the projected effects of alternative policies that might have been implemented instead of the quota. The institutional and theoretical implications of past import policy are then brought together in chapter 10 in connection with possibilities for future oil policy.

Continuity of Oil Import Policy

The assertion made above regarding the continuity of oil import policy over the past three decades deserves further emphasis, especially since, while the policy thrust has remained the same, the problem has changed. The volume of oil imports has been taken as synonymous with the degree of energy insecurity facing the United States, and energy insecurity, in turn, has been regarded as contrary to the national interest. Consequently, and consistently, the reaction has been to devise and implement schemes for reducing the quantity of imports. Also consistently, the schemes that have been implemented have had, as their basic methodology, the repudiation of market forces as a means to achieve the national security goal. In short, the nation has thought it faced the same import security problem over the past three decades, has believed that this problem has grown worse over time, and has reluctantly recognized that it has failed repeatedly to come to grips with the problem. With equal consistency it has adopted, or thought it should adopt, increasingly Draconian political solutions to the problem.

This is not to say that an energy security problem has not existed. Indeed it has. But it has not always been one that the policies adopted were capable of dealing with. Further, the nature of the problem has changed significantly with changes in domestic and international energy markets. The problem in the first part of this period was to preserve short-term U.S. oil supply flexibility;

import controls or emergency response capability was an appropriate basic policy. The more recent security problem, and one that remains for the future, is fundamentally different—it is to obtain a foreign source of oil at predictable and nonexploitative prices. This goal cannot be met through use of traditional devices—it can only be acomplished through creation of an international order based on the collective interest of nations in economic stability, and the particularized self-interest of oil producers and consumers in using oil efficiently during the transition away from dependence on this fossil fuel. The "energy independence" response of the 1950s is wrong when applied to the problem of the '70s: it would exact exorbitant costs while at the same time placing the United States, and perhaps the world, on an inefficient path for the ultimate move away from oil and gas. Domestic oil and gas would be used too fast, and the oil and gas of the nations with vast reserves of these fuels would be expensively and prematurely replaced by alternate fuels brought on-stream by forced-draft efforts, and perhaps without full recognition of their environmental and other consequences. Nevertheless, U.S. policy has consistently been one of "energy independence," and threatens to remain so in the future.

The thrust of the response to the security issue, however, has changed from time to time. It started with designation of the Naval Petroleum Reserves early in this century. In the mid-1950s, there were first informal efforts to get imports reduced, then formal voluntary programs, then a passively enforced voluntary program. Finally, in 1959, the mandatory quota program was established with active enforcement. That program was eroded over time as its political and economic cost rose with changes in domestic and world oil markets. Its philosophy remained intact, however, and very much a part of the political rhetoric.

The Arab oil embargo of October 1973 reignited concern over energy security and prompted renewed avowals of dedication to the same goal which had motivated energy policy all along—self-sufficiency. While the recognition that energy self-sufficiency was impossible came tardily, it was never part of the rhetoric to accept substantial dependence on foreign oil. Acceptance came implicitly with the actions of Congress, which reflected the wishes of a public that refused to pay the price of implementing self-sufficiency. This choice was reaffirmed with the passage of the Energy Policy and

Conservation Act of 1975 and its acceptance by President Ford. But again, despite the inadequacy of the efforts undertaken, the *policy* of the nation remained unchanged: to promote security through reducing dependence on foreign oil. The nation has been unwilling either to change this policy or to implement it.

The Changing Environment for Oil Policy

The economic and political environment of world oil has changed dramatically over the years since the mandatory quota program and its predecessors were devised. Perhaps the most dramatic change has been the shift in international market control from a cartellike group of private oil companies during the 1950s to a cartellike group of oil-exporting countries during the 1970s. This change has important implications for the security risk attached to oil imports because of the widely different motives of oil companies and exporting governments. Both may share a desire for greater net revenues, but the governments have much more complex cultural and geopolitical motives—and greater freedom to act upon them.

In the past, individual host governments could and did interrupt oil supplies, but there was no organization to coordinate export policy among oil producers. The exporting countries depended upon the oil companies to market their oil; if one country stopped production, supplies were made up from other sources, and there was little effect on consumers. The oil-exporting countries still rely on the oil companies to market the bulk of their oil, but bargaining strength has shifted. Individual companies and consuming countries face, as a matter of OPEC policy, the prospect of attempted selective boycott by several or all exporting countries. In the meantime, the OPEC countries are continuing to develop their own capacity in refining and transporting oil, and more importantly, have begun to develop an open market for oil so that they are no longer dependent on one or a few off-takers. Reliance on the oil companies for downstream facilities may be expected to decline further with time, though for the reasonable future the companies will still be necessary to the oil-exporting countries.

The tensions associated with the Arab–Israeli conflict are much the same now as twenty-five years ago. But the Arab position today is much stronger, both militarily and politically, than before. The change in control of international oil altered the distribution of income and wealth in favor of the Arab countries. They are now in a stronger position to advance their interests. In addition, Arab control over oil resources has forced oil importers to reassess their support of U.S. policy toward Israel. The Arabs now have an effective weapon to use against the United States (or others) for political purposes.

On the other hand, as the oil-exporting countries take their place in the community of influential nations, they begin to accumulate a vested interest in the economic and political institutions that surround that community and bind it together. This has a special significance with respect to future trade and financial relationships with industrialized nations. Oil is a source of economic benefit to the exporting nations only if it can be traded for goods and assets in the industrial countries. This is in contrast to oil as a source of political strength. While the oil exporters gain political strength because they possess a scarce resource which they can *deny* to the rest of the world, they gain and maintain economic strength only so long as they continue to *supply* that resource and keep the rest of the world both prosperous and cooperative. That is to say, as the oil-exporting countries gain influence and strength, they also acquire the necessity to act responsibly. They find, as did the United States after World War II, that strength breeds restraints on freedom of action. As OPEC nations store today's surplus for constructive use tomorrow, they become increasingly dependent on the stability of existing financial institutions for their future welfare.

The vast transfer of wealth to the oil-exporting countries that is now occurring could, indeed, be dissipated in an orgy of wasteful consumption. To their credit, however, the major oil-exporting nations have limited their *nouveau riche* excesses. Some countries have, of course, current productive outlets for the greatly augmented resource flows. The others, for the most part, have at least proclaimed that they intend to use current revenues to raise the permanent income of their peoples. To do so means that they must use oil as the basis for economic growth—a gradual process requiring time to convert current export surpluses into real capital for future use. Wealth not consumed today may be stored for future use by purchasing the assets of other countries. This means that they are dependent on the oil-importing countries to redeem the traded assets on future demand. Dependence of this sort is a new phenomenon to the oil-exporting countries; they have never had surplus wealth before.

The U.S. petroleum situation has also experienced important changes since the late 1950s. In 1959 the United States could choose to reduce import dependence at relatively small opportunity cost by preventing the real price of energy from falling as fast as it otherwise would. Now, reducing import dependence would require a relatively large observed cost because the real price of energy would have to rise even faster than it already has. This shift has come about because the monopsonistic world oil market of the 1950s has been replaced by the monopolistic market of the 1970s, and because domestic production capability and the domestic oil resource base have shrunk relative to domestic consumption. We describe in the body of this work some of the factors that have contributed to the pattern that evolved domestically, but in large measure it was the natural consequence of the usual process of resource exploitation over time. Its apparent suddenness and its "crisis" aspects, however, were the result of policy choices— most importantly, those which reduced the flexibility and responsiveness that we have come to expect when market forces are allowed to allocate resources over time.

The "crisis" in domestic oil supply and demand was magnified by two decades of developments with regard to oil substitutes. The regulation of the field price of natural gas reduced incentives for discovery, increased consumption, and distorted allocation among consumers. The growing demand for gas forced prices sharply higher in nonregulated intrastate markets, which absorbed new supplies. The resultant shortages in natural gas supplies in interstate markets forced consumers to switch to petroleum products, accelerating demand pressure on oil supplies. The coal industry was in poor condition to meet the growing energy demands of the 1970s. A period of secular decline, extended by the low-price policy for natural gas, left the industry with reduced production capacity, inadequate transportation equipment, shortages of skilled man-power, and reduced capacity in essential supporting industries. Just when coal demand may have been expected to grow because of prospective shortages of natural gas, the nation sought to make up for decades of neglect of its environment and brought future levels of coal consumption into question. Moreover, similar over-due environmental concerns threatened to greatly increase the cost or prohibit surface coal mining just as, again overdue, health and safety regulations reduced labor productivity in underground mines. As the final thread in this story, expectations regarding the cost and acceptability of nuclear power were excessively optimistic. This had the double-barreled effect of denying the nation antici-pated nuclear power *and* the lead time and research infrastructure to seek alternatives to it. As a result, there was a shortage of en-ergy supplies, and the residual claimant for the energy demand not supplied by these alternative energy sources was oil, which came from abroad.

The market conditions that led to the price increases of 1973–74 resulted from many separate and unexpected influences that came together at the same time. Not only was energy supply constrained, but there was an unexpectedly high growth in both U.S. and world oil demand. Most importantly, the demand increases were not localized, but general, and promised to be around for some time. The increased oil supply was to be found only in the Middle East, and it could not be obtained from other oil provinces or from other energy sources. The worldwide nature of the energy "crisis" is the first important distinction which must be drawn between 1973 and the situation in earlier years. OPEC was created in 1960 following two years of nominal price declines and several years of real price deterioration. There was a glut of oil in the world's markets that would require years of growing demand to absorb. Inexpensive oil was in the process of replacing coal in many traditional uses. Consequently, there was also surplus coal production capacity. Energy was abundant and therefore cheap. Twenty years ago plans were made in all phases of life that im-plicitly assumed energy would remain cheap and abundant in the future. All such plans and expectations must now be changed; the abrupt switch from monopsonistic to monopolistic pricing has telescoped the time available for adjustment. The organization of the market foreclosed the gradual process of accommodation that would have occurred had prices been free to adjust to shifts in underlying economic factors.

The Security Problem

These changes in the economics and politics of world oil necessarily imply changes in the nature of the U.S. security problem associated with dependence on oil imports. The problem is no longer simply a matter of supply interruption, where the United States may guard inexpensively against a spontaneous embargo or a military interdiction of supplies. Now the United States must also take into account the problems that arise from monopoly price behavior on the part of OPEC, the stability of the cartel in controlling prices in the future, and the methods by which exploitative OPEC action may be constrained.

Oil embargoes, as we have known them so far, have been initiated solely for political purposes. The producing country restricts the supply of oil to persuade consuming countries to alter international political positions. Consumers may either accede to those political demands or suffer the loss of oil or expense of replacing it while exerting counter pressure on the embargoing country. Because an embargo is a political act, it is unlikely to involve all OPEC producers. The cultural, religious, and economic differences among the members of OPEC all but preclude their common agreement on a political issue. Oil is a fungible commodity traded in a world market, and therefore an effort of one or a few producers to embargo selected consumers will be largely ineffective. It is only when the embargo is accompanied by general supply reduction, as it was in 1973–74, or when it is perpetrated by nations which can themselves bring a reduction in overall supply, that its effects are large. It is important to emphasize that prices did not rise after 1973 because of the temporary Arab embargo, but because the growth of demand outpaced the growth of supply before 1973, and because supply was limited afterward.

By its nature, an embargo is a temporary expedient which serves to demonstrate the seriousness of the political disagreement between countries. The short-term nature of an embargo is enforced by the fact that it is costly to both parties, but the cost rises over time for the initiator (as it loses current sales and prospective markets) and falls for the recipient (as it adjusts to altered energy supply patterns).

The appropriate policy response to a potential embargo is different from that to the perceived threat of military interdiction of oil supplies during wartime. In the latter case, the goal is to maintain adequate domestic energy supplies to meet prospective needs. In this sense, in the Cold War atmosphere of the 1950s, import controls to preserve the domestic industry were appropriate. When the perceived problem shifted to one of selective embargo by some oil exporters, the appropriate policy response also shifted—to one which would allow quick adjustment to short-term reductions in supplies. A short-term response is all that is needed because even if the embargo is not lifted, other supply sources can be developed. Emergency storage, domestic standby productive capacity, or preplanned means of reducing demand, among others, offer the type of response required. A further change in response is called for if the expectation is that a supply reduction by one exporter cannot be made up by others. Then, a permanent shift from dependence on petroleum may be required.

The prospect of an embargo also changes the perspective for choice of petroleum sources. The incentive will be to diversify to areas which it is hoped will offer more supply reliability, but also to diversify even among insecure sources. The greater the variety of sources, the less the chance for collusion among these sources, and the less the effect of any partial embargo on total supply. This incentive explains in part the enormous investment undertaken in the past decade in the high-cost North Sea oil provinces.

The temporary nature of an embargo also means that it does not disrupt long-run market prices or expectations regarding them. In the face of a partial embargo, prices will fluctuate as supplies are reallocated, and will rise to the extent that total supply is temporarily reduced, but producers and consumers will not alter their basic expectations about world prices. They will expect prices to return to normal when the embargo ends. An embargo may thus produce self-correcting price effects that will tend to offset the influence of a shortage. Prices will rise with an embargo, but buyers, expecting a return to normalcy, will put off purchases to the extent that inventories will allow. Any purchases moved forward will lessen the impact of the embargo on current prices.

In sharp contrast to an embargo, cartel price behavior is based on economic objectives. Thus, the cartel organization must be forged on economic principles and the actions of the organization must be consistent with the long-term self-interest of each member. Because that interest ultimately rests on the member being made economically better off by belonging to the cartel, cartel behavior is constrained by the imperatives of the marketplace. A cartel may no more act without considering the demand for its product than a domestic monopolist can ignore the demand characteristics for the product it sells. Similarly, the organization must neutralize the forces, both internal and external, that will otherwise destroy it. Internally, that means that compromises on cartel behavior must *at the least* leave each member better off inside the cartel than outside of it. Externally, the cartel must act in such a way that new producers either will be unable to take away markets or else will join in restricting output.

OPEC's cohesiveness is based on economics. It cannot expect to achieve unity on political, religious, or social goals, but it can adopt such rhetoric as is not internally threatening. The popular concept of the "third world" is relevant in this regard. The OPEC countries can proclaim themselves members of the economic underprivileged in a struggle between the haves and have-nots, so long as doing so sets up no conflicts within their own nations. The OPEC countries have been remarkably successful in obtaining the applause of the less developed countries that lack oil even as they exact more tribute from them (in terms of higher prices and lowered world prosperity) than they return in aid. OPEC as a cartel has not, however, been diligent in exporting revolution or proclaiming the right of all the world to share equally in the new oil wealth. The economic goals of some OPEC members may be only intermediate steps toward their own political or military objectives, but the economic goals themselves are alone the province of the OPEC collective.

The oil cartel must include enough of the oil supply to encompass incremental demand at current and prospective prices if it is to control the price of oil. To make controlling that price worth-

while, it must control sufficient additional oil that, even while restraining output sufficiently to hold the price at the desired level, it continues to sell enough so that its net revenue is greater than if it sought no price control at all. Consequently, the greater the proportion of world oil supply controlled, and the broader the willingness and ability to share in output constraint, the less fragile and more worthwhile the cartel becomes to its largest and dominant members. Indeed, they are willing to undertake proportionately greater supply restraint to broaden membership; any cartel influence over marginal members is better than no control at all. But all oil exporters need not belong, nor need all members constrain production equally, in order for the cartel to operate smoothly. As it happens, OPEC nations control sufficient oil to make price control both possible and profitable even for those on whom the bulk of the restraint has fallen. Whether this condition continues will depend upon the magnitudes and directions of changes in the world oil market and upon whether OPEC price changes and the shifts in market shares within OPEC continue to meet the necessary condition for cartel survival *and* reflect "equity" as perceived by the dominant members. At present the former condition appears assured; the second depends upon internal OPEC "statesmanship" or, failing that, upon economic coercion or its threat.

For the consuming nations, then, cartel pricing of oil is a long-term phenomenon. It implies long-term control over supply, thus dominating the short-term control implied by an embargo. It is thus the pricing policy of OPEC to which energy producers and consumers around the world should be giving primary attention. There is no finite time horizon to which its effect can be limited because the world will be subjected to an uncertain price for oil into the indefinite future. The usual policies provide only limited defense against this risk. Diversification among different import sources is irrelevant so long as the cartel controls incremental supplies and thus sets the price for all energy. Increased storage would provide only the flimsiest of buffers against price increases; again, the prospective incremental supply of oil someday would come from OPEC. Restriction of imports to force increased domestic production only replaces high OPEC prices with higher domestic ones—with the further disadvantage of consuming productive resources which would otherwise remain available for use somewhere in the world.

In summary, the changes in oil market conditions and the corresponding changes in the nature of the security problem suggest that the policy option appropriate to the Cold War thinking of the 1950s was not an appropriate response to the fears of a selective embargo of the early 1970s, and certainly is even more inappropriate for concern over exploitative cartel pricing behavior in the future. A new approach to the new energy import problem is required.

Themes and Conclusions
Regarding the Course of Oil Import Policy

A survey of the formulation and administration of public policy toward the oil industry reveals a number of themes that, despite changing circumstances and issues, are repeated again and again. Perhaps the most striking of these is that public policy drifted consistently toward direct government intervention in the process by which energy decisions are made. That course was not chosen lightly. Indeed, there was substantial resistance to expanded intervention—that is, successive administrations were reluctant to use government power to achieve desired goals—but when the choice was forced, the "activist" road was taken. Decisions regarding the supply and demand for oil have been politicized. In this connection, the shifting power of different special interest groups demands attention; it is notable that none of these groups alone, and especially not "big oil," dictated policy throughout this period. Given the "political" component in oil issues, it is understandable that income distribution concerns, not allocational matters, attracted the most attention. Finally, as we note in more detail below, the public attitudes which shaped political possibilities have changed little since the 1950s.

Drift Toward Government Control

The drift toward government control can be explained, perhaps, by the tendency to presume that any situation defined as a problem must have a solution, and that a solution is, *ipso facto*, worth pursuing. The decision that conditions of energy supply were a matter of governmental interest was critical; from that point the drift of policy was inexorable. Efforts to reverse this drift failed in part because at each step the decision was marginal—only a little more control was involved—and the benefits from the entire enterprise appeared substantial. Moreover, some special interests always benefited from each action, while the costs involved were sufficiently hidden and dispersed to prevent effective resistance from forming.

Strikingly, however, this drift toward government control over energy supply and consumption (which, for our purposes, culminated in the Energy Policy and Conservation Act of 1975) occurred despite great shows of reluctance. Import controls, and price controls as well, were imposed by administrations ideologically opposed to them, not by politicians who perceived these acts to be a "good" in themselves. The Eisenhower administration "studied" the oil imports question interminably before even adopting "voluntary" controls, and put on a public face, at least, of surprise and dismay that mandatory controls were later required. The nation, and especially the administration, agonized over the 1973–75 decisions to maintain price controls on oil. Government control of the petroleum industry has been implanted and expanded by those who would not accept the results of a free market in energy, but who were unwilling to embrace the idea of government control. As a result, the nation got centralized decision making and free market rhetoric.

The mandatory quota program appeared to offer general but unmeasurable benefits to all citizens in the form of greater energy security. It clearly provided substantial and tangible, though not readily visible, benefits to some groups, and its costs were largely hidden. Unlike Sherlock Holmes, who was alert to the significance of the nonbarking dog, the consumer failed to notice the nonfalling oil price. It was only when oil prices had to rise if import restraints were to be maintained that the opportunity costs of import controls became politically intolerable. A similar process occurred with price controls on petroleum. The cost of the resulting inefficient resource allocation was spread unobtrusively throughout the economy (though energy resource owners bore an obvious transfer burden), but the lower consumer prices were obvious. The future holds substantially higher imports or energy rationing or greater government expenditures. When those results become obvious, that is, when the opportunity costs always present become more visible, a reversal of the present policy drift will become feasible. However, it is by no means certain that this will occur, as the dogged continuation of natural gas field price controls attests.

Multiple Goals, Complex Instruments

When viewed as a means to achieve energy security, oil import policy was a collection of diverse and loosely articulated instruments. The regulations were cumbersome, awkward, and, in some cases, silly. Far more efficient means existed to achieve greater energy security.

The error in this view, of course, is that the policy goal was not energy security. Indeed, there was no one goal for import policy. Many goals existed; they were subsumed under the security rationale while the policy process labored to fulfill each. The very concept of energy security is murky. A program to enhance it provided, therefore, a convenient "Christmas tree" on which all sorts of special advantages could be attached in sometimes jarring juxtaposition. If the goal of the mandatory quota program is defined as promoting energy security at a minimum cost, it must be judged a failure. It did remain in force from 1959 to 1973, however, and in terms of simple survival power must be judged a success.

One reason for the "success" of the mandatory quota program was that its provisions mollified those groups whose special interests were identified, and failed to alert those groups whose interests were harmed. A roll call of the special interests in energy policy would find most of them the recipient of at least some favored treatment: small refiners, inland refiners, Northern Tier refiners, major oil companies, oil producers, petrochemical companies, northeastern utilities and other identifiable and isolatable consuming interests, deep water terminal operators, Island interests, West Coast consumers, and so forth. The coal interests lost their benefits after the mid-1960s when residual fuel oil imports were relaxed, but by that time, with the emphasis on air quality, there were few markets coal could retain on the basis of slight economic advantage. The major large group which *paid* for the benefits of the greater energy security achieved under oil import controls was the undifferentiated portion of the consuming public. With one possible exception, other identifiable functional groups were either unaffected, or actually made better off.

The "possible exception" is the international operations of major oil companies and, perhaps, those oil companies themselves. The overall restriction on imports lowered their potential market, and its administration forced them to share the already limited market with newcomers. The special provisions further eroded their position. The sliding scale, the petrochemical quota, the Islands program, the resid program, and the overriding fact that traditional importers were required to share the quota with the inland refiners all reduced the advantage of owning overseas production. Virtually every controversy was resolved against the best interests of the original major company importers, a fact with important implications when the political economy of oil is examined. The political power of oil may be great, but based on the record of the mandatory quota program, this power is not found in the international giants of the industry.

This discussion highlights the general proposition that in oil policy it was income distribution issues which dominated. While the import quota program had as its public interest rationale the improvement of energy security, the impetus for its adoption came from those interests directly benefited. A careful analysis of allocations was not performed, or at least not publicized by a public body, until the 1970 report of the Cabinet Task Force. The battle lines over provisions of the controls took on regional, sectoral, and parochial dimensions, not analytical ones.

One lesson from oil import controls is, then, that oil policy was not concerned with achieving a single goal, and hence the criteria for success or failure were not well defined. Consequently, the pattern of shifting goals and conflicting ends can be judged irrational only if irrelevant *ex post* values are superimposed upon the policy process. Oil policy has accommodated the special interests involved, and it has done so while avoiding conflict which might have threatened social stability. In this light, the broader lesson is that the failure to satisfy the criterion of economic efficiency will not prove fatal to a program unless and until that criterion is adopted by substantial groups which find its violation harmful to their interests.

The Executive and Oil Policy

Oil policy has been a constant source of difficulty, frustration, and failure for the Executive Branch. No president has benefited polit- ically from his administration's efforts to deal with the oil issue, and most have suffered. Eisenhower, with great reluctance, was forced into mandatory oil import controls. Kennedy faced extreme pressure from the New England interests and was embarrassed by having to give way to it. Johnson tried to banish import policy from the White House because of sensitivity to charges of manipu- lating it to benefit his parochial Texas interests, at a time he was trying to meld a national consensus. Nixon returned the matter to the Executive Office, where he was soon forced to make a number of no-win decisions. For a time he thought energy security was a candidate for an issue around which the country could be gathered and Watergate forgotten. Ultimately, however, the obvious help- lessness of the government in the face of OPEC and the chaos sur- rounding oil policy-making contributed to the impression that his administration was incompetent to govern. President Ford was wounded by his failure to secure his chosen energy policy. His failure to prevail, coupled with strong words and a grand design, contributed to the image of political ineptness and lack of presi- dential bearing.

Why, it may be asked, did oil policy consistently prove so detri- mental to the political fortunes of a long line of very different chief executives? Primarily, we would suggest, because there was never a national consensus on what that policy should be. The only truly national purpose, energy security, was clouded because of the pervasive suspicion of the oil industry and because this na- tional goal coincided so exactly with certain of its special interests. For the chief executive, then, oil policy was a political disaster. Any action which satisfied a single group inevitably angered many more.

These problems were not so serious for Congress. Congressmen, by the nature of their limited constituencies, could evolve and support positions which led to political benefits to them. The balance of power in the Congress with reference to oil policy shifted over time, but Congress was not beset by the ambivalence that tortured successive administrations.

Continuity and Change in Energy Policy

These are the consistent themes that can be inferred from the record of public policy toward oil and oil imports, despite the superficial appearance of discontinuity and chaos. In a sense, the charge that the nation has not had an energy policy is false. It has not had an oil policy on which all, or in fact any, could agree in its entirety. It has not had an oil policy which met any ideological test. It has not had a policy which achieved any single goal efficiently. But it has had an oil policy which accommodated a range of private interests in a manner which the nation has found satisfactory. We turn now to a discussion of what that policy has been and how it developed.

2

The Beginning of
Oil Import Controls

The role of imported energy and estimates of prospective energy supply reliability have fluctuated in the United States, and this fluctuation has been accompanied by changing views on appropriate policies toward the domestic oil industry and oil imports. The energy "crisis" of the 1970s was preceded by fears five decades earlier that the United States was potentially short of fuel. Even earlier, concern about fuel availability resulted in the creation of the Naval Petroleum Reserves (NPR).[1] The decade following World War I, however, saw escalating domestic discoveries until, by 1923, the United States became a net exporter of petroleum, a position it relinquished during World War II (see table 2-1). Following 1944, net imports began the steady climb maintained through the recent era.

The world petroleum situation was changing, as we can see from table 2-2. Especially noteworthy is the dramatic decline in the relative importance of U.S. production as a percent of the total and the equally dramatic increase in the importance of Middle East oil. While world reserves were rising rapidly, world consumption

[1] In 1909, President Taft reserved 3 million acres of publicly owned petroleum land in California and Wyoming to meet prospective defense needs; there are now four designated National Petroleum Reserves, including one on the Alaskan North Slope. Authority for leasing an NPR under certain circumstances was included in the Mineral Leasing Act of 1920 (41 *Stat.* 444). See M. Murphy Blakely, ed., *Conservation of Oil and Gas: A Legal History* (Chicago, American Bar Association, Section on Mineral Law, 1949).

followed at a slower pace. Consequently, the low-cost production from expanding regions began to find its way into U.S. markets and into markets formerly served by the United States. These changes in the international petroleum market were critical for what followed in U.S. oil import policy.

The Growth of Concern:
1954 to the First Suez Crisis

In 1950, seven major oil companies controlled the world oil market. The so-called "Seven Sisters" included British Petroleum, Royal Dutch–Shell, Mobil, Exxon, Socal, Texaco, and Gulf. A small French stepsister—Compagnie Francaise des Petroles (CFP) —deserves mention but had little influence compared with the big seven. These companies controlled virtually all of the known reserves in the less developed regions of the world and a large share of the reserves in the developed countries. A series of interlocking joint ventures were formed by the Seven Sisters in the concession areas, with the result that production plans were mutually known and agreed upon by all. Production could be programmed to avoid excess supplies and distributed into marketing areas to prevent shifts in individual company shares.

Joint control over production and distribution lessened the temptation of price competition among the companies. It also increased the bargaining power of the oil companies in relation to host governments. The host governments faced unified or single bidders for their concessions. Further, as Iran found out later, even if control over production could be wrested away from the companies, oil could not be marketed without company assistance. The oil companies also controlled the transportation, processing, and marketing facilities.

Because the major international companies were involved in all stages of the production process—exploration, production, transportation, refining, and marketing—there was little or no opportunity for open market pricing of crude and oil products until the final sale for consumption. Instead, there existed only internal accounting prices reflecting the transfer of oil from joint ventures to individual members. Firms had the flexibility to take their profits

Table 2-1. U.S. Production, Imports, Exports, and Demand for Petroleum, 1920–75

(millions of barrels)

Year	Domestic production			Imports		Exports		Net imports[b]	Domestic demand[e]	Net imports ÷ demand
	Crude oil	Nat. gas liquids[a]	Total	Crude oil	Total	Crude oil	Total			
1920	442.9	10.9	453.9	106.2	108.8	9.3	79.6	29.2	483.1	6.04
1921	472.2	12.1	484.2	125.4	128.8	9.6	71.8	57.0	541.2	10.53
1922	557.5	13.7	571.3	127.3	136.0	10.8	74.6	61.4	632.7	9.70
1923	732.4	21.8	754.2	82.0	99.6	17.5	102.2	-2.6	751.6	-0.35
1924	713.9	24.4	738.4	77.8	94.6	18.2	117.5	-22.9	715.5	-3.20
1925	763.7	28.7	792.4	61.8	78.2	13.3	114.2	-36.0	756.4	-4.76
1926	770.9	34.6	805.4	60.4	81.3	15.4	132.3	-51.0	754.4	-6.76
1927	901.1	41.6	942.8	58.4	71.7	15.8	142.0	-70.3	872.5	-8.05
1928	901.5	46.0	947.5	79.8	91.6	19.0	155.3	-63.7	883.8	-7.21
1929	1007.3	56.2	1063.6	78.9	108.7	26.4	163.5	-54.8	1008.8	-5.43
1930	898.0	55.3	953.3	62.1	105.6	23.7	156.9	-51.3	902.0	-5.69
1931	851.1	45.4	896.5	47.2	86.1	25.5	124.7	-38.6	857.9	-4.50
1932	785.2	37.3	822.5	44.7	74.5	27.4	103.5	-29.0	793.5	-3.47
1933	905.6	35.2	940.8	31.9	45.4	36.6	107.0	-61.6	879.2	-7.01
1934	908.1	38.3	946.3	35.6	50.5	41.1	114.8	-64.3	882.0	-7.29
1935	996.6	41.2	1037.8	32.2	52.6	51.4	129.4	-76.8	961.0	-7.99
1936	1099.7	45.3	1145.0	32.3	57.1	50.3	132.4	-75.3	1069.7	-7.04
1937	1279.2	52.0	1331.1	27.5	57.2	67.2	173.3	-116.1	1215.0	-9.56
1938	1214.4	53.1	1267.5	26.4	54.3	77.2	194.1	-139.8	1127.7	-12.40
1939	1265.0	54.1	1319.1	33.1	59.1	72.1	189.5	-130.4	1188.7	-10.98
1940	1353.2	58.9	1412.1	42.7	83.8	51.5	130.5	-46.7	1365.4	-3.42
1941	1402.2	84.3	1486.5	50.6	97.1	33.2	108.8	-11.7	1474.8	-0.79
1942	1386.6	85.7	1472.4	12.3	36.0	33.8	116.9	-80.9	1391.5	-5.81
1943	1505.6	90.1	1595.7	13.8	63.4	41.3	150.0	-86.6	1509.1	-5.74
1944	1677.9	102.4	1780.4	44.8	92.3	34.3	207.6	-115.3	1665.1	-6.93
1945	1713.6	114.9	1828.5	74.3	113.6	33.0	183.0	-69.4	1759.1	-3.95
1946	1733.9	117.8	1851.7	86.1	137.7	42.4	153.1	-15.4	1836.3	-0.84
1947	1857.0	132.9	1989.8	97.5	159.4	46.4	164.5	-5.1	1984.7	-0.26
1948	2020.2	147.1	2167.3	129.1	188.1	39.7	134.7	53.4	2220.7	2.40
1949	1841.9	157.3	1999.2	153.7	235.6	33.1	119.4	116.2	2115.4	5.49

22

Year										
1950	1973.6	182.1	2155.7	177.7	310.3	34.8	111.3	199.0	2354.7	8.49
1951	2247.7	205.0	2452.7	179.1	308.2	28.6	154.0	154.2	2606.9	5.92
1952	2289.8	223.9	2513.7	209.6	348.5	26.7	158.2	190.3	2704.0	7.04
1953	2357.1	239.1	2596.2	236.4	377.5	19.9	146.6	230.9	2827.1	8.17
1954	2315.0	252.6	2567.6	239.5	384.0	13.6	129.7	254.3	2821.9	9.01
1955	2484.4	281.9	2766.3	285.4	455.6	11.6	134.2	321.4	3087.7	10.41
1956	2617.3	293.2	2910.5	341.8	525.6	28.6	157.4	368.2	3278.7	11.23
1957	2616.9	295.2	2912.1	373.2	574.6	50.2	207.2	367.4	3279.5	11.20
1958	2449.0	295.2	2744.2	348.0	620.6	4.3	100.6	520.0	3264.2	15.93
1959	2574.6	321.1	2895.7	352.3	649.6	2.5	77.1	572.5	3468.2	16.51
1960	2574.9	340.4	2915.4	371.6	664.1	3.1	73.9	590.2	3505.6	16.84
1961	2621.8	361.8	2983.6	381.5	699.7	3.2	63.6	636.1	3619.7	17.57
1962	2676.2	372.8	3049.0	411.0	759.8	1.8	61.4	698.4	3747.4	18.63
1963	2752.7	401.0	3153.7	412.7	774.7	1.7	75.9	698.8	3852.5	18.14
1964	2786.8	422.5	3209.3	438.6	826.7	1.4	73.9	752.8	3962.1	19.00
1965	2848.5	441.6	3290.1	452.0	900.8	1.1	68.3	832.5	4122.6	20.19
1966	3027.8	468.7	3496.4	447.1	939.2	1.5	72.4	866.8	4363.2	19.87
1967	3215.7	514.5	3730.3	411.6	926.0	26.5	112.1	813.9	4544.2	17.91
1968	3160.9	707.7	3868.6	472.3	1039.4	1.8	84.5	954.9	4823.5	19.80
1969	3204.0	748.0	3953.0	514.1	1155.6	1.4	84.9	1070.7	5023.7	21.31
1970	3350.7	772.7	4123.4	483.3	1248.1	5.0	94.5	1153.6	5277.0	21.86
1971	3296.6	775.1	4071.7	613.4	1432.9	0.5	81.7	1351.2	5422.9	24.92
1972	3284.3	798.3	4082.5	811.1	1735.3	0.2	81.4	1653.8	5736.3	28.83
1973	3206.0	789.3	3995.3	1184.0	2283.5	0.7	84.4	2199.1	6194.4	35.50
1974	3056.9	761.7	3818.6	1269.2	2230.9	1.1	80.5	2150.4	5969.0	36.03
1975	2922.6	730.0	3652.6	1498.2	2210.3	2.1	76.4	2133.9	5786.5	36.88

Sources: 1920–67: American Petroleum Institute, *Petroleum Facts & Figures*, 1971 ed., pp. 283–288.
1968–75: American Petroleum Institute, *Basic Petroleum Data Book*, sec. VII, table 3, sec. IX, table 2, sec. X, table 1; except crude exports: U.S. Bureau of Mines, Crude Petroleum, Petroleum Products, and Natural Gas Liquids, annual issues 1969–75, table 1.

a Prior to 1968, benzol and other hydrocarbons were included; thus 1968 and later data are not strictly comparable with those of prior years.
b Total imports minus total exports.
c Total domestic production plus net imports.

Table 2-2. Percent of World Petroleum Production by Geographic Areas
for Selected Years, 1925–75

Year	U.S.	Latin America	Middle East	Far East & other Asia	Africa	Rest of world
1925	70.9	15.4	3.1	3.5	0.1	7.0
1929	68.0	16.3	2.7	3.6	0.1	9.3
1933	62.6	14.7	3.6	3.9	0.1	15.1
1938	60.8	15.5	5.7	3.6	0.1	14.3
1950	52.7	18.9	15.9	2.2	0.5	9.8
1955	45.3	17.9	20.0	2.3	0.3	14.2
1960	34.9	18.0	23.9	2.5	1.3	19.4
1965	27.5	15.6	26.7	2.1	6.9	21.3
1966	25.6	14.1	28.8	2.1	8.7	20.7
1967	24.7	13.7	28.1	2.3	8.8	22.4
1968	23.7	13.0	29.3	2.4	10.4	21.2
1969	22.3	12.2	29.9	2.6	12.1	20.9
1970	21.4	11.5	29.8	3.0	13.3	21.0
1971	19.8	10.5	33.9	3.3	11.8	20.7
1972	18.6	9.5	35.7	3.7	11.2	21.3
1973	16.7	9.3	38.4	4.1	10.7	20.8
1974	15.8	8.6	38.9	4.1	9.6	23.0
1975	15.7	8.1	36.8	4.1	9.3	26.0

Sources: 1927–65: Joel Darmstadter, Perry D. Teitelbaum, and Jaroslav G. Polach, Energy in the World Economy: A Statistical Review of Trends in Output, Trade and Consumption since 1927 (Baltimore, Johns Hopkins University Press for Resources for the Future, 1971) pp. 185–220.
1966: International Petroleum Encyclopedia, 1974 (Tulsa, Okla., Petroleum Publishing Co., 1974) pp. 306–308.
1967–75: International Petroleum Encyclopedia, 1976 (Tulsa, Okla., Petroleum Publishing Co., 1976) pp. 300–302.

at whatever stage in the production process was most beneficial, given competition and tax policies. This flexibility, coupled with the absence of competition for concessions, perhaps reduced payments to host countries below a competitive level. Moreover, when the monolith of the Seven Sisters was fractured after mid-1950, and excess supplies began to show up, the host countries shared part of the decline in product prices.

A number of factors combined to undermine the control of the Seven Sisters, but the most important was the entry of newcomers in the prolific Middle Eastern and North African oil regions. Entry was possible because of increasing access to concessions and to consumer markets. The ability to get concessions depended preeminently on the freedom to try. The decline of colonialism opened some areas to negotiations. In addition, the U.S. government insisted on more open dealings and required that independents be permitted into some operations. Finally, host governments opened concessions in new provinces to newcomers in an effort to gain additional sources of revenue.

Many of the newcomers were crude-short U.S. firms anxious to take advantage of higher domestic prices and to expand into foreign markets. Prorationing controls maintained the U.S. price above the world level by restricting domestic production. In addition, U.S. tax laws permitting payments to foreign governments to be subtracted from U.S. taxes made access to foreign crude all the more lucrative. The incentives to enter the international market were there, and downstream outlets for products were consequently created. Outside the United States, several national and private firms developed refining and marketing facilities. The great independent tanker magnates formed the vital transport links, loosening another area of control of the market.

The entry of newcomers bid up the price of concessions, thus alerting host governments to the low returns they were forced to take before. An important lesson had been learned in the bargaining game when dealing with diverse as opposed to unified interests. Furthermore, the entry of newcomers expanded total production, creating a surplus in world markets and eroding world prices. Another lesson would be learned by the host countries and kept for future reference. The major companies responded to the surplus by attempting to reduce production and per barrel payments to host governments. The host governments resisted these moves because their revenues were vitally dependent on continued production and the tax rate. Ultimately, of course, the host governments succeeded in formulating a bond based upon their community of interest.

For the United States, surplus world production and eroding prices meant increased imports (see table 2-1). Efforts to maintain the domestic price by prorationing controls forced domestic producers to cut back on the rate of output. The result was an increase in excess capacity in the United States. The rise of imports and the decline in the rate of capacity utilization in the United States led to increased support among domestic producers for ways to control imports, and the initiatives that were launched received growing public support. The public policy rationale for import restriction was found in military dependence on petroleum. This view held that secure petroleum supplies could only be obtained from a domestic industry. It was sustained and reinforced by memories of the vulnerability of tankers to submarines, even in U.S. coastal trade, during World War II, and the knowledge that petroleum shortages affected both the German and the Japanese war efforts. The untested conclusion was that the only (or the most efficient) way to maintain a secure domestic supply of petroleum was to encourage the buildup of a large domestic industry through the production incentive of a high price protected from foreign competition. The Cold War that began in the late 1940s, the international tensions in the Middle East which led to threatened U.S. intervention against the U.S.S.R. in Iran, the later Iranian oil takeover, the military action in Korea, followed by further potential U.S. intervention in Indochina and, finally, the Suez crisis of 1956, all combined to generate receptivity to national security arguments. It is not surprising that formal actions protecting the domestic petroleum industry from foreign competition have been based from the first on the rationale of military exigency, and have been implemented through application of acts legally based on national defense considerations. While the major sources of the perceived insecurity shifted over time from interdiction of supplies by an adversary in time of war to restriction of output or limitation of access to oil on the part of the exporting countries, national security, broadly defined, has remained the primary drive behind oil import policy. The prospective economic gain to the oil industry from restriction of imports does not explain the broad support import controls received.

By July 1954, sufficient concern over the import problem had arisen to persuade President Eisenhower to establish the Cabinet (Advisory) Committee on Energy Supplies and Resources Policy to study possible policy actions required to maintain and strengthen the U.S. defense posture regarding energy supplies.[2] Before the committee reported, however, the president at a news conference announced his opposition to petroleum quotas at a time when free

[2] The White House Report on Energy Supplies and Resources Policy, February 26, 1955, reprinted in *The Oil Import Question*, A Report on the Relationship of Oil Imports to the National Security by the Cabinet Task Force on Oil Import Control (Washington, GPO, 1970) pp. 163–168.

trade was an important element of administration policy.[3] Nevertheless, the committee report found that oil import control was an important element in national defense, specifically stating that should the ratio of imports to domestic production rise above 1954 levels, security problems would be created for the United States. The committee concluded that this condition would create insufficient incentives for exploration and discovery of new sources of supply and "endanger . . . military and civilian supplies and reserves that are necessary to the national defense." Despite the strong language of the committee report, it concluded that formal mandatory government intervention should be avoided through "voluntary individual action of those who are importing."[4] Table 2-3 provides annual data on crude oil imports by source so that the developing pattern of trade in oil during this crucial period can be followed.

An instrument for measuring and monitoring the flow of imports was established in the Trade Agreements Extension Act of 1955, section 7, subsection (b). This act, which became law on June 21, 1955, required the director of the Office of Defense Mobilization (ODM) to keep the president informed of any situations in which the size of imports might threaten national security. It also authorized increased restrictions on trade in these circumstances.[5] The cabinet committee's judgment that any significant increase of imports relative to domestic production in 1954 would be harmful provided a reference point for those seeking to minimize

---

[3] "We are trying to liberalize trade. . . . I would deplore seeing us going backward." Press conference of February 9, 1955, *Public Papers of the President*, p. 263.

[4] The White House Report on Energy Supplies and Resources Policy, February 29, 1955, reprinted in *The Oil Import Question*, p. 166.

[5] Section 7 of the act established a two-step procedure to increase restrictions on imports: an opinion by the director of ODM that specific imports are threatening to impair the national security, followed by a determination by the president of the facts and appropriate action. This procedure was amended in section 8 of the 1958 Extension Act to authorize the president to take whatever action, for such time deemed necessary to limit imports threatening national security, and to consider certain criteria, such as the impact of imports on domestic production needed for defense and the effect of foreign competition on individual domestic industries, to determine whether any consequent weakening of the economy impairs national security. These provisions were incorporated into section 232 of the Trade Expansion Act of 1962. P.L. 87-794 (1962), 19 U.S.C., para. 1862 (1964).

(thousands of barrels)

Table 2-3. Imports of Crude Oil by Source, 1950–60

Year	Canada	Mexico	Venezuela	Other Western Hemisphere	Middle East	Other	Total
1950	5	9,840	107,726	15,915	40,434	a	173,920
1951	473	12,889	105,857	16,903	37,809	3,543	177,474
1952	1,113	8,344	119,325	16,234	57,223	5,253	207,492
1953	2,650	4,342	116,059	15,290	80,445	14,426	233,212
1954	2,606	5,151	129,737	14,023	77,300	13,828	242,645
1955	16,395	6,159	148,829	9,590	101,419	11,778	294,170
1956	43,227	6,094	177,199	11,443	103,551	13,213	354,727
1957	53,804	3,187	209,049	10,619	85,123	24,427	386,209
1958	30,621	999	191,559	12,025	124,658	23,845	383,707
1959	33,902	229	195,240	13,506	114,834	24,235	381,946
1960	40,866	766	200,528	18,038	111,135	29,513	400,846

Source: U.S. Department of the Interior, Bureau of Mines, *Minerals Yearbook*, 1951, p. 1045; 1953, p. 453; 1955, p. 416; 1957, p. 451; 1959, p. 453; 1961, p. 469.
a Less than 500 barrels.

imports. In late July 1955, twenty-seven senators, primarily from oil- and coal-producing states, wrote the ODM director pointing out that imports for the first 6 months of 1955 had increased significantly over 1954 (11.2 percent rather than 10.34 percent for crude oil; 6.72 percent rather than 6.24 percent for residual fuel oil), and that it was the responsibility of ODM to act to correct the situation.[6]

Partially in response to this and similar pressure, the director of ODM requested oil-importing companies to make available to him statistics on imports for the first 7 months of 1955 and their plans for imports for the next 11. Additionally, he requested a statement of policy on imports from these companies. The Cabinet Fuels Committee also announced that it was going to reconvene to determine if its recommendations for limiting imports were being followed.[7] It was becoming evident that part of the problem was arising from the incipient breakdown of the international petroleum cartel discussed above, which was showing up in increases in imports from firms which were not large importers in 1954.[8]

When Arthur S. Flemming, director of ODM, received the comments of the companies, he concluded that imports had indeed exceeded the levels set by the cabinet committee. He found that there had been a 15 percent increase in crude imports during the first 7 months of 1955 and a 23 percent increase in residual fuel imports, compared with a 5 percent increase in domestic production. One-half of the companies reporting had exceeded the prescribed ratio for crude, and three-fourths for residual oil. Oil imports had reached the point where some action should be taken,

[6] "Imports Cut Asked," Oil and Gas Journal August 8, 1955, p. 76.

[7] Reported in Oil and Gas Journal August 15, 1955, p. 99. The part played by the cabinet committee in the evolution of mandatory controls was diverse, to put it mildly. Its avowed intention was to control imports by any possible nonregulatory plan, to which end it negotiated with the industry, the Congress, the exporting nations such as Venezuela and Canada, and other executive offices. It was to this committee that the House Ways and Means looked for an effective plan for voluntary controls when it held extensive hearings in March 1976 on rewriting the Reciprocal Trade Bill.

[8] See also the discussion in Douglas R. Bohi, Milton Russell, and Nancy McCarthy Snyder, Oil Imports and Energy Security: An Analysis of the Current Situation and Future Prospects, Report of the Ad Hoc Committee on the Domestic and International Monetary Effect of Energy and Other Natural Resource Pricing of the Committee on Banking and Currency, House of Representatives, 93 Cong. 2 sess. (September 1974) chapter II, pp. 39 ff.

the director concluded, but he gave the importing firms an opportunity to arrive at a voluntary program to restrict imports, in order
to avoid direct government controls.[9]

In November 1955, in a presentation to the Cabinet Fuels
Committee, ODM Director Flemming revealed that he had con-
tacted the forty petroleum importing companies and told them
that, on the assumption that Western Hemisphere imports would
not increase substantially, import levels from those sources could
be ignored. A 7 percent reduction in imports of crude oil from
other areas during the last 8 months of 1955 was required, however. This overall reduction would fall solely on imports during
the last 2 months of the year. Imports at the reduced pace of 7 percent below the recent record would bring the industry into compliance with the intent of the law and hence not threaten national
security. He further reported that residual fuel imports had declined sufficiently during 1955 to conform with the public interest.
The ODM again repeated its (and the administration's) preference
for voluntary compliance, but expressed a determination to act
directly if necessary.[10]

As the data in table 2-3 show, the requests made by the ODM
did not lead to lower imports, however much some companies proclaimed their voluntary compliance with efforts to lower dependence on foreign oil. Western Hemisphere petroleum imports did
rise, contrary to Flemming's assumption, and Eastern Hemisphere
petroleum imports rose somewhat rather than fell. Imports from
Canadian sources increased substantially as the western fields in
that country came into production; Canadian exports tripled between the first and fourth quarters of 1955. The effect of imports
on the U.S. industry was perceived to be serious. Imports were
blamed for the prospect of limiting production, even from wells
previously exempt from market demand prorationing. Wells on
prorationing in Texas were restricted to about half of their allowable production, despite growing output limitations in other states
(see table 2-4). Import control began to take on an emotional
dimension previously lacking. Industry spokesmen began to argue
that the national interest, even beyond national defense, was at

[9] Letter from Flemming, reported in *Oil and Gas Journal* September 19, 1955, p. 88.
[10] Letter from Flemming, reported in *Oil and Gas Journal* November 7, 1955, p. 71.

Table 2-4. Annual Average of Monthly Production Allowables for Four
States, 1948–67

(percent of MER per well)

Year	Texas	Louisiana	New Mexico[a]	Oklahoma
1948	100	b	63	c
1949	65	b	61	c
1950	63	b	69	c
1951	76	b	74	c
1952	71	b	68	c
1953	65	90	63	c
1954	53	61	57	c
1955	53	48	57	60
1956	52	42	56	53
1957	47	43	56	52
1958	33	33	49	45
1959	34	34	50	41
1960	28	34	49	35
1961	28	32	49	31
1962	27	32	50	35
1963	28	32	54	31
1964	28	32	54	28
1965	29	33	56	27
1966	34	35	65	38
1967	41	38[d]	74	50

Source: Stephen L. McDonald, *Petroleum Conservation in the United States: An Economic Analysis* (Baltimore, Johns Hopkins University Press for Resources for the Future, 1971) p. 164.

[a] Southeast area only. Normal unit allowables converted to market demand factor based on 70 barrels per day as maximum normal unit allowable.

[b] No fixed allowable schedule.

[c] Comparable data not available.

[d] Not exactly comparable with preceding figures because of the introduction in this year of the new "intermediate zone" allowable schedule, which effectively increased the base to which the market demand factor applied.

stake because "excessive imports were threatening conservation practices and even the political viability of the statutes designed to prevent physical waste."[11]

Committed to voluntary compliance, and at the same time strongly interested in strengthening and placating the domestic petroleum industry, the administration watched import increases with mounting concern and some frustration. Action was finally forced. In mid-May 1956, ODM Director Flemming revealed that yet another study of the import situation was underway. This re-

[11] Editorial: "Imports Are Too High if They Hamper Conservation," *Oil and Gas Journal* April 9, 1956, p. 61.

view of the situation was to determine whether oil importers would be in compliance with the cabinet committee recommendations by September 1. According to information then available, for the period since voluntary restraint was requested, the first half of 1956 would exhibit substantial compliance in residual fuel oil imports; they would only be 5,000 bbl/day above the recommended level. Further, there was a reduction in Middle East imports of 8 percent between November 1955 and April 1956, a satisfactory level of restraint. District V (i.e., Washington, Oregon, California, Nevada, Arizona, Alaska, and Hawaii) imports were removed from further consideration because of the generally satisfactory situation there. Prospects for the second half of the year, however, were not as bright as the early 1956 experience indicated. Imports had risen dramatically after April 1, and plans for accelerated imports were in the offing, especially from Canada and Venezuela, but also from the Middle East.[12]

Response to the Flemming report and the announced new study—which had the effect of side-stepping any immediate effective action—was predictably hostile from both the industry and interested political figures. Producing-state congressmen Frank Ikard of Texas (who later became president of the American Petroleum Institute) and John Jarman of Oklahoma were the leaders of the House attack on Flemming and the ODM decision.[13] Calls for mandatory, if not Draconian, action were tied to the severely depressed state of the domestic industry.

Undoubtedly reacting to a threat of congressional action, and in an effort to again regain the initiative for the Executive Branch, Flemming requested a further reduction of Middle East imports by 4 percent during the third quarter, compared with the first half of 1956.[14] The 4 percent decrease, though small in relation to actual imports during the first 6 months, represented a full 25 percent reduction from what the firms had intended to import during the third quarter. This potential reduction created the most severe strain on voluntary compliance that had been placed on the importing companies. The requested self-denial of economic gain, more-

12 Letter from Flemming, reported in *Oil and Gas Journal* May 21, 1956, p. 140.

13 For instance, see "Disruptive Increases in Imports of Foreign Oil," *Congressional Record* June 12, 1956, pp. 10125–33.

14 Letter from Flemming, reported in *Oil and Gas Journal* July 2, 1956, p. 64.

over, was expected from some of the companies least likely to comply—the firms with new production in the Middle East just coming on-stream.[15] Stressing that the cuts urged were "voluntary," Flemming nonetheless proffered the view that if the cuts took place, it would be unnecessary to conduct the already proposed fall 1956 hearing designed to explore the implementation of mandatory controls. The implication was clear: conform or face punitive action. The response was equally predictable: imports would not be restricted. No mechanism existed to convert the potential collective gain from avoidance of mandatory controls on imports to an incentive for individual companies to make the profit sacrifices entailed. The market structure model implicit in the expectation that voluntary compliance would be forthcoming was one of monopoly or at least reasonably tight oligopoly. That condition had disappeared by 1956, if indeed it had ever existed regarding domestic refiners, and was to be further eroded as access to oil abroad was gained by additional potential oil importers.

Congressional pressure on ODM continued through July, when thirty-one senators formally submitted a letter to its director requesting information and action. Clear warnings of congressional intent to act quickly to create a mandatory program were issued. The estimates of the senate group were that imports were considerably *above* the amounts suggested by ODM, and that restraints must be greater than those announced as anticipated if imports were to be maintained at 1954 proportions.[16]

In the first part of August 1956, nineteen domestic trade associations presented a joint petition under the Trade Act of 1955 formally requesting a restriction on oil imports. In their petition it was noted that in 1954 the rate of oil imports, compared with domestic production (which was to be the criterion for a peril point under both the cabinet committee recommendation and the 1955 Trade Act), was 16.6 percent. In 1955, imports were 18.3 percent of domestic production and in the first 6 months of 1956 imports had risen to 19.5 percent. If import plans were validated for

15 Bohi, Russell, Snyder, *Oil Imports*, pp. 43–49.

16 Senator M. Neely (W.Va.) expounded the senators' point of view on the floor. See *Congressional Record* vol. 102, pp. 15022–24; also *Oil and Gas Journal* August 6, 1956, p. 54. (In instances where documents are not readily available to the general reader, reference is made to convenient sources such as the *Oil and Gas Journal*.)

the second half of 1956, imports would reach 21.7 percent of domestic production. The trade associations urged that some (unspecified) action be taken to limit imports. The petition argued that of all the alternatives available, only one should be foreclosed—the "voluntary" restraints policy which had proven so ineffective.[17]

Despite intense pressures, and with little obvious support from groups other than the importing companies themselves, ODM recommended no mandatory action to restrict imports. Indeed, public pronouncements by Flemming and others in the administration reiterated the intense ideological hostility to government coercion, even though the policy goal of import limitations was supported. Though there was obviously sentiment to do more, ODM again limited itself to requesting lowered imports for the fourth quarter of 1956 on a voluntary basis. The importing firms were told that *total* imports for 1956 (already running far above the standard) should be brought in line with the 1954 standard—with the total restriction to be achieved in the last quarter, an almost obvious impossibility.[18]

In a parallel development on the policy side, the Cabinet Fuels Committee reported in early October that a new basis for determining allowable imports was appropriate. The committee concluded that Middle East imports should not exceed 299,600 bbl/day for 1957, which amounted to only a 1 percent reduction from the level of imports during the first half of 1956. The anticipated 5 percent increase in domestic demand for 1957 would, presumably, keep the ratio of imports to domestic production satisfactory through that year. Hence a minor reduction in imports would suffice, in a growing economy, to protect the domestic petroleum producing industry. The obviously easier task of restraining increases rather than reducing existing levels of imports was thought to be possible through voluntary action. The president took this opportunity to reaffirm his preference for a voluntary program, again for reasons of both ideology and flexibility in administra-

[17] In a petition to Flemming, producers claimed that the "plans of the importing companies show that during the next six months the excess of petroleum imports over the 1954 relations will be greater . . . unless positive action is taken to restrict them," as quoted in *Oil and Gas Journal* August 13, 1956, p. 85.

[18] Letter from Flemming, reported in *Oil and Gas Journal* September 19, 1956, p. 92.

tion. Several exemptions from the new voluntary rules were proposed by the Cabinet Fuels Committee. First, residual fuel oil was not mentioned. Canadian oil, despite its rapidly increasing share of the import market, was not included in the basis for setting allowable imports. Venezuelan oil was similarly excluded, but in a separate action Venezuelan officials "voluntarily" agreed to keep that nation's exports within the original formula, some 405,000 bbl/day. This latter agreement, if acted upon, would have required an absolute decline in imports from Venezuela during 1957, except to District V. District V was again specifically excluded from even voluntary controls. Additionally, importers were again urged to give preference to Western Hemisphere fuel sources.[19]

Implementation of the voluntary program on the revised basis required that the "new importer" problem be faced. The growth in imports by these firms, partly due to niches created in the market by limitations on the more visible major firms, made them impossible to ignore even while they were difficult to police on a voluntary basis. Newcomers for the most part were not constrained by the unofficial sanctions that could be imposed on large, multinational, established firms. They were less affected by public or industry opinion. Moreover, some were not involved in domestic production and thus did not even have the incentive to restrain imports that would follow from sharing production losses within the United States if collective restraint on imports failed. Newcomers, then, were in the usual position of the small and unimportant—so long as they could convince others that they could not be deflected from behaving in their own self-interest, room would have to be made for them. If the overall import levels consistent with the relaxed guidelines of the revised Cabinet Fuels Committee were to be honored, firms which had previously been importing within their limits would be forced to restrict their imports still further. Observers were not sanguine about the prospects that they would, again because there was no agreed-upon mechanism to allocate collective responsibility. As newcomers gained access to greater quantities of importable oil, a shift could be discerned in the in-

[19] Executive Office of the President, Office of Defense Mobilization, press release, October 17, 1956; also *Oil and Gas Journal* October 29, 1956, pp. 122–125.

terest of established multinational firms. Given the politically disadvantaged position of the visible large firm in a voluntary system, it is clear that its future well-being might best lie in action to
scuttle the voluntary program in exchange for a mandatory program under which fairer allocations might be anticipated. In a
formal program, visibility and size, and with it regulatory expertise
and political influence (which were handicaps under voluntary
controls), might become a means of getting higher levels of access
to markets. As we shall discuss below, there were also reasons
for the major firms to support mandatory import controls because
such controls would also tend to restrict entry of new firms into
the international oil market.

The flurry of activity surrounding the future of voluntary controls culminated in late October 1956, with ODM hearings requested by nineteen domestic trade associations (as required by the
1955 Trade Act). Broad issues were opened to scrutiny. A recurrent theme, one of particular concern to the domestic industry,
was that the creation of exempt categories, as in the Cabinet Fuels
Committee recommendations, had provided precedent for still
wider exemptions in the future. As hearing witnesses pressed the
Legislative Branch's case against the Executive, congressmen re-
counted the legislative history of the oil protective clause in the
Trade Agreements Act of 1955. They stated that there was no intent to exclude from import restraint such categories as residual
fuel oil, Canadian or Venezuelan oil, or shipments to District V.
Domestic producer groups asserted that the observed reduction of
exploration and development was associated with growing imports.
Importers, on the other hand, pointed out the lower delivered
costs and consequent national economic benefits from foreign oil;
they noted that competitive pressure on petroleum-based products,
both national and international, required minimum cost fuel inputs. Traditional importers argued that their established market
relations were being threatened by newcomers. On the other hand,
refiners without access to foreign oil argued that they would suffer
destructive disadvantages without imports of foreign crude on an
equitable basis.[20] Developments in the Middle East made these de-

20 Ibid.

liberations appear irrelevant, however, as concern turned from an
oil surplus to a prospective shortage. The positions taken during
these hearings became timely again only after resolution of the
Suez controversy.

Oil Import Policy and the Suez Crisis

The Suez crisis of 1956 dramatically altered the situation of world
oil. The Egyptians blocked the Suez Canal with sunken ships.
The result was that for the period of hostilities and for several
months thereafter, oil from the Persian Gulf could reach western
markets only by way of the long, slow, and expensive journey
around Africa. Diversion of the oil flow increased shipping costs,
created significant refueling and refining demands on inadequate
South African port facilities, and halved the crude carrying capacity of the world's tanker fleet because of the longer journey. The
Suez crisis led to other fuel flow disruptions as well. Other Middle
Eastern countries took direct action against further shipments to
the British and French. Pipelines were destroyed; embargoes on
shipments to Britain and France were instituted; and production
of firms owned by British and French nationals was hampered.

The Suez crisis had supply and demand effects on the U.S. industry and both served to abate the immediate demand that import controls be implemented. U.S. refineries were cut off from
much of the 300,000 bbl/day they had been importing, and other
countries (primarily Venezuela) that had been supplying oil to the
United States were called upon to meet European demands. While
the bottleneck in supplying oil to consuming markets was at first
the shipping facilities, it was soon evident that without the full
flow of Middle Eastern supplies to market, additional producing
capacity and higher rates of reserve utilization elsewhere would be
required. The U.S. industry was in an excess stock position at the
time of the crisis, and this lessened the supply disruptions' immediate effect on consumers.

Industry planning in the face of the oil emergency was hampered by two uncertainties. The first of these was how long the
closure would last. A short closure of the Suez Canal, along with

an early reopening of Middle Eastern production and pipeline facilities, would exacerbate excess supply problems if a major effort were undertaken to reestablish high levels of capacity utilization in the depressed U.S. market. On the other hand, an exceptional marketing opportunity would be lost if Middle East output were closed in for a long time and U.S. industry failed to respond. The second uncertainty was compounded by confusion regarding the position of the U.S. government. The Eisenhower administration strongly condemned Britain and France for their actions against the Egyptians. Did this condemnation extend, however, to refusal to facilitate the supply of fuel for those countries through financial and operational assistance? Without such direct signals as exemption from antitrust prosecution for cooperating firms' pooling efforts, the effectiveness of the fuel supply activities of American firms would be reduced. Government action to increase the tanker fleet through demothballing and through facilitation of more efficient scheduling answered some industry doubts on this issue.

The U.S. industry response to the Suez crisis was important as an indication of its flexibility and of the level of excess capacity. The demand for U.S. crude oil immediately rose both domestically and abroad. Actual deliveries were hindered somewhat, however, by the lack of adequate transport facilities to provide all producing areas with equal access to markets. The most important conflict over how to handle the increased demand focused on Texas, where most of the excess capacity existed. West Texas and New Mexico crude, for example, was unable to get to tidewater markets. Pipeline facilities had been developed to meet only the requirements of traditional prorated production levels, not full-flow output. Because allowables were set at a level where all producers could bring an equal proportion of potential output to market, the result was output limitations at coastal sites even though export markets went unserved. Producers that did have access to markets, supported by consumer interests, called for geographically split allowables which would free producers to sell all they could, while those without adequate access to markets would have their allowables restricted in order to allocate available throughput capacity. This proposal was opposed by the producing interests without outlets, who concluded that transport facilities would be brought on-stream if supply pressures were sufficient. Indeed, some action of this sort did occur; pipeline flows were reversed and new transport channels for West Texas crude opened. The Texas Railroad Commission (TRC), through its actions and through the comments of its leader and chairman, General Ernest O. Thompson, took the side of the producers without access to markets. The view of the TRC was that the Suez closure provided an opportunity to bring industry stocks into balance with prospective demand and to rectify the excess supply problem which had been building for some time. As is to be expected, the crisis over Suez firmed prices and brought about a desired reduction in stocks.

Continued blockage of the canal brought some increases in prices of Venezuelan crude and brought an immediate jump in sales from the U.S. Gulf Coast. By the end of November 1956, the additional sales from the United States had reached almost 600,000 bbl/day, about three-fourths of which were going to Europe and one-fourth to the East Coast to make up for interrupted imports. Later reports put the expected additional shipments at up to 850,000 bbl/day.[21]

The large increase in demand for exports made it possible for the domestic industry to work off its surpluses of crude and heavy fuel oils, but left excessive stocks of gasoline and other products. Had all demands been met, in fact, the higher sales may have increased some of these surpluses because of the relatively fixed proportions in refinery output and because of the equity requirements of market demand prorationing in the face of transportation bottlenecks and nonhomogeneity of crude.

The Middle East crisis, and the industry response to it, opened conflict between the domestic independent segment of the industry and the international majors. The focus of the controversy was on the Middle East Emergency Committee (MEEC), organized to coordinate supplies for Europe. Justice Department representatives met with the MEEC to monitor potential anticompetitive behavior, but their presence did not prevent suspicion from being expressed about possible manipulation of the shortages. The Inde-

---

[21] Bureau of Mines, *Minerals Yearbook,* 1957, pp. 348–349, shows overall stocks declining by 104 million barrels over November to March, which exceeds the normal winter decline by 54 million barrels. Total exports over these same months were about 70 million barrels above normal. As one might expect, stock levels rose to record highs after reopening of the Suez Canal.

pendent Petroleum Association of America (IPAA) stated that the majors continued to import too much, and did not "allow" sufficient increases in domestic production to meet the crisis. It was in the major international oil companies' interest, of course, to minimize the role of the domestic industry in meeting U.S. and European oil needs. To allow new firms into these markets during the crisis would threaten control over those same markets for the future. Additionally, to provide lucrative markets for excess capacity during the crisis would make the loss of those markets all the more painful when normal trade channels opened, and make restriction on imports more difficult to resist. The IPAA hence charged that, for their own purposes, the international majors sought to place the blame for inadequate supplies on tankers and port facilities, not on the real bottleneck, available crude supplies.[22]

By the end of March a further change in conditions was evident. The TRC cut allowables back to 15 days a month for April amid reports that the European markets no longer needed additional crude or products and that stocks were rising beyond desired levels.[23] All Suez had meant was 2 months of higher production, some drawdown of excess stocks, and some firming of petroleum prices. The canal was restored to some usefulness by early April, and by mid-April oil was moving and the U.S. government removed its support for MEEC.[24]

In the face of the turnaround from rising imports to substantial net exports, ODM Director Flemming had stated in December 1956 that imposition of further import controls would be held in abeyance until the end of the emergency, even though pre-Suez crisis plans for 1957 imports would have triggered section 7 of the Trade Agreements Act.[25] In his view, had these plans materialized, the quantity of oil imports would have threatened national security. Flemming's statement signaled the end of the "laissez-faire with bombast" policy and its replacement by administration resolve not to let imports rise to their previously predicted levels. It

[22] "Seaton Says Europe Gets More Oil Than Promised," *Oil and Gas Journal* February 18, 1957, pp. 102–103.

[23] April allowables were reduced from an all-time record high in March; see *Oil and Gas Journal* March 25, 1957, p. 101.

[24] "Oil Lift Suspended," *Oil and Gas Journal* April 22, 1957, p. 89.

[25] Executive Office of the President, Office of Defense Mobilization, press release, December 4, 1956.

was evident by late winter of 1957 that action would be required to implement this resolve.

The import question, never totally forgotten, surfaced at the end of February 1957 when data on 1956 imports became available. Oil imports amounted to approximately 350,000,000 barrels in 1956, despite the disruptions occasioned by the Suez closedown. These imports were 11.77 percent of U.S. crude oil demand, compared with 10.68 percent in 1955, 9.54 percent in 1954, 9.12 percent in 1953, and 8.41 percent in 1952. Imports for all of 1957 were expected to approach those for 1956, even if Persian Gulf oil did not flow unhindered until the third quarter. Given these prospects, in early March ODM notified importers that a filing of import intent for the 6 months following the reopening of Suez was required so that surveillance could be maintained.[26]

The Suez emergency gave rise to considerable study of the imports program in a new context. In general, the event strengthened the hand of procontrol forces. First, the temporary spurt in U.S. demand increased the domestic production base and made explicit the economic loss domestic firms experienced from imports. The desirability of surplus domestic output capacity was underscored, but it became obvious that the security thus bought had come almost exclusively at the cost of the well-being of the domestic industry. Second, the vulnerability of foreign oil supplies lent validity to attempts to improve national security by strengthening the domestic production base. It was easier to defend deterrence of low-cost imports as being in the "national interest." Controls became more impervious to criticism from both foreign exporting countries and from consumer spokesmen.

The Impetus for Controls

Serious consideration of implementing import controls was finally started in mid-April 1957 when the new director of ODM, Gordon Gray, certified to President Eisenhower that he had reason to believe the level of imports threatened to impair national security.[27]

[26] Executive Office of the President, Office of Defense Mobilization, press release, March 6, 1957.

[27] Executive Office of the President, Office of Defense Mobilization, "Memorandum for the President: Gordon Gray, Director," April 23, 1957.

Gray based this conclusion on the import plans reported by some sixty importing companies. Altogether they estimated their imports for the last half of 1957 at 1,261,000 bbl/day, or 17.4 percent of estimated domestic production, 500,000 bbl/day above the level which would fulfill the earlier goal of a 1954 imports/production ratio. The administration, even after Gray's announcement, appeared to be seeking some means of avoiding voluntary controls, and certainly a mandatory program. Eisenhower announced an independent study commission but it never got off the ground. Meanwhile, political pressure, indicated in part by the flood of proposed bills in Congress, continued to mount. Finally, with an anticipated increase in imports from May to July alone of 236,400 bbl/day, mostly from the Middle East, with further increases in imports anticipated for the last 6 months of 1957, and with the decision of the TRC to reduce allowables to 13 days in July, some action became unavoidable. President Eisenhower abandoned the plan for an independent commission and formed a new cabinet committee which first met on June 24, 1957. The committee consisted of the secretaries of Commerce, Defense, Treasury, State, Interior, and Labor.

Controls over imports became inevitable the moment the political pressure to appoint a study group could no longer be resisted. Observers could also have foreseen the inevitability of mandatory controls, given the breakdown in the international company cartel that had in an earlier time been able to share out production for export. The national security argument deterred opposition to controls almost as effectively as the expectation that controls would at worst mean stable rather than falling prices. Price increases were ruled out in the opinion of most analysts because of the world-wide oil glut and the political vulnerability of the oil industry. The cartel was assumed to be capable of assuring that import controls would not raise prices from the historic level, but only "stabilize" them.[28]

---

[28] The failure to focus on the opportunity costs of controls was pervasive during the entire program. The price-stabilizing effects of prorationing had apparently mesmerized the public—and the industry as well—into interpreting increases in imports as altering the source of oil, but not its price. In no other way can the special treatment of products, especially residual fuel oil, and of imports into District V, be reconciled with the main thrust of import controls.

The long and varied efforts to move the United States away from the laissez-faire policy toward oil imports which it had followed since the 1920s came to an end with the president's acceptance on July 29, 1957 of the report of the Special Committee to Investigate Crude Oil Imports.[29] While opposed by the Oil Jobbers Association,[30] whose interests would be harmed because the resulting higher prices would restrict its market while limiting competition among suppliers, for most energy groups this step was accepted with apathy, resignation, or glee.

To see why most interests were appeased, before proceeding with a description of the voluntary import control scheme, it is useful to review the various interests involved in the debate and what each may have expected to gain by limiting imports. A fuller analysis of the effects of import controls is given below.

To begin with, the domestic oil industry was constrained by state conservation regulations that focused almost exclusively on maintaining the price of crude oil in the United States. If imports entered the United States at a lower price, the entire market would gravitate toward the lower import price. In order to prevent price deterioration, the state conservation authorities forced domestic producers to reduce output. Domestic producers were understandably distressed at being forced to accommodate foreign oil and argued that imports be limited instead.

Since imports could undersell domestic oil, the implication is that the marginal cost of foreign oil was less than that of domestic. If the U.S. market remained open to competition from abroad, the volume of imported oil would continue to increase and displace higher cost domestic oil until only equally competitive domestic operations remained in the market. How much displacement would take place is a matter of speculation, though some estimates are given in chapter 8. No such estimates were provided during the debate over import controls; instead the argument seemed to

[29] Report to the President of the Special Cabinet Committee to Investigate Crude Oil Imports, reprinted in *The Oil Import Question*, A Report on the Relationship of Oil Imports to the National Security, prepared by the Cabinet Task Force on Oil Import Control (Washington, GPO, 1970) appendix C-2, pp. 181–190.

[30] Letter to the President from Otis Ellis, counsel for National Oil Jobber's Council, reported in *Oil and Gas Journal* July 15, 1957, p. 61.

be that any displacement would be deleterious to national security and should be prevented.

As a practical political matter, however, this extreme position could not be implemented. There were other interests involved that would preclude complete autarky. Within the oil industry there were numerous American firms producing abroad that depended on the U.S. market. There were also domestic refineries built to process imported oil. In addition, if the government were to cut off access to foreign oil, a higher domestic price would be necessary to elicit additional domestic production. This would mean American consumers would have to pay increasingly higher prices for petroleum products than the world price would dictate. The government would be in the uncomfortable position of openly forcing consumers to sacrifice for the benefit of the oil producers. Finally, relations with governments in the exporting countries would be strained by a severe reduction in sales to the United States.

Thus, the government was in the difficult position of balancing diverse interests: protecting domestic industry from foreign competition; avoiding a precipitous increase in oil prices to consumers; and placating those interests already attached to oil imports. As we shall see below, the easiest way to balance these interests was to limit any additional growth of imports. That way, interests already established would continue, no immediate change in prices would be observed, and yet no further inroads in the domestic market would be achieved. The market thus becomes insulated from competition from abroad, meaning that the domestic price may remain above the world price.

The spread between the domestic and foreign price means, in turn, that those who are able to import, either by virtue of their geographical location or because of their historical connection with imports, stand to make a windfall gain because of the scarcity value of imports. Refiners processing imported crude oil have lower average input costs than those processing domestic crude. Because the prices of finished products will tend toward a single level for all refiners, those with the highest proportion of imported feedstocks stand to make the highest profit margins. With the later adoption of mandatory quotas tied to the volume of domestic crude used as feedstocks, the marginal cost of production (as well as the average cost of production) of importing firms would be reduced relative to nonimporting firms, thereby affecting relative competitive positions.

The gains associated with importing cheaper foreign oil created a variety of tensions that plagued the administration of import controls. Those receiving the gains complained when newcomers were permitted to enter the field because the gains would be spread over more firms or because the total gains would be reduced. Those on the outside were anxious to receive a share of the windfall and pressed for participation. Consumer interests complained because they had to pay for the additional benefits received by importers. Finally, the government used the benefit associated with the right to import as an incentive to achieve goals unrelated to the national security goal of maintaining a healthy and viable domestic petroleum industry. These tensions will be described in the following sections as they arose and affected the development and implementation of the import controls.

Implementation of Voluntary Controls

The first phase of the "voluntary" import control program[31] was revealed on July 29, 1957, when President Eisenhower accepted the report of his Special Committee to Investigate Crude Oil Imports, which recommended that national crude oil imports should not exceed 1,031,000 bbl/day (about the pre-Suez level) compared with the 1,266,700 bbl/day planned by importers for the last half of 1957.[32] The plan to implement this goal restricted crude oil imports into Districts I–IV; West Coast imports, residual fuel oil, and other petroleum products were not affected. The rationale for not restricting either West Coast crude oil imports or imports of residual fuel oil was that in each case imports supplemented domestic production but did not displace it. Domestic producers, even at

[31] The controls of the pre-1957 period were voluntary in the sense that firms were urged to restrain imports, but no formal quotas on a firm-by-firm basis, set by government, were implemented. The designation "voluntary control program" is reserved for the period of formal activity beginning in 1957.

[32] Report to the President of the Special Cabinet Committee to Investigate Crude Oil Imports, reprinted in *The Oil Import Question,* appendix C-2, pp. 181–190.

full output, could not saturate these two markets at existing price levels. Imports of petroleum products other than residual fuel oil were not taking place in sufficient volume to affect the domestic market—or at least not enough to require action.

The allowed level of crude oil imports chosen was 12 percent of domestic production. The control proposal, as issued, provided for approximately 756,000 bbl/day of imports into Districts I–IV, not a great deal less than was coming in, but much below planned imports. The report also offered a basis for company-by-company allocations. The seven established importers were to be cut back 10 percent from their average imports of 1954–56. The fifteen small importers were to be allowed imports equal to those reported to ODM in July; these amounts were not much greater than these same firms actually imported for the same period in 1956. Newcomers were to advise the Department of the Interior 6 months before they wished to begin importing. Upon such notification, a determination would be made as to the quantity of imports they would be allowed under the voluntary constraint program, and as to whether those increases would require a further reduction of other importers or could be handled through demand growth.[33] The philosophy adopted was that stated in the report: "New importers should have the opportunity to enter and share in a reasonable manner in the United States market."[34]

With respect to District V, the report recommended that imports should continue to fill the gap between demand and domestic production (at an unspecified price), until the development of an economical means of interregional transportation. Consequently, no voluntary import limitations were proposed at the time. It was expected that District V imports would not exceed 275,000 bbl/day for the last half of 1957, an amount equal to 29.8 percent of expected production in that area.

When the voluntary program was announced, twenty-two known importers were given a quota. After the announcement, however, it was discovered that fourteen additional importers were active in Districts I–IV. These other fourteen were small, and some had no plans to import in 1957. It was decided that imports of these firms could be accommodated without disturbing the quota allocations

---

[33] Ibid., pp. 188–189; also *Federal Register* vol. 22, p. 6804 (August 22, 1957).
[34] *The Oil Import Question*, p. 187.

of the others because the total volume in question would not be significant. Implementation of the control program included a request to the importing firms that they inform the Department of the Interior of their intent to comply with the import limits. All firms replied, and of the twenty-two known importers, fourteen stated unreservedly that they would go along. One firm, Sun Oil, said that it would not comply because its legal counsel foresaw possible antitrust implications in the program. Five companies wanted some adjustment of the actual quotas they received, though agreeing in principle with the program. Some of these did not commit themselves to follow the guidelines as they were issued because they considered their quota allocation inequitable. Tidewater and Atlantic Refining Co. asked for an immediate hearing where they could demonstrate the special problems and conditions which should lead to an upward revision of their quota. Sinclair and Atlantic argued that they were being punished, by the procedure adopted, for their earlier compliance with the requests to limit imports.[35] "Voluntary" compliance with the quota was all the program officially required but, nonetheless, firms realized that precedents were being established that made it worth their while to seek revisions in their allocations under the program. The companies certainly perceived the existence of sanctions, however unofficial, and supported creation of machinery to hear and consider claims of inequity under the program.

Five topics surfaced with President Eisenhower's announcement of the program. These were: industry and public response to the program, appeals and how they would be handled and resolved, the perennial issue of the proper treatment of new importers, the problems imposed by exceptions to controls, and most sticky, the question of compliance with and enforcement of a putatively voluntary program.

Response to the program was somewhat positive though most observers considered it far from ideal. The producing interests were disturbed that products, West Coast imports, and residual fuel oil were not included, and that the program had no enforcement teeth. Their representatives, notably the Independent Petroleum Association of America (IPAA), nevertheless supported the

[35] Department of the Interior press release, August 9, 1957, reported in *Oil and Gas Journal* August 12, 1957, pp. 71–73.

program because controls were essential for domestic producers.[36] Importers, especially historical importers, feared their positions would be undercut by new firms and resented bearing all of the import reduction. Ideological opposition also existed, even among those who stood to gain from controls, but the voluntary face placed on the program subverted some of this opposition. The industry in its discussion of the program frequently referred to it as an "international application of prorationing," implying that the prorationing view of the world was more familiar, and perhaps less frightening, than import controls *per se*. In summary, the program was sufficiently innocuous to hamper opposition from those harmed, but sufficiently promising to cause those for whom it was designed to adopt a wait-and-see attitude.

Requests for access to the appeals machinery were not long in coming. These requests took two forms: either notice that there had been an error, as with the firms left off the importer list, or else a claim that the program worked an inordinate hardship on a firm because of special circumstances. The more serious of the "hardship" problems were associated with firms such as Tidewater that had made commitments for expanded facilities based on imported crude. Compliance would make these facilities inoperative or unprofitable. Tidewater described the quotas as tantamount to the confiscation of its $200,000,000 Delaware City refinery, which had yet to open.[37] It had closed one of its refineries in anticipation of opening the new one, and had hence reduced its historic import base. The new refinery had not gone on-stream to contribute to the import base as applied in the quota allocation. Tidewater's quota, it argued, thus did not even represent the stationary state without the increased capacity from its new plant. Moreover, Tidewater had invested $35 million in the refinery for special equipment to process low-gravity, high-sulfur foreign oil, had entered into firm contracts for tankers for durations as long as twelve years,

[36] Ibid.; and presentations at the 28th Annual Meeting of the IPAA, reported in *Oil and Gas Journal* November 4, 1957, pp. 82–83. Captain Matthew Carson, administrator of the Oil Import Administration, explained the goals of the program and replied to its critics at the IPAA meetings. His presentation was released to the press at the Department of the Interior, October 28, 1957.

[37] Statement before special panel of four, including Administrator Carson; see *Oil and Gas Journal* September 16, 1957, pp. 101–102.

and had committed itself to charter seventeen tankers to be built by 1961. Finally, it had committed itself to purchase foreign oil in specified amounts expressly for this new refinery. Understandably, then, Tidewater was opposed to all forms of import controls and was expressly and explicitly against those based on historical import patterns, as applied. The first round of appeals resulted in only minor increases in quotas in two cases, both involving basic data errors.

In the first application of the quota program to a newcomer, Crown Central Petroleum Corp. was allowed a 5,000 bbl/day quota, compared with its request for 20,000 bbl/day. Crown Central could demonstrate that its import plans predated controls, going back to March 1957. The quota to Crown Central was fitted into imports through the anticipated increases in domestic demand. The administrator, in effect formulating policy, stated that he would allow a portion of the increases in domestic demand to flow to those who wanted to initiate imports, but some of the increase should be reserved for old importers.[38]

Potential new importers were served notice that they would not obtain a quota by wishing for one—a meaningful production relationship between imported crude, a facility, and a market was required. Captain Matthew Carson, administrator of the program, in an interview stated that to be considered seriously for a quota, a potential importer would have to have a direct interest in the oil *imported*—he could not just have production abroad or merely seek to act as a broker of crude oil.[39] Hence, an inland refiner would not be allowed to participate in the program because it could not run the crude itself in a tidewater plant. Further, a central element in allocating quotas to new importers would be whether the prospective importer had a market area competitive with refiners that did have low-cost imports.[40]

Import controls as initially applied and formulated were inadequate to resolve two problems which soon were to occupy much of the administrator's attention. These were imports into District

[38] "How Oil Imports Will Be Controlled During the Months Ahead," interview of Administrator Carson by the *Oil and Gas Journal* November 4, 1957, pp. 84–86.

[39] Ibid.

[40] *Federal Register* vol. 22, p. 8988 (November 8, 1957); also see *Oil and Gas Journal* December 2, 1957, pp. 62–63.

V and imports of products, especially residual fuel oil. Consideration of the District V matter began formally in November 1957,
with hearings on limiting imports into that region. As anticipated,
import controls were expanded to the West Coast following these
hearings.[41]

District V was an area of perennial domestic crude deficit. No
case could thus be made for limiting imports on grounds that foreign oil directly displaced domestic output in the West, and apparently there was no will to make the case based on the fact that
import restriction would allow an increase in the price. Trans-
Rockies transport was negligible, and the two parts of the nation
formed essentially independent petroleum markets at prospective
prices for domestic and foreign crude in the absence of import
controls. The conclusion that the markets were independent, and
the reasoning and policy based upon it, became confused in late
1957 because of indications that a crude oil pipeline was being
considered to link the western regions with the crude-surplus areas
of the Southwest. That District V was a crude-deficit area was correct, but not dispositive, if it was free imports that precluded the
development of facilities which would open these lucrative markets
to southwestern producers. Once import controls were possible,
the markets became joined, and the issue of import controls in
the West to prevent displacement of domestic crude was alive. The
hearing did not settle this issue, but the fact it was held and the
arguments presented did signal policy options for 1958 and
beyond.

The District V quotas adopted in the order signed December 12,
1957 provided for a reduction of almost 130,000 bbl/day from the
planned imports for the first half of 1958. The allocations were 15
percent less than the average for 1956–57 for the eight established
importers. The total allowed imports were 220,100 bbl/day, compared with the estimated 275,000 bbl/day for 1957. As a first reaction, the companies appeared to have decided to comply, however
reluctantly.[42]

Residual oil imports offered a similar problem because, while
U.S. refineries did not cover U.S. demands for this fuel, higher
prices for residual could induce more domestic output. It would

[41] *Federal Register* vol. 22, p. 12772 (December 12, 1957).
[42] "U.S. Asks Heavy Import Cutbacks for West Coast," *Oil and Gas Journal* December 30, 1957, pp. 108–109.

likewise induce a long-run shift toward greater coal consumption —an important alternative fuel in the electric generation market. Structural shifts in the fuel market in the long run, then, rather than displacement of actual U.S. refinery products, was the essential issue here. In anticipation of formulating a control policy, importers of residual oil were asked to report on their level of imports for 1957. Complaints of excessive imports had been mounting from those harmed, including coal producers. The ODM requested these reports as the first invocation of section 7 of the 1955 Reciprocal Trade Agreements Act.[43]

Imports of other petroleum products were small. The prospect of refining cheap foreign crude oil into products which could be imported freely into the U.S. market, however, attracted considerable attention. New export-oriented refineries outside U.S. territories would be required for this purpose. The government indicated that it would not allow the quota program to be subverted in this fashion—product import controls would be imposed if substantial flows threatened—but the possibility continued to be discussed.

Erosion of the Voluntary Program

The voluntary program failed to achieve universal acceptance even at its initiation, and the support that did exist eroded rapidly early in 1958. Compliance with both its letter and spirit progressively deteriorated, but that is not surprising. In effect, importers were asked to voluntarily sacrifice their individual self-interest in additional imports for the direct benefit of domestic producers. In exchange, they were promised the possible avoidance of mandatory controls in the event that other importers similarly restricted imports; in other words, they were expected to exchange an individual cost for a collective benefit of dubious worth and uncertain achievement. And for many of the participants, the allocation of the costs among them was considered manifestly unfair.

Moreover, observers, especially those disadvantaged, alleged that in a number of ways the purpose of the program was being subverted. Charges were made that pipeline subsidiaries of importers

[43] "Residual Check Due," *Oil and Gas Journal* November 4, 1957, p. 81.

were refusing to connect wells of small operators in deference to the interest in larger imports of their parent. Military purchases abroad also aroused criticism. It was charged that military buying in the Caribbean created a market for light products from refinery operations, which made it feasible to produce heavy products, which in turn could be imported into the United States without restriction. Domestic producers and refiners thus lost light product sales and had the market for residual fuel oil depressed by imports which could not have been produced in the absence of the military sales. The loss of markets was therefore much greater than that indicated by direct military consumption alone.

In the light of this situation, several firms, the most important of which was Tidewater, refused to follow the voluntary program guidelines. Others did not take a public position but nevertheless violated their quotas. In response, the government planned to obtain compliance by bringing public pressure on the firms that refused to accept voluntary import limitations. Carson made this strategy clear when he spoke before the API and identified the three then noncomplying firms as Eastern States Petroleum Co., Sun Oil Co., and Tidewater Oil Co.[44] He assured API that limiting oil imports was the settled policy of the administration. If the voluntary controls were not successful, mandatory controls would be inevitable.

The compliance problems which threatened the program during 1957 worsened in early 1958. They were exacerbated by the depressed economic conditions which frustrated industry goals and restricted industry profits. The problem posed by growing imports into District V was intimately tied with the rising levels of exportable surplus production in Canada. Canada began exporting to the United States in volume in 1955; its exports to the West Coast rose rapidly through 1956 and 1957. Consequently, basing future imports on the historical level of activity, as would occur if the voluntary program were applied to Canadian crude, would be particularly restrictive. Canada could be expected to resort to intense diplomatic maneuvering to keep the U.S. market open. Restriction of Canadian exports also posed a domestic political

[44] Department of the Interior press release, November 13, 1957, reported in *Oil and Gas Journal* November 18, 1957, p. 137.

issue. Canadian exports could not be classified as uncertain in an emergency and Canadian output was already restricted to market demand. Hence, the arguments for restriction of Canadian imports could not be based on either national security or prospective exploitative dumping.

Old line importers, who benefited from a reasonably stable, non-coercive program compared with a mandatory one, and who were open to sanctions, continued to keep their imports under the quota limits during the new year despite the incentives to do otherwise. These importers—Atlantic, Gulf, Sinclair, Sunoco, Mobil, Socal, Standard of New Jersey, and the Texas Company—brought in 420,400 bbl/day in December 1957, and planned an average of 483,000 bbl/day for January–May; their allocation was 493,100 bbl/day. The new importers, on the other hand, actually imported 339,000 bbl/day in December and planned imports for the January–May period of 326,000 bbl/day, as against an allocation of 278,300 bbl/day. One small importer, Delta Refining Co., began importing without even applying for a quota. There was no direct and forceful action the government could take to restrain noncompliance.[45]

Not only were the smaller importers ignoring the quotas, their number was growing rapidly. As noted above, the growth of new-comers was induced by easier access to concessions in the export-ing countries and to markets in importing countries. They were especially attracted to the lucrative U.S. market by significant price differentials for crude that were not eliminated because of voluntary restraint on the part of large importing firms and the prorationing of output by domestic firms. The earlier hope that newcomers could be accommodated by demand growth was scut-tled by the continued depression in product sales; consequently, if the overall import ceilings were to be maintained, traditional importers would be required to suffer even greater cuts than antic-ipated earlier. Imports as they were distributed, moreover, gave tidewater refineries a considerable cost advantage over competitors in some markets, leading to further demands for more stringent controls or at least fairer sharing of import rights. Finally, if the

---

[45] "New Storm Brews over Imports Plan," *Oil and Gas Journal* January 27, 1958, pp. 125–126.

traditional importers were not to move over for the aggressive new-comers, domestic producers would be forced to do so. Action against imports was sought from many directions.

By the middle of March 1958, political pressures for further action on the oil import question approached unrestrainable levels. The IPAA, reversing its earlier policy, called for mandatory controls. Legislators in both houses of Congress had issued calls for action; hearings were underway, and bills submitted. Output was down to 9 days in Texas, and similar market demand prorationing restrictions were in force elsewhere. A special commission on oil industry developments, formed by the Texas Railroad Commission, reported severe financial problems in Texas due to depressed conditions in the oil industry, which in turn was caused by excessive imports. Finally, applications for import quotas from new importers for the second half of the year were up to 400,000 bbl/day, on top of requests for 1,000,000 bbl/day by established importers. Total import quotas for Districts I–IV were set at 713,000 bbl/day for the last 6 months of 1958, 8 percent less than before. If imports were actually held to this level, they were expected to amount to approximately 12 percent of District I–IV production.[46]

In the face of deteriorating compliance with the program, President Eisenhower's Special Cabinet Committee to Investigate Crude Oil Imports attempted to salvage its voluntary nature from a Congress which was rapidly approaching willingness to pass mandatory legislation. As a result of its deliberations, Executive Order 10761 "Government Purchases of Crude Petroleum and Petroleum Products" was issued; it authorized sanctions against violators of the "voluntary" quota.[47] Using the Buy American Act[48] for authority, the president ordered all government agencies to purchase only domestic or "complying" foreign-origin crude. Thus when it became evident that voluntary controls would not restrict imports,

[46] The conversion of Texas Railroad Commissioners to the mandatory standard came relatively late, and they sometimes echoed Administrator Carson's view that imports played a minor role in Texas supply problems; see *Oil and Gas Journal* March 24, 1958, p. 56. The 12 percent figure, which most parties respected as the boundary between safe and unsafe levels of imports per production, was first proposed several years before by the cabinet committee, on the basis of historical trend statistics. See *Oil and Gas Journal* March 31, 1956, p. 50.

[47] *Federal Register* vol. 23, pp. 2067–69 (March 28, 1958).

[48] March 3, 1933; 47 *Stat.* 1520, 41 *U.S.C.* 1970 ed., 10A–10C; 13 *Stat.* 1024, 41 *U.S.C.* 1970 ed., 10D.

the administration's choice was to reject its ideology rather than to change its goals. This order started the nation onto the road to the mandatory controls of 1959.

Executive Order 10761 was interpreted to mean that a firm which could not obtain a certificate of compliance would be boycotted by federal agencies. Firms were required to be in compliance for the month in which the contract was performed *and* for the 3 previous months, though they were given 30 days from the issuance of Order 10761 to achieve compliance. Regulations were issued at the end of April by the Oil Import Administration. While details are not important, the spirit of these regulations is. They were tightly drafted to leave no opportunity for firms to avoid compliance by setting up subsidiaries, by complying in only one part of their operations, or by attempting to segregate "domestic" and/or "complying" oil from unsanctioned imports.[49] The action taken was expected to defuse the congressional drive for rigid mandatory controls and to achieve actual import restraint.

The administration was disappointed if it expected the Buy American sanction to resolve the political and economic problems of oil imports. Not only did congressional efforts to mandate controls continue, but the industry remained depressed, the program was attacked in the courts, violations of the import levels continued, and prospects for even greater imports mounted. The amount of imports exceeded quotas during the months of March and April, and implementation of the Buy American program ran into considerable difficulty. Many importers and sellers had, for one reason or another, failed to meet their quota restrictions for the previous 3 months. Few complying firms existed to supply necessary products. The department of defense, in order to meet its military purchase needs, requested that it be allowed to purchase products from firms who promised in the *future* to obey any import restrictions.[50]

---

[49] *Federal Register* vol. 23, pp. 2872–73 (April 30, 1958).

[50] "Imports Exceed Quotas," *Oil and Gas Journal* April 28, 1958, p. 60. Continuing difficulties in qualifying sellers led to further relaxation of requirements as experience was gained in the program. In September 1958, the criteria were relaxed to allow importers to show cause for their noncompliance and to average inputs over the April–December period to achieve compliance (*Federal Register* vol. 23, pp. 70006–7, September 10, 1958). In December, in a further effort to entice firms to remain with the program and to add flexibility to procurement, the compliance period was extended to February 28, 1959 (*Federal Register* vol. 23, pp. 10389–90, December 25, 1958).

Efforts to increase the demand for domestic crude through this program were further hindered because, to the extent that there was some restraint on crude imports, the incentives for product imports grew. Clearly, firms with refinery capacity both within and without the United States could profitably alter the utilization rates of their domestic and external facilities. Consequently, not only did U.S. operations suffer in whatever export markets remained, but added product imports into the United States further displaced domestic crude oil sales and refinery operations (see table 2-1). The independent refiners, and marketers dependent upon them, were especially harmed by the shift in import mix generated by limiting the quotas to crude oil.

The continued differential in crude costs caused more and more potential importers to request quotas as the second half of 1958 began. When previously faced with prospective new entrants, the administrator reduced quotas of existing importers and gradually phased newcomers onto the list. By August 1958, the authorized import level stood at 713,100 bbl/day, while fourteen historical importers were requesting additions to their quotas of 208,080 bbl/day and sixty-two newcomers were requesting new quotas for 393,684 bbl/day.[51]

The burgeoning demand for quota allocations threatened the viability of the program even if the compliance problem were resolved. The Oil Import Administration found itself with no objective way to allocate the valuable import quotas at its disposal. Each prospective importer stood on the same plane as any other; no compelling ethical (or legal) case could be made for giving an asset to one party rather than to another. The added degree of restraint prospectively required for 1959 transformed the decision process to one where the ad hoc approach, which was tolerable before, would be politically, and perhaps now legally, unacceptable. A fresh approach to limiting imports was required. One alternative was to bow to pressure for mandatory controls; another was to restructure the voluntary program to relieve some of the pressures building up on it. The administration chose the latter course, but was required first to defeat congressional initiatives that would have rigidly limited imports through use of the law.

51 "Import Quota Bids Mushroom," *Oil and Gas Journal* August 11, 1958, p. 78.

The administration attempted to counter pressures for mandatory controls in several ways. First, it split the political forces favoring controls by offering subsidies to domestic metal producers, who had earlier joined with the oil forces; this group was thus neutralized, and logrolling among primary materials producers was thus eliminated. Second, the administration promised to present a mandatory control program if the voluntary controls broke down. Third, it began to limit the importation of products. The constraints on the importation of crude oil had led to increased refining abroad and to the transportation of petroleum products into the United States. Not only did this uneven handling of fuel imports threaten overall import controls, it also distorted the choices open to the oil industry and tended to transfer refining outside the United States.[52] Consequently, on July 14, 1958, the President's Special Committee to Investigate Crude Oil Imports concluded that product imports had grown to the point where further increases would constitute a threat to the voluntary program and to the national interest. The president accepted the recommendation "that importing companies voluntarily limit their imports of such unfinished gasoline and other unfinished oils to this level during the remainder of the calendar year, 1958." The level established was the average barrels per day imported during May and June 1958. To achieve compliance and remain eligible to sell to the federal government, firms were required to limit their imports to this level. No limits were set on asphaltic crude and some other products. Firms were requested to make reports of the levels of the imports during May or June 1958, and to report on their future imports.[53]

Despite these moves, controversy continued within Congress and in the press over the desirability of a mandatory bill. The administration's actions, the mood of hostility against further government intervention, and perhaps some consumer realization of self-interest led to the defeat of mandatory controls when it came to a test in the House. The bill that was passed instead extended the Reciprocal Trade Agreements Act without legislated oil import

[52] See Glenn P. Jenkins and Brian D. Wright, "Taxation of Income of Multinational Corporations: The Case of the United States Petroleum Industry," *Review of Economics and Statistics* vol. LVII, no. 2 (February 1975) pp. 1–11.

[53] *Federal Register* vol. 23, pp. 5399–5400 (July 16, 1958).

control.[54] It included amendments clarifying and making more explicit action required under the National Security Amendment, but left discretion to the Executive Branch as to when and how such action would be taken. However, this act was widely thought to provide both the policy test (imports of an article or derivatives of the article are not to be so large as to threaten the "investment, exploration and development necessary to assure" growth to meet future needs) and the teeth to limit imports.

Efforts to Restructure the Voluntary Program

With legislated controls dead for the time being, further attention could be paid to the problem of making voluntary controls work. The crucial issues were enforcement and a legitimitized method of distributing the quotas among the many applicants. As noted before, by late August, when applications for the new allocations were in, the problem had reached the point where some action was required. A proposed new program for Districts I–IV (District V remained under study) was announced September 11, 1958, with a call for comments. While this effort was to fail, it did provide the forum within which the analysis and ultimate compromises behind the mandatory program were formed. The concept of voluntary controls was not abandoned in the proposal, but there was an effort to alter the basis of determining and allocating imports to place controls on a defensible footing. An analysis of the reasoning behind the actions that followed, and a history of control devices previously utilized, was published as a guide to those trying to formulate company policy.[55] Extensive hearings, comments, and industry and government discussion followed.

The first element in the restructuring was a change in the method of determining the amount of allowed imports. The quantity was set by first estimating U.S. production for the year ending June 30, 1959—6,261,000 bbl/day. The special committee criterion which was an imports to production ratio of 12 percent, when applied to this estimate, yielded allowed imports of 751,300

[54] U.S.C. 1352a.
[55] Federal Register vol. 23, pp. 7088–89 (September 12, 1958).

bbl/day, to which 75,000 bbl/day were added for imports of unfinished oils. Total imports allowed, then, would be 826,300 bbl/day, or 10.1 percent of the independently estimated total demand of 8,173,000 bbl/day. Based on these factors, the decision was reached to determine allowed imports for the future at 10.1 percent of estimated demand, not 12 percent of production. On this basis, for 1959 the total of imports and estimated production would be 7,087,300 bbl/day, slightly over one million barrels per day *short* of estimated demand. This shortfall was to provide the economic incentive to the domestic industry to increase its output and capacity utilization.[56]

The allocation of import quotas was also changed in this proposal. First, in the transition period from September 11 through December 31, 1958, no change in allocations would be made. Beginning in 1959, however, all allocations were to be based on refinery inputs, with all refineries eligible whether or not they had an import history. All importers with a historical allocation were allowed that allocation, subject to a minimum of 6 percent (for those with zero imports as well) and a maximum of 37.5 percent of inputs for the first 6 months of 1959. During the last 6 months, minimum imports would be raised to 9 percent of refinery runs for the year ending March 31, 1959, with a compensating reduction to a new ceiling for refiners with the highest proportion of foreign crude. Beginning January 1, 1960, the historical differential would be eliminated and allocations made on the basis of equal percentages of inputs, with absolute quantities for each refinery adjusted each 6 months thereafter. An escape clause existed for refineries with no ready source of domestic crude. Such refineries were allowed a nontransferable allocation to be used in a specific facility. Asphalt produced from foreign crude was allowed as an offset against the quota on a barrel-for-barrel basis. No importer was allowed to take more than 10 percent of his allocation as unfinished oil.

New operations and expansions of capacity by existing refineries were rewarded with proportionate quotas when facilities came onstream during a quota period; they entered the program on an equal basis thereafter. Importers not possessing operating refineries

56 Ibid.

were gradually phased out of the program. No transfer of quotas was allowed—which meant that each firm had to clear imports through customs, but could then dispose of the oil as it saw fit (except for the special hardship allocations mentioned above). Puerto Rican refineries were allowed allocations based on imports during July–September 1958, and were to apply for additional allocations on the same basis as continental refineries.[57]

The effect of the proposed regulations was important. They moved controls from a basis of domestic production to consumption and they altered significantly the distribution of the quotas. No longer was it possible for the benefit from low-cost imports to flow to nonpetroleum firms or to firms without refinery facilities. Within the industry, distributional shifts were also important. Coastal refiners with a long history of imports would be severely harmed by this shift in policies; inland refiners were favored. Elimination of the "two-price" system and of the developing market segmentation in the United States was achieved by this shift. Of the eighty applicants for new quotas filed before this proposed regulation shift, seventeen (245,500 bbl/day requested) were ineligible under the proposed requirements. The sixty-three remaining new applicants had requested quotas of 573,000 bbl/day, of which only 52,000 bbl/day would be granted under this proposal. The quota distribution under the proposed scheme in Districts I–IV, after elimination of the historical factor, would have looked like this in profile: sixty-three new applicants, 11.1 percent of quota; twenty-four old applicants, 84.1 percent of quota; seventy-one nonappliers, 4.8 percent of quota.[58]

This announced proposed restructuring of import controls was met by frantic controversy. Few were satisfied. Not only were the benefits of quotas (and hence costs to consumers) made explicit, and prospective sharing of the benefits foreclosed for those left outside, but established beneficiaries were harmed by elimination of the historical differential. The controversy mounted, and in late

[57] Ibid.
[58] "What the Imports Control Plan Means," *Oil and Gas Journal* September 15, 1958, pp. 104–107.

October the Cabinet Fuels Committee decided that it was un-
realistic to leave to the OIA the role of assessing comments on the
proposed changes and formulating a finished program. It became
obvious that any program was going to be essentially political in
its operation, and hence needed political input in its formulation.
The committee thus took over the responsibility for reformulating
policy, relieving Captain Carson and the OIA from the political
pressure that threatened to overwhelm continued operation of the
existing program. The year ended without any change taking place
in allocations, methods, or application. Quotas were simply extended on an ad hoc basis.

The inability to achieve agreement on a new policy did not
signify agreement with the old. The Cabinet Fuels Committee
could not obtain agreement as to what advice should be given the
president, so it therefore requested yet another study by the Office
of Civil and Defense Mobilization. This study was to address the
basic issue of whether imports threatened to impair the national
security. This new study could be viewed as a device to reestablish
legal justification for controls. No policy was formulated before
the February 28 expiration of controls, and the voluntary program
was simply extended to March 10.[59] On March 10, 1959, President
Eisenhower issued Executive Order 3279 abolishing the voluntary
program and substituting a mandatory program in its stead.[60]

The period of voluntary controls ended with the industry in
much the same condition as when the controls began. Excess supplies existed at all marketing levels, domestic production was restricted well below the private optimal level, and imports were
being blamed. The sanctions established during 1958 were not
perceived to be adequate by those harmed by imports. In fact,
however, actual imports were not substantially higher than those
allowed, even though the program was only voluntary. Replacement of voluntary controls was required, however, because political and economic pressures were building up to the point where an
acceptable level of compliance was not likely to hold in the future.

[59] *Federal Register* vol. 24, pp. 1573 (March 3, 1959).
[60] Proclamation 3279, in *Federal Register* vol. 24, pp. 1781–84 (March 12, 1959).

Most observers were convinced that the voluntary program could not long survive because of the great difference between the world and the domestic price, differences in the ability of firms to utilize foreign crude, and the vast differences in interests between major firms and new entrants. The last gasp of the voluntary program, the proposal to assign imports based strictly on refinery inputs, had surfaced but no agreement was possible among conflicting interests. Refinery-based import controls clearly would require some mandatory powers.

3

The Mandatory Quota Program

The presidential proclamation which brought mandatory controls did not change the underlying economic reality that oil could be imported at a lower price than it was bringing domestically. What it did was to limit access to foreign oil, in the process increasing the consumer cost of petroleum and redistributing income and wealth within the United States and among the United States and foreign countries. It also increased the level of domestic petroleum production and reduced the proportion of the energy supply coming from abroad, compared with the "no restraint" case. The means by which these ends were achieved, and the effects of achieving them, are considered in this chapter and in those that follow. In this chapter we describe the control mechanism that was set up.

The decision that mandatory controls were required followed the determination that voluntary controls were not sufficient to meet public policy objectives. We have yet to explain, however, why an administration ostensibly dedicated to noninterference in private business activities, and an administration acting to expand international trade, would choose to restrict imports of an important material in so forthright and forceful a manner, and how it would justify that choice. Though we have mentioned rationales for import controls above, and though we will return to the matter at greater length in later chapters, it is useful for us here to cite the changing rationales for control over time as a backdrop to the subsequent discussion.

Rationale for Import Controls

The decision to impose mandatory oil import controls was, of course, in an important sense political; the interplay of special interest groups, essentially veiled from *ex post* analysis, explains much of what occurred. Our explication in later sections of the gainers and losers from specific actions will indicate, but cannot demonstrate, where the balance of political power lay. Nonetheless, these decisions were played out in a public forum, and the limits of actions were set by an appreciation for the national interest.

Import controls were legally based on the national security provisions of the Trade Agreements Extension Act of 1954 as amended in 1958; it was necessary that they bear a connection with defense efforts and threats to national security, however defined. The closure of the Suez Canal in 1956 provided evidence for the importance of standby capacity in U.S. oil production facilities. The essential level of such capacity was presumed to include not only sufficient flexibility to cover U.S. needs in case of a restriction of imports, but an ability to fuel our overseas allies as well. The maintenance of standby capacity is, of course, expensive, and the domestic petroleum industry made the case that an appropriate level would not be provided if the industry were faced with growing imports of foreign crude which would lower the effective price received by domestic producers.[1]

---

[1] The quantity of excess capacity maintained was a function of the price received by the producers and the rate of curtailment of supply to market demand (through prorationing) required to obtain that price. In the absence of imports, the higher the price, the lower the production rate and the higher the level of standby capacity which could be sustained without a diminution of investment in new supplies. Given that market demand prorationing was used to maintain the nominal domestic price, oil imports, of course, lowered the rate of utilization in the industry and thus made marginal reservoirs uneconomic to develop. If imports had been allowed to erode price instead, they would have led to abandonments of marginal producing reservoirs, non-development of marginal potential reservoirs, but higher utilization rates in low-cost reservoirs. In either case, if oil imports were allowed unlimited entry, no excess capacity would be maintained. At the limit, either the domestic price would be held above the world price but none of it would be sold—and hence no supplies developed —or else the domestic price would fall to the world level and all reservoirs which could produce or be developed at that price would be fully utilized.

The argument was placed in a dynamic framework so that the *continued* future capacity to meet energy needs, in the face of declining incentives, was the touchstone of the defense rationale. It was not based on a present threat of cutoffs of essential fuel supplies. While the rationale, then, for the restriction of imports was national security, it also included requirements for excess capacity.

The Kennedy administration shifted the focus of national security through its emphasis on building effective trading partners, especially in the Western Hemisphere. Trade policy in oil, as in other areas, reemphasized the interconnection of markets and emphasized international collective security as against a limited national viewpoint. This revised goal was identified as an oil policy which provided markets for Western Hemisphere crude, and accepted the responsibility for supplying friendly nations in periods of distress—such as that which accompanied the second closing of Suez in 1967.

A further rationale for protection was the effect of oil imports on the U.S. balance of payments. While this concern was expressed in the early days of controls under Eisenhower, its fullest fruition occurred after 1965 when trade deficits were severe, the fuel component of imports appeared to be increasing, and the nation had not faced up to progressive shifts in relative currency values.

Underlying some part of the movement toward protection—but to an often unspecified and never determinable degree—was the quasi-populist rationale of protecting the smaller U.S. independent producers from the multinational oil companies which controlled foreign supplies. Domestic producers most susceptible to displacement were those who had marginal production, including stripper well producers, producers outside the prolific Southwest, and fringe firms who survived by close attention to the detail that makes the difference between marginally profitable and unprofitable production. These producers—and their representative trade organizations—felt estranged if not divorced from the operations of the multinational firms. These groups supported controls on imports as a means of retaining additional productive capacity in the United States. The frequency with which the various small business committees of Congress and the self-ordained protectors of the smaller firms defended existing controls and sought their extension testifies to the strength of these values.

This brief discussion of the rationales for oil import controls points up the array of goals a single set of regulations was presumed to fulfill. The actual application of the mandatory quota program suffered from the diversity of tasks that it attempted to perform. The divergence of goals also opened the program to various interpretations of its mission. This meant that there were no criteria which could—or could not—be applied when allocations were made. Policy was adrift because the rationale for policy was both imprecise and ambiguous.

Despite these conceptual difficulties, decisions about allocations were required in the mandatory control program. We turn now to the institution of the program and to the decisions made.

The Mandatory Quota Program: Establishment and Major Provisions

The mandatory quota program was established by Presidential Proclamation 3279, "Adjusting Imports of Petroleum and Petroleum Products into the United States," dated March 10, 1959, under the authority provided by Section 2 (b) of the Trade Agreements Extension Act of 1954.[2] This action followed a report by Leo A. Hoegh, Director, Office of Civil and Defense Mobilization, which, after a brief review of history and current evidence concluded that: "crude oil and the principal crude oil derivatives and products are being imported in such quantities and under such circumstances as to threaten or impair the national security."[3] On the basis of this report, the President's Special Committee to Investigate Crude Oil Imports recommended on March 6, 1959, a mandatory program placed on a footing different from that of the voluntary program it replaced.[4] The committee's report set out in

2 *Federal Register* vol. 24, pp. 1781–84 (March 12, 1959). It is reprinted in the appendix to this chapter, along with summaries of amendments through 1973.

3 Office of Civil and Defense Mobilization, "Memorandum for the President," February 27, 1959, reprinted in *The Oil Import Question*, A Report on the Relationship of Oil Imports to the National Security, prepared by the Cabinet Task Force on Oil Import Control (Washington, GPO, 1970) pp. 207–211.

4 Report of the Special Committee to Investigate Crude Oil Imports, reprinted in *The Oil Import Question*, pp. 203–206.

considerable detail the outline of such a program; the president's proclamation substantially embodied the terms of the report.

The light in which the situation was seen in government circles appears in the statement of the president which accompanied the issuance of Proclamation 3279.[5]

> I have today issued a Proclamation adjusting and regulating imports of crude oil and its principal products into the United States.
>
> The Voluntary Oil Import Program has demonstrated to me the willingness of the great majority of the industry to cooperate with the government in restricting imports to a level that does not threaten to impair security. I commend them, and to me it is indeed a cause for regret that the actions of some in refusing to comply with the request of the Government require me to make our present voluntary system mandatory.
>
> The new program is designed to insure a stable, healthy industry in the United States capable of exploring for and developing new hemisphere reserves to replace those being depleted. The basis of the new program, like that for the voluntary program, is the certified requirements of our national security which make it necessary that we preserve to the greatest extent possible a vigorous, healthy petroleum industry in the United States.
>
> In addition to serving our own direct security interests, the new program will also help prevent severe dislocations in our own country as well as in oil industries elsewhere which also have an important bearing on our own security. Petroleum, wherever it may be produced in the free world, is important to the security, not only of ourselves, but also of the free people of the world everywhere.
>
> During the past few years, a surplus of world producing capacity has tended to disrupt free world markets, and unquestionably, severe disruption would have occurred in the United States and elsewhere except for cutbacks in United States production under the conservation programs of the various state regulatory bodies.
>
> The voluntary controls have been and the mandatory controls will be flexibly administered with the twin aims of sharing our large and growing market on an equitable basis with other producing areas and avoiding disruption of normal patterns of international trade.
>
> The Director of the Office of Civil and Defense Mobilization will keep the entire program under constant surveillance, and will inform the President of any circumstances which in his opinion indi-

[5] The White House, Statement by the President, March 10, 1959, reprinted in *The Oil Import Question*, pp. 195–196.

cate the need for any further Presidential action. In the event price increases occur while the program is in effect, the Director is required to determine whether such increases are necessary to accomplish the national security objectives of the Proclamation.

The United States recognizes, of course, that within the larger sphere of free world security, we, in common with Canada and with the other American Republics, have a joint interest in hemisphere defense. Informal conversations with Canada and Venezuela looking toward a coordinated approach to the problem of oil as it relates to this matter of common concern have already begun. The United States is hopeful that in the course of future conversations agreement can be reached which will take fully into account the interests of all oil producing states.

Proclamation 3279 laid out the general lines of policy and assigned to the secretary of interior the responsibility of drawing up the regulations required for translating the policies into administrative reality. Its effective date was April 1, 1959. The main provisions of the proclamation may be summarized briefly:

1. Three geographical areas were specified, to be subject to different regulations:
   a. Districts I–IV,[6] the area east of the Rocky Mountains, identified as an area "in which there is substantial oil production capacity in excess of actual production."
   b. District V, the West Coast states, identified as an area "in which production is declining and in which, due to the absence of any significant inter-area flow of oil, limited imports are necessary to meet demand."
   c. Puerto Rico.
2. Residual fuel was differentiated from imports of crude oil, unfinished oil, and refined products, for treatment under separate rules.
3. The secretary of interior was to provide for a system of allocation of authorized imports upon the basis of a "fair and equitable distribution among persons having refinery capacity . . . in relation to refinery inputs during an appropriate period or periods . . . and may provide for distribution in such manner as to avoid drastic reductions below the last allocations under

6 "Districts" refers to Petroleum Administration for Defense (PAD) districts (see frontispiece).

the Voluntary Oil Import Program." The persons receiving quotas were free to trade them for domestic oil to process in their own refineries, but quotas could not be sold.

4. For District I–IV the maximum level of imports, except residual fuel oil, was to be approximately 9 percent of estimated total demand in these districts ("demand" being undefined). Finished products were to be limited to an amount not to exceed the level of such imports during calendar 1957, and unfinished oils were not to exceed 10 percent of permissible imports of crude and unfinished oils.

5. In District V, the level was to be determined by the difference between estimated total demand and the supply available from domestic sources of production, as determined by the Bureau of Mines. The finished product and unfinished oils provisions were the same as those for Districts I–IV.

6. Starting from an initial level of 1957 imports, imports of residual fuel oil were to be kept under review and adjusted at the discretion of the secretary of interior.

7. Imports into Puerto Rico were placed at the 1958 level, subject to the discretion of the secretary. He was empowered to adjust the level of imports to conform to changes in local demand or in export demand.

8. Provision was made for importing fuel in bond for both ship and airplane use.

9. An Oil Imports Appeal Board (OIAB) was established and empowered to grant relief on grounds of hardship, error, or other relevant special consideration, but the granting of additional importing authority to any prospective importer was to be balanced by a reduction in imports allowed for others.

The policy effects of the mandatory quota program were to be monitored by the director of the Office of Civil and Defense Mobilization. His office was assigned the responsibility of suggesting to the president alterations in the allowed levels of imports of petroleum and petroleum products. It was required to consult with the State, Defense, Treasury, Interior, Commerce, and Labor departments before making its recommendations. Importantly, the proclamation included the provision: "In the event prices of crude oil or its products or derivatives should be increased after the effective date of this proclamation, such surveillance shall include a

determination as to whether such increase or increases are necessary to accomplish the national security objectives of the act. . . ."[7]
An effort was thus made to assure consuming groups that import
controls were not to be used to force prices up; their effect in preventing price erosion was left unstated. For the producers whose
output was limited to market demand, an increase in output and
consequent decline in excess capacity amounted, of course, to a
once and for all increase in value of existing properties.

Proclamation 3279 did not, of course, include specific rules pertaining to allocation of quotas to specific refineries, nor did it include answers to other questions about how the quotas were to be
administered. These issues were handled in Oil Import Regulation
1 of the Oil Import Administration, Department of the Interior.[8]
The major provisions of the regulation were as follows:

1. The initial allocation period for crude was from March 11 to
   June 30, 1959, and thereafter in 6-month periods; for products
   the period began April 1.
2. Allocations of crude oil were made only to firms which could
   demonstrate refinery capacity and output for the previous
   period; to receive a finished product or residual fuel oil quota,
   an importation record for calendar year 1957 was required (for
   a quota for finished products into Puerto Rico, the last half of
   1958 was the relevant period).
3. Allocations were made on a "sliding scale," with incremental
   inputs receiving smaller quota allocations.
4. The allocation ratios were different for Districts I–IV than for
   District V because of the different control theory involved.
5. A historical factor based on the last allocation under the
   voluntary control program set a lower bound for import allocations to historical importers. Each importer received an allocation based on the greater of (1) his historical entitlement or
   (2) his refinery runs allocation.
6. No allocation was permitted to be "sold, assigned, or otherwise
   transferred." Hence, each quota was required to be imported
   to the account of the quota holder before being traded for
   domestic oil usable to the quota holder, should trading prove
   desirable.

[7] *Federal Register* vol. 24, p. 1784 (March 12, 1959).
[8] *Federal Register* vol. 24, pp. 1907–11 (March 17, 1959).

7. Firms which were unable to obtain crude from domestic sources by ordinary or continuous means could obtain special import allocations, but were then ineligible for the usual import quotas.
8. Finished product imports were allocated to each eligible applicant in the proportion that his imports bore to the imports of products during 1957 by all eligible applicants.
9. Puerto Rican imports were established at the level of imports during July through September of 1958.
10. The exchange of crude oil was predicated on meeting four requirements. The exchange was required to be:
   a. in kind for domestic crude oil or unfinished oils;
   b. not otherwise unlawful;
   c. operated on a current basis, with not more than 90 days elapsing between the deliveries of the foreign and the domestic oil; and
   d. reported to the Oil Import Administrator.[9]

The operation of the mandatory quota program can best be understood within the context of the controversies about its major provisions. These are discussed in detail in chapters 4 and 5. Two important procedural elements of the mandatory quota program deserve further attention here—the quota exchange system and the Oil Imports Appeals Board.

Quota Exchange Rules and Procedures

Integral to the operation of the mandatory quota program was the process by which quotas of interior, nonimporting refiners were converted to a flow of foreign oil to coastal refiners. The import control program as adopted required that every refiner, but only refiners, be given an import quota; even refineries with no intent or ability to import were given grants of authority to do so. The reasoning which led the government to include nonimporting refineries in the program is unknown, but it probably included both an equity and an efficiency argument. To deny broad access to the benefits of imported crude would be to handicap one portion of

9 Further clarification of the oil exchange procedure came in *Federal Register* vol. 24, p. 2361 (March 26, 1959).

the refining industry in its efforts to compete with another, and to redistribute income and wealth among them. If eligibility for imports had been limited to those facilities which actually processed foreign crude, tidewater refineries would have had substantial cost advantages which could have been realized in the short run through higher profit margins and in the long run in deeper penetration into the interior product markets. Interior refiners would have had first their profits and then their market share decline as they were forced to match lower prices based on foreign crude. The dividing line between the market spheres of coastal and interior refiners, which depends solely on transport costs if crude costs are equal, would have shifted to the disadvantage of the latter, and preexisting commercial patterns would have been disrupted. Some disturbance of such markets, of course, did follow the creation of the mandatory quota program because nonrefiner importers under the voluntary program had their quotas removed, and quotas of refiners were changed. The loss of a quota to nonrefiners, however, had little efficiency effect, and perhaps this explains in part the government's willingness to proceed without compensating the losers.

General distribution of quotas among refiners had efficiency and security benefits compared with granting them only to refineries which could run imports. The higher proportion of imports in total runs that would have occurred if quotas had been limited to coastal refineries would have made eligibility for the quota more valuable than it was with general eligibility. Consequently, expansion of coastal facilities would have been encouraged while interior refineries would have been used less intensively or abandoned. This tidewater expansion would have been accompanied by shipment of domestic oil to the coastal refineries to provide the nonimported proportion of inputs for the expanded facilities. In addition, products would bear higher average transport costs as refining became more concentrated on the coast. Concentration of refining in the coastal regions had security implications as well. Coastal refineries were perceived to be less defensible during war. Moreover, a concentrated industry, wherever located, would be less likely to survive hostilities than would a dispersed one. Finally, surviving elements in a dispersed industry could serve the national need better if transportation links were disrupted. Allocation of imports among only those refineries with access to foreign crude, instead of a general distribution of quotas, thus would have led to a greater concentration of refineries along the coasts, to premature abandonment of facilities, to excess refinery capacity in the short run, and to higher transport costs. All of these results argued for sharing quotas among all refiners.

By allowing all refiners access to imported crude, the control program did, however, alter preexisting competitive relationships to the detriment of those refiners whose operations were established to utilize foreign raw materials. In an effort to mitigate the disruptive effects of the control program on such importers, they were given higher quotas based on their historical import pattern, and, as noted earlier, the subsequent reductions in their quota were phased in. The differential impact of the control program on different segments of this industry was thus recognized, and a compromise was enunciated that allowed historical importers access to the benefits of foreign oil on terms more favorable than those for nonimporters, but allowed nonimporters some of the benefits. It is necessary to understand the implications of this program before its procedures and institutions can be understood.

The program adopted meant that the marginal cost of crude oil among refiners differed, but according to the different quota proportions that each received, not because some used imported oil and others did not. The marginal cost of crude for all refiners was determined by the average of the domestic and imported prices of crude, weighted by the proportion of quota and nonquota inputs. The size of a firm's allocation thus depended upon its level of inputs; a right to a quota allocation arose only through processing oil. An example of how the system worked to affect the marginal cost of crude would be useful here. Assume firm H had an historically based quota of 37 percent, and firm I, an inland refiner, had a marginal allocation of 6 percent, based on the sliding scale and the size of its operations. If domestic oil were \$3.50/bbl and imported oil were \$2/bbl, then the marginal cost of crude for firm H would be \$3.087 $[= (3.50 + 0.37 \times 2)/(1 + 0.37)]$ and for firm I, \$3.415 $[= (3.50 + 0.06 \times 2)/(1 + 0.06)]$.[10] Had each

---

[10] See chapter 7 for the derivation of this formula and for an argument as to why refiners would not be inclined to pass along the savings resulting from cheaper imports to consumers.

firm received an equal 9 percent quota, then the marginal input cost for both would be $3.376. These results can be compared with those from alternative systems that could have been selected. Had firm H been allowed to import all its oil and had firm I been required to depend upon domestic sources—the situation prior to controls—then firm H would have had a marginal cost of $2/bbl and firm I one of $3.50. So long as market demand prorationing maintained the domestic price above the world price, and some domestic oil were used, firm H would have earned substantial rents. These would have disappeared over time as the expansion of imports swamped the price-props in the domestic market. On the other hand, if the system were based on giving some firms (H) a volumetric quota rather than one based on levels of output, and on giving other firms (I) no quota at all, both would have had the same marginal input cost, $3.50/bbl. Each would have depended upon the same domestic market for its incremental supplies; the average cost of firm H would, of course, be lower, and it would earn inframarginal rents.

We can now examine the procedures and institutions by which the tidewater refiners got the oil and inland refiners were compensated for giving up the right to import it. This was done through a paper oil barter exchange system which was superimposed upon a system by which firms in the industry had traditionally adjusted crude supplies and refinery requirements without buying and selling crude oil through a cash market.[11]

Exchanges of imported oil and domestic oil were authorized under the condition that "oil be exchanged for oil" and that the recipient of the domestic oil process it in his own refinery. This latter rule prevented creation of a market in exchanges *per se*. There was no parallel rule that the recipient of the foreign oil

---

[11] Crude oil differs in characteristics and location. Additionally, the ownership of crude oil from a given field or well is fragmented even though it flows in an undifferentiated stream through gathering facilities. Refineries also differ in the characteristics of preferred crude oil input and by location. Thus firms often cannot run "their" crude in "their" refineries without expensive mismatching of crudes and facilities, similarly expensive cross-hauling, and costly duplication of production and gathering facilities. Rather than buy and sell crude oil or reserves in a cash market to achieve the proper mix of refinery input and to minimize production, gathering, and transportation costs, firms have instead "traded" crude oil among themselves to gain this end. This institution has developed in part because of tax advantages and in part because of the greater security of supply that firms think they can obtain through it.

must process it in his own refinery. The foreign oil, once exchanged, could be bought and sold in subsequent transactions.
Exchanges between Districts I–IV and District V were prohibited;
exchanges among crude and unfinished oils were allowed within
each area. Oil imported under most hardship cases or special provisions was required to be utilized in the quota recipient's own
facilities, while in other cases such recipients were excluded from
this requirement entirely by the Oil Import Appeals Board. The
regulations provided that money could not change hands, nor
could accounting take place on a monetary basis, in the accom-
plishment of the exchanges between foreign and domestic oil.[12]

The provision that money could not change hands was, of
course, unenforceable—side payments merely required some leger-
demain or disguise. The *Oil and Gas Journal* noted that higher
prices for products, different transportation charges, and other
such payments were sometimes used in effecting exchanges of oil
with different value.[13] Each exchange involved a whole range of
separate circumstances, including transportation responsibility,
quality of crudes, timing (within limits), plus the vagaries of the
domestic and international market. Depending on these and other
factors, the ratio of the volume of domestic to imported oil exchanged was determined, subject only to the requirement that
such exchanges must be reported to the administrator of the Oil
Import Administration. The regulations regarding side payments
(and the timing of the actual use of the oil) were relaxed in 1973,
but the oil-for-oil principle was maintained even after the quota
was replaced by an import fee on oil not qualifying under the
quota provisions.[14]

Usually exchanges were accomplished by a contractual agreement between an interior refiner who held a quota and a coastal
refiner who directly or through some affiliate was also a producer
of foreign oil. The inland refiner agreed to buy, as if in the coun-

[12] The general pattern of quota exchanges was set out in Proclamation 3279, section
3 (b) (3), see *Federal Register* vol. 24, p. 1783. They were structured as regulations in
C.F.R. Title 32A, National Defense Act, appendix, chapter X: Oil Import Administration, Department of the Interior, section 17, "Use of Imported Crude Oil and Unfinished Oils"; these appear in *Federal Register* vol. 24, pp. 1907ff. (March 17, 1959).
[13] "Crude-Oil Men Are Having a Field Day," *Oil and Gas Journal* April 27, 1959,
pp. 83–85.
[14] *Federal Register* vol. 38, p. 16195 (June 21, 1973).

try of origin, a stated amount of foreign oil of specified grades produced by the coastal refiner (or designee) and to deliver it duty paid at the port of the refiner. In return, the tidewater refiner agreed to deliver to the inland refiner a stated amount of domestic oil of specified grades. The remaining terms of the agreement then consisted of a formula which determined the ratio at which the foreign oil would exchange for domestic oil. The terms were flexible in the sense that provision was made for adjustment if the grades of oil delivered did not conform precisely to the specifications of the contract.

The exchange agreements were arrived at by a process of search and negotiation. When the quota program was first instituted, there was considerable disarray in the negotiations, and bargains were struck over a sizable range of exchange terms. No "purchaser" of quotas had any clear idea of what he might have to pay; no "seller" of a quota had a clear idea of what he might expect to receive in exchange. The disparity in terms was rapidly diminished as the exchanges became institutionalized and knowledge of market conditions became known. Additionally, of course, the underlying terms also changed as world market conditions adjusted to the new situation in the United States. Among other changes, the equilibrium values among foreign crudes were affected. Once the market had achieved an orderly character and adjustments were worked out, contracts were extended and amended without serious difficulty and continuing relations were established among particular interior and coastal refiners.

Institutionalization of the exchange program was facilitated by actions of the National Petroleum Refiners Association (NPRA), the trade group for the large (over 30,000 bbl/day) refiners. Each exchange, and its terms, was required to be reported to the administrator of the Oil Import Administration. The NPRA compiled these exchanges and published them for use by the industry and the Oil Import Administration, which was supplied copies so that it would have a common reference with the industry.[15] The *Digest*

---

[15] National Petroleum Refiners Association, *Oil Import Digest,* mimeo, loose leaf, variously dated, Washington, D.C. The NPRA collected and interpreted regulations and administrative and judicial decisions and reported crude oil exchanges among companies. This material was continuously updated. The authors are indebted to NPRA for making this and other material available.

further facilitated communication between refiners, the Oil Import Administration, and the Oil Import Appeals Board because it also presented in a convenient form the basic documents dealing with the program, and an "official" interpretation of them.

Since in the common case the coastal refiner was affiliated with a company that had foreign crude production, the essence of the exchange process was that the importing refiner was selling his own foreign production to the quota holder at one price and buying it back at a higher one.[16] While each contract had the *appearance* of being an exchange of oil for oil at a certain ratio, the heart of the bargain lay elsewhere—in the monetary value implicitly placed upon the quota rights. In negotiating the domestic-to-foreign oil ratio, the parties considered the value of a barrel of foreign oil to be the market price in the country of origin, plus freight to the East Coast point of entry, plus import duty. The value of a barrel of domestic oil was the market price in the field plus gathering and marketing cost for transporting it to the specified point of delivery. The ratio between the two represented the bargain struck as to the value of the import quota.

The exchange process was merely a veil covering the transfer to inland refiners of some of the benefits of importing cheap foreign oil. No productive function was changed in maintaining the facade that something was actually happening. The substance of the matter remained that the coastal refiner went about arranging his total imports from customary sources—from his foreign production, exchanges with other foreign producers, or purchases from other foreign producers. Similarly, the interior refiner went about arranging his total requirements of domestic oil from customary sources. A substantial amount of formal paperwork, however, was performed to make it appear that each party acquired some actual oil and traded it to the other.

A cash market for quotas could have achieved the same goals and been more efficient, but the exchange system satisfied important political needs.[17] First, its effect was direct in providing a

---

[16] The refiner receiving the quota did not in all cases want to receive the foreign production of his own company, but that was a matter which could be taken care of by the normal processes of exchange among foreign producers.

[17] If quota holders sold for cash, and the amount of their quotas depended on the size of their refinery inputs, the marginal cost of crude oil to them would be the same

visible market for domestic production; its results could be seen—
they did not need to be inferred. Second, the distributional effect
was veiled. A cash market for quotas would have opened to public
scrutiny the level of subsidy of domestic production. Public support for direct transfers of income from consumers to producers
was limited, even if their purpose was to sustain domestic production for national security reasons. Direct and obvious transfers of
cash among refiners may also have disturbed the public and participants, and thus threatened the political viability of what was
clearly thought by the administration to be an essential program.
The exchange program approached demand enhancement directly
and redistribution indirectly, as contrasted to a cash market for
quotas, and consequently was politically more secure.[18] Discussion
of replacing the exchange system by direct cash payments recurred
throughout the life of the mandatory quota program, but it never
resulted in changes in the regulations.

The Oil Imports Appeals Board

Proclamation 3279 establishing mandatory controls directed the
secretary of interior to form an Oil Imports Appeals Board
(OIAB) consisting of representatives of the departments of In-

---

as under the costless exchange program. Since cash purchases and sales would lower
transactions costs, the marginal cost of crude would be even lower for inland refiners
under a quota sale program than under the system adopted. Given that the form of
the subsidy to inland refiners had no effect on demand for products, the quantity of
output of inland refiners would increase slightly as the result of the lower transactions
costs of a cash payments system. Consequently, holding other things constant, the demand for domestic crude would increase with a cash payment system as against the
unwieldy exchange program that evolved.

[18] It is interesting to contrast the quota exchange program under import controls
with the entitlements program under the price control program of 1974–75. After
1973, the high-cost crude was foreign and the low-cost crude was domestic controlled
oil. Again, the decision made was to "equalize" the cost of crude oil among refineries,
but in this case the equalization was performed through a centralized cash payments
process rather than through the facade of enforced crude oil exchanges. The Federal
Energy Administration determined the quantity of low-cost controlled oil each refinery was "entitled" to run as its share of the total, the value of each "entitlement,"
and supervised the cash payments from those refineries using more than their share to
those who used less. The publicity and comment in the nontrade press regarding such
payments was striking, and demonstrated the public relations wisdom of the procedure followed in the quota program.

terior, Defense, and Commerce at the deputy assistant secretary level or higher. The OIAB was empowered to adjust quotas and to review revocation or suspension of allocations or licenses "on grounds of hardship, error or other relevant special considerations, but within the limits of the maximum level of imports established. . . ."[19] Section 21 of Oil Import Regulations established the OIAB. The chairman was to be elected from among its membership, and its decisions were to be final.[20] In an amendment filed in December, it was announced that relief in the form of modifications of quotas was to take effect during the succeeding allocation period.[21] The operating procedures adopted by the OIAB were adjusted in a revision of rules and procedures issued later in the same month.[22]

The procedures of the OIAB were relatively informal throughout its operation. Firms had 30 days, generally, to appeal a decision of the Oil Import Administration. Petitions were to be in writing stating the decision appealed, the relevant provisions of the regulation, the grounds for relief, the relief sought, and the justification for the relief sought. A hearing could be requested, but would only be granted if a valid basis for relief was presented in writing. Expert testimony was first discouraged and then explicitly forbidden in a revision of the regulations issued on June 26, 1964.[23] Hearings were public and informal; provision was made for supporting or opposing presentations by interested parties; and a transcript of hearings was kept. Decisions were to be made purely upon the record. Approval by two members of the OIAB constituted a binding decision.

The central feature of the OIAB through the first decade of its operation was that it refused to consider any appeals except those

[19] *Federal Register* vol. 24, p. 1784 (March 12, 1959). The Defense Department representative was replaced by a representative of the Department of Justice in 1970, signaling in part the replacement of a narrow "defense" focus in the OIAB with one more concerned with general economic and administrative issues (Proclamation 3969, *Federal Register* vol. 35, p. 4321, March 11, 1970). The requirement that the member be at the level of deputy assistant secretary or higher was eliminated in 1963 (Proclamation 3531, *Federal Register* vol. 28, p. 4077, April 25, 1963).

[20] *Federal Register* vol. 24, p. 1910 (March 17, 1959).

[21] *Federal Register* vol. 24, p. 10076 (December 12, 1959).

[22] *Federal Register* vol. 24, p. 10444 (December 23, 1959).

[23] *Federal Register* vol. 29, pp. 8211–12 (June 30, 1964).

very narrowly conceived. It did not accept comments or petitions
that had policy overtones. There were four bases for action by the
OIAB as formalized in a presidential action at the end of 1959.
These included relief designed to modify allocations because of
exceptional hardship or error, to grant allocations to those with
importing histories but which did not otherwise qualify for allocations, to grant finished product allocations in hardship cases, and
to review administrative revocations and suspensions of licenses.[24]
Of these, the first was most important. The second, the "import
history" provision, was apparently a "grandfather" clause specifically entered to benefit one importer—Gabriel Oil Co.—though it
was stretched to cover a few other cases. The "finished product"
category was added after the original regulations were drafted in
order to make a grant of this sort possible, but this authority remained unused until 1967. The "revocation or suspension" section was never of general importance.[25]

The "exceptional hardship or error" provision, was, then, the
crucial category under which the OIAB worked for most of its life.
After the very strict constructionist Eisenhower era, the board was
sympathetic to a variety of appeals, but error was restricted primarily to error on the part of the government or a third party, not
of the petitioner, except in a case of exceptional hardship. Error by
government or a third party, on the other hand, did not require a
showing of hardship. With reference to an appeal based on hardship alone, there was an early tendency to consider unprofitability
a certifiable hardship, but in October 1962 this criterion was reversed. Hardship, then, became a matter of natural disasters or
strikes which reduced output during the base period.[26]

The first OIAB began work in April 1959 under regulations
established by the secretary of interior.[27] During the first appeal
period (March–June 1959) the OIAB received eighty-one appeals
of which it granted only six. The appeals granted in two cases were
based on an error by the Oil Import Administration in overlook-
ing eligible importers. In each case the OIAB decided there had

24 Proclamation 3328, *Federal Register* vol. 24, p. 10133 (December 16, 1959), as
implemented in regulations found in *Federal Register* vol. 24, p. 10444 (December
23, 1959).

25 *Oil Import Digest* vol. 1, pp. A303–304 (July 19, 1968).

26 Ibid., pp. A302–303.

27 *Federal Register* vol. 24, p. 2622 (April 4, 1959).

been an overly restrictive definition of inputs or outputs. Two positive decisions were based on hardship: in one instance (Tropical Gas) the traditional supplier shut down, leaving foreign feedstock the only source of supply; in the other instance (Signal Oil and Gas) a fire had temporarily eliminated production during the base period. The narrow definition of appeals worthy of relief was reinforced by the consistent denial of petitions by the OIAB through the remainder of the Eisenhower administration. Only one other (Douglas Oil Co., owned by Continental Oil) appeal was granted; it was based on a late filing.[28]

The Kennedy appointees to the OIAB in May 1961 took a different view of their responsibilities and were more responsive to appeals for relief. The previous board's position had reduced the number of petitions filed, but in its first decisions the Kennedy board approved four.[29] The response, of course, was that firms began to bring more cases before the OIAB. Policy was reversed in three of the four initial grants of relief by the new board. In one of the reversals an allocation was granted because the firm had not received a quota to which it had been entitled under the voluntary program, and thus it deserved a historical quota. In the other two reversals the issue was extreme hardship; the refiners were losing money. Administrative error in calculating the permissible imports into District V was the issue in the fourth case; it resulted in a revision of the regulations which increased the allocation for all West Coast refiners.[30]

A common complaint against implementation of the historic quota provision—that it penalized those firms which had reduced imports and complied with the voluntary program—came to the OIAB in 1962. Socony argued successfully before the OIAB that it had acted responsibly and that its quota had suffered accordingly. It was granted an increased quota, but this policy was not generalized for other firms.[31]

Further increases in allocations during the first half of 1962 convinced policy makers that continued grants by the OIAB could subvert the import restrictions unless the policy of giving them

28 *Oil Import Digest* vol. 1, pp. A301–302 (January 19, 1968).
29 "Imports Board Grants Appeals of Four Firms," *Oil and Gas Journal* July 10, 1961, p. 77.
30 *Oil Import Digest* vol. 1, p. A302 (January 19, 1968).
31 Ibid.

immediate effect were reversed. As it was, the actual level of imports during a period was not constrained by the import formula. Beginning in the second half of 1962, provision was made for OIAB allocations to take effect only in the subsequent period, and consequently to come within, not on top of, allowed imports.[32] A different means of handling this problem was later devised: the OIAB was itself given a quota, as part of the import allocation within the overall formula, from which successful appeals could be satisfied.

The OIAB proceeded without substantial change in operation or function until 1968 when it began to be used increasingly to resolve general policy problems created by the quota program. Starting during this period, the OIAB granted import authority for finished products in response to local pressures for greater imports.[33] The OIAB increasingly became a vehicle for loosening import controls while minimizing resulting political repercussions from producers. Its action could be dismissed as "administrative interpretations" which did not signal a substantial policy shift or a precedent which would have been threatening to interested groups. In fulfilling this role, the OIAB served as an important safety valve during both the Johnson and Nixon administrations. This later activity of the OIAB can more properly be discussed in the next chapter within the context of the controversy over the allowed level of imports.

Modification of the Mandatory Quota Program

Minor changes in the mandatory quota program were incorporated over the life of the program. They included adjustments required by altered conditions. While such changes affected numerous parties, they were relatively uncontroversial and could be handled through routine administrative action. In another class of changes, however, there were periodic revisions of the quantities allowed

32 "New Allocation Formula Proposed for Imports," *Oil and Gas Journal* June 18, 1962, p. 68; and "Imports-Control Policy Near House Test," *Oil and Gas Journal* June 25, 1962, pp. 88–89.
33 "Fuel Oil Dealers Due Emergency Import Quotas," *Oil and Gas Journal* February 19, 1968, p. 52.

to be imported and of allocations among refineries within this total. While straightforward, administratively simple, and within the context of settled policy, such changes were so significant to affected parties as to always lead to strenuous opposition and spirited support. Finally, modifications of the basic nature of the program were proposed and sometimes instituted. Characteristically, these changes broadened the range of eligible importers and altered the basis of the program from one designed to maintain capacity in the domestic industry to one with broader social aims. Again, the distributional impact of such changes made them inherently political; they demanded resolution at the highest levels.

It is unnecessary to examine the numerous minor modifications in the control system.[34] The controversies around proposed changes that brought large income redistributions, however, serve to illuminate the nature of the control system itself and to demonstrate its broader effects on the economy. An extended discussion of these controversies, only some of which resulted in changes, is reserved for the next two chapters; but identification of the most important of them, and an overview of the special programs to which the general oil import controls gave rise, will be useful to the reader here.

A principal and continuous controversy surrounded the level of imports to be allowed. The distributional issue was sharply drawn between producers (especially those with solely domestic operations) and consumers; and between domestic producers and those who controlled oil output abroad. This controversy was played in public primarily as a conflict between the "public interest" as defined by the consumer benefits of free trade, and the "public interest" as identified with energy security. The stakes were very large, and the conflict commensurately bitter. To the extent that the public interest was focused on limitation of imports, it was indifferent to the allocation of import authority among import quota recipients. The recipients were not indifferent, and efforts to influence the allocation absorbed much time and political energy. The original controls had two discriminatory provisions: the first, the special historical quota, was designed to protect individual

[34] The NPRA *Oil Import Digest* reported on each of these changes as it occurred, and periodically summarized the steps in the development of the program. The interested reader is referred to that document as a starting point for further elaboration on any specific aspect of the operation of the program.

firms from serious immediate and direct harm. The second, the sliding scale provision which gave higher allocations to smaller refiners, was designed to appeal to a broader range of public opinion and to sustain or increase the number of firms in the industry for reasons of competition.

Treatment of imports from the Western Hemisphere, especially overland from Canada and Mexico, confused the rationale for import controls and again was the subject of controversy. The crux of the issue with reference to overland supplies was whether the goal of the program was to protect the domestic industry or whether insecure supplies were to be limited. If the former was the case, to the extent imports from Canada were not to be limited they must be subtracted from the import levels allowed the rest of the world. If not, Canadian oil could be allowed to displace domestic production. The "special" relationship with Western Hemisphere nations further confused and complicated this issue.

Another theme running through controversies over the mandatory quota program was the urge to modify it to foster other goals. Schemes surfaced to use the program to the special benefit of some segments of the refining industry and some domestic producers and marketers; to promote economic development of certain areas and enhanced air quality; and to aid various special consumer groups. Among the most important of these were schemes involved in freeing up imports of residual fuel oil. Residual fuel oil import policy was critical to East Coast consumers, the domestic coal industry, Venezuela, and the Caribbean-based refineries which relied on Venezuelan oil. Special quotas for petrochemical companies, another recurrent proposed modification in the mandatory quota program, were highly controversial because they meant either a reduction in refinery quotas or an increase in imports. Petrochemical companies complained that unfair competitive conditions were created to the extent that refiners could benefit from the import control program and they could not, despite the fact that their inputs, processes, and products overlapped with those of refiners. Petrochemical firms also argued that quotas for them would increase U.S. net exports and thus serve balance of payments goals, without compromising protection of the domestic oil producers or of national security. In yet another effort at changing the basis of the mandatory quota program, U.S. possessions in the Caribbean sought special treatment so that refineries located there could contribute to economic development of those poor and economically depressed islands.

Each of these special programs tended to dilute the effectiveness of oil import control or else to redistribute its costs. They also increased the complexity of its administration. Yet, the basic form of the mandatory quota program remained relatively unchanged throughout its life. By late 1970, however, it was clear that Districts I–IV were soon to face the same crude insufficiency that had always existed in District V. Rather than hold to a restrictive formula which would drive crude prices up, the decision was made to divide the rising oil demand between domestic and foreign producers. With Proclamation 4210 of April 18, 1973, of course, the mandatory quota program was suspended.[35] It was replaced with an import fee which, because it was not collected on volumes previously imported under the quota, initially lowered the cost of imported oil. The demise of quantitative import controls was thus finally the result of a gap between domestic energy supply and demand so great as to require intolerable price increases in order to close it.

The domestic oil situation changed substantially during the life of the mandatory quota program. As the program began in 1959, imports made up less than 10 percent of demand, the domestic industry was woefully overextended with excess productive capacity, prices on the world market were substantially below domestic prices, and imports were rising rapidly. Fourteen years later, imports were about a third of consumption, domestic excess capacity had been eliminated, and the price of imported oil was beginning to drive domestic prices higher. Quantitative controls could not stop these basic shifts in underlying economic conditions, but they did slow the domestic response to these changes. Some of the important consequences that followed are considered in later chapters.

[35] *Federal Register* vol. 38, p. 9645 (April 19, 1973).

Appendix: Proclamation 3279 and Amendments

A. Presidential Proclamation 3279: Adjusting Imports of Petroleum and Petroleum Products into the United States

March 10, 1959 (*Federal Register* vol. 24, pp. 1781–84, March 12, 1959)

WHEREAS, pursuant to section 2 of the act of July 1, 1954, as amended (72 Stat. 678, 19 U.S.C. 1352a), the Director of the Office of Civil and Defense Mobilization has made an appropriate investigation to determine the effects on the national security of imports of crude oil and crude oil derivatives and products and, having considered the matters required by him to be considered by the said act of July 1, 1954, as amended, has advised me of his opinion "that crude oil and the principal crude oil derivatives and products are being imported in such quantities and under such circumstances as to threaten to impair the national security"; and

WHEREAS, having considered the matters required by me to be considered by the said act of July 1, 1954, as amended, I agree with the said advice; and

WHEREAS I find and declare that adjustments must be made in the imports of crude oil, unfinished oils, and finished products, so that such imports will not so threaten to impair the national security; and

WHEREAS I find and declare that within the continental United States there are two areas, one, east of the Rocky Mountains (Districts I–IV), in which there is substantial oil production capacity in excess of actual production, and the other, west of the Rocky Mountains (District V), in which production is declining and in which, due to the absence of any significant inter-area flow of oil, limited imports are necessary to meet demand, and that accordingly, imports into such areas must be treated differently to avoid discouragement of and decrease in domestic oil production, exploration and development to the detriment of the national security; and

WHEREAS I find and declare that the Commonwealth of Puerto Rico largely depends upon imported crude oil, unfinished oils, and finished products and that any system for the adjustment of imports of such commodities should permit imports into Puerto Rico adequate for the purposes of local consumption, export to foreign areas, and limited shipment of finished products to the continental United States:

NOW, THEREFORE, I, DWIGHT D. EISENHOWER, President of the United States of America, acting under and by virtue of the authority vested in me by section 2 of the act of July 1, 1954, as amended, do hereby proclaim as follows:

Sec. 1. (a) In Districts I–IV, District V, and in Puerto Rico, on and after March 11, 1959, no crude oil or unfinished oils may be entered for consumption or withdrawn from warehouse for consumption, and on and after April 1, 1959, no finished products may be entered for consumption or withdrawn from warehouse for consumption, except (1) by or for the account of a person to whom a license has been issued by the Secretary of the Interior pursuant to an allocation made to such person by the Secretary in accordance with regulations issued by the Secretary, and such entries and withdrawals may be made only in accordance with the terms of such license, or (2) as authorized by the Secretary pursuant to paragraph (b) of this section, or (3) as to finished products, by or for the account of a department, establishment, or agency of the United States, which shall not be required to have such a license but which shall be subject to the provisions of paragraph (c) of this section.

(b) Until the Secretary of the Interior is able to make allocations and issue licenses, he may, subject to such conditions as he may deem appropriate, temporarily authorize such entries and withdrawals without licenses and the quantities so entered or withdrawn shall be deducted from any allocation subsequently made by the Secretary to any person who has made any such entry or withdrawal.

(c) In Districts I–IV, District V, and in Puerto Rico, on and after April 1, 1959, no department, establishment, or agency of the United States shall import finished products in excess of the respective allocations made to them by the Secretary of the Interior. Such allocations shall be within the maximum levels of imports established in section 2 of this proclamation.

Sec. 2. (a)(1) In Districts I–IV the maximum level of imports of crude oil, unfinished oils, and finished products, except residual fuel oil to be used as fuel, shall be approximately 9% of total demand in these districts, as estimated by the Bureau of Mines for periods fixed by the Secretary of the Interior. Within this maximum level, imports of finished products, exclusive of residual fuel oil to be used as fuel, shall not exceed the level of imports of such products into these districts during the calendar year 1957 and imports of unfinished oils shall not exceed 10% of the permissible imports of crude oil and unfinished oils.

(2) In Districts I–IV the imports of residual fuel oil to be used as fuel shall not exceed the level of imports of that product into these districts during the calendar year 1957.

(b) In District V the maximum level of imports of crude oil, unfinished oils, and finished products shall be an amount which, together with domestic production and supply, will approximate total demand in this district as estimated by the Bureau of Mines for periods fixed by the Secretary. Within this maximum level imports of finished products shall not exceed the level of imports of such products into this district during the calendar year 1957 and imports of unfinished oils shall not exceed 10% of the permissible imports of crude oil and unfinished oils.

(c) Such additional imports of crude oil may be permitted in addition to the maximum levels established in paragraphs (a) and (b) of this section as are necessary to meet the minimum requirements of refiners, and pipeline companies using crude oil directly as fuel, which are not able to obtain sufficient quantities of domestic crude oil by ordinary and continuous means, such as by barges, pipelines, or tankers.

(d) The maximum level of imports of crude oil, unfinished oils, and finished products into Puerto Rico shall be approximately the level of imports into Puerto Rico during all or part of the calendar year 1958, as determined by the Secretary of the Interior to be consonant with the purposes of this proclamation, or such lower or higher levels as the Secretary may subsequently determine are required to meet increases or decreases in local demand in Puerto Rico or demand for export to foreign areas.

(e) The Secretary of the Interior shall keep under review the imports into Districts I–IV and into District V of residual fuel oil to be used as fuel and the Secretary may make, on a monthly basis if required, such adjustments in the maximum level of such imports as he may determine to be consonant with the objectives of this proclamation.

(f) The levels established, and the total demand referred to, in this section do not include free withdrawals by persons pursuant to section 309 of the Tariff Act of 1930, as amended (19 U.S.C. 1309), or petroleum supplies for vessels or aircraft operated by the United States between points referred to in said section 309 (as to vessels or aircraft, respectively) or between any point in the United States or its possessions and any point in a foreign country.

Sec. 3. (a) The Secretary of the Interior is hereby authorized to issue regulations for the purpose of implementing this proclamation. Such regulations shall be consistent with the levels established in this proclamation for imports of crude oil, unfinished oils, and finished products into Districts I–IV, into District V, and into Puerto Rico, and shall provide for a system of allocation of the authorized imports of such crude oil, unfinished oils and finished products and for the issuance of licenses pursuant to such system, with such restrictions upon the transfer of allocations and licenses as may be deemed appropriate to further the purposes of this proclamation.

(b)(1) With respect to the allocations of imports of crude oil and unfinished oils into Districts I–IV, and into District V, such regulations shall provide, to the extent possible, for a fair and equitable distribution among persons having refinery capacity in these districts in relation to refinery inputs during an appropriate period or periods selected by the Secretary and may provide for distribution in such manner as to avoid drastic reductions below the last allocations under the Voluntary Oil Import Program. Such regulations also shall provide for allocations of crude oil to persons having operating refinery capacity or having pipeline facilities using crude oil directly as fuel who show inability to obtain sufficient quantities of domestic crude oil by ordinary and continuous means, such as barges, pipelines, or tankers.

(2) Such regulations shall provide for the allocation of imports of crude oil and unfinished oils into Puerto Rico among persons having refinery capacity in Puerto Rico in relation to refinery inputs during all or a part of the calendar year 1958 as the Secretary may determine.

(3) Such regulations shall require that imported crude oil and unfinished oils be processed in the licensee's refinery except that exchanges for domestic crude or unfinished oils may be made if otherwise lawful, if effected on a current basis and reported in advance to the Secretary, and if the domestic crude or unfinished oils are processed in the licensee's refinery. However, persons receiving allocations of crude oil on the basis of inability to obtain sufficient domestic crude by ordinary and continuous means shall not be permitted to make exchanges.

(4) With respect to the allocations of imports of finished products into Districts I–IV, District V, and Puerto Rico, such regulations shall, to the extent possible, result in a fair and equitable distribution of such products among persons who have been importers of finished products during the respective base periods specified in section 2 of this proclamation.

(c) Such regulations may provide for the revocation or suspension by the Secretary of any allocation or license on grounds relating to the national security, or the violation of the terms of this proclamation, or of any regulation or license issued pursuant to this proclamation.

Sec. 4. For the purpose of hearing and considering appeals or petitions by persons affected by the regulations issued by the Secretary of the Interior, he is authorized to provide for the establishment and operation of an Appeal Board, comprised of one representative each from the Departments of the Interior, Defense, and Commerce to be designated, respectively, by the heads of such Departments. Such representatives shall be of the rank of Deputy Assistant Secretary or higher. The Appeal Board may be empowered, on grounds of hardship, error, or other relevant special consideration, but within the limits of the maximum levels of imports established in section 2 of this proclamation (1) to modify any allocation made to any person under the regulations issued pursuant to section 3 of this proclamation, (2) to grant allocations of crude oil and unfinished oils in special circumstances to persons with importing histories who do not qualify for allocations under such regulations; and (3) to review the revocation or suspension of any allocation or license. The Secretary may provide that such decisions by the Appeal Board shall be final.

Sec. 5. Persons who apply for allocations of crude oil, unfinished oils, or finished products and persons to whom such allocations have been made shall furnish to the Secretary of the Interior such information and shall make such reports as he may require, by regulation or otherwise, in the discharge of his responsibilities under this proclamation.

Sec. 6. (a) The Director of the Office of Civil and Defense Mobilization shall maintain a constant surveillance of imports of petroleum and its primary derivatives in respect of the national security and, after consultation with the Secretaries of State, Defense, Treasury, the Interior, Commerce, and Labor, he shall inform the President of any circumstances which, in the Director's opinion might indicate the need for further Presidential action under section 2 of the act of July 1, 1954, as amended. In the event prices of crude oil or its products or derivatives should be increased after the effective date of this proclamation, such surveillance shall include a determination as to whether such increase or increases are necessary to accomplish the national security objectives of the act of July 1, 1954, as amended, and of this proclamation.

(b) The Special Committee to Investigate Crude Oil Imports is hereby discharged of its responsibilities.

Sec. 7. The Secretary of the Interior may delegate, and provide for successive redelegation of, the authority conferred upon him by this proclamation. All departments and agencies of the Executive branch of the Government shall cooperate with and assist the Secretary of the Interior in carrying out the purposes of this proclamation.

Sec. 8. Executive Order 10761 of March 27, 1958, entitled "Government Purchases of Crude Petroleum and Petroleum Products" (23 F.R. 2067) is hereby revoked as of April 1, 1959.

Sec. 9. As used in this proclamation:

(a) "Person" includes an individual, a corporation, firm, or other business organization or legal entity, and an agency of a state, territorial, or local government, but does not include a department, establishment, or agency of the United States;

(b) "Districts I–IV" means the District of Columbia and all of the States of the United States except those States within District V;

(c) "District V" means the States of Arizona, Nevada, California, Oregon, Washington, Alaska, and the Territory of Hawaii;

(d) "Crude oil" means crude petroleum as it is produced at the wellhead;

(e) "Finished Products" means any one or more of the following petroleum oils, or a mixture or combination of such oils, which are to be used without further processing except blending by mechanical means:

(1) Liquefied gases—hydrocarbon gases recovered from natural gas or produced from petroleum refining and kept under pressure to maintain a liquid state at ambient temperatures;

(2) Gasoline—a refined petroleum distillate which, by its composition, is suitable for use as a carburant in internal combustion engines;

(3) Jet fuel—a refined petroleum distillate used to fuel jet propulsion engines;

(4) Naphtha—a refined petroleum distillate falling within a distillation range overlapping the higher gasoline and the lower kerosenes;

(5) Fuel oil—a liquid or liquefiable petroleum product burned for lighting or for the generation of heat or power and derived directly or indirectly from crude oil, such as kerosene, range oil, distillate fuel oils, gas oil, diesel fuel, topped crude oil, residues;

(6) Lubricating oil—a refined petroleum distillate or specially treated petroleum residue used to lessen friction between surfaces;

(7) Residual fuel oil—a topped crude oil or viscous residuum which, as obtained in refining or after blending with other fuel oil, meets or is the equivalent of Military Specification Mil–F–859 for Navy Special Fuel Oil and any other more viscous fuel oil, such as No. 5 or Bunker C;

(8) Asphalt—a solid or semi-solid cementitious material which gradually liquefies when heated, in which the predominating constituents are bitumens, and which is obtained in refining crude oil.

(f) "Unfinished Oils" means one or more of the petroleum oils listed in paragraph (e) of this section, or a mixture or combination of such oils, which are to be further processed other than by blending by mechanical means.

IN WITNESS WHEREOF, I have hereunto set my hand and caused the Seal of the United States of America to be affixed.

DONE at the City of Washington this tenth day of March in the year of our Lord nineteen hundred and fifty-nine, and of the (SEAL) Independence of the United States of America the one-hundred and eighty-third.

DWIGHT D. EISENHOWER.

By the President:
CHRISTIAN A. HERTER,
   Acting Secretary of State.

B. Summaries of Amendments to Proclamation 3279 Through 1973

Proclamation 3290; April 30, 1959 (*Federal Register* vol. 24, pp. 3527–29, May 2, 1959).

1. Excludes from allocation controls crude oil, unfinished oils or finished products which are transported to the United States by pipeline, rail or other means of overland transportation from the country where they were produced; which country, in case of unfinished oils or finished products, is also the country of production of crude oil from which they were processed or manufactured. This clause would exempt from controls imports from Canada.
2. The quantities subject to allocation shall not be reduced because of product imports, except in District V where the level of allocation is to be reduced to cancel the effect of above relaxation.
3. Restriction removed on the exchange of crude among domestic refiners.

Proclamation 3328; December 10, 1959 (*Federal Register* vol. 24, pp. 10133–34, December 16, 1959).

1. Sets the maximum level of imports of crude oil and finished products in District V at total demand minus domestic production. However, the import of finished products must not exceed the level of imports in 1957.
2. The level of allocations in Districts I–IV will not be reduced because of imports which are exempted from allocation controls.

Proclamation 3386; December 24, 1960 (*Federal Register* vol. 25, p. 13945, December 30, 1960).

1. Sets the maximum level of imports of all petroleum products, except residual fuel oil in Districts I–IV, at 9 percent of the total demand.
2. Imports of finished petroleum products are not to exceed the level of imports in 1957. Unfinished product imports are not to exceed 10 percent of the permissible imports of crude oil and unfinished oil.

Proclamation 3389; January 17, 1961 (*Federal Register* vol. 26, p. 507, January 20, 1961).

1. Imports of residual fuel oil into District I and into Districts II–IV not to exceed the level of imports into the respective areas in calendar year 1957.
2. Permits the entrance of new importers and establishes a redistribution of import licenses.
3. Redefines Districts I–IV: 'District I' includes the states of Maine, New Hampshire, Vermont, Massachusetts, Connecticut, Rhode Island, New York, New Jersey, Pennsylvania, Maryland, Delaware, West Virginia, Virginia, North Carolina, Georgia, Florida and the District of Columbia. All other states formally in Districts I–IV are redefined as Districts II–IV.

Proclamation 3509; November 30, 1962 (*Federal Register* vol. 27, pp. 11985–88, December 5, 1962).

1. Links the maximum level of imports into Districts I–IV to domestic production of crude oil and natural gas liquids.
2. The maximum level of all imports subject to allocation, except residual fuel oil into Districts I–IV, shall be an amount equal to the difference between 12.2 percent of the quantity of crude oil and natural gas liquids produced in these districts and the quantity of imports from oil-producing countries which are not subject to allocation.
3. Imports of finished products other than residual fuel oil not to exceed the level of imports of such products in calendar year 1957.
4. Import of unfinished oils not to exceed 10 percent of the permissible imports of crude oil and unfinished oils.
5. The maximum level of imports as determined above to be adjusted by 9 percent of the amount by which total estimated demand fell

short or exceeded the actual demand for the same period in the previous year.

6. In all districts the distribution of allocations to be related to refinery inputs, excluding the imported inputs from oil-producing countries not subject to allocation controls.

Proclamation 3531; April 19, 1963 (*Federal Register* vol. 28, p. 4077, April 25, 1963).

Establishes the constitution and operations of the Oil Import Appeals Board.

Proclamation 3541; June 10, 1963 (*Federal Register* vol. 28, p. 5931, June 13, 1963).

1. The maximum level of imports into Districts I–IV of all petroleum products except residual fuel oil subject to allocation shall be an amount equal to the difference between 12.2 percent of the quantity of crude oil and natural gas liquids which the secretary of interior estimates will be produced in these districts and the quantity of imports from oil-producing countries exempted from allocation.

2. Imports of finished products other than residual fuel oil not to exceed the level of imports of such products in the calendar year 1957.

3. Imports of unfinished oils not to exceed 10 percent of the permissible imports of crude oil and unfinished oils.

4. Deletes clause concerning adjustment of imports to fluctuations in demand.

Proclamation 3693; December 10, 1965 (*Federal Register* vol. 30, pp. 15459–61, December 16, 1965).

1. Brings imports into foreign trade zones and Puerto Rico under the allocation controls. This, however, does not include previously exempted imports.

2. The maximum level of imports into Districts I–IV, except residual fuel oil, subject to allocation shall be an amount equal to the difference between 12.2 percent of the quantity of crude oil and natural gas liquids estimated by the secretary to be produced in these districts and the quantity of exempted imports from oil-producing countries and from Puerto Rico during comparable base period in the calendar year 1965.

3. Import of finished oils other than residual fuel oil shall not exceed the level of imports during the calendar year 1957.

4. The maximum level of imports of finished products into Puerto Rico shall be approximately the level of imports during the calendar year 1958.

5. Allocation of imports of crude oil and unfinished oils into Puerto Rico based on the estimated requirements in calendar year 1964.

6. Shipments or sales of unfinished oils or finished products from Puerto Rico to Districts I–IV in excess of that shipped or sold in a corresponding base period in 1964 or 1965 will reduce allocations for the next period by the amount of excess.
7. Allows for the establishment of new processing facilities in Puerto Rico which would promote employment and industrial development of Puerto Rico.
8. Imported crude oil or unfinished oils must be processed in licensee's facilities.

Proclamation 3779; April 10, 1967 (*Federal Register* vol. 32, p. 5919, April 13, 1967).

Directs the secretary of interior to review demand and supply of asphalt in all districts and Puerto Rico and allows imports of asphalt with or without licenses at his discretion.

Proclamation 3794; July 16, 1967 (*Federal Register* vol. 32, p. 10547, July 19, 1967).

1. Aims at ensuring an adequate supply of low-sulfur residual fuel oil in support of air pollution controls.
2. The maximum level of imports of residual fuel oil into Districts I–V will be the level of imports in calendar year 1957, as adjusted by the secretary of interior.
3. Provides for fair and equitable distribution of residual fuel oil among importers where the maximum sulfur content is to be specified by the secretary.

Proclamation 3820; November 9, 1967 (*Federal Register* vol. 32, pp. 15701–02, November 15, 1967).

1. Allows for the development of petrochemical facilities in the Virgin Islands.
2. Allows for import of finished products other than residual fuel oil from Virgin Islands into Districts I–IV, up to a maximum limit of 15,000 average barrels per day in any allocation period.

Proclamation 3823; January 29, 1968 (*Federal Register* vol. 33, pp. 1171–73, January 30, 1968).

1. Regulates shipments from Puerto Rico to District V.
2. Deals with the supply disruption following the 1967 Middle East crisis.
3. Controls imports of liquids derived from tar sands.
4. The maximum level of imports of crude oil into Puerto Rico shall be established, taking into account shipments from Puerto Rico to Districts I–V and the demand for finished products within Puerto Rico.

5. Provides for fair and equitable distribution of allocations among persons having refinery capacity in Districts I–V, on the basis of:
   (a) level of refinery inputs
   (b) level of input or output of petrochemical plants
   (c) export of finished products or petrochemicals
   (d) imports of inputs from oil-producing countries which are exempted from allocation controls are to be excluded in determining the allocations
   (e) gradual reduction of historical allocations, but not less than the allocation computed on the basis of refinery inputs.
6. Import allocations in Puerto Rico based on refinery capacity in 1964 and maintenance of shipments to Districts I–V at 1965 levels.
7. Allows license holders unable to fully utilize their licenses in 1967 because of Middle East crisis to do so in 1968 or 1969.

Proclamation 3969, March 10, 1970 (*Federal Register* vol. 35, pp. 4321–22, March 11, 1970).

1. Imports of Canadian crude oil and unfinished oils into Districts I–IV to be subject to voluntary controls; limited to 395,000 average barrels per day in the period March 1, 1970 through December 31, 1970.
2. The secretary of interior shall make allocations for Canadian imports.

Proclamation 3990; June 17, 1970 (*Federal Register* vol. 35, pp. 10091–92, June 19, 1970).

1. Allows the import of an additional 100,000 barrels of No. 2 fuel oil per day from Western Hemisphere sources into District I.
2. No license or allocation shall be required in connection with the transportation to the United States by pipeline through a foreign country of crude oil, unfinished oils or finished products produced in the customs territory of the United States.

Proclamation 4018; October 16, 1970 (*Federal Register* vol. 35, pp. 16357–58, October 20, 1970).

1. Allows for imports of 14.6 million barrels of No. 2 fuel oil during 1971 from Western Hemisphere sources; to be allocated to independent deepwater terminal operators.
2. Natural gas liquids produced in Canada may be imported into the United States without license.
3. Ethane, butane, and propane produced in the Western Hemisphere may be imported into the United States without reducing other allocations.
4. Crude oil produced in Canada may be imported into District I for use as boiler fuel without reducing other allocations.

Proclamation 4025; December 22, 1970 (*Federal Register* vol. 35, pp. 19391–95, December 23, 1970).

1. The quantity of crude oil, unfinished oils, and finished products that may be imported into Districts I–IV continues to be determined on the basis of 12.2 percent of the quantity of crude oil and natural gas liquids which the secretary of interior estimates will be produced in these districts.
2. Canadian component of imports set at approximately 100,000 barrels per day during 1971.
3. Allows for Mexican imports at a level of 30,000 barrels per day.

Proclamation 4092; November 5, 1971 (*Federal Register* vol. 36, pp. 21397–99, November 9, 1971).

1. Extends indefinitely the provision permitting the import of No. 2 fuel oil into District I. Allows the import of an average of 45,000 barrels per day of No. 2 fuel oil from Western Hemisphere sources to be allocated to persons in District I who do not have crude oil import allocations for Districts I–IV.
2. Enables the holders of allocations of No. 2 fuel oil to import from Puerto Rico, but not to exceed an average of 5,000 barrels per day.
3. The director of emergency preparedness may advise the secretary of interior to suspend the requirement that No. 2 fuel oil imports must be produced in the Western Hemisphere, if that requirement restricts the availability of No. 2 fuel oil in District I.

Proclamation 4099; December 20, 1971 (*Federal Register* vol. 36, pp. 24203–04, December 22, 1971).

1. Allows increased licensed imports into Districts I–IV for 1972, including the Canadian component of those imports, by approximately 100,000 barrels over the 1971 level of imports.
2. The quantity of crude oil, unfinished oils, and finished oil products that may be imported into Districts I–IV continues to be determined on a basis of 12.2 percent of the quantity of crude oil and natural gas liquids which the secretary of the interior estimates will be produced in those districts.

Proclamation 4133; May 11, 1972 (*Federal Register* vol. 37, p. 9543, May 12, 1972).

1. Permits an increase in import licenses for Districts I–IV to meet demand requirements for the remainder of 1972.
2. The maximum level of imports of crude oil, unfinished oils, and finished products is increased from 965,000 barrels per day to 1,165,000 barrels per day.
3. The Canadian component of imports is increased from 540,000 barrels per day to 570,000 barrels per day.

Proclamation 4156; September 18, 1972 (*Federal Register* vol. 37, pp. 19115–16, September 19, 1972).

1. Allows for increased imports to meet the rapid increase in demand.
2. The secretary of interior may allocate an additional 5,000 barrels of No. 2 fuel oil during the period January 1, 1972 through December 31, 1972.
3. Increases allocations of crude oil, unfinished oils, and finished products for the remainder of 1972, up to a maximum of 10 percent of the existing allocations held, providing such additional allocations be deducted from any allocation made for the period of January 1, 1973 through December 31, 1973.

Proclamation 4175; December 16, 1972 (*Federal Register* vol. 37, pp. 28043–44, December 20, 1972).

1. Occasional shortages of certain finished products may be relieved by additional imports from the Virgin Islands.
2. The secretary of interior is authorized to make additional allocations of crude oil, unfinished oil, and finished products to meet the shortages of these products. However, such additional allocations will be deducted from subsequent allocations made to that importer.

Proclamation 4178; January 17, 1973 (*Federal Register* vol. 38, pp. 1719–21, January 18, 1973).

1. Permits an increase of 915,000 barrels per day in licensed imports into Districts I–IV, including the Canadian component of those imports.
2. Fixes the Canadian component of import allocations into Districts I–IV at a maximum of 675,000 barrels per day.
3. The maximum level of imports of crude oil, unfinished oils, and finished products is set at 2,025,000 barrels per day, reflecting the increase of 915,000 barrels per day.
4. The average level of imports of No. 2 fuel oil into District I is set at 50,000 barrels per day for the period May 1, 1973 through December 31, 1973.
5. Permits No. 2 fuel oil to be imported freely into Districts I–IV for the period January 1, 1973 through April 30, 1973.

Proclamation 4202; March 23, 1973 (*Federal Register* vol. 38, pp. 7977–78, March 27, 1973).

Empowers the appeals board to make allocations in cases of exceptional hardship or special circumstances to persons who do not qualify for allocations based on import history within the limits of maximum level of imports, as established by section 2 of Proclamation 3279.

Proclamation 4210; April 18, 1973 (*Federal Register* vol. 38, pp. 9645–46, April 19, 1973).

1. Suspends tariffs on imports of petroleum and petroleum products and replaces them by license fees. The license fees may be adjusted from time to time in order to control the level of imports.
2. Calls for encouragement of investment in domestic refining, petro-chemical plants, and exploration.
3. The maximum level of imports shall be the difference between sup-ply and estimated demand.
4. Establishes the maximum levels of imports, not subject to allocation or license, from Canada, Mexico, and other sources.
5. Any additional imports are made subject to licensing fees.
6. The maximum level of imports not subject to licensing fees shall be gradually reduced and by April 30, 1980, the system of issuing alloca-tions and licenses not subject to fees shall be abolished.

Proclamation 4227; June 19, 1973 (*Federal Register* vol. 38, pp. 16195–201, June 21, 1973).

1. Establishes the level of licensing fees on imports from Canada over and above the level of imports set in section 2.
2. Sets the level of licensing fees on motor gasoline, unfinished oils, or finished products imported from American Samoa, Guam, Virgin Islands, or other foreign trade zones at the rate applicable to feed-stocks.

4

Major Controversies Within the Mandatory Quota Program

The mandatory quota program was controversial because it involved matters of great private and public importance. It altered the distribution of income and wealth and the allocation of resources. Its provisions directly and obviously improved the position of some individuals and firms at the expense of others and affected the regional distribution of income. Direct and parochial economic interests thus accompanied broader national concerns in the formulation of the mandatory quota program.

Among the public interest concerns was the role imported oil played in national security. Quite divergent views were held on this issue, and ranged from a position that sought petroleum autarky in order to achieve security to one which argued for enlarged imports to avoid "draining America first." Concerns about long-run energy resource availability and environmental quality were brought into the debate on oil import policy, especially toward the end of the program. The strain of shifting from an international trade export surplus to a deficit on current account was an important factor in molding the views of some people on oil import policy. The importance of these issues, and the attitude toward "big oil" which tended to place oil imports in the center of any situation in which they played any part at all, explains much of the fervency with which controversies about the control program were joined. Additionally, of course, positions ostensibly based on these public policy issues were advanced by those with corresponding private interests, which added to the stridency if not to the logic of the debate. Finally, the regional effects of import controls led to political leaders, especially in Congress, formulating and communicating positions favorable to their constituencies.

There were almost limitless ways to handle import controls, and conflicts arose over which would be chosen. There were six major issues with important national economic, political, and distributional consequences that ran through the life of the mandatory control program. The first was the question of what level of imports was to be allowed. The second issue was whether import quotas were to be open to all refiners, just to those refiners in the industry when controls were imposed, or to other types of firms as well. Once it was determined that quotas were to be given "newcomers," the focus of this controversy shifted to the criteria for allocation of import authority between them and the historic importers. The third issue was the distribution of quotas among recipients by size. The fourth controversy concerned the distribution among oil exporters of the right to export to the United States. Western Hemisphere oil producers sought special access to the U.S. market, and the question was whether they were to get it. A continuing issue, never really resolved, was whether the mandatory quota program should be replaced by an altogether different import control alternative. Finally, the most serious and certainly most complex issue was whether import controls should be used for any purpose other than simply regulating imports—whether, that is, their goal might be broadened to affect the distribution of income or to achieve other ends.

The development of the basic structure of the mandatory quota program can be understood better through examination of these issues than through a chronological recounting of events. These issues, in turn, are illuminated by an understanding of what lay behind them—what economic and other factors led interest groups to adopt the positions and arguments that they did. Consequently, each issue is taken up below and followed through to the last stages of the mandatory quota program. In the next chapter special provisions of the program that had important effects, either on the industry or on the economy, are discussed separately.

Level of Imports

The level of oil imports to be allowed into the nation under the restrictive program was the cornerstone issue throughout the mandatory quota program. It set the boundaries on the importance of the restraint and determined the potential size of the overall impact of the program. It was the central issue in the debate over the wisdom of import control. Positions regarding this issue were discussed above, but may be summarized here as an introduction to developments between 1959 and 1973.

The domestic fuel industries (petroleum and its substitutes) supported restriction on imports because imports of oil reduced the value of the invested capital of energy producers, the rents of those who owned mineral rights to energy sources, and the quasi-rents of specialized resources, including labor, devoted to production of fuel. The interest of these groups as producers was in restricting imports as much as possible. Protection from potential fuel supply interdiction for reasons of national security, strictly defined, would lead to a similar posture of minimizing imports.[1] On the other hand, looked at in the short run, consumers as consumers would prefer an import–domestic oil mix that would minimize current fuel cost—which implies no control over imports. For the long run, consumers would prefer a policy which minimized the current discounted value of the stream of fuel costs over time, which, given certainty, could imply import restrictions or import subsidies as well.

Two other positions existed, though they were neither precisely formulated nor based on reasoning that recognizes a maximizing test. An isolationist–primitive mercantilist thread is found in expressions of those against imports during the period of controls. This body of opinion wished the nation to be free of reliance upon foreign sources of oil, just as it wished it to be free of other foreign entanglements. The negative emotional response to growing world interdependence was reinforced, or sometimes rationalized, by the recurring argument that jobs were being exported or wealth sent

---

[1] It is important to remember that military security at this time was still keyed to views of a war of attrition, such as World War II, when military fuel consumption could be a much greater portion of total fuel use than in later decades.

to foreigners. That this reasoning and line of thought failed common tests of economic rationality did not make it any the less important as a political force. Another theme, one with divergent implications for imports, was the "conservation" position that resisted a policy which it saw as promoting "drain America first." Fear of resource inadequacy in oil has a long history, and while this concern was not acute during the period in which controls were being established, it certainly was pervasive by the late 1960s when the allowed level of imports was again an important issue. Even in the early days of the control issue, this position had sufficient support to require an explicit refutation by the Special Cabinet Committee to Investigate Crude Oil Imports.[2] Environmental concerns joined concern about resource adequacy during the latter part of the control period and influenced views of the appropriate mix between imported and domestic oil, oil and coal, and the appropriate level of energy consumption.

In each general grouping of interested parties there were subgroups whose interests diverged from those of the rest of the group. It is therefore neither accurate nor useful to suggest that positions were always aligned with broad groupings of actors. Functions within the same firm could even be affected differently by imports and thus different divisions could favor different levels of import constraint, whatever position they were required to take by the central management of the firm. For example, while major integrated international oil companies owned domestic reserves and processing facilities which would benefit from import restraints, they were also in a position to benefit from unlimited imports because of their favored position in world markets. Imports provided them an exclusive benefit, while they shared the much more competitive domestic producing market with others. In general, then, the overall interest of such firms was complex; it would diverge from either the simple "no restraint" or the "no imports" postures of others. Within each interest group similar tradeoffs were required, and the final position taken by each depended upon the net effects of the quantity of imports and upon views of the public

[2] Special Committee to Investigate Crude Oil Imports, report to the president, "Petroleum Imports," July 29, 1957, reprinted in *The Oil Import Question*, A Report on the Relationship of Oil Imports to the National Security, prepared by the Cabinet Task Force on Oil Import Control (Washington, GPO, 1970) pp. 181–190.

interest in restraining dependence on foreign oil. The net effect, in turn, was often determined by the actual provisions of the import control mechanisms. The point to be made is this: *a priori* determination of the private interest of a firm or pressure group in the level of imports is not always possible. The decisions taken were the result of the interplay of very complex forces and influences, and any attempt to infer the power of conflicting interest groups from the decisions made is likely to be misleading. One thing, however, is certain: changes in the overall level of imports created and destroyed enormous private wealth, and controversy surrounded each such decision.

Given the importance of the decision on level of imports, one would have hoped for detailed policy analysis and justification for the level selected. Such analysis is not apparent from the record. Four major reports were prepared on the import question and there is no evidence in any of them of careful consideration of the issue of what an appropriate level of imports would be. Though distressing to the purist analyst, it is not surprising to the politically attuned observer that the rationale for the levels chosen was not articulated and perhaps never formulated: no unambiguous criteria existed, and decisions based on any criterion, if made explicit, could easily have been refuted or challenged.

The President's Cabinet Advisory Committee on Energy Supplies and Resources Policy in its report, issued by the White House on February 26, 1955, made no reference to the basis of its conclusion that

> if the imports of crude and residual oils should exceed significantly the respective proportions that these imports of oils bore to the production of domestic crude oil in 1954, the domestic fuels situation could be so impaired as to endanger the orderly industrial growth which assures the military and civilian supplies and reserves that are necessary to the national defense. There would be inadequate incentive for the exploration and the discovery of new sources of supply.[3]

The task force on whose recommendations this cabinet committee relied did not offer further documentation as to why the 1954 pro-

---

[3] Presidential Advisory Committee on Energy Supplies and Resources, *Report,* February 26, 1955, reprinted in *The Oil Import Question,* pp. 165–166.

portion was chosen.[4] With reference to residual fuel oil, on the other hand, the task force was more precise in its criteria, implying that a coal industry of at least 500 million tons should be protected and that East Coast residual imports should be limited to the proportionate increase in heavy fuel (including coal) demand *unless* coal output was above 500 million tons.[5] On the basis of these reports, one is left with the conclusion that the 1954 proportion of imports (10.3 percent nationwide; 11.3 percent in Districts I–IV; 5.2 percent in District V) was chosen because it was the last year on which data existed. Additionally, of course, by recommending that the existing import levels be stabilized, the problem of taking positive action which would harm particular interests was avoided—no rollback in import levels was indicated.

The second major policy document, that of October 17, 1956, from the reconvened Cabinet Committee on Energy Supplies and Resources, made recommendations, again with no underlying analysis made public. Its conclusion was that non-Western Hemisphere imports should be limited to the 1954 proportions of domestic oil production in Districts I–IV, that Western Hemisphere imports should be closely watched, and that the informal agreement with Venezuela to maintain a voluntary quota should be monitored. It suggested a course of watchful waiting on the situation in District V, as it was apparent that a crude deficit existed there. No policies were adopted regarding residual fuel oil because the level of imports of this heavy fuel were not deemed troublesome, but continued periodic surveillance was suggested.[6] Again, analytical formulation, much less determination, of the optimal rate of imports was not present in the report. The year 1954 was again adopted as a standard, and future divergence from this *status quo ante* position was taken as a signal for more forceful action restricting imports.

The third study, that by the Special Committee to Investigate Crude Oil Imports, similarly picked a convenient, though analytically unsupported, figure as the magic number for allowed im-

---

[4] Task Force Report of the Cabinet Committee on Energy Supplies and Resources Policy, November 24, 1954, reprinted in *The Oil Import Question*, pp. 169–175.

[5] Ibid., p. 172.

[6] Presidential Advisory Committee on Energy Supplies and Resources, *Report*, October 17, 1956, reprinted in *The Oil Import Question*, pp. 176–178.

ports—12 percent of domestic production or 9.6 percent of demand in Districts I–IV, and the difference between the amount demanded and the amount supplied "on a reasonably competitive basis" for District V.[7] The actual level of District I–IV imports during 1956 was 12.3 percent, an increase of 1 percent over 1954. This rate was lowered, however, by the Suez crisis, and thus the standard set in the 1957 report implied an actual reduction in the proportion of the U.S. market that imports should be allowed to take.

Finally, of course, the mandatory quota program, based on the March 6, 1959 report of the cabinet committee, established 9 percent of Bureau of Mines (BOM) estimated petroleum product demand (excluding residual) as the standard for Districts I–IV.[8] This proclamation required a considerable reduction in the actual level of imports and a reduction in the ratio of imports to demand that had held in the past. Again, no analytical criterion could be ascertained from the level of imports chosen.

The absence of a clear criterion left import policy with no basis to which all parties could refer. Since the ratio of allowed imports chosen was not founded on any obvious exogenous or predetermined standard, it was free to be changed through the operation of political forces. Groups with special interests in the level of imports were thus encouraged to exercise maximum efforts at the political level. In a situation such as oil import controls, where there are no criteria for fulfilling a public policy, as well as no unambiguous means of determining that the policy itself is in the public interest, maximum opportunity exists for the play of naked political power and gross corruption. It is thus interesting to view the changes in the allowed level of imports in part as responses to developments in the distribution of political influence.[9]

Incentives for increasing imports were present from the institution of mandatory controls. The price of foreign oil was lower

[7] Special Committee to Investigate Crude Oil Imports, *Petroleum Imports,* July 29, 1957, reprinted in *The Oil Import Question,* pp. 187–188.

[8] Presidential Proclamation 3279, *Federal Register* vol. 54, pp. 1781–84 (March 17, 1959).

[9] Residual fuel oil occupied a market effectively isolated from both crude oil and other products. For that reason, the argument over the level of residual imports is reserved for chapter 5 where this program is considered separately.

than that of domestic, and equilibrium in imports had not been established, even in 1959. Consequently, just maintaining imports at the same ratio required action against ever-stronger economic pressures. Since the basis for restriction was security of domestic fuel supply in the event of import disruption, any evidence of economic deterioration in the industry was used to support yet another appeal to restrict imports. Nevertheless, implict in the posturings of such supporters of import controls as the independent producer groups was the realization that the level of imports set in Proclamation 3279, 9 percent of prospective demand, was the best that could be expected. Protecting this position against steady erosion became their most important goal.

Explicit onslaughts were one thing; in addition, however, producer representatives had to contend with unforeseen factors which undermined the import limits. Two such factors arose very soon after controls were instituted: overestimates of demand and overland imports. The prospective demand figures on which import quotas for the next period were determined were based on estimates made by the Bureau of Mines. Unfortunately for the producing interests, the bureau projections seemed consistently to fall on the high side, and extra imports ensued. No adjustments to erroneous estimates were made. To avoid this upward creep in allowed imports, producers wished to have the basis for quotas shifted to domestic petroleum production for the previous period. Not only would a firm number, one not subject to biased estimation, be substituted, but this basis had the added benefit to producers of understating required imports in a period of output growth. The second unforeseen development eroding the market was the growth in overland imports. In 1959, when by special proclamation overland imports were exempted from controls,[10] imports of Canadian oil into Districts I–IV amounted to only 56,000 bbl/day. Imports were not much higher in 1960, but by 1961 they were at 91,500 bbl/day, by 1962 at 109,200, and by 1963, 119,200 bbl/day, and rising.[11] Coming into the country under the peculiar "Brownsville shuffle" (discussed below) was another 30,000 bbl/day

[10] Presidential Proclamation 3290, *Federal Register* vol. 24, p. 3527 (May 2, 1959).

[11] Semiannual Department of the Interior, Oil Import Administration, press releases, issued February and September. The same data can be calculated from Bureau of Mines petroleum statistics releases.

of oil exempt from controls. Despite the supposed limitation of imports to a proportion of demand, then, absolute and relative imports were rising at a time when the domestic industry was uncomfortably underutilized. The victory for the producing interests represented by the mandatory quota program was slipping away.

Presidential Proclamation 3509 resolved both of these issues. Canadian crude could continue to be imported freely, *but* the estimated prospective amount of Canadian imports was to be subtracted from the amount of import quotas otherwise available for allocation.[12] Additionally, the basis for import quotas was shifted from 9 percent of estimated demand to 12.2 percent of actual production, resulting in an estimated 70,000 bbl/day lower imports in the first half of 1963 compared with what would have occurred under the preexisting program.[13]

From this time on, political success or failure by producer interests on import matters was measured by the relative security of the 12.2 percent ratio. The remainder of the struggle over import controls was essentially fought as a rear-guard action against forces seeking to pierce this ceiling. Unfortunately for the producer interests, consistent underestimates of prospective Canadian imports were made, and total imports continued to exceed the new specified percentage. Moreover, in Presidential Proclamation 3541, the basis of calculating domestic production was changed from actual to prospective production.[14] Again, biased or faulty estimating procedures could lead to imports above 12.2 percent. Moreover, the amount imported, even if the estimate were correct, would be based on current domestic production rather than on that of the previous period, a potentially significant difference in a growing market. The producing interests were unable to withstand the pressure for proportionately greater imports obtained in this manner.

In their efforts to restrict imports, producers perceived their power to be centered in Congress. There, it was felt, dedicated and powerful oil state interests might be able to write the 12.2

---

[12] Presidential Proclamation 3509, *Federal Register* vol. 27, p. 11985 (December 5, 1962).

[13] "U.S. Producers to Benefit Most," *Oil and Gas Journal* December 10, 1962, pp. 49–50.

[14] *Federal Register* vol. 28, pp. 5931–32 (June 13, 1963).

percent formula into legislation where it would be immune from discretionary administrative adjustments. These efforts never succeeded, partly because of the growing strength of northeastern consumer representatives, partly because of the opposition of strong presidents who did not wish to see their discretion limited, and partly because of the inertia that must be overcome when significant change is sought in a tolerably successful policy. Congressional pressure did, however, prevent frontal assault on the 12.2 percent criterion. It served to keep imports within some bounds, to the probable distress of presidents who sought more imports in part because of their potential contribution to foreign policy objectives.

There were several periods when serious legislative efforts to obtain greater control over imports were mounted. The strenuous efforts of 1964 achieved some benefits in terms of program adjustment that led to greater demand for domestic production, but did not result in legislative change.[15] Continued expansion of imports and erosion of domestic producer economic conditions led to another major legislative effort in 1967. Both TIPRO and IPAA decided to take the legislative route, using the trade bill as their vehicle. Other industries, including steel and textiles, were expected to join with oil producers in attempting to obtain quota protection.[16] The administration argued against the loss of flexibility inherent in the proposed import control bill, while producers pointed to the necessity for greater rigidity to reduce the 140,000 bbl/day brought in outside the 12.2 formula in 1966. Producers pointed to the drop in crude prices (15 percent in constant dollars between 1957–59 and 1967), and to the declines in geophysical activity, active rotary rigs, exploratory and developmental wells drilled, and oil-related employment.[17] This effort to alter the import quota program, like the others, failed, and in retrospect it can be seen that the producers were never to come as close again.

15 "Producers Want More Than Token Relief," *Oil and Gas Journal* June 1, 1964, pp. 36–37; "Independents to Try Political Attack," *Oil and Gas Journal* July 6, 1964, pp. 76–78; "Independents Seek Legislative Relief," *Oil and Gas Journal* July 20, 1964, pp. 60–61; "Interior Agrees on Import Help," *Oil and Gas Journal* July 20, 1964, pp. 60–61.

16 "Independents Gear for Imports Battle," *Oil and Gas Journal* May 15, 1967, pp. 44–45.

17 "Udall, Independents Clash on Imports," *Oil and Gas Journal* October 23, 1967, pp. 44–45.

While independent producers were concerned with restricting imports to 12.2 percent of production, fuel consumers and, quietly, their overseas suppliers, sought to increase imports—not so much by frontal assault on the 12.2 percent as by special programs. Temporary shortages, restrictive business practices (an accusation of jobbers against their suppliers), excessive prices, and special needs which required the subsidy of extra low-cost oil imports were among the situations that proponents used to justify additional imports, even while potential domestic production was adequate. There were further ruptures in the control program as fuel availability got progressively tighter after 1970. Even before that time, however, there were numerous developments which upped imports. Among these were misestimations by the Bureau of Mines, shipments from U.S. islands possessions, excess imports from Canada and Mexico, Defense Department purchases abroad, fuel imported in bond but actually used within the United States, special imports of No. 4 and No. 2 fuel oil, bonus quotas for low-sulfur residual oil production, and special quotas for asphalt. (These programs are discussed in detail in the next chapter.) Residual fuel imports, of course, were effectively freed from controls during most of the control period. Market pressure, and the indefensibility on objective grounds of the import formula chosen, led, then, to gradual weakening of import controls and to proportional as well as absolute increases in the role of imported crude in U.S. consumption. Controversy over the level of imports was a continuing feature of the control era.

The final breakdown in the 12.2 percent formula came when domestic production was unable, at prevailing prices, to cover the petroleum needs of the nation. The discussion of this situation is reserved for chapter 6.

Allocation of Import Quotas

The allocation of import quotas among importers distributed valuable rights (an estimate of which is given in chapter 8) and consequently was a matter of controversy just one step removed from determining the overall level of allowed imports. Many issues were involved in allocating quotas. First, were there to be qualified importers other than refining firms, and, if so, for those firms, what were to be the criteria for allocation? Allocation among refining firms was complicated by the existence both of firms which had been historic importers and of firms which had not been users of foreign feedstocks but which would be placed at a competitive disadvantage if traditional importers had a protected source of cheaper raw materials. Were only historic importers—or, perhaps those with tidewater facilities which could process foreign crude— to be allowed the cheaper inputs? Further, were refiners to be discriminated among on the basis of size?

An additional complication was created by the possibility of importing finished or semifinished petroleum products rather than crude oil. If product imports were not limited, the crude oil import control program would break down. Logical relationships were confounded if refiners were given product import allocations, yet to allow product users to import cheap products would be unfairly competitive to domestic refining firms. Finally, of course, U.S. firms had established refineries outside the national borders for the express purpose of supplying products for the domestic market; restricting these imports severely could virtually eliminate the market served by those refineries, with predictable serious consequences for the firms. No obvious or externally correct solution existed as to how the import quotas were to be distributed. As with the level of imports, then, the distribution of quotas represented the result of a large number of conflicting forces of different strengths—and those forces yielded different distributions over time.

Import patterns by firms were already changing at the time mandatory controls were instituted. A minority of refineries were importing crude oil; a shrinking majority were not. Large numbers of newcomers were appearing under the voluntary controls that existed prior to 1959; the growth in their number and volume of throughput was one of the reasons for the need to switch the program mode. The major importing firms, however, had adjusted their operations to dependence upon foreign inputs. Refinery location, capital decisions, marketing arrangements and production and supply patterns, however, had suffered some disruption when the voluntary controls of 1957 were instituted. These patterns would be more dramatically altered by mandatory controls if those controls altered the status quo markedly. Consequently, a standing in equity was perceived to exist with regard to a further shift in policy affecting those firms which would bear the commercial brunt of import controls.

Those established importers could not be protected completely from restrictions on imports, however, because to allow those firms to continue importing the same amount as before would foreclose participation by inland refiners in access to low-cost foreign oil. Inland refiners, and the producers who served them, would then have been faced with an intolerable competitive disadvantage. The lower costs to tidewater refineries would allow those refineries to penetrate further into the interior, restricting markets for inland refiners and for producers supplying them. Coincidentally, inland refineries were more likely to be independent of the integrated firms, and hence they were a prime market for the domestic independent producer whose future was tied in some degree to the vitality of the inland refinery industry. Hence, some access to quota rights for refiners with neither an import history nor capability was politically opportune. It was also probably legally necessary if challenges to the constitutionality of the import controls were to be defeated.

In view of the considerations outlined above, it is not surprising that the government in the end turned to the system of granting quotas to all refiners and permitting exchanges.[18] It represented a defensible plan in terms of oil logistics and possessed fewer political drawbacks than other plans considered. Even so, the introduction of such a system had to depend on finding a satisfactory method of administration. The means lay directly at hand. The system arrived at for Districts I–IV was to at once cut the "historic" importers back to 80 percent of their last allocation under the voluntary program and then to divide the remaining allowed imports among all other refiners according to their refinery runs. A sliding scale which favored smaller refiners was used in the latter allocation.[19] Each firm was allowed to choose that basis which would maximize its quota entitlement.

The system arrived at was in substance one by which import quota holders not prepared to process foreign oil were subsidized

---

[18] See the discussion on pages 71–78 and the literature cited there.

[19] *Federal Register* vol. 24, pp. 1907–11 (March 17, 1959).

by the actual refiners through their right to "exchange" oil. It was a fairly simple mechanism for channeling an enormous transfer of wealth between two groups of private businesses. This process was also well designed to provide a wide base of political support for the control system. It forced the large integrated oil companies to share the advantages of imports with independent producers and refiners, who would otherwise have felt themselves menaced by the competitive strength of the "majors." The system did not, or did not appear to, consolidate and extend the domain of economic power occupied by the international majors. It provided some benefits to domestic majors as well as to the smaller independent refiners and producers. The domestic majors were keen supporters of the quota system, as it evolved, because it gave them a big cut of the low-cost foreign oil which they could "sell" (exchange) at a profit.[20]

The rationale for a historical basis of allocation was to allow time for adjustment to import controls. Consequently, it was anticipated that the historical allocation would shrink over time and all firms would end up with an allocation based on throughput, and thus with roughly equal crude oil input costs. The allocation of imports on the historical rather than refinery run base was a controversial issue, especially as the historical allocation shrank too fast from the view of those benefited, and not nearly fast enough for the others. As in the case of the overall level of imports, no obvious or clearly appropriate rate of decline in the historical basis existed. The decision was arbitrary, which is not to say it was not extensively argued.

Arguments regarding quotas for inland versus traditional tidewater refineries, and their respective levels, touched upon doctrines of equity, national security, and market structure. Equity arguments featured the view that historic importers had no right in perpetuity to maintain their favored position; they had been amply rewarded for their earlier investment. On the other side, it was obvious that inland refiners had made no investment, absorbed no risk, and taken no action which conceivably could

---

[20] In fact, the great preponderance of quota recipients *did* trade off their quotas. *Petroleum Week* March 24, 1961 ("Petroleum Comments: Who's Kidding Whom," p. 17) stated that of 151 refiners receiving quotas, 115 traded off their entire quota, 20 traded off most of it, and only 16 used most of the imported oil.

justify their receipt of a quota worth variously up to $1.50 per barrel.

National security arguments were presented by interior refiners. They noted that without universal allocation of quotas, the economic disadvantage they suffered would drive refining to tidewater locations, bring about its concentration, and hence make it more vulnerable to foreign attack. A dispersed system of refineries, attainable only with a quota-based subsidy, was required to enhance security of essential refinery supplies in time of national emergency. The historic importers' contrary position was that this argument was fallacious because no national security rationale regarding refinery location was established, so allocations to nonprocessors failed the legal test required by the program's authorization under the defense and security provisions of the Trade Agreements Act.

The final argument for a sharing of quotas among all refiners, and ultimately for a "phase-out" of historical quotas, was based on an effort to counteract a supposed trend of concentration in the petroleum industry. Assistant Attorney-General Lee Loevinger stated with reference to residual fuel oil, for example, that "Use of the historic pattern as the principal basis of allocation, other than for temporary purposes, . . . [is] . . . antithetic to the normal process of growth and change through competitive efforts. By virtue of the competitive advantage in costs of imported over domestic residual, what changes in industry structure do occur are in the direction of growing concentration and increasing domination by the principal historic importers."[21] Views with regard to crude oil undoubtedly were similar. It was perceived that giving some importers, and the largest international integrated oil companies at that, a permanent advantage would create faulty structural incentives in the industry. The fact that historic quotas went almost exclusively to the largest firms was further adduced to their detriment, given antipathy toward further concentration, if not toward "big oil" itself.

Whatever the rationale, and however lacking in economic analysis the decisions made, the policy of granting quotas to all refiners and allowing exchanges was adopted. Historic importers, however,

21 "Justice Low-Rates 'Historic' Quotas," *Oil and Gas Journal* May 20, 1963, p. 102.

were given an advantage which declined over time. The efforts to expand the mandatory quota program to include petrochemical and firms in other phases of the industry are discussed in the next chapter. As we will see there, eligibility for a quota allocation was ultimately expanded beyond even the refinery segment. Allocation of the quota remained controversial throughout its existence. Arguments on both sides of the issue, and especially over the level of historic input, were trotted out with regularity each time the mandatory program was reviewed. Consensus was impossible on these issues as well as on the distribution of the quota by refiner size.

The Sliding Scale

A decision that inland refiners were to get quotas for oil that they could not run in their own refineries left unsettled whether those quotas were to be proportional to runs or in some fashion regressive—and if regressive, to what degree. Controversy thus arose around what became known as the "sliding-scale" provision.

The sliding-scale feature of the allocation system was political in its origins, in a rather narrow sense. It was designed to fend off attacks upon the system based upon the prevalent bias toward "small business." At many points where government touches private business, as in the awarding of defense contracts, special provisions are included to favor participation by small firms. In the oil refining industry, for example, a precedent existed in the "set-aside" program by which the Defense Fuel Supply Center placed small refiners in a favored position in awarding contracts for jet fuel. Contemporary accounts suggest that it was anticipated by those devising the allocation system that if they provided a formula for sharing that was proportionate to refinery runs, Congress would modify the system by introducing some sort of similar set-aside provisions. Because of the desire to avoid legislation on this topic, the sliding-scale formula was adopted to foreclose this source of future congressional interference.

The sliding scale favoring smaller refiners was designed to provide sufficient incentive to keep them in business on the assumption that many would fail without it. This goal was supported because of the presumed need for dispersion of refining facilities for national security purposes and because small refineries were thought to provide competition to the integrated firms and thereby to improve the functioning of the industry. These arguments, if they are to be supported analytically, must be founded on diseconomies of scale in refining or on external economies in either marketing or resource acquisition. If small refineries have a systematic cost disadvantage that makes them noncompetitive, then subsidies are required to keep them in business.[22] In either case, reason would dictate that some ascertained basis for the size of the relative subsidy differential must be available and utilized in establishing the actual schedules chosen. Policy on the sliding scale benefited from no such analysis. Not only were estimates of these factors not made, or at least not presented for the record, but it is not obvious that the issue of the sliding scale was even formulated in this fashion. In essence, small refineries (and their owners) were "good," and some extra subsidy was to be granted to them. Again, special interests dominated the comments on the sliding scale. Only the play of power and administrators' decisions as to a desirable rate of subsidy can explain the differentials that were created and sustained.

The actual sliding scales in Districts I–IV and in District V, over the history of the program, responded to these forces. Two noteworthy changes occurred over time. First, the number of steps was reduced, and second, the smaller refiners received relatively greater allocations. Numerous attempts were made to simplify the scales even more, but these were not successful. The importance of the quota to small refiners led to their organizing to exert political influence. The American Petroleum Refiners Association was formed in 1962 for the specific purpose of providing a unified voice for the smallest refiners.[23]

A final issue with the sliding scale deserves mention. The basis for the different incremental levels of quotas was the amount of refinery runs by firm, not by plant. It was advantageous, then, for refinery ownership to be fragmented. This policy had predictable

---

[22] The wisdom of keeping them in business depends, of course, on the size of the subsidy required and the level of national security and industry structure benefits received.

[23] "Little Refiners Ask Bigger Quotas," *Oil and Gas Journal* January 22, 1962, p. 29.

effects. First, it reduced the value of a small refinery as a merger prospect for an established refining firm. Second, it provided incentives for the formation of "concubine" relationships with large firms which could acquire informal control, but not integrated ownership, of small firms without losing the preferential quota of the small firm. The history of the program contains charges of concubinage but the extent of its existence is unknown. Finally, the sliding scale encouraged small refineries, or preserved their existence, by the additional revenues obtained through the sale of import tickets.

Level of Imports, Historical Preferences, and the Sliding Scale—The Results of the Controversies

The general rules that governed allocation of imports of crude, unfinished oil and oil products (excluding residual fuel oil) into Districts I–IV were (1) the formula by which the level of imports was determined and (2) the historic and sliding-scale formulas by which this total was divided among refining companies. These formulas do not quite cover the whole ground; if they are understood, however, the special features of the program fall into place. Imports into District V were allocated among refiners in the same general way, but the criterion for the level of imports was quite different. While this discussion centers on Districts I–IV, it applies equally well to District V, except for the overall import formula.

Originally, the level of imports was fixed by formula at 9 percent of the domestic demand for oil products, as estimated for the next allocation period by the Bureau of Mines.[24] Imports from overland sources (Canada and Mexico) were exempt. This exemption permitted an unregulated growth of total imports due to an increasing rate of imports from Canada. The level of imports also grew more rapidly than domestic production because the base was inflated by a rapidly growing rate of residual fuel oil imports. As of July 1, 1963, a new formula was applied which limited imports (including those from Canada) to 12.2 percent of domestic production of crude oil and natural gas liquids. The new formula yielded

[24] Information in this section is drawn from chapter 2 and from the *Oil Import Digest, passim* cited there.

a total approximately equal to the old formula plus then-current imports from Canada, but it removed the mechanism by which much of the import growth had been taking place. After 1965, a number of new programs complicated the allocation picture under the 12.2 percent formula, but the outline of the program can be seen without reference to these special situations and to the progressive ad hoc relaxation of controls which occurred later.

It is interesting to see how the historical factor, the entry of new importers, and the sliding scale have affected the respective interests of various segments of the industry over time. Eighty-eight percent of crude oil imports to Districts I–IV in 1954 was in the hands of the seven large "established importers." Of the remainder, two-thirds was in the hands of four other East Coast refiners. Five interior refiners accounted for the rest. By 1956, crude oil imports had risen by 150,000 barrels per day over 1954, and all but 20,000 barrels of this increase was accounted for by other than the seven original established importers. The number of new importers had risen from nine to fifteen, and the amount of their imports to more than 25 percent of the total.

When the voluntary program was started in 1957, and after appeals were settled, the seven "established" importers were cut back by 10 percent of their 1954–56 average, while the other fifteen were given 35 percent of the total.[25] In the last allocation under the voluntary program (1958), the seven "established" companies had been cut back to 59 percent of the total, while the "new" importers, which had risen in number to fifty-four, were given the remaining 41 percent of the allowed imports. This was the point at which the voluntary program began to fall apart, as noted in chapter 2. Imports of crude oil ran well ahead of allocations, and a large volume of imported products outside the allocations (in addition to residual fuel oil) made their appearance.

When the mandatory program was initiated in 1959, the original formula specified that importers under the voluntary plan should receive 80 percent of their last quota under that plan, with the remainder to be distributed to all other refiners on the basis of their refinery runs and the sliding scale. From this time on, all

---

[25] On appeals, six other companies were awarded quotas, bringing the total number of importers to twenty-eight.

refiners were "importers." Twenty-two companies, representing 65 percent of total allocations, found it advantageous to use the historical basis. The number of companies using the historical basis was never higher than at the beginning of the program; the historical allocation was eliminated for periods following 1971. Under the original allocation scheme, the established seven importers were cut back to 47 percent of the total imports for the last half of 1959 rather than the 59 percent they had enjoyed under the voluntary program. Five other East Coast refiners received 17 percent, and interior refiners 36 percent.

The sliding scale and the historical allocation were joined in 1962 by an allocation to overland importers—the Northern Tier refiners—who were given a different quota after Canadian imports came under control (see below). The pattern that resulted is shown in table 4-1 for Districts I–IV and in table 4-2 for District V. The historical, and consequently the overland, allocation was abolished in 1971, having declined throughout the program. This decline, along with the changing proportions allocated to refiners of different size, led to a progressive bias toward the smaller refiners during the program. This change was more marked toward the smallest refiners in District V than in Districts I–IV. The mandatory quota program was set aside in 1973, but the allocations under its mechanism were continued as the criterion for rebate of a portion of the special license fee which was imposed in its stead. The mandatory quota program grew in complexity, of course, with coverage of products, with new provisions to control Canadian oil, with the Islands program and with other special arrangements. In the course of the program the proportion of imports coming to refiners under the basic crude oil quota shrank, and other provisions accordingly increased in importance. Tables 4-3 and 4-4 bring together the volumes of imports entering the nation under different arrangements. Residual fuel oil, of course, was not a part of the mandatory quota program proper, but the level of imports of this product is shown here as well. Refiners of other than Canadian oil received virtually all of the import quota in Districts I–IV, which were predominantly crude oil, in the early days of the program, about 85 percent. By 1972, as the program approached an effective close, those refiners received only about half of the quota as established by formula, and that quota itself was exceeded

Table 4-1. Districts I–IV Import Quota Allocations to Refiners by Basis, 1959–75

(percent of inputs)

	Historical basis	Overland basis	Input basis: Refinery throughput in average bbl/day								
			0–10,000	10,000–20,000	20,000–30,000	30,000–60,000	60,000–100,000	100,000–150,000	150,000–200,000	200,000–300,000	300,000+
1959: Mar–Jun	80.0		12.0	11.0	10.0	9.0	8.0	7.0	6.0	5.0	4.0
Jul–Dec	75.7		11.4	10.4	9.5	8.5	7.6	6.6	5.7	4.7	3.8
1960: Jan–Jun	75.7		13.0	11.9	10.8	9.7	8.7	7.5	6.5	5.3	4.3
Jul–Dec	75.7		11.8	10.8	9.8	8.8	7.9	6.9	5.9	4.9	3.9
1961: Jan–Jun	72.0		11.5	10.5	9.6	8.6	7.7	6.7	5.7	4.7	3.8
Jul–Dec	70.0		11.1	10.2	9.3	8.3	7.4	6.5	5.5	4.5	3.7
1962: Jan–Jun	72.8		11.6	10.7	9.7	8.7	7.7	6.7	5.7	4.7	3.8
Jul–Dec[a]	70.0	70.0	12.0	10.2			8.2			5.2	
1963: Jan–Jun	67.5	63.75	12.5	10.7			8.6			5.3	
Jul–Dec	65.0	58.75	12.5	11.5			9.2			5.4	
1964: Jan–Jun	63.0	55.75	14.0	11.9			9.3			5.45	
Jul–Dec	61.0	52.75	15.0	11.2			8.9			5.28	
1965: Jan–Jun	59.0	49.75	17.0	11.6			9.2			5.53	
Jul–Dec	57.0	46.75	18.0	11.9			9.4			5.64	
1966: Jan–Dec	54.0	42.25	18.0	11.4			8.9			5.26	
1967: Jan–Dec	51.0	37.75	20.0	11.4			8.0			4.28	
1968: Jan–Dec[b]	45.0	33.25	19.0	10.2			6.7			2.74	
Jan–Dec[c]	45.0	33.25	18.8	10.1			6.6			2.7	
1969: Jan–Dec	40.0	27.25	19.5	11.0			7.0			3.0	
1970: Jan–Dec	30.0	24.5	19.5	11.0			7.0			3.0	
1971: Jan–Dec			20.0	12.0			7.0			3.5	
1972: Jan–Dec[d]			21.7	13.0			7.6			3.8	
1973: Jan–Dec			21.7	13.0			7.6			3.8	
1974: Jan–Dec			21.7	13.0			7.6			3.8	
1975: Jan–Dec			21.7	13.0			7.6			3.8	

Source: National Petroleum Refiners Association, Oil Import Digest, vol. 1, for 1959–71: p. A-51 (3/13/71); 1972–74: p. A-21 (8/25/74); 1975: p. A-51 (8/18/75).

a Scale change.
b First 182 days.
c Last 184 days.
d Historic basis and overland basis abolished.

Table 4-2. District V Import Quota Allocations to Refiners by Basis, 1959–75

(percent of inputs)

	Historical basis	Refinery size—average bbl/day input basis							
		0–10,000	10,000–20,000	20,000–30,000	30,000–60,000	60,000–100,000	100,000–150,000	150,000–200,000	200,000+
1959: Mar–Jun	80.0	25.0	20.0	15.0	10.0	9.0	8.0	8.0	6.0
Jul–Dec	80.0	37.5	30.0	22.5	15.0	12.0	11.0	10.0	8.0
1960: Jan–Jun	75.5	35.4	28.3	21.2	14.1	11.3	10.3	9.4	7.5
Jul–Dec	80.0	45.0	36.0	26.9	17.9	14.4	13.1	11.9	9.5
1961: Jan–Jun	66.5	40.0	31.3	22.7	13.5	10.9	10.0	8.9	7.2
Jul–Dec	70.3	42.1	32.9	23.8	14.1	11.3	10.3	9.3	7.4
1962: Jan–Jun	65.9	39.6	30.8	22.4	13.2	10.7	9.7	8.7	6.9
Jul–Dec[a]	70.0	52.0	34.9			15.6		11.0	
1963: Jan–Jun	67.5	52.0	32.0			10.5		10.5	
Jul–Dec	57.0	50.0	25.9			8.57		8.57	
1964: Jan–Jun	55.0	52.0	29.0			9.57		9.57	
Jul–Dec	53.0	55.0	33.0			20.0		14.08	
1965: Jan–Jun	51.0	60.0	33.7			20.4		14.1	
Jul–Dec	49.0	53.5	25.7			14.1		9.54	
1966: Jan–Dec	46.0	48.5	22.0			11.9		7.3	
1967: Jan–Dec	43.0	48.5	18.2			9.8		6.0	
1968: Jan–Dec[b]	28.5	45.0	11.0			5.2		2.2	
Jan–Dec[c]	28.5	44.3	10.7			5.0		2.2	
1969: Jan–Dec	23.5	40.0	9.3			4.3		1.9	
1970: Jan–Dec	13.5	40.0	9.3			4.3		1.9	
1971: Jan–Dec[a]	—	60.0	15.0				5.0		
1972: Jan–Dec	—	67.5	16.9				5.6		
1973: Jan–Dec[d]	—	67.5	16.9		5.6	5.6	5.6	5.6	
1974: Jan–Dec[d]	—	67.5	16.9		5.6	5.6	5.6	5.6	
1975: Jan–Dec[d]	—	67.5	16.9		5.6	5.6	5.6	5.6	

Source: National Petroleum Refiners Association, Oil Import Digest, vol. 1, for 1959–71: p. A-75 (3/13/71); 1972–74: p. A-21 (8/25/74); 1975: p. A-76 (8/18/75).

[a] Scale change.
[b] First 182 days.
[c] Last 184 days.
[d] The percentages shown were used to calculate the proportion each refinery received of the initial allocation; that proportion was then used to allocate the remaining overall allowed imports.

Table 4-3a. Districts I–IV Import Allocations, 1959–64

(bbl/day)

	1959 Mar.-June	1959 July-Dec.	1960 Jan.-June	1960 July-Dec.	1961 Jan.-June	1961 July-Dec.	1962 Jan.-June	1962 July-Dec.	1963 Jan.-June	1963 July-Dec.	1964 Jan.-June	1964 July-Dec.
Total quota[a]	NA	754,650	795,330	771,840	785,790	772,290	792,540	786,330	907,680	938,180	956,529	950,014
Deductions												
Canada	—	—	—	—	—	—	—	—	120,000	125,000	133,500	145,000
Mexico									30,000	30,000	30,000	30,000
Other[b]	—	—	—	—	19,260	24,570	11,790	9,000	(25,650)	—	—	—
Maximum level of imports subject to allocation	NA	754,650	795,330	771,840	766,530	747,720	780,750	777,330	783,330	783,180	793,029	775,014
Total finished products	76,172	76,631	76,631	76,634	76,634	76,634	76,634	76,634	76,634	76,634	76,634	76,634
Total crude and unfinished oils	NA	678,019	718,699	695,206	689,896	671,086	704,116	700,696	706,696	706,546	716,395	698,380
Refiners												
Historic basis	454,480	441,020	438,732	437,159	438,552	433,537	450,355	357,833	343,347	305,282	293,580	283,373
Input basis	314,793	241,687	280,209	267,132	251,165	241,483	256,234	342,958	363,059	401,177	422,702	414,816
Other[c]	NA	(4,688)	(242)	(9,085)	179	(3,934)	(2,473)	(95)	290	87	113	191
Residual fuel oil imports[d]	609,734		618,205		622,077		684,923		728,597		782,402	

Sources: Gulf Oil Corporation, *Petroleum Import Statistics Under Oil Import Control Programs by Import Periods Through First Half of 1968* (May 1968) pp. C-1 and C-3. Residual fuel oil imports: American Petroleum Institute, *Basic Petroleum Data Book*, sec. IX, table 6.

[a] Quota based on 9 percent of Bureau of Mines estimate of total demand during 1959–62, and then on basis of 12.2 percent of crude oil and natural gas liquids production thereafter. Canadian overland imports exempt from quota 1959–62; starting in 1963, along with the formula change, estimated Canadian imports were subtracted from the quota; Mexican overland imports had a similar trend, but were limited to 30,000 bbl/day (see text). NA = Not available.

[b] Includes adjustment for over and under estimates of basis on which quota was determined. Parentheses indicate negative numbers.

[c] Includes overages and allocations on appeals. Parentheses indicate negative numbers.

[d] Provided to supply a complete picture of imports. Resid was not covered by the control system which governed other petroleum imports. Calculated from total resid imports for the year.

Table 4-3b. Districts I-IV Import Allocations, 1965–72

(bbl/day)

	1965 Jan.–June	1965 July–Dec.	1966	1967	1968 Jan.–June	1968 July–Dec.	1969	Actual allocations[a] 1970	Actual allocations[a] 1971	Actual allocations[a] 1972
Total quota[b]	974,292	995,276	1,009,550	1,064,328	1,101,416	1,101,416	1,152,412	1,205,238	1,250,000	1,271,000
Deductions										
Canada	154,500	168,500	180,000	225,000	280,000	280,000	306,000	414,816	475,000	540,000
Mexico	30,000	30,000	30,000	30,000	30,000	30,000	30,000	30,500	31,225	36,000
Puerto Rico	—	—	—	3,750	30,800	30,800	34,800	44,800	67,000	64,300
Maximum level of imports subject to allocation	789,792	796,776	799,550	805,578	760,616	760,616	781,612	715,122	676,775	630,700
Total finished products	76,634	76,634	76,634	76,636	76,636	76,636	76,636	96,800	75,000	80,000
Virgin Islands (Hess)	—	—	—	—	15,000	15,000	15,000	15,000	15,000	15,000
OIAB	—	—	—	—	7,000	7,000	7,000	13,279	—	—
No. 2 oil (District I)	—	—	—	5,000	—	—	—	20,164	40,000	45,000
Other	76,634	76,634	76,634	71,636	54,636	54,636	54,636	48,357	20,000	20,000
Total crude and unfinished oils	713,158	720,142	722,916	728,942	683,980	683,980	704,976	618,322	601,775	550,700
Petrochemical	—	—	30,000	40,084	52,000	72,224	77,690	90,100	94,549	93,606
Refiners										
Historic basis[c]	273,481	229,103	248,751	229,371	202,382	216,025	177,602	562,239	640,178	657,750
Input basis	439,490	490,874	441,063	455,485	389,595	344,168	389,869	—	—	—
Other[d]	187	165	3,102	4,002	40,003	51,563	59,815	(34,017)	(132,952)	(200,656)
Residual fuel oil imports[e]	916,337		1,015,151	1,072,279	1,102,257		1,243,438	1,513,030	1,559,775	1,717,650

Sources: National Petroleum Refiners Association, *Oil Import Digest* vol. 1, 1965–70: p. A-53 (1/9/70) 1970–72 actual: p. A-54. Residual fuel oil imports: American Petroleum Institute, *Basic Petroleum Data Book*, sec. IX, table 6.

a From 1970 forward, quota quantities were no longer strictly restricted, and consequently the calculated maximum level of imports of crude and unfinished oils based on the 12.2 percent formula was exceeded in the allocations actually granted. The amounts entered here are the quotas actually granted—which exceed the calculated amount available for allocation. The extra allocations were granted under various special exceptions discussed in chapter 6.

b 12.2 percent of Bureau of Mines estimated crude and natural gas liquids production.

c Includes OIAB (Gabriel Oil Co.).

d Includes: OIAB (set aside); OIAB grants, court orders set aside; Sequoia (1967 error); Husky (1968 error); carry-over (one-half); sec. 25 "starters" (refinery and petrochemical); not allocated. Parentheses indicate negative numbers.

e Provided to supply a complete picture of imports. Resid was not covered by the control system which governed other petroleum imports. Calculated from total resid imports for the year.

Table 4-4a. District V Import Allocations, 1959–64

(bbl/day)

	1959		1960		1961		1962		1963		1964	
	Mar.-June	July-Dec.	Jan.-June	July-Dec.	Jan.-June	July-Dec.	Jan.-June	July-Dec.	Jan.-June	July-Dec.	Jan.-June	July-Dec.
Total quota[a]	NA	265,500	279,000	326,000	280,000	305,000	330,000	407,000	389,000	356,000	388,000	464,000
Less: exempt imports[b]	NA	22,005	52,000	51,000	40,000	64,000	103,600	124,600	133,000	125,600	141,000	144,500
Maximum level of imports subject to allocation	NA	243,495	227,000	275,000	240,000	241,000	226,400	282,400	256,000	230,400	247,000	319,500
Total finished products	10,621	10,619	6,753	10,619	10,679	10,679	10,679	10,679	10,679	10,679	10,679	10,679
Total crude and unfinished oils	NA	232,876	220,247	264,381	217,821	230,321	215,721	271,721	245,321	219,721	236,321	308,821
Refiners												
Historic basis	130,560	101,740	115,745	63,893	50,808	69,415	49,458	37,170	35,034	23,199	19,525	—
Input basis	69,827	131,630	104,350	201,291	167,106	172,189	180,704	233,740	210,315	196,529	216,765	308,822
Other[c]	NA	(494)	152	(803)	(93)	(11,283)	(14,441)	811	(28)	(7)	31	(1)
Residual fuel oil imports[d]	NA	NA	18,975		44,411		39,225		18,671		25,716	

Source: Gulf Oil Corporation, *Petroleum Import Statistics Under Oil Import Control Programs By Import Periods Through First Half of 1968* (May 1968), pp. D-1 and D-3. Residual fuel oil imports: American Petroleum Institute, *Basic Petroleum Data Book*, sec. IX, table 6.

[a] Bureau of Mines estimated difference between domestic supply and total demand. NA = Not available.

[b] Canadian crude and products.

[c] Includes overages and allocations on appeals. Parentheses indicate negative numbers.

[d] Provided to supply a complete picture of imports. Resid was not covered by the control system which governed other petroleum imports. Calculated from total resid imports for the year.

Table 4-4b. District V Import Allocations, 1965–70[a]

(bbl/day)

	1965		1966	1967	1968		1969	1970
	Jan.–June	July–Dec.			Jan.–June	July–Dec.		
Total quota[b]	474,000	421,000	395,000	370,000	322,000	322,000	392,000	482,000
Less: exempt imports[c]	141,000	155,000	155,000	144,000	135,000	135,000	181,000	225,425
Maximum level of imports subject to allocation	333,000	266,000	240,000	226,000	187,000	187,000	211,000	246,575
Total finished products	10,679	10,679	10,679	10,679	10,679	10,679	10,679	10,679
Total crude and unfinished oils	322,324	255,323	229,321	215,321	176,321	176,321	200,321	235,896
Petroleum	—	—	2,000	4,259	3,169	3,000	3,000	3,239
Refiners Historic basis	—	—	—	152,650	143	143	—	—
Input basis[d]	322,324	255,323	226,223	194,417	154,877	152,875	144,946	148,140
Other[d]	—	—	1,098	1,380	18,132	20,303	52,357	84,517
Residual fuel oil imports[e]		29,381	17,164	12,485	17,765		21,249	16,408

Source: National Petroleum Refiners Association, *Oil Import Digest*, vol. 1, 1965–70: p. A-76 (3/13/71). Residual fuel oil imports: American Petroleum Institute, *Basic Petroleum Data Book*, sec. IX, table 6.

[a] Announced quotas and allocations are misleading for the post-1970 period due to frequent revisions. It was not possible to construct (ex-post) consistent series which, with confidence, could be said to represent what happened.

[b] Bureau of Mines estimated difference between domestic supply and total demand.

[c] Canadian crude and products.

[d] Includes: OIAB (set aside); low sulfur; sec. 25 "starters"; carry-over; not allocated.

[e] Provided to supply a complete picture of imports. Resid was not covered by the control system which governed other petroleum imports. Calculated from total resid imports for the year.

substantially. Thus the "basic" allocation to refiners in Districts I–IV by 1972 amounted to only about 40 percent of imports other than residual fuel oil. Since residual fuel oil had also grown in importance as an import during this period, the declining role of the refiner-importer was even greater than the halving implied by these comparisons. The effect of changes in the program over time were not nearly so important in District V. The part the "hemisphere" programs played in eroding the role of the refiner-importers is discussed below; the other means by which the primary right to import was slowly removed from these firms is described in the next chapter.

Hemisphere Preference: Special Programs for Canada, Mexico, and Venezuela

A "hemisphere preference"—a special relationship with Western Hemisphere oil exporters—was a continuing issue throughout the mandatory quota program, and indeed before. While the concept taken by itself was popular in the abstract, operational implementation of discriminatory treatment was extremely controversial. Preferential treatment for these exporting countries was seen to dispossess the markets of other exporting countries, domestic producers, or both. Hence the treatment of Western Hemisphere nations was a source of tensions among the U.S. authorities, exporting countries, differentially placed international oil companies on whose account prospective imports were produced, and domestic producing and refining interests.

The result of conflicting pressures was to provide direct special benefits to Canada and Mexico in the form of special treatment of imports from those nations. Preferences of a less direct sort were granted to Venezuela and other Latin American exporters. These latter benefits consisted mainly of attempting to require Western Hemisphere feedstocks as a condition for special import quotas under some programs, and of urging a Western Hemisphere preference on District V importers. The relatively free import of residual fuel oil, directly against the interests of the domestic coal industry, also was of special benefit to Venezuelan producing interests. Not only was the crude oil produced there of low gravity, especially suited for residual fuel oil production, but the U.S. market could be used to balance refinery mixes at a low level of processing, which meant lower-cost refining operations for the Caribbean facilities using Venezuelan crude. An analysis of the reasoning behind the hemisphere preference is given below, followed by separate consideration of the treatment of each Western Hemisphere exporter.

There were several reasons for a hemisphere preference, an important one being U.S. preoccupation with assuring that its sphere of influence in both North and South America was not threatened. The extensive business ties with both Canada and Latin America were under attack by nationalistic forces in both areas, and preferential access to U.S. markets was viewed as one means of assuring those nations that benefits from hemispheric ties were reciprocal. U.S. business during the late 1950s and early 1960s was engaged in aggressive expansion into both Canada and Latin America, implanting investment and expanding markets. During this "trade-not-aid" era, every effort was made to convince these nations that open access to U.S. enterprise could be the cornerstone on which their economic development could be based. Additionally, of course, U.S. foreign policy sought to sustain friendly governments, especially in Latin America where the Cuban problem was manifest, and depended upon the support of these governments in the United Nations and elsewhere. The mandatory quota program, in this context, was viewed as a self-serving repudiation of the principles on which the United States had been urging other nations to rely. A preference for Western Hemisphere crude oil was one means for softening this dismay—and Venezuela, in particular, made a sustained effort to achieve such a preferential status.

Oil imports from the Western Hemisphere—especially overland—also fulfilled national security goals as they were conceived in the early days of import restriction. The tragic experience with submarine warfare during World War II demonstrated that transport over long sea lanes was vulnerable, especially if an extended military effort were required. Even though U.S. policy featured "massive retaliation" through the 1950s, there was concern that if hemispheric sources of crude oil supply were to be diminished due to lack of demand, supplies from the Middle East, Africa, and the Far East could be interrupted. The later strategic shift toward the feasibility of limited or conventional war made secure access to crude oil even more important. As the potential supply of domestic fuel relative to domestic demand fell, this argument took on additional force.

Finally, there were political and legal reasons for a preference for Western Hemisphere crude. As we have noted before, there was no direct legislative mandate for the mandatory quota program, or for any other import restrictions. The program was based upon a national security finding under the Trade Agreements Extension Act. Challenge to those findings would certainly have had greater standing if preference were not granted to demonstrably more secure sources of crude. While the national security argument was broadened throughout the life of the program, it would have been more difficult to sustain had, for example, Canadian crude not been given preferential standing. The political problem was similar. Constantly under attack by importing interests, the political viability of the program would have been threatened even more if the national security rationale became untenable because of restrictions on crude imports from geographically neighboring suppliers.

Implementing a hemisphere preference, however, was difficult. The problems posed by finding an acceptable method to discriminate in favor of imports from each Western Hemisphere supplier—Canada, Mexico, and Venezuela—were unique, and not made easier by the fact that special interests were harmed by each preference granted. The simple solution, general country quotas, was rejected in favor of allocation by refineries. Consequently, more complex alternatives were required.

The Canadian Program

Under the voluntary program, imports from Canada were subject to quota allocations, the same as imports from elsewhere. The refiners receiving them were a group of five companies, known as the "Northern Tier" firms.[26] When the mandatory quota program was

[26] The five companies are Great Northern Oil Co., Northwestern Refining Co., International Refineries, Murphy Oil Co., and Dow Chemical Co. (Bay Refining). (See frontispiece for locations.)

set up, they, like other importers, received quotas based on historical imports. However, only a few weeks after the program was initiated (March 10, 1959), on April 30, 1959, the president amended the proclamation to exempt from import restrictions crude, unfinished oils, and finished products entering the United States by means of overland transport from the country where they were produced.[27] Though clothed in general terms, in deference to the diplomatic practice of avoiding the appearance of trade discrimination among countries, the exemption could apply only to Canada and Mexico. Thus the hemispheric preference was exercised through a means defensible on national security grounds because overland transport was not, presumably, subject to military interdiction.

The most striking feature of the new rule was that the exempt Canadian oil imports were outside the formula for controlling the level of total imports. The Canadian imports, being outside the quota, directly competed for the share of the market available to domestic producers. The Canadian producers were, in fact, more favorably placed than the American ones. Most American production was subject to market-demand prorationing by state regulatory commissions, while Canadian production, though subject to conservation controls, was allowed to increase as rapidly as it could find a place in the American market. This open-ended Canadian entry into the U.S. market was unacceptable to domestic producers; as imports of Canadian oil increased, the objections became more vociferous.

This anomaly, or "loophole," was ended beginning January 1, 1963. The basic import control proclamation was amended November 30, 1962, to establish a new formula to govern total imports into Districts I–IV; the import level was set at 12.2 percent of production rather than at the preexisting 9 percent of total demand.[28] The Canadian exemption from import control was continued but the estimated amount of Canadian imports was to be deducted to establish the amount allocated to refineries from overseas sources. Canadian imports thus replaced foreign, not domestic oil, as imports from Canada rose after 1963. The conflict between

[27] Proclamation 3279, *Federal Register* vol. 24, pp. 1781–84 (March 12, 1959); and Proclamation 3290, *Federal Register* vol. 24, p. 3527 (May 2, 1959).

[28] Proclamation 3509, *Federal Register* vol. 27, pp. 11985–87 (December 5, 1962).

Canadian and domestic producers was resolved for the moment, but a new one was created between Canadian interests and international oil companies whose major production was not Canadian, and between Canada and other oil exporters. The apparently systematic underestimates of prospective Canadian imports did cause concern among domestic producers; they argued that the Bureau of Mines estimates were biased in the same fashion as the estimates of demand discussed earlier in this chapter.

An odd feature crept into the situation of the historic Northern Tier refineries. When the mandatory quota program started, they received quotas based on their imports under the voluntary program. When a few weeks later Canadian imports were made exempt, the initial quotas were not rescinded—it is commonly supposed simply by administrative oversight. So, in addition to free access to Canadian oil, those refineries also continued to receive quota tickets which they could exchange at a profit for domestic oil—a practice soon labeled the "double dip." In May 1960, a proposed regulation to end these quotas was published,[29] but it ran into a political snag and was dropped. The quota ticket exchange provided the only market for about 12,000 barrels per day of oil, mainly from North Dakota. The wells were not connected with the refineries by pipeline; without the quota subsidy, the oil was too expensive, and would have been replaced at the refinery by Canadian oil. Regional political support was exerted and the quotas were continued. It was decided, however, that refinery runs of Canadian oil could not be counted as part of the inputs on which import quotas were calculated.[30] Historic quotas of Northern Tier refiners were reduced more rapidly than those of other refiners in the set of compromises adopted for the 1963 quota year. For example, for the first period of 1963 the historic quota for refineries, except those with overland imports, was 67.5 percent, while for Northern Tier refineries, the rate was 63.75 percent.[31]

Canadian imports rose dramatically in Districts I–IV and in District V. The replacement of first domestic and then later other

<hr>

[29] *Federal Register* vol. 25, p. 4137 (May 10, 1960).

[30] *Federal Register* vol. 25, p. 4960 (June 4, 1960); also *Oil Import Digest* vol. 1, pp. A-23 and A-24 (March 1, 1968).

[31] "How New Imports Setup Affects Individual Refiners," *Oil and Gas Journal* December 17, 1962, pp. 54–55.

foreign crude created severe strains, and even in 1963 efforts were being made to restrain Canadian oil imports, especially into Districts I–IV. The peculiarities of the Canadian petroleum market then, with its somewhat artificial division between domestic and import areas, confused the situation for exports to the U.S. market.

Canadian oil is produced in the west and normally finds its U.S. market in District V or in the North Central states. Since foreign oil transferred by ship historically was cheaper, eastern Canada was being furnished petroleum from overseas during the mandatory quota program. In effect, the United States provided a market for Canadian production at the protected (higher) U.S. price, making Canadian producer interests happy, while the large Canadian consuming markets were happy with oil imported at the (lower) world price. Part of the internal conflict between producers and consumers, which was so bitter in the United States, was avoided, as oil imports simply redirected Canadian crude into the United States. Conflict over market zones in Canada remained, with imported oil threatening to extend further westward. This conflict was settled with the establishment of an artificial "energy line" moving up the Ottawa Valley, demarcating the limit beyond which imported oil was not to be shipped after 1969 (see frontispiece). This Canadian policy tended to restrict that country's exports to the United States because the line was drawn eastward of the point at which an equilibrium based on transport cost would have been reached.

One issue of great concern to U.S. energy security planners was that the reliability of imports from western Canada was directly related to the security of eastern Canada imports. To the extent that Canadian producers would, or could, be required to supply home markets in the case of emergency, the western Canadian crude would be diverted from U.S. to Canadian markets. U.S. supplies were not secure so long as Canadian imports were not secure, and Canadian imports faced the same insecurity as did U.S. imports arriving by sea. Delivery bottlenecks caused by lack of pipeline connections vitiated rapid diversion of Canadian crude away from U.S. markets in the event of sudden disruption of Canadian overseas supplies but did nothing to protect against longer term displacement. Indeed, as events following the Arab embargo of 1973 were to demonstrate, Canadian oil was no different from OPEC oil in terms of security long-run access.

Apparently efforts were made throughout the early 1960s to restrict imports from Canada. These efforts culminated in a secret agreement in 1967 which set limits on these imports. No enforcement machinery was established, however, and the result was that the agreed-upon limits were very shortly exceeded.[32] Again, the opposition to Canadian crude oil flowing into the United States came from other exporters and from domestic producers who saw, period after period, that estimated imports from this source were exceeded by actual shipments.

Finally, on March 10, 1970, the president announced (Proclamation 3969) mandatory controls on Canadian overland imports, limiting them to 395,000 bbl/day from March 1, 1970.[33] These controls were quite different from those for overseas shipments. The regulations did not permit exchanges (except under specialized, constrained conditions), allowed for a minimum of a 5 percent growth from the base period, allowed all imports to be unfinished oils, and limited imports to 35 percent of operating capacity of the recipient firms as of January 1, 1969. Provisions prohibiting the pyramiding of quotas for foreign oil were also introduced.[34]

The final development affecting restrictions on Canadian imports occurred on October 2, 1970, when imports by ship from Canada on inland waterways were first treated as if they were imports overland, imports of natural gas liquids from Canada were allowed without being charged to import quotas, imports of crude for topping (from any source—including Canada) were allowed into District I, and imports of Canadian crude for use as boiler fuel were allowed at the discretion of the secretary of interior. In effect, crude oil for topping and for direct use was to be considered within the residual fuel oil definition.[35] Following this period, the

---

[32] "Overland-Import Policy Falling Apart," *Oil and Gas Journal* October 27, 1969, pp. 42–43.

[33] Proclamation 3969, *Federal Register* vol. 35, p. 4321 (March 10, 1970) and "Nixon Slows Oil Imports from Canada," *Oil and Gas Journal* March 16, 1970, pp. 100–101.

[34] *Federal Register* vol. 35, pp. 10296–97 (June 24, 1970).

[35] Proclamation 4018, *Federal Register* vol. 35, p. 16357 (October 20, 1970). "Topping" is the process by which very light fractions (natural gasoline, liquid petroleum gases, etc.) are removed from the crude oil. It is necessary to do this before crude oil can be used as boiler fuel because otherwise the light fractions, with their very low boiling points, may vaporize prior to the burning process and create dangerously explosive conditions.

132   LIMITING OIL IMPORTS

pattern of U.S. oil import needs shifted; additional oil flows were required to meet basic U.S. demand. As discussed in chapter 6, the progressive relaxation of import restrictions favored all importers, and Canada got first call on the expanded U.S. market. For reasons that go beyond our immediate concern, at the very time the United States was relaxing import restrictions against Canadian crude, conditions were developing which led Canada to impose progressively more stringent export restrictions which were designed to lead to a phaseout of oil imports from that country, except perhaps of heavy oils, by the early 1980s.

Canada, then, has always occupied a special place in U.S. oil import policy, though that place changed over time. Other Western Hemisphere countries have also been given differential treatment, though the role of Mexico in the U.S. oil pattern has been the most anomalous.

The Mexican Program

Mexico, though long a producer of petroleum, has had a varied pattern of exports to the United States, but these exports were never particularly significant in either the United States or the Mexican markets. Mexico, like Canada, shares a border with the United States, and hence geography placed it in a position to benefit from the "overland" exemption through which Canadian crude moved. Mexico, however, had no overland transportation facilities available to move economically significant quantities of crude from its producing regions to the United States. A crevice in the import controls was exploited, however, to bring Mexican oil under the overland exemption. Mexican crude was moved by tanker from its producing regions to the U.S. port of Brownsville, Texas, on the Mexican border, unloaded in bond and then shipped into Mexico in trucks, which made a U-turn, and promptly reentered the United States. On reentry, the crude was taken out of bond, duty was paid upon it, and it officially entered the United States under the overland exemption. Because a market for only a fraction of the Mexican oil existed in Brownsville, most of it was reloaded upon tankers and shipped to East Coast U.S. ports as "domestic" oil.[36]

[36] "There's More Than One Way to Import Crude," *Oil and Gas Journal* January 16, 1961, p. 47.

It was apparently at the instigation of the U.S. State Department that this "Brownsville shuffle" was implemented. Import controls had deprived the Mexican government's oil company, Petroleos Mexicanos (PEMEX) of a 30,000 bbl/day sale to Texaco (primarily asphaltic residual). The primary alternative market for this product was Cuba, which at that time the United States was attempting to isolate economically. The State Department approached both the U.S. customs and the Oil Import Administration (OIA) and got unofficial approval of the "Brownsville shuffle" on assurances that only Mexican-origin petroleum would be shipped. The arrangement was that approximately 15,000 bbl/day were to be imported, and that the imports would be residual fuel oil. As it worked out later, however, topped crude made up the bulk of the imports; it was used as refinery input, and there was no effective limit on quantity.[37]

While the imports through Brownsville were at a level of about 7,000 bbl/day in December 1960, they increased to 10,000 bbl/day in January 1961, 20,000 bbl/day in March, and to an average of 30,000 bbl/day in April, with the estimated April rate reaching 43,000 in its last week.[38] The highest imports based on actual data, compiled later, were at the rate of 50,000 bbl/day.

Clearly, imports at this level (and higher levels were predicted) could not be countenanced by the OIA without substantially undercutting the whole import control program. An agreement was reached among Interior Secretary Stewart L. Udall, Interior Assistant Secretary John M. Kelly, Mexican embassy officials, and representatives of PEMEX to limit imports to 30,000 bbl/day. PEMEX could, then, administer this "country quota" as it saw fit, assuring the transfer of much of the scarcity value of the import license to the Mexican company.[39] The ludicrous program of transshipment, openly recognized, continued to be revalidated from time to time after the original three-year agreement expired. Finally, in Proclamation 4025 the "overland exemption" facade

37 "Border Oil Shuffle Vexes Import Officials," *Oil and Gas Journal* April 17, 1961, p. 84.

38 Ibid.; "There's More Than One Way to Import Crude," *Oil and Gas Journal* January 16, 1961, p. 47; and "Rising Brownsville Imports Curtailed," *Oil and Gas Journal* May 1, 1961, p. 80.

39 Department of the Interior press release, May 4, 1961, reported in *Oil and Gas Journal* May 8, 1961, p. 65.

was eliminated and a country quota given Mexico beginning January 1, 1971.[40] Nevertheless, the fear of sudden disruption and unemployment in Brownsville was such that at first only the actual shipment back and forth across the Rio Grande was eliminated. The requirement was that the petroleum would continue to be landed at Brownsville, unloaded, and then reloaded on tankers to the East Coast.[41] First the waste, then creation of putative property rights in waste, then government protection of waste, all as a result of the quota program, was nowhere else so clearly demonstrated.

Venezuela in the Oil Import Program

Venezuela created special problems for the U.S. control program. On the one hand, Venezuela depended upon the U.S. market, and, in turn, the United States preferred Venezuelan imports. This preference was based on the U.S. interest in Western Hemisphere solidarity and on advantages of the relatively more secure passage from Venezuela than from other foreign oil sources.[42] On the other hand, the national security rationale, good world diplomatic relations, and the domestic oil industry's political pressure would not allow Venezuela either special preference for quotas or quota-free access to U.S. markets, such as that enjoyed by Canada. The result was a constant tension between the mutually exclusive goals of preference for Venezuela and equal treatment for foreign suppliers.

Venezuela reacted strongly, of course, to the import controls. It was harmed economically by the restriction on its sales, by the lower expected sales for the future, and by the price reductions that coincided with the mandatory quota program. The growing world oil surplus was particularly acute for Venezuela because of its distance from European markets compared with that of its competitors in the Middle East and Africa. The difficulties this nation faced in marketing its crude, even at lower prices, and at a time when it was undertaking extensive economic development programs, led to new sympathy toward organizing with other oil-

40 *Federal Register* vol. 35, pp. 19391–95 (December 23, 1970).

41 Kenneth W. Dam, "Implementation of Import Quotas: The Case of Oil," *Journal of Law and Economics* vol. 14, no. 1 (April 1971), pp. 1–60.

42 Interestingly, the voyage from Venezuela to East Coast U.S. ports is approximately the same distance as is the trip from Gulf Coast U.S. ports to the same destinations. Both routes are about equally exposed militarily.

exporting nations to achieve better terms of trade for oil. Indeed, Perez Alfonso, the Venezuelan oil leader, apparently in part in response to the frustrations involved in seeking freer access to the U.S. market, was willing to join and in fact led in the formation of OPEC; it is certainly true that the more experienced and better-trained Venezuelan oil establishment supplied much of the analysis and impetus in the early, somewhat floundering years of that organization.

The result of these tensions was a series of stopgap measures, which fully satisfied none of the parties. It can be inferred that the operative policy toward Venezuela was to provide it such preferences as were possible without formal abrogation of controls or overt discrimination against other exporters which would violate existing trade policy. In pursuit of this end, the special "Island" importers were enjoined to prefer Venezuelan crude when possible, importers of residual fuel oil were encouraged, if not required, to buy Western Hemisphere source products, and other such preferences were established. These provisions are considered at greater length in chapter 5. Additionally, in providing access to Canadian oil, the United States facilitated Venezuelan marketings in that country because Canadian crude was absorbed elsewhere. The freeing of residual fuel oil imports, which took place over time but was completed in 1966, was of special assistance to Venezuela because low-gravity Venezuelan crude has a particularly high heavy oil yield. Similar benefits occurred when, in a later effort to free up additional imports, No. 4 fuel oil and topped crude were added to the products treated like residual. In the later stages of the control program, other special assistance to Venezuela was offered. Proclamation 3990, for example, specifically provided for importation of 40,000 bbl/day of No. 2 fuel oil if it was manufactured in the Western Hemisphere from Western Hemisphere crude.[43] Later changes (Proclamation 4018) enhanced sales of Venezuelan crude and products, including ethane, propane, butane, and No. 2 fuel oil in District I.[44] Further shifts in the role of Venezuelan petroleum in U.S. markets followed upon the general reorganization and lifting of controls described in chapter 6.

---

[43] *Federal Register* vol. 35, pp. 10091–92 (June 19, 1970).
[44] *Federal Register* vol. 35, p. 16357 (October 20, 1970).

Alternative Approaches

Controversy over the method used to restrict imports continued over the life of the program even though there was never a serious prospect that an alternative approach would be adopted. Three major alternatives were considered. These were quota auctions, exporting country quotas, and protective tariffs. The protective tariff alternative is discussed in chapter 6 because the major thrust for its adoption came in the transition period from 1970 forward.

Quota auctions would transfer the scarcity value of low-cost petroleum imports to the U.S. treasury and away from the refinery recipients. Such auctions would, of course, equate the effective marginal cost of imported oil and domestic oil as refinery inputs. Those refiners best able to utilize the imported oil would bid the higher prices, leading, presumably, to optimal allocation of resources. The effect of this shift would be to take the government out of the allocation process and implant market, rather than political, distribution of imports among potential recipients. It was this factor, elimination of the opportunity to use the import control program to provide special incentives or rewards to otherwise uneconomic activities, which led to its support among some oil industry observers.[45] A quota-auction approach would also open the import market to competition. It would facilitate bids from any source, and hence open the program to persons who did not share economic interests with refiners. Finally, of course, by nationalizing the scarcity value of imported oil, the quota auction would minimize inequities in the distribution of public largesse. Domestic producer groups, most notably TIPRO, advocated adoption of the auction for yet another reason: it was thought that quota bidding, by neutralizing the special advantages of imported oil, would help prevent the erosion of controls.[46]

While the above arguments supported the movement to quota bidding, other countervailing concerns existed. The first problem with shifting to quota bidding was that it would upset many of the adjustments that the industry had made to the existing system.

[45] "A New System Is Needed to End Oil-Quota Scraps," Editorial, *Oil and Gas Journal* December 28, 1968, p. 69.

[46] "Interior Mulls Import Quota Bidding," *Oil and Gas Journal* March 25, 1968, p. 82.

The adjustment process would bring expensive and disruptive changes and shifts in the operation and organization of financial aspects of the industry, as well as in production processes. Among objections to quota bidding, mentioned in the task force report, *The Oil Import Question,* was that this system would lead to a shift in oil sources.[47] The previous quota arrangement had induced importing firms to adopt country-of-origin patterns which maximized their overall return, both foreign and domestic. These patterns turned out to include imports from high cost, but more secure, areas such as Venezuela. Auctioning of quotas would widen the participation of potential importers and would thus force even established firms to seek out the lowest-cost oil—Persian Gulf, for the most part—and hence would upset existing producing and marketing arrangements. Not only would such an eventuality be painful for established firms, but it would be contrary to established national policy. That is, the existing quota program was recognized to be inefficient, but its very inefficiency was said to promote the national interest in dispersed, and especially Western Hemisphere, crude sources. Because this result could not be achieved directly, retention of the refinery-based allocation system, it was argued, would be preferable.

Whatever the views of participants or the merits of their arguments, the force of precedent and the disinclination to upset existing arrangements, since costly adjustments had already occurred, was sufficient to bury the proposal for auctioning quotas. The publication of *The Oil Import Question,* with its strong support of tariffs as the restrictive device of choice, eliminated quota auctioning as a viable alternative during the life of the mandatory program. The changed nature of the oil security problem, and efforts to find some means to restrain the power of OPEC as a cartel, led to new interest in the quota auction system following the Arab embargo and OPEC price increases of 1973.

Country quotas as a restrictive device against oil imports were never particularly popular, perhaps because they shifted the scarcity value created by import restriction to oil-exporting countries.[48] Country quotas would allow oil exporters to exact additional revenues from potential importers. The total return to oil sellers

---

[47] *The Oil Import Question,* p. 86, paragraph 321.

[48] It is noted above that a country quota was given to Mexico, but under highly specialized circumstances.

would be equal to the difference between their resource cost and the cost of marginal U.S. domestic supplies, and the benefit compared with the mandatory quota program could be roughly equal to the value of the import "tickets," or up to $1.50 per barrel during some periods. None of the scarcity value created by the quota would flow to domestic interests. Despite this effect, U.S. policy has provided for country quotas for some primary products such as sugar and coffee. The relatively small magnitude of the resulting shifts in income, the fact that they are attuned to security of commodity supplies not considered to be available in the United States at comparable costs, the fact that the ensuing transfers are to poor countries toward which we feel some affinity, and general public failure to understand the effects of such programs may together explain our political willingness to countenance these transfers. Certainly they have been used as foreign policy instruments; and removals of quotas have occasionally been used to signal U.S. disapproval of positions taken by foreign governments. This instrument has not been similarly used in the petroleum trade, perhaps because it does not fit the characteristics mentioned above which make country quotas acceptable for other commodities.

One desirable trait of the country quota technique made it attractive. Country quotas allow the selection of import sources and thus provide a mechanism for exercising preferences for more secure supplies. For example, the higher cost of Venezuelan crude would have forced it increasingly out of the U.S. market had special advantages not been given Western Hemisphere sources. It was those advantages—extralegal pressure applied to importers and the willingness of major multinational oil firms to sacrifice short-term gain for other ends—that prevented further reliance on more distant reserves during the mandatory quota program. A country-quota program could have achieved this goal directly.

Alternatives to importer quotas were therefore contemplated both before and during the operation of the mandatory quota program. The continued reliance on the technique chosen—importer quotas—can be explained by equity and political factors. Selection of importer quotas as the control policy did not dictate, however, the choice of refineries as primary quota recipients. Other recipients, for other purposes, were contemplated, as is shown in the following section.

The Mandatory Quota Program
as an Economic Policy Instrument

Import controls, and their administration, were ostensibly designed to enhance the national security, however defined. In general, this goal required maintenance of a larger domestic petroleum industry than would otherwise exist, and one secure from attack. In pursuing this goal, the control program created valuable property rights in import licenses and distributed them primarily to refineries. Other interests understandably coveted the wealth thus transferred and sought to divert the import control program to achieve still other ends and different distributive effects. Once the subsidy–wealth–transfer character of quotas was recognized, it became increasingly difficult for the authorities to deny other "worthy" causes entry into the program.

Several of the efforts to use the opportunities created by import restriction to foster other goals came to fruition. Among these were the special treatment of residual fuel oil, the Island programs, allocations for petrochemical companies, and allocations for the asphalt content of imported crude, each discussed in the next chapter. Generally less successful, but no less controversial uses of oil import restrictions were also contemplated. These included use of controls (or their selective relaxation) to affect prices, to provide special incentives for petroleum producers, to provide import quotas in exchange for exported products, and to foster competition in product markets.

Proclamation 3279 establishing the mandatory program specifically required the director of the Office of Civil and Defense Mobilization (later Office of Emergency Preparedness) to monitor the operation of the program with reference to its effect on prices.[49] Most of the efforts to affect price behavior were focused on products rather than crude, until the early 1970s. Through most of the life of the program the implicit view seemed to be that the price maintenance efforts of the mandatory quota program would be ignored by government so long as petroleum product prices remained constant or fell in nominal terms; price increases, however, would trigger concern which might lead to an official response.

---

[49] *Federal Register* vol. 24, p. 1784 (March 12, 1959).

Action in this regard first came in the early-1967 confrontation between the industry and the Johnson administration. The Chairman of the Council of Economic Advisers, Gardner Ackley, and Acting Secretary of Interior Charles F. Luce (Secretary Udall was out of the country) were the principal government officials involved. As early as December 1965, Secretary Udall, in announcing 1966 quota levels, pointedly remarked that controls had protected the domestic industry's prosperity and stability, and that the industry, therefore, should not raise crude or product prices, especially on gasoline.[50] During 1966, the *Oil and Gas Journal* reported industry executives had been asked to rescind or reduce crude price increases.[51] In the face of firming gasoline prices during 1966, imports were relaxed slightly to make more gasoline and light products available without altering the overall import level. The *Oil and Gas Journal* also reported that selected oil executives had been given a private warning from the White House in December of that year that general price increases would be frowned upon.[52]

During the first two weeks of February 1967, price increases in Districts I–IV were announced by many firms. Luce, acting in concert with Ackley, sent telegrams urging that the increases be rescinded. Along with this "persuasion," public discussion was initiated regarding possible action by government to force prices down through market influences. In late February news reports quoted a "top Interior official," (later identified as Luce) as saying that the administration would flood the country with imported gasoline, and that other actions would also be taken, if the companies did not relent.[53] Some of the firms reduced prices, meeting the deadline that Luce had imposed.[54] The result of the threat to use the quota program to control product prices was a residuum of hostility and suspicion which surrounded controls through the remainder of their existence. An indication of the bitterness

[50] Department of the Interior press release, December 10, 1965, reported in *Oil and Gas Journal* December 10, 1965, pp. 40–41.
[51] "Oil Sits Tight on Gasoline Price Hike," *Oil and Gas Journal* February 20, 1967, pp. 46–48.
[52] Ibid.
[53] Gene T. Kinney, "Feds Ready Imports Club in Price Hassle," *Oil and Gas Journal* February 27, 1967, pp. 68–70.
[54] "Pressure Ebbs in Gasoline Price Battle," *Oil and Gas Journal* March 6, 1967, pp. 54–55.

created is found in statements of oil company executives quoted in the *Oil and Gas Journal* and in editorials appearing during the conflict.[55]

Price change as a criterion for import policy arose again shortly after the close of the Luce-led attack on gasoline prices. Secretary Udall asked for presidential authority to increase imports of asphalt and asphaltic crudes. Price increases in March and April 1967, along with reports of bid-rigging in the highway program, raised the issue.[56] Further discussion of special treatment of asphalt imports is found in the next chapter.

The last phase of the Johnson administration's use of import policy to affect petroleum prices was concluded in a special hearing on controls held in May 1967. At that time Secretary Udall specifically rejected the use of import control restrictions, or their relaxation, to discipline the price behavior of firms. Moreover, in an even more striking turnaround, he refused to accept responsibility for the threatened use of the import program in February for that purpose.[57] Though the administration had apparently abandoned the price weapon, Congress was not so constrained. Following the Suez war of the summer of 1967, domestic prices again rose. Northeastern senators and congressmen endorsed legislation to push up imports of heating oil to contain price increases. They also called for an OEP study as to whether the price increases which were occurring were necessary under the national security clause.[58]

The expected price effects in a period of inflation motivated the gradual lifting of restrictions after 1970. The OEP, in fact, announced that, pursuant to Proclamation 3279, it was instigating an investigation of the recent price increases with the cooperation

[55] *Oil and Gas Journal*, "Feds Ready Imports Club in Price Hassle," February 27, 1967, p. 69; "Don't Let Washington Get Away with This," February 20, 1967, p. 31; "The Knock at the Door at Midnight," February 27, 1967, p. 61; "How the Administration Lost Oil's Confidence," March 6, 1967, p. 49; "Why We Need a Clear National Energy Policy," March 20, 1967, p. 73; "How the Government Should Use Its Power Over Prices," March 27, 1967, p. 41.

[56] "Udall Bids for Asphalt-Import Power," *Oil and Gas Journal* April 10, 1967, pp. 60–61.

[57] Opening statement for hearings May 22–24, 1967; see Department of the Interior press release April 16, and *Oil and Gas Journal* May 29, 1967, pp. 35–38.

[58] See, for example, "Interior and Defense Departments Must Free More Oil to Assure Adequate Winter Supply for New England," *Congressional Record* November 1, 1967, pp. 30850–52.

of the Department of Justice and other departments.[59] The earlier
publication of *The Oil Import Question* had brought the price
effects of import controls to the public's attention and perhaps required the OEP action for political purposes. Further consideration of the use of selective import relaxation after 1971 as a price
control device is considered in chapter 6.

The other uses of import quotas for special ends were less important and less widely supported. Though controversial, the low
probability of their acceptance reduced the public discussion of
them. For example, a recurring effort was made by small-producer
groups to have the quotas granted directly to them, with allocation perhaps based on exploration and development activities.[60]
The view of producers was that, dollar for dollar, greater incentive
for domestic exploration and development would come if the subsidy (albeit a somewhat camouflaged one) were granted directly,
rather than indirectly in the form of higher rates of allowed output. In terms of exploration and development effects, of course,
their position was probably correct; but the political ramifications
of making the subsidy so obvious were perhaps enough in themselves to doom the plan.

Quotas were also proposed for independent marketers, as were
greater set-asides for independent refiners and small businesses.
The purported public interest purpose of special quotas at this
stage of the industry would be to foster competition and to assure
product supplies. Richard W. McLaren of the antitrust division
of the Department of Justice developed just such a plan. It was
designed to prevent the special allocative powers of the integrated
firms from affecting the ability of some segments of the industry to
compete on an equal footing. A different distribution of product
quotas, plus the special power that import quotas would give,
would preclude restrictive behavior on the part of the international and integrated domestic firms, according to this view.[61]

---

[59] *Federal Register* vol. 35, p. 17682 (November 17, 1970).

[60] "Producers May Seek Import Quotas," *Oil and Gas Journal* August 7, 1961, p. 96;
"New Plan Pushed for Import Quotas to Domestic Wildcatters," *Oil and Gas Journal*
May 23, 1966, p. 106.

[61] U.S. Department of Justice, Richard W. McLaren, Assistant Attorney General,
Antitrust Division, letter of September 23, 1969 to Philip Areeda, Executive Director,
Cabinet Task Force on Oil Import Control.

Finally, when balance of payments problems became perceived as acute in the United States, special use of import controls to facilitate exports was urged. The export issue was important in both the petrochemical and the free trade zone programs, which are discussed in the next chapter. Over and above these programs, however, specific efforts to establish an "import-for-export" principle of allocation persisted.[62] These efforts were finally successful in late 1967, when Secretary Udall announced that beginning in 1968, petrochemical plants would be allowed to import petroleum feedstock to the extent that it was converted into petrochemicals which were exported.[63] When the quotas were later announced, it was learned that up to 60,000 bbl/day (later reduced to 30,000 bbl/day) could be earned in this fashion. President Johnson signed Proclamation 3823 confirming the "import-for-export" program on January 29, 1968.[64] The predicted result of this new departure in quota allocations varied, depending upon the interest involved. It was either to be a great increase in domestic construction of petrochemical plants, with positive balance of payments effects (the chemical companies), or great additional balance of payments outflows (IPAA).[65]

The elements of controversy over special aspects of the mandatory quota program illuminate the interests that constantly sought differential treatment. The adjustments that resulted from these rather minor controversies allowed the program to adjust to changed conditions without dramatic revision. The special programs discussed in the next chapter were far more significant. Together, the working out of these compromises and special allocations maintained the viability of the program until inflation, combined with the growing pressure on domestic oil production capacity, required fundamental relaxation of controls.

[62] "Chemical Firms Ask Unlimited Imports," *Oil and Gas Journal* November 27, 1967, p. 56.

[63] "Chemical Firms Win Bigger Field Quotas," *Oil and Gas Journal* December 25, 1967, p. 104; "Bonus Import Quotas to Top 12.2 Ratio," *Oil and Gas Journal* January 1, 1968, p. 33.

[64] *Federal Register* vol. 33, pp. 1171–73 (January 30, 1968).

[65] "Imports Pie Enlarged, but Slices Smaller," *Oil and Gas Journal* February 5, 1968, p. 114; "Chemical Firms Campaign for Still-Larger Quotas," *Oil and Gas Journal* January 15, 1968, p. 50.

5

Special Programs
in the Import Control System

The mandatory quota program was never applied in an across-the-board fashion as the exceptions discussed in the preceding chapter show. Special conditions led to differential application of the policy. Application of the program was also adjusted to contribute to social goals far removed from the national security objective of strengthening the domestic petroleum industry. There were three special programs in the import control system in addition to hemispheric preferences cited above which significantly affected its application during the period before general relaxation of controls became a factor. These were the special treatment of residual fuel oil, broadening eligibility for quotas to include petrochemical firms, and the Islands programs. This chapter will describe these programs, discuss how they came about, and suggest their effects on the special interests involved, including other quota recipients. Also included is a discussion of the less important case of asphalt, the abortive attempt to create free trade zones, and the relaxation of controls on No. 2 fuel oil in 1970, the forerunner of general decontrol.

Residual Fuel Oil

One of the most important special programs within the import control scheme was that for residual fuel oil (resid). Resid is the

144

viscous residuum of the refining process which strips the lighter molecules from crude oil. Because of its consistency—it sometimes cannot be pumped unless heated—resid cannot be transported long distances economically except by water, and therefore is used primarily in large installations served by water transport. Though resid contains more heat value per unit volume than other, lighter, petroleum products, its extra handling cost, limited application, and the availability of substitutes lower its price per barrel relative to lighter fuel oils or gasoline. The primary U.S. market for resid is as a utility and industrial fuel and most of it is used in District I, the East Coast (table 5-1).

While resid is a joint product in crude oil refining, the degree of processing determines the proportion of the crude oil stream which is converted to this heavy product. Thus resid is produced in fixed proportions only in the short run; in the long run the proportion is responsive (within limits) to the relative price of resid versus lighter products and to the cost of additional processing. The U.S. refining industry has, until the early 1970s, found it economical to minimize resid fractions, thus causing the output of resid per barrel of crude to be much lower in this nation than elsewhere. Characteristics of the crude going into the refinery also determine the proportion of the input that ends up as resid. California crudes are much "heavier" (lower gravity) than those of the midcontinent, and therefore refinery yields of resid in California were proportionately much higher than in the rest of the nation. During much of the control period, District V exported resid on net to District I. In short, resid was treated as a by-product in the United States, its domestic production depended primarily on the rate of refinery output of lighter products, and the unsatisfied domestic market for resid was filled by imports. Because of these characteristics, resid imports during the import control period were seen as supplementing, not supplanting, the domestically produced product, and thus controls on resid were handled differently than were controls on other products or on crude oil.

This view of imported resid as not affecting the domestic petroleum market was in large measure correct, but not because of the characteristics of domestic resid supply, or of freer imports of resid. As noted before, resid can be produced from crude in variable proportions. Had the price of resid been substantially higher than

Table 5-1. U.S. Residual Fuel Oil Consumption and Imports, 1951–74

(thousands of barrels)

Year	Total domestic consumption	Imports				Imports as a percent of consumption
		District I	Districts II–IV	District V	Total	
1951	563,388	NA[a]	NA	NA	119,166	21.2
1952	556,273	NA	NA	NA	128,479	23.1
1953	564,729	NA	NA	NA	131,533	23.3
1954	520,714	NA	NA	NA	129,124	24.8
1955	556,983	NA	NA	NA	152,035	27.3
1956	561,538	NA	NA	NA	162,869	29.0
1957	543,950	NA	NA	NA	173,229	31.8
1958	531,367	NA	NA	NA	182,306	34.3
1959	554,352	219,341	3,212	18	222,571	40.1
1960	550,536	211,788	14,475	6,945	233,208	42.4
1961	542,986	214,453	12,605	16,210	243,268	44.8
1962	548,433	237,565	12,432	14,317	264,314	48.2
1963	538,522	252,785	13,153	6,815	272,753	50.6
1964	556,632	274,306	12,053	9,412	295,771	53.1
1965	574,118	318,634	15,829	10,724	345,187	60.1
1966	613,972	357,907	12,623	6,265	376,795	61.4
1967	639,539	383,260	8,122	4,557	395,939	61.9
1968	669,484	394,528	8,898	6,502	409,928	61.2
1969	722,529	440,983	12,872	7,756	461,611	63.9
1970	804,287	536,968	15,288	5,589	557,845	69.4
1971	838,045	558,771	10,547	8,382	577,700	68.9
1972	925,647	616,990	11,670	8,741	637,401	68.9
1973	1,030,177	639,611	16,539	20,075	676,225	65.6
1974	957,811	538,573	19,725	20,859	579,157	60.5

Source: American Petroleum Institute, *Basic Petroleum Data Book* (October 1975), sec. VII, table 12 and sec. IX, table 6.

[a] NA indicates data not available.

it was, then a larger resid fraction in domestic operations would have been economic, and domestic refinery throughput would have been increased to meet the total demand for petroleum products, including resid. Additionally, the price of a joint product affects the return to the entire operation, and thus a higher price for resid would have led to a higher optimal output, even if proportions were fixed. That the resid price was not higher is explained from the demand side. The demand for residual fuel oil is closely associated with that for coal and natural gas in the boiler fuel market. Consequently, the price of residual fuel oil is bounded by inter-fuel competition from coal and natural gas. Restrictions on resid imports would have been fruitless in terms of driving prices beyond the bounded range—the effect would have been instead to increase the demand and possibly raise the price for coal and natural gas.[1]

These characteristics of resid demand and supply affected the resid control program because they defined the special interests involved. On the demand side, it was District I (the Atlantic coast from New England to Florida) that was primarily interested in ample resid imports to hold down the cost of fuel. Consumers in the remainder of the nation were not much affected by resid. On the supply side, domestic oil producers and refiners were not much affected by resid imports, for reasons given above. Coal producers, and to a lesser extent natural gas producers, were very much affected, as were the ancillary services such as rail transportation of coal. Resid import policy was also a matter of great concern to Venezuela, the source of much crude from which resid was made, and to the Caribbean refineries which were established in part to process Venezuelan crude into residual fuel oil for the U.S. market.

As this discussion attempts to make clear, the issues around resid imports were distinct from those affecting overall oil import policy. The level of resid imports, in turn, had only a small impact on the

---

[1] This market changed radically in the early 1970s. Coal use has been restricted because of environmental standards and thus has become noncompetitive—the prices of resid and coal no longer vary directly. Natural gas is no longer available for boiler fuel use. Finally, for historic reasons relating to the mandatory quota program, price controls on resid were not binding, and its price under the price and allocation controls rose relative to other products. Consequently, domestic refineries were planned and built to concentrate on resid output, and the product mix of domestic refineries was no longer so heavily weighted toward light products.

profitability of domestic oil production and upon incentives to find and produce oil. For this reason, analysis which starts by summing resid imports with crude imports is misleading; such data provide little information of value.

The Development of Resid Controls

The efforts to include resid in the oil import control program came from pressure exerted by the coal industry, not from the oil industry, but the oil industry sometimes joined in the lobbying effort in order to broaden the support base for crude oil import restriction. For example, the coal and oil industries joined forces in backing the unsuccessful Simpson bill of 1951 which consolidated a number of bills calling for protection against several mineral imports. In 1955, independent oil producers and the coal industry again jointly backed the Neely amendment to the Reciprocal Trade Agreements Act, which would limit both crude oil and resid imports to 10 percent of domestic demand for each category.[2] The Neely amendment was defeated, but Congress added a section in the Trade Agreements Extension Act of 1955 authorizing the director of the Office of Defense Mobilization (ODM) to advise the president if there was reason to believe that oil imports posed a threat to national security, and authorizing the president to take action to restrict imports if necessary (see p. 66 ff.).

Residual oil imports were not found to be a threat to national security during the four years prior to the start of the mandatory quota program. In early 1959, however, the director of ODM reported to the president that "crude oil and the principal crude oil derivatives and products are being imported in such quantities and under such circumstances as to threaten to impair the national security."[3] The report did not specifically include or exclude residual oil from "principal derivatives and products." However, the

[2] See "If the Neely Bill Passes," *Oil and Gas Journal* March 21, 1955, pp. 122–123, for an interesting opinion on how the coal interests were using the oil producers' support to benefit primarily the coal industry under the Neely bill.

[3] Director of the Office of Defense Mobilization, "Memorandum for the President" (February 27, 1959), reprinted in *The Oil Import Question*, A Report on the Relationship of Oil Imports to the National Security, prepared by the Cabinet Task Force on Import Control (Washington, GPO, 1970), p. 210.

Special Committee to Investigate Crude Oil Imports, on the basis of the national security finding by the director, recommended to the president a mandatory control program that specifically included residual fuel, but under special rules different from those applicable to crude oil and other products. Proclamation 3279 thus included the following provisions:[4]

Sec. 2(a)(2).   In Districts I–IV the imports of residual fuel oil to be used as fuel shall not exceed the level of imports of that product into these districts during the calendar year 1957.

Sec. 2(e).   The Secretary of the Interior shall keep under review the imports into Districts I–IV and into District V of residual fuel oil to be used as fuel and the Secretary may make, on a monthly basis if required, such adjustments in the maximum level of such imports as he may determine to be consonant with the objectives of this proclamation.

Late in 1959, Proclamation 3328 was issued to give the secretary of interior the power to raise the maximum levels of residual oil imports above the 1957 levels if the need arose.[5] The reduction in domestic output of resid plus the onset of a severe winter made it clear that, if imports were not allowed to rise, there would be substantial price increases and even shortages of heavy fuel oil.

In the original plan, allocations among individual importers were made solely on a historical basis. Each importer received an allocation which bore the same percentage relation to total imports during that year.[6] There was no provision for newcomers. Allocations were for 6-month periods until July 1, 1960, when they were put on a quarterly basis.

This system of controls lasted until early 1961 when public and congressional pressure ultimately forced some changes. Throughout the period there was no provision made for newcomers who might wish to become importers. This troubled some consumers who had no choice but to deal with established importers. Proclamation 3389 in January 1961, in response to these concerns, altered

[4] *Federal Register* vol. 24, p. 1783 (March 12, 1959).

[5] *Federal Register* vol. 24, pp. 10133–34 (December 16, 1959) .

[6] The total was exclusive of (1) imports brought in under bond to be used by vessels in foreign trade and (2) military imports subsequently reexported. As these items are included in the Bureau of Mines import figures, that statistical series differs from that of the Oil Import Administration.

the conditions surrounding resid import controls.[7] Among other provisions, it recognized that imports of resid into Districts II–IV were inconsequential and singled out District I for detailed regulation. It also opened the door to other than historical resid importers by giving 15 percent of the District I quota to owners of deepwater terminals in District I, on the basis of terminal inputs for the year ending September 30, 1960. As the controls were eventually implemented by the Kennedy administration, a sliding scale was applied so that importers with small inputs got a larger percentage factor to apply than did importers with larger inputs.[8] After newcomers were allowed to import resid, historical importers were limited to 85 percent of their 1957 import volumes, rather than 100 percent as in 1959 and 1960. Subsequently, the percentage was revised downward in allocating the allowed imports among the enlarged and growing group of eligible firms.

The District I resid import quota was to be determined by the Bureau of Mines by estimating total District I demand for resid and subtracting from that estimate the amount of projected resid output in District I and shipments of resid into District I from Districts II–IV and Puerto Rico. The expected excess of demand over supply determined the total amount of the District I quota. No mention was made of the price at which the demand estimate was to be made. Thus, as of April 1, 1961, the resid import control program was, for most purposes, limited to District I, and had the feature of presuming to allow imports to make up the deficit between domestic demand and domestic supply, a practice already found in District V crude oil import regulations. Allocations were made for 12-month periods, April 1 to March 30, and were distributed by quarters on a permissible percentage of the annual total basis specified by the secretary of interior. In 1965 this was changed to a semiannual basis. A distinction was made in 1963 and 1964 between importers with and without a crude oil allocation. In 1964, the last applicable year of the distinction, the first group received 78.5 percent and the second group 81.5 percent of their 1957 volumes. A differentiation on the same ground, but at a lower percent of inputs, was also made among terminal operators. They

[7] *Federal Register* vol. 26, p. 507 (January 20, 1961).

[8] *Federal Register* vol. 26, pp. 2121–24 (March 11, 1961); *Oil Import Digest* vol. 1, pp. A-85, A-86 (August 4, 1967).

also were granted quotas on the basis of their historical terminal inputs, but with a sliding scale awarding higher allocations to those with lower volumes.[9]

These changes—admission of terminal operators (newcomers) and the sliding scale based on inputs—while placing the resid program on the same conceptual basis as the crude oil program, did nothing to placate marketers in the northeastern region. On the contrary, some of them complained that the changes made it more difficult to meet their requirements from their customary sources of supply.[10]

Starting April 1, 1966, the allocation system was eliminated in District I. Thereafter, no maximum level of imports was fixed; allocations and licenses were issued to eligible importers in such amounts as the applicant certified to have been sold and/or delivered to customers during the allocation period. Thus, no limit was placed upon either the total level of imports into District I or upon the amount any individual importer might bring in, but a skeleton system through which effective controls could be reinstituted was maintained; the controls formally remained in existence. The steps leading to this freeing of resid imports, which was a blow to the coal industry but essentially irrelevant to oil producers, will be examined in the next section.

Easing Resid Controls

In May 1961 the Office of Civil and Defense Mobilization (OCDM) initiated an investigation to determine the effect from the national security standpoint of the existing import controls on residual fuel oil.[11] For whatever reasons, including, presumably, a disinclination to face the political repercussions of any recommendations, the investigation lasted a long time before producing a report in February 1963, *Memorandum for the President,* by a new director of the agency [newly named the Office of Emergency

---

[9] *Oil Import Digest* vol. 1, p. A-86 (August 4, 1967).

[10] In a submission to OEP, June 7, 1965, the New England Council stated that "yearly quotas on fuel oil are not consistent with the national security interests of the United States" (p. 1). See also in the *Oil and Gas Journal,* "Resid Control Critics Step Up Attack," February 3, 1963, pp. 54–55, and "Resid Imports Rule Suspended," May 19, 1969, p. 74.

[11] *Federal Register* vol. 27, p. 1779 (February 24, 1962).

Planning (OEP)].[12] The investigation was requested by several groups; foremost among them were consuming interests in New England and Florida and the congressional delegates from these areas.

The investigation was an extensive and detailed one in which interested parties were asked to submit written statements on their positions and rebuttals to the arguments made by others. Those favoring retention of controls were the coal industry, coal-carrying railroads, coal miner labor unions, several oil companies (including Sinclair and Standard Oil of Indiana), and several independent oil producer trade associations (including IPAA and TIPRO). Those favoring decontrol included the New England and Florida consuming interests, several major oil companies (Atlantic, Humble, Shell, Standard Oil of California, Texaco, and Cities Service), and several oil jobbing and marketing companies and groups.

The approach of the report to the problems at issue may best be presented in the director's own words:[13]

> The prime consideration with which any inquiry on imports must be concerned is their effect on the availability of adequate resources to meet requirements in any type of emergency. As the Trade Expansion Act of 1962 indicates, it is primarily from the standpoint of capability to meet requirements that circumstances such as requirements of growth and the importation of goods are to be judged.
>
> The adequacy of resources is not a strictly national problem—is not one for which one looks for an answer within the geographical limits of the United States. Our military strategy is built on a system of alliances. Security assumes mutual obligations and mutual logistical support. It assumes that in wartime the resources of allies will be available to the common cause. And where the countries involved are those of this hemisphere the case for mutual support is particularly strong. . . .
>
> In addition, it is evident also that alliances which will be strong in emergencies do not spring from unfriendly actions and mis-

---

[12] Office of Emergency Planning, *Memorandum for the President* (Relating to the National Security Considerations in the Residual Oil Control Program), February 13, 1963. The request for comments and statements was not issued until February 1962, with submissions due in April of that year, "OEP Finally Ready for Import Study," *Oil and Gas Journal* February 19, 1962, p. 77.

[13] Ibid., Office of Emergency Planning, pp. 4–6.

understandings in normal times. In our national security interest there are forceful reasons for unhampered trade relations with other free world countries and an obligation to avoid actions which will weaken their economies and make it more difficult for them to maintain democratic institutions . . .

The threat to the national security posed by residual imports cannot be assessed solely in terms of the adequacy of the supplies of residual in an emergency or even in terms of the effect of such imports on crude oil availability. Although the oil import program in its declared purpose was directed solely to insuring availability of oil in emergencies (through adequate exploration and development of reserves), it has been plainly necessary to extend this inquiry to the effect of residual imports on other related fuels. Residual, coal, and natural gas long have been competitive with each other in varying degrees. And the effect of residual imports on coal-carrying railroads, in terms of the service which they may furnish in emergencies, is also an issue. I propose, therefore, to examine in turn, beginning with residual supply, the effect which residual imports have had and may be expected to have on emergency availability of sufficient fuels.

The most striking feature of the report was the thoroughness of the analysis of the coal industry's position. This was the correct emphasis, since the issues with respect to resid imports very largely centered upon the respective positions of coal and resids in the boiler-fuel markets of the Northeast. The secretary of labor strongly urged retention of controls because he was "seriously concerned with the possible impact of elimination of controls over residual fuel imports on the domestic coal industry." Recognizing that the coal industry had suffered a severe decline, the report traced the difficulties primarily to other sources. The director came to the following conclusion:[14]

I do not question the desirability of continuing measures to remedy hardships in the coal region. Of course these measures should be continued. But I do not believe that the national security section of the Trade Expansion Act can under the showing of this investigation be the medium for Government assistance.

More specifically to the security issue, the coal industry had said that it might not be able to meet the greatly increased demand for

14 Ibid., p. 30.

coal in the event of national emergency if productive capacity were allowed to deteriorate further. The director concluded otherwise, despite protests from the Department of the Interior. With respect to vulnerability of overseas supplies from the Caribbean area, the director noted that domestic supplies to the East Coast also involved sea transport of residual or crude oil. The importation of resid from the Caribbean would thus not markedly increase the level of security responsibility of the defense establishment in the event of war.[15] The Kennedy administration decided not to take the OEP advice and instead maintained the resid program. It did, however, increase imports by 10 percent, improve the position of terminal operators, and announce provision for further increases in imports in the event of emergency needs (presumably including higher prices) for additional resid in the District I market.[16]

The controls on resid were relaxed further in succeeding years, as if, in effect, the intention was to allow resid to be imported in such quantities as necessary to cover District I demand at the existing price. For example, the winter of 1965 was severe, and rising levels of economic activity led to threatened shortages of resid. Emergency allocations were granted and though the facade of requiring subsequent reductions in imports was maintained, in fact controls were relaxed.[17] Whatever the rationale, the effect of controls became primarily to prevent price increases. The level of imports required for this purpose rose through the control period as shown by the figures for District I:[18]

Period	Amount Allocated (bbl/day)
4/1/61–3/31/62	461,427
4/1/62–3/31/63	507,000
4/1/63–3/31/64	575,000
4/1/64–3/31/65	638,000
4/1/65–3/31/66	797,612

[15] Ibid., and "OEP Favors Relaxation of Resid Controls," *Oil and Gas Journal* February 18, 1963, pp. 54–55.

[16] "Imports Going Up 10 Percent Under New Program," *Oil and Gas Journal* March 18, 1963, p. 73.

[17] *Federal Register* vol. 30, pp. 2212–13 (February 18, 1965).

[18] Gulf Oil Corporation, *Petroleum Import Statistics Under Oil Import Control Programs, By Import Periods Through First Half of 1968* (Pittsburgh, Pa., May 1968) p. F-4.

The total allocation for 1965–66 was originally set at 755,000 bbl/ day, up from the previous allocation due to expected decreases in domestic supply and increases in demand.[19] This amount was later further adjusted upward due to market pressures as determined by the OEP. Though the OEP at the time had a second national security investigation underway on resid, it concluded that more imports were needed even before the study was complete. In a letter to the secretary of interior, OEP recommended that "the residual fuel oil import level should be increased substantially for the remainder of the current fuel oil year and should be set as high as possible for the year beginning April 1, 1966."[20] In response to this recommendation, allocations were increased by almost 100,000 bbl/day for the last quarter of the 1965–66 allocation.[21]

The sensitivity of this issue was reflected in President Lyndon Johnson's request for a classified report from Secretary of Defense McNamara. Apparently President Johnson was concerned that the intense political pressures that were being mounted might lead to failure to reflect the national interest—he was especially concerned about the implications of additional resid imports for the coal industry. Secretary McNamara gathered a group of government and private experts who were virtually sequestered for the period until their report was prepared. When completed, the report—though never released—supported the recommendation that import controls on resid could be relaxed without serious effects on national security and with far less serious effects on the coal industry than those being claimed.[22]

Subsequent action by the secretary of interior virtually removed restrictions from residual oil imports into District I.[23] In announcing the new residual fuel oil program, Secretary of the Interior Udall issued a news release which read in part as follows:[24]

> The 1966 revisions will assure, to the maximum extent possible under Presidential Proclamation 3279, as amended, that individual

[19] *Federal Register* vol. 30, p. 4415 (April 6, 1965).

[20] Letter dated December 18, 1965, attached to a Department of the Interior press release, December 22, 1965.

[21] *Federal Register* vol. 31, p. 580 (January 18, 1966).

[22] Discussion with participants in the study.

[23] *Federal Register* vol. 31, pp. 5071–72 (March 29, 1966).

[24] Department of the Interior news release, March 25, 1966.

import allocations of residual fuel oil will be responsive to market requirements.

This will be accomplished by a major change relating allocations for participants to actual sales as evidenced by invoices, bills of sale, and contractual commitments.

The new program is designed to eliminate the premiums that have attached to import licenses and which have had the effect of forcing the smaller consumers to pay higher prices for residual fuel oil.

Secretary Udall indicated that the new program would "combat inflation by encouraging fuel [sic] and free competition in the market place."

The revisions are responsive to the advice of the Director of the Office of Emergency Planning, who, in a letter to the Secretary of the Interior dated December 18, 1965, pointed out: "A thorough consideration of all issues covered by my residual fuel oil investigation indicates that control of these imports could be substantially relaxed without impairment to the national security. This is consistent with recent advice from the Secretary of Defense which takes into account the current military situation."

The new system introduced in 1966 did not wholly abandon allocation procedures. What the regulations did was to widen the eligibility for an allocation and guarantee all eligible applicants quotas to the full amount of their sales contracts, or other evidence of sales, followed by licenses upon evidence of delivery.[25] It was a backhanded sort of system, allowing importation of what had already been sold, and licenses for what had already been delivered. Eligible importers had previously been restricted to those of record in 1957 and persons with ownership of deep water terminals capable of accepting full tanker cargoes. Eligibility was now extended to most large-scale wholesalers.

Resid imports into Districts II–IV and into District V, while less important than those into District I, continued to be limited to 1957 historical importers until 1967. The effect of controls on these districts was primarily on the allocation among importers, though unlike District I, in those markets, a perpetual resid deficit did not exist. Some positive price effects with reference to refiners were, therefore, in evidence. When the proclamation was amended for Districts II–V, the change encouraged imports of low-sulfur resid, and crude used to manufacture low-sulfur resid, to help

[25] *Federal Register* vol. 31, pp. 5960–61 (April 19, 1966).

abate air pollution.[26] At the same time the definition of residual oil was changed to include No. 4 fuel oil (along with No. 5 and 6 fuel oils) so that the sulfur content of the heavy fuel oil produced domestically could be reduced through blending. These actions followed closely the adoption of regulations by federal, state, and local government agencies requiring the use of low-sulfur resid as part of the program to reduce air pollution. Advocates supported the changes in the regulations to provide for freer crude imports to produce low-sulfur resid by arguing that continuation of controls would only result in the development of foreign processing facilities to supply U.S. demand.

The new authorization was first implemented in District V by providing bonus allocations of crude oil on a barrel-for-barrel basis to refiners who supplied low-sulfur fuel oil to "customers required to burn such fuel in order to comply with local government requirements."[27] According to Interior Secretary Udall, the bonus quotas were intended to deal with "a serious and immediate air pollution problem" in Los Angeles County.[28]

The new regulation did not create much controversy when it was applied only to District V. However, when the Oil Import Administration proposed on May 23, 1968 to extend bonus import quotas for the production of low-sulfur resid fuel in Districts I–IV,[29] several interest groups were mobilized. Coal interests complained about the unnecessary increase in oil imports, suggesting instead that the problem of sulfur oxides could be solved by treatment of stack gases. Inland refiners objected because they could not participate in the proposed program since the regulations limited the bonuses to firms delivering low-sulfur fuel oil to areas complying with air pollution regulations (i.e., New York City, New Jersey, and Washington, D.C.). Other refiners and producers objected because windfalls would accrue to a select few at the expense of the rest of the industry. They did not want the 12.2 percent ceiling on nonresid imports violated east of the Rockies.[30]

[26] *Federal Register* vol. 32, pp. 10547–48 (July 19, 1967).

[27] Ibid., p. 13856 (October 5, 1967). These rules avoid mentioning Los Angeles by name and prefer the circumlocution "a large metropolitan area in District V."

[28] *Federal Register* vol. 33, p. 18374 (December 11, 1968).

[29] *Federal Register* vol. 33, p. 7822 (May 29, 1968).

[30] "Cross Fire Lashes Import Bonus Plan," *Oil and Gas Journal* August 12, 1968, p. 47.

As a result of the negative response, the government dropped the plan to award bonus crude oil import quotas in Districts I–IV. Instead, in December 1968, the government adopted a set of rules authorizing bonus quotas for imports of Western Hemisphere residual fuel oil for processing into heavy fuel containing less than 1 percent sulfur. The regulations required the desulfurization of residual fuel oil imports containing at least 2 percent sulfur. They were intended to encourage the construction of U.S. plants capable of desulfurizing foreign resid. This was significant because up to this time resid imports were barred in Districts I–IV except for direct use as a fuel. With processing allowed, imports of resid threatened the effectiveness of the limitation on crude oil imports. The controversial regulation was described as a bonanza to the few quota recipients.[31] Only three firms received bonus quotas (amounting to 241,500 bbl/day) under this arrangement before it was suspended in May 1969 by the new Secretary of the Interior Walter J. Hickel.[32] Hickel ordered the suspension pending a review of oil import policy by the newly established Cabinet Task Force on Oil Import Control.[33]

The suspension did not end the special exemptions to controls for imports for antipollution purposes. During 1970 the Oil Import Appeals Board assumed responsibility for supplying low-sulfur resid quotas in Districts II–IV, where import controls were still binding. Quotas were granted, however, only in special cases. In March 1970, the board recommended, and Secretary Hickel granted, a special quota to Commonwealth Edison for 4.5 million barrels of foreign resid to come into the Chicago area. Hickel explained that the action was required to curb air pollution because low-sulfur domestic fuels were not available. Although Secretary Hickel based the decision on "a very special set of circumstances,"[34] the combination of clean air regulations and shortages of low-sulfur fuels generated widespread claims for hardship exemptions.

[31] *Federal Register* vol. 33, p. 18374 (December 11, 1968); see also *Oil and Gas Journal* December 16, 1968, p. 66.

[32] *Federal Register* vol. 34, p. 7535 (May 14, 1969).

[33] See the discussion in chapter 6 on the recommendations of the task force.

[34] Granting a special exemption was always a controversial action, and accusations of favoritism had plagued Secretary Udall from the outset of his administration. See *Oil and Gas Journal* March 30, 1970, p. 75, on Hickel and March 25, 1968, on Udall.

In response to the growing problem, on October 16, 1970, President Nixon amended the oil import proclamation to permit increased imports of fuel oils and crude oil to be distilled as residual fuel oil, with the resid output not to be counted against the import quota.[35] In December the proclamation was further amended to permit imports in excess of the 12.2 percent ratio to domestic production, without reference to resid production.[36] At this time all oil import controls were relaxed in response to growing energy shortages, with implications discussed in the next chapter.

Concluding Comments on Resid Controls

Import controls that would increase the price of fuels used primarily for electricity generation in District I were a political liability to the administration and to the oil industry, and were correctly viewed by the latter as of little benefit. Consequently, these controls were eliminated, but not without substantial effects. The increase in resid imports provided a wider market for foreign crude and made possible the further development of Caribbean refinery capacity. The unbalanced demand for resid led domestic refineries to be built with additional processing to minimize resid output, so that lighter products were more expensive to produce (see chapter 8). The relative decline in U.S. refinery capacity in some part thus resulted from uncontrolled imports of resid into District I.

Uncontrolled residual oil imports were most important in contributing to the decline in coal production and utilization, and in lowering the incentive to develop cleaner methods of burning coal. The emerging emphasis on environmental quality during the 1960s did not translate into substantial efforts to reduce pollution associated with burning coal because residual fuel oil was available. The progressive shift away from coal and toward oil (and natural gas) was thus exacerbated, with well-known implications for the 1970s.

The decision to free resid imports for District I was predicated upon acceptance of a separation of the political and economic aspects of oil import controls from the national security issue. The

---

[35] Proclamation 4018, *Federal Register* vol. 35, p. 16357 (October 20, 1970).

[36] Proclamation 4025, *Federal Register* vol. 35, p. 19391 (December 23, 1970).

national security rationale was not strong enough to prevail without the political support of the domestic oil industry. The argument that seaborne oil from any Western Hemisphere source was equally vulnerable to attack was correct but turned out to be ineffective because the substitute for resid was domestic coal and natural gas, not domestic oil. Free imports of resid did in fact lead to a greater proportion of the U.S. fuel supply being exposed to military threat, and led as well to a lower proportion of U.S. fuel requirements being met from domestic sources. This meant that later a larger proportion of the U.S. fuel supply was affected by the OPEC price increases. The harm to the domestic economy from the events of 1973 was greater because of the rundown state of the coal industry during the 1960s.

The decision to grant bonus quota allocations and special control exceptions for the purpose of fighting air pollution exemplifies another important issue. In this case, as in others described below, the incentives granted through preferential access to low-cost foreign petroleum supplies could be used to further other public goals. Utilities, and refiners supplying utilities, made compelling arguments because clean air regulations forced them to search for low-sulfur fuels at a time of growing scarcity.

The role of the Oil Import Appeals Board was expanded as a result of the policy clashes surrounding resid imports. While the board had been in existence since the beginning of the mandatory quota program, it at first played a minor role in ameliorating special hardships. Over time, however, the board's role and authority was extended because it offered an instrument to achieve flexibility in administering a rigid program. This first occurred with resid imports, but was extended later to other petroleum products, as will be discussed below.

The resid import control program was always peripheral to the crude oil control program, but it was important both politically and in terms of its ultimate effects on the U.S. fuel economy. Resid policy represented the victory of the consuming eastern states over the coal interests. It resulted in relatively low-cost energy in the industrial Northeast which countered, to some degree, the attraction of other regions which sought to pull industry away from that region. In retrospect, the relatively free importation of resid during the 1960s made the major resid-using regions much more vulnerable when world oil prices rose. Not only were those regions more dependent on heavy oil as an industrial fuel and as a source of electricity, but the erosion of domestic resid-producing capacity made it impossible to administer the domestic price controls in such a way as to hold resid prices below the world market level. The worldwide industrial recession, and the consequent glut of resid output which led to this product being priced at surplus disposal levels through 1976, made the adjustment less severe than it otherwise might have been.

The Petrochemical Program

Chemical companies argued from the beginning that they should be included along with refiners in the mandatory quota program. They contended that their exclusion discriminated against them in two significant ways: (1) the program gave domestic refineries, who were competitors in the petrochemical field, an unfair cost advantage in domestic and foreign markets, and (2) the program reduced the competitiveness of the U.S. petrochemical industry in world markets. This latter contention was expanded by the assertion that the differential treatment was forcing U.S. companies to build plants abroad rather than in the United States, a potent argument in this period when capital investment was considered inadequate and when balance of payments problems attracted public attention. Nonetheless, the petrochemical firms were not allowed quotas, nor were their arguments given official expression until 1962.

These issues were raised in a report to the president in 1962, along with the idea of special treatment for the petrochemical industry.[37] No action was taken, however, and the issue was not pushed with sufficient vigor to surface again until 1965. In that year an interagency task group was established to consider the question of how the oil import program could be revised to reward exports, as part of the government's general program of improving the U.S. balance of payments situation.[38] This led into a considera-

[37] Interagency Petroleum Study Committee, *A Report to the President* (September 4, 1962).
[38] "High-Level Group Starts Import Study," *Oil and Gas Journal* July 12, 1965, p. 56.

tion of petrochemicals, and hearings were scheduled to explore the issues.[39] The Commerce Department supported the petrochemical company position, advocating very generous treatment in access to foreign feedstocks. The Interior Department at first denied that there was any reason for special treatment. During the year a research study commissioned by a group of petrochemical companies presented their case on the issues.[40] The study was challenged by the oil companies, leading a group of them to commission another study which came to drastically different conclusions.[41] Oil companies were opposed to special relief for the petrochemical industry because it would result in lower quotas for the oil companies or in a larger volume of imports. In addition, oil refiners enjoyed a competitive advantage relative to petrochemical firms where their products overlapped.

Hearings were held by the Department of the Interior on October 28–29, 1965 to consider proposals for admitting petrochemical companies to the oil import program. The proposals of the petrochemical companies ran toward (a) permitting imports of foreign feedstocks into foreign-trade zones free from import control but with access of finished products into the United States and/or (b) import quotas similar to those of oil refiners. The emphasis was on the prognosis that domestic feedstock costs would rise relative to foreign feedstock costs, threatening loss of foreign markets and construction of new plants abroad instead of at home. The oil companies, in opposition, challenged the evidence on prospective feedstock costs, on the incentives to plant location abroad, and on the balance of trade argument in general. In addition, on national security grounds, they argued against any basis of allocation not related to the purchase of domestic crude oil. The hearings of 1965 were for the most part anticlimactic in that Secretary Udall opened them with the announcement that the decision had been taken to grant import allocations to petrochemical companies.[42]

[39] *Federal Register* vol. 30, p. 12079 (September 22, 1965).

[40] Arthur D. Little, *Oil Import Quotas and the U.S. Balance of Payments in Petrochemicals*, a report to the Dow Chemical Co. and Monsanto Co. (March 1966).

[41] Stanford Research Institute, *Petrochemical Feedstock Imports and Their Effects on the U.S. Balance of Payments*, 2 vols. (September 1967).

[42] "Udall Favors Petrochemical Plant Import Quotas," *Oil and Gas Journal* November 1, 1965, pp. 30–31; "IPAA Favors Import Curbs on Gas, Petrochem Feedstocks," *Oil and Gas Journal* November 1, 1965, p. 36; and *Oil Import Digest* vol. 1, p. A-97 (August 20, 1971).

Easing Controls on Petrochemical Feedstocks

Import allocations for petrochemical companies were authorized by Presidential Proclamation 3693, dated December 10, 1965.[43] Under the regulations proposed pursuant to this proclamation, the allocation by the Oil Import Administration would amount, for the petrochemical sector for 1966, to about 30,000 barrels per day (within the 12.2 percent formula) in Districts I–IV and 2,000 barrels per day in District V.[44] The quota was allocated to companies having petrochemical plants on the basis of a percentage of feedstock inputs. Whether by coincidence or design, the original 30,000 bbl/day allocation was about equal to the level of exports of petrochemicals. Beginning with 30,000 bbl/day in 1966, District I–IV allocations rose to 40,000 in 1967, and to 52,000 bbl/day in 1968 (and up to 94,000 in 1972). These figures represent, respectively, 6.7, 7.6, and 8.35 percent of petrochemical plant inputs during the first three years as defined for allocation purposes; they continued at similar or higher levels throughout the program.[45] Allocations to individual firms were based on a uniform percentage of inputs, thus departing from the sliding-scale method applied to oil refineries. The allocations went in part to oil companies that owned and operated petrochemical facilities—of the 40,000 bbl/day "petrochemical" allocations in 1967, for example, 32 percent went to oil companies.

The amounts thus allocated did not represent the entire amount of imports allocated to petrochemical production. Some petrochemical companies were credited with refinery inputs for their operations which produced feedstock, and for this they secured quotas under the regular crude oil allocation system. Similarly, oil companies secured quota credit on oil turned into feedstocks, in addition to quota credit for feedstock input into their own petrochemical facilities. Thus, at the 1967 level, all parts of the petrochemical import program had quota credits in the amount of about 67,000 bbl/day, rather than the nominal 40,000 for feedstock inputs. The total was raised to 79,000 bbl/day for 1968. This procedure to a degree provided quota credit on the same oil twice. This was known colloquially as the "double dip," and was similar

[43] *Federal Register* vol. 30, pp. 15459–61 (December 16, 1965).
[44] Ibid., pp. 15434–35 (December 15, 1965).
[45] See table 4-3, and *Oil Import Digest* vol. 1, p. A-99 (July 24, 1968).

in effect to the provision enjoyed for a period by the Northern Tier importers of Canadian oil.

Other administrative problems arose out of the technical difficulty of defining a petrochemical plant as distinct from a refinery, and of defining feedstocks for inclusion within the program. Both oil companies and petrochemical companies could fall into two distinct quota groups. Oil companies received additional petrochemical quotas if they had petrochemical facilities; petrochemical companies received additional quotas if they had oil refining facilities. The original proposed regulation said that persons eligible for oil import allocations and petrochemical allocations "would not receive two allocations but would receive an allocation computed on whichever basis would result in the larger allocation."[46] This statement brought protests from the oil companies, who argued that the policy would discriminate against their petrochemical operations. Thus, an amended regulation was adopted on May 25, 1966 that provided that a company could receive an allocation based on refinery inputs and another allocation based on petrochemical plant inputs.[47]

Apart from the different allocation formulas governing the two programs (sliding scale versus fixed percent of input), there was also a difference in what could be imported. The nominal rule for petrochemical inputs was the same as that for crude oil and unfinished oil in general—namely, (1) that importers must process in their own plants either the oil imported or the oil received in exchange for it and (2) that unfinished oil could make up not more than 15 percent of the quota. However, petrochemical feedstocks are unfinished oils; consequently, the administrator was authorized to adjust this latter percentage up to 100 percent in the case of unfinished oils to be processed in the importer's own plant.[48]

During 1967 the large chemical companies used the existing balance of payments crisis to press their case for access to additional

---

[46] *Federal Register* vol. 30, pp. 15434–35 (December 15, 1965).

[47] The Office of Import Administration issued an ambiguous Bulletin No. 2 on April 15, 1966, which appeared to reestablish the "one allocation" rule for a plant, but the bulletin was later withdrawn and was followed by appeals from companies claiming losses were incurred because they were misled. *Oil Import Digest* vol. 1, p. A-97 (August 20, 1971).

[48] "Oil Import Regulations," paragraph 213.9 (c) in *Oil Import Digest* vol. 1, p. A-126 (May 1, 1975).

imports of foreign feedstocks.[49] The so-called Chemco group also proposed to a receptive administration that petrochemical producers receive additional import quotas to the extent of the quantity of their petrochemical exports.[50] The basic proclamation was amended in late January to authorize the secretary of interior to make special allocations related to exports.[51] Secretary Udall announced that the petrochemical firms would receive an estimated 30,000 bbl/day in quota bonuses during 1968 in the new import-for-export program, but he did not act immediately. The Chemco group immediately responded that this was not enough. They argued that higher-cost domestic feedstocks would force them to build plants abroad to serve both foreign and U.S. markets from foreign locations.[52] While both Udall and Commerce Secretary Trowbridge announced their opposition to the Chemco request for unlimited import bonuses related to exports, plans for partial bonuses proceeded. Nonetheless, no bonuses were issued throughout 1968 within the import-for-export program, and the incoming Nixon administration was expected to be no more responsive to the chemical companies' request.[53]

The Nixon administration turned this issue over to the Cabinet Task Force on Oil Import Control, which received the same Chemco recommendation for an immediate increase in petrochemical quotas, bonus allocations based on exports, and the gradual phaseout of all controls on imports of petrochemical feedstocks. The task force report, released in February 1970, recommended that one of two possible programs be established: free access to imports for use in exports or completely free access to foreign feedstocks.[54] Nixon chose not to act upon these recommendations of

[49] "Chemical Firms Ask Unlimited Imports," Oil and Gas Journal November 27, 1967, p. 56.

[50] "Udall Boosts '68 Import Levels but Postpones Setting Quotas," Oil and Gas Journal December 25, 1967, p. 104; and "Bonus Import Quotas to Top 12.2 Ratio," Oil and Gas Journal January 1, 1968, p. 33. Chemco consisted of Celanese, Dow Chemical, DuPont, Eastman Kodak, Monsanto, National Distillers, Olin Mathieson, Publicker, and Union Carbide.

[51] Federal Register vol. 33, p. 1171 (January 29, 1968).

[52] "Chemical Firms Campaign for Still-Larger Quotas," Oil and Gas Journal January 15, 1968, p. 50.

[53] "Nixon Expected to Avoid Sudden Oil Policy Shifts," Oil and Gas Journal November 18, 1968, pp. 99–102.

[54] The Oil Import Question, p. 136.

the task force, following considerable adverse reaction from most parts of the industry (see the discussion in the next chapter). The continual delay and ultimate defeat of the import-for-export plan was in part due to adverse reaction from the oil industry and in part to the difficulty of formulating a feasible set of regulations to be applied to the complex petrochemical industry. By the latter half of 1970, the incentive behind the push for the export bonus program began to disappear. Increasing world oil prices were reducing the advantages of access to foreign feedstocks and thus the intensity of the efforts of the petrochemical firms to obtain special import advantages. Nonetheless, an import-for-export provision was finally added in 1972, along with other provisions which increased imports allowed petrochemical companies.[55] These elements of loosening import restrictions were part of the general shift in control policy which sought to broaden access to foreign supplies, not special programs to assist petrochemical firms. These changes preceding the abolition of the mandatory quota program are detailed in chapter 6. Petrochemical companies retained their fee-free allocations under the special fee program that superseded quotas. The fee-free 1974 base to which the schedule was applied amounted to 11.2 percent of petrochemical inputs in Districts I–IV and 11.9 percent in District V.[56] Thus the petrochemical firms did obtain special treatment under the mandatory quota program, but never at the level they sought.

Concluding Comments on the Petrochemical Program

The petrochemical industry based its case for import quotas on grounds of equity with similarly placed refiners and on the promise that additional quotas would increase the industry's contribution to the U.S. balance of payments. The oil companies responded with two main arguments to the request for additional quotas: (1) the balance of payments evidence was not valid, and (2) the import program was devised to promote the limited purpose of stimulating the oil industry and should not be diverted to the pursuit

[55] *Oil Import Digest* vol. 1, p. A-95 (August 18, 1975), and "Oil Import Regulations," paragraphs 213.10, 213.11, in *Oil Import Digest* vol. 1, pp. A-126 to A-130 (May 1, 1975).

[56] *Oil Import Digest* vol. 1, p. 91 (August 18, 1975).

of other public purposes. Oil companies were in no position to argue against equivalent quotas on equity grounds. Arguments about the expected contribution of petrochemical exports to the balance of payments depended most crucially upon the projected difference between foreign and domestic feedstock prices. The projections made by the Chemco group in 1967, when the export bonus plan was first seriously proposed, were rendered obsolete by 1970; ironically, the bonus was granted only after balance of payments arguments were obsolete.

The balance of payments argument, however, was merely a handy issue upon which to solicit special favors. To discuss the petrochemical import program solely in terms of the balance of payments issue ignores the most important point raised in the controversy: the distribution of the economic rents created by the quota program. When the petrochemical companies were included in the quota structure in 1966, they simply joined the group of other refiners who had enjoyed the subsidy benefits of import quotas from the beginning of the program. The great stake of the petrochemical companies in the long run was the extent to which they would lose their market share to petrochemical production by oil and gas companies. The distribution of the quotas, when viewed in this light, is entirely divorced from the public purpose of stimulating investment in the discovery of new oil reserves in the interest of national security. Some additional petrochemical capacity may have been retained in this country by the quota allocation. Whether or not the cost in the form of exported refinery capacity was greater than the benefits received is impossible to determine. Unlike the case of the resid program, developments since these decisions were taken do not illuminate their wisdom—or lack of it.

The Islands Program

The discussion up to this point has described the use of the mandatory quota program to achieve public goals associated with air pollution and the balance of payments. This section describes the role assigned to the quota program in connection with the U.S. island possessions of Puerto Rico, the Virgin Islands, and Guam:

the promotion of economic development. As we shall see later, special deals were arranged by the secretary of interior to distribute quota allocations to refiners on the condition that they build refinery facilities on the islands, provide employment for locals, and otherwise contribute to the well-being of the local economy.

Puerto Rico

Puerto Rico is inside the customs territory of the United States, so the customs laws apply there as in the fifty states. However, under Proclamation 3279, the secretary of interior was authorized to fix a separate level of oil imports into Puerto Rico. Quotas were allocated on a historical basis to companies that had refining capacity in Puerto Rico, with no provision for newcomers. This limited quotas to two refining companies, Commonwealth Oil Refining Co. and Gulf Oil Corp., and to W. R. Grace and Co. for feedstock for its fertilizer plant. The general rule was to limit imports to the average daily rate of a 3-month period in 1958; quotas to the two eligible applicants were to be based on their respective imports (changed to inputs in 1961) for the same period. The general rule was flexible, however, in that the secretary might increase or decrease the level to meet changes in demand in Puerto Rico or for export to foreign areas, but not to the U.S. mainland.[57]

The reason for the special status assigned to Puerto Rico from the beginning of the program had to do with the island's dependence on Venezuelan crude oil for its refineries. It was reasoned that without the special status described above, it would be cheaper to import refined products from the mainland than to import U.S. crude oil for processing in Puerto Rico. Permission to import Venezuelan crude was necessary for the continued operation of local refineries.

At the outset, total allocations of crude and unfinished oils were approximately 80,000 bbl/day, about three-quarters to Commonwealth and one-quarter to Gulf Oil Corp. By the second half of 1965, when the general rule was changed, imports of crude and unfinished oils had risen to 138,000 bbl/day. The refining proc-

[57] *Federal Register* vol. 24, p. 1783 (March 12, 1959).

esses in Puerto Rico created an overflow of coproducts which was sent to the mainland. The amount of products shipped from Puerto Rico to the mainland, omitting residual fuel oil, rose from 26,000 bbl/day in 1959 to about 38,000 bbl/day in 1965.[58] The rising amount of such exports to Districts I–IV, and outside the 12.2 percent formula, was one of the "loopholes" in the import program of which the oil producers complained.[59]

In July 1965, the Department of the Interior held hearings devoted to all aspects of the Puerto Rican program. The principal subject at issue was allocations to a new program of petrochemical production. At the same time the general program was reviewed, especially with respect to complaints against the overspill of products to the mainland. As a result, on December 10, 1965, the regulations were modified by Proclamation 3693.[60] For each allocation period, the maximum level of imports of crude and unfinished oils into Puerto Rico was to be fixed by the secretary. Those eligible for allocations were persons who had refining capacity in Puerto Rico in 1964, thus limiting them to the two original companies. The allocation to each company was to be based upon separate estimates of the requirements of each applicant. The rising flow of products to the mainland was dealt with by the rule that if an allocation holder shipped, or sold to be shipped, a larger amount than he shipped in 1965 to Districts I–IV, the excess would be deducted from his allocation in the next period. This limited the shipment of products (other than resid) to about 38,000 bbl/day—33,000 by Commonwealth and 5,000 by Gulf—outside the 12.2 percent formula.[61] While respecting this limit on shipments, the secretary of interior could authorize any amount of imports of crude oil and unfinished oils into Puerto Rico so long as the products were either used locally or exported to other countries.

[58] Department of the Interior, Bureau of Mines, *Minerals Yearbook*, annual.

[59] For example, the following articles in the *Oil and Gas Journal:* "Impact of Puerto Rican Plant Feared," August 10, 1964, pp. 46–47; "Phillips Woos Support for Puerto Rico Project," January 18, 1965, p. 51; "Phillips Scores Puerto Rican Critics," March 29, 1965, pp. 76–77; "Jersey Starts 'Me-Too' Line on Naphtha for Puerto Rico," May 10, 1965, p. 111; and "Third Company Seeks Puerto Rico Imports," June 14, 1965, p. 77.

[60] *Federal Register* vol. 30, p. 15459 (December 16, 1965).

[61] *Oil Import Digest* vol. 1, pp. A-25 and A-26 (April 26, 1968).

The Puerto Rican Development Program: Petrochemicals

The hearings in July 1964 were largely devoted to the proposal of the Commonwealth of Puerto Rico that imports of feedstocks be authorized to support the building of a petrochemical complex. Early in the life of the mandatory quota program, the Economic Development Administration of Puerto Rico had envisioned this as a possible extension of its highly successful program of introducing industrial activities. The proposal gained the interest of the Department of the Interior, which is the agency of the American government responsible for supervision of Puerto Rican affairs, quite apart from its duties with respect to oil imports. Proposals had been solicited from American companies for setting up the core facilities for such a petrochemical development. From among the proposals submitted, one by Phillips Petroleum Co. was found generally acceptable by the Puerto Rican agency; and it was especially on account of this proposal that the secretary of interior called the hearings of July 31, 1964.[62] Representatives of a large number of oil producers and refiners spoke in opposition to the proposal as an enlargement of the Puerto Rican "loophole." But the Department of the Interior finally adopted a favorable attitude.[63]

Proclamation 3693 provided that the secretary might make "allocations of imports of crude oil and unfinished oils into Puerto Rico to persons as feedstocks for facilities which . . . in the judgment of the Secretary will promote substantial expansion of employment in Puerto Rico through industrial development . . ."[64] This was done simultaneously with the amendment authorizing allocations for petrochemical feedstocks in Districts I–IV and District V, described previously, giving it the status of part of a petrochemical "package," rather than just a benefit to Puerto Rico. Under this authority, effective January 1, 1966, an allocation of 50,000 bbl/day of unfinished oils from Western Hemisphere sources was made to Phillips Petroleum Co., to remain in effect

[62] "Phillips-Puerto Rico Contract Signed," *Oil and Gas Journal* June 28, 1965, p. 53, and *Oil and Gas Journal* July 12, 1965, p. 56.

[63] "Udall Favors Petrochemical Plant Import Quotas," *Oil and Gas Journal* November 1, 1965, pp. 30–31.

[64] *Federal Register* vol. 30, p. 15461 (December 16, 1965).

for ten years, pursuant to the terms of the contract between the company and the Commonwealth of Puerto Rico. The allocation carried with it the privilege of shipping to the mainland up to 24,800 bbl/day of finished products. Unlike shipments under the general Puerto Rican program, these shipments fell within the 12.2 percent formula. An equivalent therefore had to be deducted from the quotas of mainland refiners.[65]

In return for these privileges, Phillips Petroleum agreed to: (1) invest a minimum of $45 million for a core chemical facility capable of processing 50,000 bbl/day of unfinished oils; (2) invest all profits from the operation of the core facility in construction of satellite plants deriving feedstocks from the core chemical facility, until an additional $55 million is invested in such satellite plants; (3) offer to Puerto Rican companies the right of first refusal, at competitive prices, of any and all volumes yielded from the core facility which would otherwise be sold outside of Puerto Rico; (4) use its best efforts, in cooperation with the Economic Development Administration, to induce other chemical companies associated with Phillips to build satellite plants in Puerto Rico; and (5) offer to Puerto Rican investors up to 25 percent equity participation in the corporation which owns and operates the core chemical facilities.[66]

It is worth noting that, simultaneously, the regulations were revised to prevent any increase of Puerto Rican shipments of products to the mainland under the basic program *outside* the 12.2 percent formula.[67] This had the appearance of a trading point to soften the opposition of domestic producers and refiners.

Another special feature of the petrochemical program was that all allocations to it must, with discretionary exceptions, be from Western Hemisphere sources. This was unusual, since no other allocations under the import program designated a geographical source. As noted above, the purpose was to placate Venezuela, already much perturbed by the way in which unlimited entry of

65 "Petrochemical Plants Will Absorb Increase in Oil Imports," *Oil and Gas Journal* December 20, 1965, pp. 40–42.

66 Letter from Interior Secretary Udall to the Governor of the Commonwealth of Puerto Rico and the President of Phillips Petroleum Company, dated May 11, 1965. Department of the Interior news release.

67 *Federal Register* vol. 30, p. 15459 (December 16, 1965).

Canadian oil cut into the demand for Venezuelan oil. In the news release of December 10, 1965, announcing the new petrochemical and Puerto Rican programs, the secretary of interior also "pointed out that representatives of the Administration have been in frequent consultation with the Government of Venezuela concerning the probable impact of the control system on future imports of petroleum from Venezuela. . . ."[68]

The approval of the Phillips project did not end the pressures to enlarge the Puerto Rican share in the oil import program. Even earlier, other companies had been negotiating with the Puerto Rican government; and afterward, there was no reason why all the benefits of future development should accrue to only two refiners and one petrochemical project. One estimate placed the cost advantage of shipping gasoline refined in Puerto Rico to the mainland at 4 cents per gallon below the cost of U.S. manufactured gasoline.[69]

The government welcomed additional proposals; and a number of companies applied for allocations as a basis upon which to negotiate. The number of proposals required that hearings be held on the generic issues involved.[70] These hearings, held in April 1967, provided the opportunity for a full-dress exploration of the issues involved in the Islands program. The oil industry cited the premise of the mandatory quota program—to encourage the domestic oil industry—and drew the obvious lesson on the basis of the interpretation presented here: "This single premise can be broadened to include price controls, job opportunities in depressed areas and a host of others." That interpretation, it concluded, was wrong. The oil industry took the position that Puerto Rico and the Virgin Islands should be treated as part of the United States or as foreign, with reference to oil imports, but not as both. Charges of favoritism reflected the widespread view that the Department of the Interior no longer had a broad consensus of support as the administrator of an established policy. Competitors specifically attacked the special programs which were under consideration; the Union Carbide proposal, if granted, was estimated to save that firm

68 Department of the Interior news release, December 10, 1965.

69 "Third Company Seeks Puerto Rico Imports," *Oil and Gas Journal* June 14, 1965, p. 77.

70 *Federal Register* vol. 32, p. 4508 (March 24, 1967).

$15,000,000 per year in feedstock costs, compared with domestic feedstock, or alternately to save it $24,000,000 in tariffs if it were foreign.[71] In general, the hearings provided an opportunity for the oil industry to highlight the disintegration of the control program as a simple national security policy.[72]

On December 15, 1967, it was announced that Commonwealth Oil and Refining Co., under authority of the amended proclamation, had been granted permission to ship 10,000 bbl/day to Districts I–IV, within the 12.2 percent formula, in addition to the 32,928 bbl/day under the regular program outside the 12.2 percent formula. At the same time, it was announced that Commonwealth would cease to ship 10,000 bbl/day of products to District V.[73] The episode had the appearance of "one-upmanship" on the part of Commonwealth at the expense of the Oil Import Administration. The OIA had set the rule that if shipments into Districts I–IV exceeded the level of of 1965, the excess should be deducted from the next allocation. Nothing was said about shipments to District V. So, while obeying the rule regarding Districts I–IV, Commonwealth shipped at a rate of 10,000 bbl/day into District V instead, incurring no penalty. While no explanation was offered, the new District I–IV quota appeared to be a way of avoiding the necessity of compelling Commonwealth to cut back its rate of operations in closing the District V loophole inadvertently left open. Sun Oil subsequently became the only company authorized to ship into District V from Puerto Rico.

A further arrangement was made to increase imports using a foreign trade zone at Penuelas, Puerto Rico. Because the facility was designated a free trade zone, feedstock imports did not require an import license (as did the feedstock imports of all other companies operating in Puerto Rico). An arrangement similar to that of Sun Oil and Commonwealth Oil was developed to permit petrochemical product shipments to the United States. The new program

[71] "Imports Set-up Slated for Full-Dress Hearing This Month," *Oil and Gas Journal* May 1, 1967, pp. 102–105.

[72] Editorial: "Import Hearings: An Opportunity for Industry and Government," *Oil and Gas Journal* May 8, 1967, p. 47.

[73] Department of the Interior news release, December 15, 1967; "Two More Puerto Rico Deals Approved," *Oil and Gas Journal* December 18, 1967, p. 56, and *Oil Import Digest* vol. 1, p. A-25 (April 26, 1968).

authorized imports of 39,500 bbl/day of unfinished oil or 45,000 bbl/day of crude, or some combination of the two, to increase capacity of the existing Union Carbide free trade zone facility. It was operations like this—utilizing cheaper foreign feedstocks to make petrochemicals sold into the U.S. market in competition with domestic petrochemical firms—that motivated the petrochemical companies to seek the advantages discussed above. As in the other two cases, the import allocation to Union Carbide required that Venezuela be the source of Western Hemisphere feedstocks.[74]

The final major allocation to Puerto Rico-based facilities came with another "development" grant—this one to Sun Oil Co. In April 1968, a plan was approved to grant a 60,000 bbl/day import quota for a new refinery, and to approve shipment of 29,500 bbl/day (not to include gasoline) into the continental United States within the 12.2 percent formula. Sun was authorized to ship a portion of this amount into District V. The details of the plan paralleled that of Phillips with one significant addition: payment of 25 cents per barrel into a Puerto Rican conservation and development fund. In this more direct fashion, Sun Oil was forced to transfer part of the subsidy element of the import quotas to the government of Puerto Rico.[75]

The Virgin Islands

Unlike Puerto Rico, the Virgin Islands are outside the customs territory of the United States. This means that oil could be imported into the islands without regard to the oil import control program, but that a license was required to ship oil or products from the islands to the mainland.

The Hess Oil & Chemical Corp. operated for some time a refinery on the island of St. Croix without the right to ship products to the mainland.[76] Following the same principle as the special program for Puerto Rico, the government of the Virgin Islands (which

---

[74] Ibid.; *Oil Import Digest* vol. 1, p. A-25 (April 26, 1968).

[75] "Sun Gets Puerto Rico Quota," *Oil and Gas Journal* April 22, 1968, p. 116, and *Oil Import Digest* vol. 1, p. A-26 (April 26, 1968).

[76] D. H. Stormont, "Hess Aims at Huge St. Croix Complex," *Oil and Gas Journal* January 9, 1967, pp. 47–48.

was also under the supervision of the Department of the Interior) applied for entrance into the import program to support refinery and petrochemical operations. Negotiations proceeded for some time between Hess, the local government, and Interior, but the proposals were brought into the open for the first time in April 1967 at the same public hearings during which the Puerto Rican program was reviewed. The proposal by Hess was similarly aimed to promote economic development and employment opportunities in the Virgin Islands. It entailed granting Hess the right to ship petroleum products made from foreign crude to the U.S. mainland.

On November 4, 1967, Interior Secretary Udall announced the approval of a plan under which Hess would be permitted to ship 15,000 bbl/day of oil products from the Virgin Islands to the mainland.[77] The allocation was conditioned upon a defined program of petrochemical development and employment, including the creation of employment for no less than 400 locals; investment of no less than $70 million for the construction of refining facilities (plus $30 million for petrochemical facilities); and royalty payments of $7,500 per day into the Virgin Islands conservation fund. Hess was urged to obtain its crude supply from Western Hemisphere—meaning Venezuela—sources. The allocation was to be included within the 12.2 percent formula for Districts I–IV. It did not, therefore, increase the total of oil imports, but previous individual finished product quotas had to be adjusted downward to accommodate the Hess allocation. The decision was implemented in Proclamation 3820.[78]

The general philosophy underlying approval of the Virgin Islands project was essentially the same as that implemented in the Puerto Rico program. In each case allocations were committed to private companies for a period of ten years to induce them to carry through a program of industrial development for the benefit of the island economies. In announcing approval of the Hess project, the secretary of interior took pains to point out that the effects

[77] Department of the Interior news release, November 4, 1967, and "V.I. Quota to Put Hess in Import Lead," *Oil and Gas Journal* November 13, 1967, pp. 70–72.

[78] *Federal Register* vol. 32, p. 15701 (November 15, 1967); "LBJ Signs 'Hess' Imports Amendments," *Oil and Gas Journal* November 20, 1967, p. 142; and "Hess Deal Hinged to Imports of No. 2," *Oil and Gas Journal* December 18, 1967, p. 60.

would be "minimal" and "consistent with the basic objectives of the mandatory oil import control program." Udall announced that a similar proposal by Coastal States Gas Producing Co.[79] was turned down and that he made a "firm and final" decision to reject any further applications for refinery and petrochemical facilities in the Virgin Islands in order "to protect and conserve the incomparable reefs and beaches which represent the finest asset of these beautiful but fragile islands."[80]

No explanation was given by Secretary Udall why Hess Oil was chosen in preference to other applicants. One observer implied that the agreement was the result of political pressure employed by Leon Hess, founder and principal stockholder of the company.[81] It was well known that the Hess agreement was preceded by open lobbying in Washington by Leon Hess.[82] It also deserves mention that the Virgin Islands scheme was all the more lucrative because the Jones Act requirement that specifies U.S. bottoms for shipments between U.S. ports does not apply to the Virgin Islands (but does to Puerto Rico).[83] The Virgin Islands program, controversial from the first, typified the use of exceptions to the mandatory quota program for purposes alien to its original intent. The political controversy surrounding the program—and its potential for subverting the appearance if not the reality of responsible government—was also highlighted. In this case Secretary Udall felt constrained, for example, to assert full reponsibility for the decision. He denied discussing it with the president, with whom the secretary had an agreement to keep import matters *away* from the White House.[84]

The controversy over the Hess project seemed justified almost four years later when it became public that Amerada Hess, successor to Hess, had not fulfilled its obligations with regard to Virgin Island development. In November 1970 official notice was

---

[79] Department of the Interior news release, November 4, 1967. The Coastal States' proposal (for a 100,000 bbl/day complex) was reported in "Coastal Awaits Imports Ruling," *Oil and Gas Journal* September 26, 1966, p. 61.

[80] *Oil and Gas Journal* November 13, 1967, pp. 70–72.

[81] Kenneth W. Dam, "Implementation of Import Quotas: The Case of Oil," *Journal of Law and Economics* vol. 14, no. 1 (April 1971) pp. 46–47.

[82] "Leon Hess Never Plays It Safe," *Fortune,* January 1970, p. 141.

[83] *Oil Import Digest* vol. 1, p. A-26 (April 26, 1968).

[84] *Oil and Gas Journal* November 13, 1967, pp. 70–72.

taken that Hess had made no expenditures, nor obligated funds with regard to the promised $70 million upgrading of its refinery due within one year of the quota grant (by December 1968), nor done anything observable toward the $30 million petrochemical facility for which its due date was December 1970. There were fewer than the required 80 percent Virgin Islanders on the Hess payroll, and Hess was not paying the agreed-upon royalty of $7,500/day (that is, 50 cents per barrel) to the Virgin Islands development and conservation fund.[85] Hess had responded to the OIA threat to cut off its quota with objections and with promises to conform, but no action followed. When these same issues were brought up almost a year later, Amerada Hess was again held by the Department of the Interior to have failed to meet the obligations it undertook in obtaining the valuable 15,000 bbl/day import right. Again, Interior did not revoke the quota but instead ordered Amerada Hess to negotiate with the Virgin Islands to remedy its violations. There was disagreement between Interior and Amerada Hess as to whether its investment obligations had been met because of definitional issues, but the native hiring condition was unambiguously violated.[86]

Guam

Like the Virgin Islands, Guam also lies outside the customs territory of the United States. At the time the special arrangements were being made for Puerto Rico and the Virgin Islands, there was no refinery located on Guam. In 1968 two proposals were made to locate a refinery on Guam under the condition that import allocations were received for shipments to the mainland.[87] The distance of Guam from the mainland, plus the location of a major U.S. military installation on the island, led to a different arrangement with respect to oil imports.

An agreement was reached with the Guam Oil and Refining Co. to sell products to the U.S. military, to sell products on the island

[85] "Amerada Faces Revocation of Virgin Islands Import Quota," Oil and Gas Journal August 16, 1971, p. 52.

[86] "Amerada Charged with Import-Rules Violation," Oil and Gas Journal June 12, 1972, p. 68.

[87] Oil Import Digest vol. 1, p. A-26 (April 26, 1968).

of Guam and possibly export to other countries, but not to sell to
the U.S. mainland. The refinery on Guam was defined as a U.S.
refinery for the purpose of selling products to the U.S. government, but a foreign refinery in all other respects, with no license
to sell to the U.S. mainland.[88]

Concluding Comments on the Islands Program

The peculiarities introduced into the mandatory quota program
in relation to Puerto Rico and the Virgin Islands were important
and dramatic. First, of course, the import program was used to
stimulate economic development, no part of its original intent.
Second, the companies had to "pay" for their allocation by making
contributions to the local economies in which they were located.
That the returns to the host economies fell short of expectations is
not surprising now; the experience of virtually all such "indus-
trialization" programs of the 1960s was similar. The current tendency to view such efforts with cynicism benefits from hindsight not
available at the time. Surely, though, experiences such as those of
the Virgin Islands are now understandable; firms attracted by subsidies are by definition marginal, and excess returns to the local
economy should not have been expected. Third, the allocations
designated a geographical source of feedstocks—effectively Venezuela. The Islands program was thus to return with one hand what
the mandatory quota program had taken away with the other.
Western Hemisphere markets were strengthened by this move, but
only at the cost of some of the benefits designed in the first place
for the intended direct recipients of the largesse. Fourth, the administration of the program reached the heights of ad hoc decision
making as each arrangement was different for each company. Even
the most basic question of including the allocation of shipments
to the United States within the 12.2 percent rule was handled differently for different firms. The result was to call the integrity of
the entire program into question. From the high public purpose
of national security it appeared to descend as far as political ex-
pediency. However intricately wrought and carefully articulated
the rationales for each action, the impression was inescapable that
the mandatory quota program was being treated as a source of

[88] Ibid., p. A-30 (August 25, 1974).

unappropriated funds available for a variety of putative public purposes.

Taken together with the petrochemical program, the Islands program represented a considerable shift in philosophy governing the administration of the import control programs. In each case, economic rents at the disposal of government, originating in the artificial scarcity created by government and paid for by consumers, were withdrawn from domestic refiners in order to support some other public purpose. Domestic refiners attempted to frame an argument that the new programs tended to lower the demand and weaken the price of domestically produced oil, thus seeking to attack the new provisions on the basis that the fundamental premise of the mandatory quota program remained its original national security rationale. The argument stood on weak ground in those cases where the new programs did not increase the aggregate volume of oil and products entering the United States—where the 12.2 percent limit was not breached. But, the principle on which benefits were originally distributed having been abandoned, domestic producers and refiners had an understandable fear that the formula governing the levels of imports would be discarded altogether. In fact, as we see in the next chapter, changes in the petroleum market made the controls first too expensive to maintain in any event, and then rendered them obsolete as originally intended. Nonetheless, the domestic industry view was correct: the Islands program helped destroy the legitimacy of the mandatory quota program, whatever other public purposes it performed.

Other Special Cases

This chapter concludes with three separate cases involving special exemptions under the oil import control program: foreign trade zones, asphalt, and No. 2 fuel oil. Each case involves a relatively minor volume of imports, but each is significant in its own way in the history of the import control program and of its relaxation.

Foreign Trade Zones

The precedents established by the Islands program generated a number of unsuccessful proposals for foreign trade zones to be located in the continental United States.[89] The best-known and most controversial proposal was that developed by Occidental Petroleum in 1968 to designate a foreign trade zone at Machiasport, Maine.[90] Occidental was one of the independents which had gone abroad with great success; its Libyan production was prolific. It sought a U.S. outlet for its crude, and concluded that the best way to achieve that goal was through a foreign trade zone scheme. The Occidental proposal was controversial because it included a provision to grant special exemptions from oil import controls to ship finished products into the U.S. customs territory. Normally, imports are permitted to enter a foreign trade zone free of restrictions for processing or storage, and may be reexported, but cannot enter the U.S. customs area without the same controls as all other imports.

Occidental proposed to build a refinery at Machiasport to process 300,000 bbl/day of predominantly Libyan crude oil, with authorization to ship 100,000 bbl/day of various finished products into U.S. customs territory. In addition, residual fuel oil would be imported from the zone into District I under existing regulations. Following the precedent established in the Islands program, and in an effort to allay fears of pollution—especially due to what was alleged to be a narrow and dangerous inland passage through partially Canadian waters—Occidental proposed to make payments of 20 cents per barrel into an environmental conservation fund.[91]

Arguments for and against the Occidental proposal resembled those in connection with the Islands program. Proponents argued that the Machiasport project was important to the economic de-

---

[89] A foreign-trade zone existed in Puerto Rico from 1962 until it was made unnecessary by authority to import oil into Puerto Rico through the Islands program. Firms using the foreign trade zones processed foreign feedstock and both exported petrochemicals and supplied raw material for a firm (Union Carbide) located in Puerto Rico, which then shipped quota-exempt products to the U.S. mainland (*Oil Import Digest* vol. 1, p. A-33, May 1, 1967; *Oil Import Digest* vol. 1, pp. A-25 and A-26, May 4, 1973).

[90] Among the other petroleum-based free trade zones established (but not operated) were two by Dow Chemical in Bay County, Michigan, and one by Union Carbide in Taft, Louisiana. Ibid. See frontispiece for location of Machiasport.

[91] "Oxy Trade Zone 100,000 b/d Quota under Heavy Attack," *Oil and Gas Journal* October 14, 1968, pp. 78–79, and "Commerce Ends Hot Hearing on Maine Zones," *Oil and Gas Journal* October 21, 1968, p. 52.

velopment of New England, would increase the supply of low-sulfur resid, and would lower petroleum products prices in the Northeast. Opponents argued that additional special deals would destroy the mandatory quota program. Indeed, the Machiasport proposal would have represented an "exception" on the grand scale; Occidental from that one facility would have been given a finished product quota greater than that of all other firms combined.[92] The proposal received considerable attention in the latter months of 1968, but was abandoned when the Nixon administration took office in 1969 and announced that no further exemptions from oil import controls would be made until after a cabinet-level review. Before that happened, however, a last-ditch effort to vitalize the foreign trade zone program resulted in a proposal issued by the Department of the Interior in December 1968.[93] The enabling presidential proclamation was not forthcoming before Nixon was inaugurated.

Asphalt

As table 5-2 shows, imports of petroleum asphalt were not very significant, either before or after the implementation of the import control program. They were never greater than 1 percent of all petroleum imports. Nonetheless, control policy toward asphalt was treated as if it were an important issue, and required a grossly disproportionate amount of attention from the federal authorities. The reason was that any proposal to change controls at once faced adverse interests, those interests occupied positions of political influence, and the quota program, by its nature, was susceptible to manipulation in response to changes in the relative power of the contending parties. The five identifiable parties were: (1) state and federal highway departments, who generally favored relaxation in order to assure supplies, or to hold prices in check; (2) a few companies capable of supplying finished asphalt from their refineries; (3) several East Coast refineries prepared to produce asphalt from imports of crude or unfinished oils; (4) interior refiners engaged in asphalt production who did not want their markets weakened

92 Ibid., "Oxy Trade Zone."
93 "Import Rules Proposed for Trade Zones," *Oil and Gas Journal* December 16, 1968, p. 69.

Table 5-2. U.S. Production, Domestic Demand, and Imports of
Petroleum Asphalt, 1945–75[a]

(thousands of barrels)

Year	Production	Domestic demand	Imports
1945	39,196	38,350	809
1950	58,240	58,677	1,795
1955	83,121	84,286	3,325
1960	98,671	104,696	6,143
1961	101,819	107,753	6,609
1962	109,576	114,122	6,625
1963	111,948	117,354	6,211
1964	114,879	120,155	5,912
1965	123,604	127,597	6,302
1966	129,579	134,070	6,104
1967	127,767	131,125	6,447
1968	135,460	141,151	6,236
1969	135,691	143,290	4,761
1970	146,658	153,477	6,201
1971	157,039	158,526	7,216
1972	155,294	163,788	9,263
1973	167,884	182,602	8,444
1974	164,237	168,733	11,252
1975	143,957	147,384	4,956

Sources: 1944–73, U.S. Bureau of Mines, *Minerals Yearbook;* 1974–75, U.S. Bureau
of Mines, "Annual Petroleum Statement."

[a] Exports and stock changes, which are not given here, balance production, domestic demand, and imports.

by increased imports; and (5) domestic oil producers who automatically opposed any plan likely to increase the total imports of crude oil and products.

From the beginning of the program, proposals were made for exempting from control imports of asphalt or of imported oils used to produce asphalt. In September 1958, the Interior Department proposed the exemption of asphalt under the voluntary program to assure an adequate supply of materials for the Federal Interstate Highway Program.[94] Public comments on the proposal were critical, so the proposal was withdrawn and asphalt came to be included under the mandatory quota program in 1959.

In 1960 a group of asphalt distributors and road-building companies petitioned the Office of Civil and Defense Mobilization for decontrol of asphalt, but with the amount of asphalt imported to be deducted from the general level of permissible imports. This

[94] *Oil Import Digest* vol. 1, p. A-32 (March 1, 1968).

event is of some significance as one of the first efforts to breach the mandatory quota program for a special purpose. After the proposal was circulated for comment, no action was taken on the proposal. In 1963 a similar proposal was circulated by the Office of Emergency Planning (the successor to OCDM), but again led to no recommendation, the proposal being formally denied in March 1964.[95]

After a quiescent period, and without prior public discussion, on April 10, 1967, the president issued Proclamation 3779 amending the basic proclamation to provide for easing of import controls on asphalt, if and when the demand–supply situation made it desirable.[96] The amendment did not prescribe a method, but placed in the hands of the secretary of interior discretionary authority to prescribe a maximum level of asphalt imports and (1) to establish a special system of allocation or (2) to permit entry for consumption without allocation. Secretary of Interior Udall explained the action as necessary so the government would be in a position to head off shortages which threatened the interstate highway program. He also cited the declining domestic yields of asphalt due to more complete processing of crude, the increasing concentration of the asphalt industry, and price increases in the East Coast market.[97] An OEP study was announced, but its results were not released. In a perhaps unrelated move, the Oil Imports Appeals Board granted an "exceptional hardship" allocation of 900 bbl/day of asphalt.[98]

On August 24, 1967, Secretary Udall issued two alternative proposals designed to authorize an increase in asphalt supply, but nothing ever came of them.[99] As usual, a variety of views were expressed from industry sources concerning what, if anything, needed to be done. Independent producers and refiners in general discounted the need for additional imports. Domestic asphalt refiners did not agree that there was a supply problem, but argued that

[95] Ibid.

[96] *Federal Register* vol. 32, p. 5919 (April 13, 1967).

[97] Department of the Interior press release, April 10, 1967, reported in *Oil and Gas Journal* April 17, 1967, pp. 126–128.

[98] "U.S. Cracks Door on Imports of Asphalt," *Oil and Gas Journal* May 15, 1967, p. 47.

[99] *Federal Register* vol. 32, p. 12621 (August 31, 1967).

any relief should come from imports of unfinished asphalt to be refined domestically.[100]

The authority to ease controls on asphalt imports continued to exist, but was not used until the supply problems that developed during 1970 became obvious and the secretary had to act to abate the upward pressure on prices. On January 13, 1971, the secretary of interior announced that, for the year 1971, all persons who certified their need for imports of asphalt to meet contractual obligations and manufacturing requirements were authorized to import all they needed.[101] In December of that year it was announced that the same provisions would extend through 1972, and asphalt imports were not again controlled.[102] The action eliminating the mandatory quota program specifically excepted asphalt from the special license fees imposed on other petroleum imports.[103]

The basis of the decision to relax import controls on asphalt imports, to meet demand requirements at existing market prices, is a forerunner of subsequent decisions to relax all oil import controls to ease general inflationary pressure.

No. 2 Fuel Oil

No. 2 fuel oil is used primarily for home heating. It ranks second only to gasoline as the industry's most important product. Import control exemptions were sought by consumer interests in the Northeast to reduce the price of this product and to increase competition among its suppliers. The pressure began to be intense in late 1967, as supplies were tight going into the heating season.[104] While no general relaxation of controls followed, Secretary Udall directed Hess to use its 15,000 bbl/day quota during the first quarter of

[100] "Industry Weighs Rival Asphalt Proposals," *Oil and Gas Journal* September 4, 1967, pp. 78–79.

[101] *Federal Register* vol. 36, pp. 775–776 (January 16, 1971).

[102] *Federal Register* vol. 36, p. 24115 (December 21, 1971).

[103] *Oil Import Digest* vol. 1, p. A-32 (May 4, 1973). It is interesting, however, that the Energy Policy and Conservation Act of December 22, 1975 reimposed license and price controls on asphalt. See chapter 6 for a discussion of the formulation of energy policy following the suspension of the mandatory quota program.

[104] "New Attack on Imports Control Readied," *Oil and Gas Journal* September 25, 1967, pp. 76–77.

1968 to import No. 2 fuel oil.[105] The other response of the administration was to use the OIAB to provide specific relief. It was empowered to grant special allocations to individual marketers "suffering exceptional hardship attributable to oil import controls." In an early decision, in September 1967, it granted allocations to three firms to import 3,000 bbl/day of No. 2 fuel oil. This became the camel's nose under the import control tent. The precedent created in September of making hardship allocations was followed in February 1968 with the award of 7,000 bbl/day to twelve petitioners for the rest of the year.[106]

These decisions met with considerable negative reaction. Among those opposing the action were the refiners supplying heating oil to the affected region, independent oil producers, and other jobbers without allocations. It is especially worth noting that the National Oil Jobbers Council was opposed, denying a shortage existed and stating that the quotas "will create an unreasonable market advantage and discriminate between favored quota recipients and others with whom they compete."[107] The importance of the No. 2 fuel oil decision, from the point of view of domestic producers and refiners, was not in the imports themselves, but in its role as the forerunner of a movement in support of extensive relaxation of import control restrictions over finished oil products. The subject of No. 2 oil imports outside the original program therefore became a firm item (1) in the resistance of oil producers to breaching the 12.2 percent formula and (2) in the resistance of refiners to product imports which deprived domestic refiners of benefits from processing crude oil, even within the formula.

Some of the fears of the oil producers and refiners eventually came to pass, but primarily within the context of the general relaxation of controls. The controls on No. 2 fuel oil imports were successively lightened beginning in 1970. In June of that year it was announced that 40,000 bbl/day of No. 2 would be allowed

---

[105] "Hess Deal Hinged to Imports of No. 2," *Oil and Gas Journal* December 18, 1967, p. 60.

[106] "Fuel Oil Dealers Due Emergency Import Quotas," *Oil and Gas Journal* February 19, 1968, p. 52.

[107] As reported in "OIAB Grants Quotas to East Coast Marketers," *Oil and Gas Journal* March 4, 1968, p. 38.

into District I for the next 6 months. Along with other actions taken at the same time, the 12.2 percent limitation was substantially exceeded for the first time.[108] In November 1971 there was a further increase in No. 2 quotas, and a relaxation of the Western Hemisphere criterion.[109] A year later there were further moves along the same line, accompanied by efforts to get larger outputs of No. 2 from domestic refiners. The demand for light oil was strong because, apparently, it was being blended with resid so that composite sulfur standards could be met to comply with air quality requirements.[110] Finally, in January 1973, President Nixon suspended controls on imports of No. 2 oil through Presidential Proclamation 4178; he announced that a No. 2 license would be issued to any company for which imports were required to meet contractual obligations or purchase orders from customers in Districts I–IV.[111]

The special import rights granted to No. 2 fuel oil wholesalers followed an effective campaign waged by northeastern politicians, and may have been gained as a salve to New England for rejection of the Machiasport proposal. The effect was to increase the region's dependence on imported oil products and necessitate a new campaign after 1973 for special subsidies to offset hardships created when foreign oil became more costly than domestic oil.

Concluding Comment

The special exemptions and general relaxation of controls described above led to growing criticism of the mandatory quota program during the late 1960s. The program, so criticism within the industry went, was losing its primary purpose of protecting domestic production in the interests of national security. At the

108 *Federal Register* vol. 35, p. 10091 (June 19, 1971).

109 *Federal Register* vol. 36, p. 21397 (November 9, 1971).

110 *Federal Register* vol. 37, p. 28043 (December 20, 1972) .

111 *Federal Register* vol. 38, p. 1719 (January 18, 1973) . See "President Loosens Clamp on Oil Imports," *Oil and Gas Journal* January 22, 1973, pp. 45–46, for reactions to the announcement and the reported flood of complaints about shortages of No. 2 fuel oil and diesel fuel.

same time, pressures for more exemptions continued, leading to suggestions for alternative restrictive measures or for no controls at all. In response to the general dissatisfaction with the mandatory quota program, President Nixon formed a cabinet-level committee to study the issues surrounding the relationship between oil imports and national security and to recommend policy action. The committee's conclusions and recommendations are discussed in the next chapter. As we shall see, however, other events were moving rapidly to seal the fate of the mandatory quota program.

6

The End of the Quota and the
Search for a New Energy Program

The mandatory quota program did not survive the changes in the world and national petroleum markets that were already manifest in the special exceptions to the program described in chapters 4 and 5. Put simply, a quota program that would have reserved over 85 percent of the non-resid petroleum market to domestic production became too expensive to maintain once excess capacity was wrung out of the producing industry; substantially higher costs would have been incurred to supply the energy demanded. The effective demise of the program, which came well before it was officially abandoned, was hastened by shifts in political power against the producing industry and by the overwhelming concern with rising prices that became the preoccupation of national economic policy after 1969. These conclusions were not obvious at the time, however, and changes in policy to meet what were later seen to be new realities did not come readily. In retrospect, some of the fiercest battles over the mandatory quota program were fought after the issue had already been decided.

This chapter illuminates the policy transitions that took place between 1970 and 1975. We start with the Cabinet Task Force report on the oil import question and its principal recommendation that the mandatory quota program be discarded and replaced by a tariff.[1] While the recommendations of the report were not ac-

[1] *The Oil Import Question,* A Report on the Relationship of Oil Imports to the National Security prepared by the Cabinet Task Force on Oil Import Control (Washington, GPO, 1970).

188

cepted by President Nixon, and the quota program continued, controls were substantially relaxed. General inflationary conditions had developed in the U.S. economy during 1970 and showed signs of worsening. Nixon responded in 1971 with a price control program that was inconsistent with the limitation of oil imports. Domestic oil supplies, indeed domestic energy supplies in general, became increasingly tight. Either prices had to rise to encourage additional supplies and discourage consumption, or additional oil imports had to be permitted to fill the gap. In short, the quota program was creating more problems than it was worth. On May 1, 1973, the quota program was eliminated and a license fee system substituted in its place. The fee system soon became superfluous, however, with the Arab oil embargo of October 1973 and the subsequent quadrupling of world oil prices. This event led to a search for a "new" energy strategy, initially labeled "Project Independence."

The Oil Import Question

The special exceptions and direct penetrations of the 12.2 percent ceiling made it evident to many that a fundamental rethinking of the existing mandatory quota program was required. The developments were numerous and significant, but were not coordinated: residual fuel oil imports were permitted in District I essentially free of control; the "clean air proclamation" extended special exemptions to imports of crude and other oils used to produce low-sulfur resid; imports of asphalt were decontrolled; import quotas were extended to petrochemical manufacturers; refiners located in Puerto Rico and the Virgin Islands obtained rights to import crude and to sell products to the United States; and imports from Canada and Venezuela were given special preference. Even while industry spokesmen charged that each of these steps had further undermined the control program, consumer spokesmen were dissatisfied.[2] The industry charged that the Department of the Interior was no longer in control of the program; that it was bending to strong economic and political pressures originating

---

[2] See, for example, the editorial: "How Import Controls Keep Crumbling Away," *Oil and Gas Journal* August 7, 1967, p. 75, as well as editorials in subsequent issues over the next several years.

from congressmen representing the northeastern states. Beyond these interests clashing over the level of imports, there were still others criticizing the discriminatory and inefficient aspects of the program.

In response to these and other concerns, the Department of the Interior initiated two efforts which resulted in a broad review of the program. The first of these were the hearings held in May 1967, which attracted numerous witnesses. Secretary Udall used the hearings as an occasion to pledge not to violate the 12.2 percent formula, or to use the imports program to control prices, but neither petroleum producers nor refiners were satisfied.[3] While it was unlikely that any substantial changes would have been wrought in the program in any case, the outbreak of the second Suez war shortly after the hearings ended reduced the impetus for change. The next major consideration of basic control policy surfaced in February 1968 with a Department of Interior call for comments on proposals to eliminate historical quota allocations (discussed in chapter 4) and to switch to a license auction as the means to distribute import rights.[4] The Texas Independent Producers and Royalty Owners Association (TIPRO) supported the latter proposal on the grounds that the alternative was a prospective breakdown in import controls altogether. TIPRO argued that auctioning would (1) ease the administrative difficulties, (2) remove political pressure for allocations, (3) eliminate allocation decisions for individual companies, (4) neutralize the economic advantages of import licenses, and (5) be consistent with the free market system. Furthermore, auctioning would remove the occasion for alleged favoritism on the part of the administrators of the program or the government as a whole. The members of TIPRO had no vested interest in the method of distribution of quotas, but were concerned with preserving the rents accruing to lease owners and land owners due to high crude oil prices and thought that

    [3] See, all from the *Oil and Gas Journal:* "Imports Set-up Slated for Full Dress Hearing This Month," May 1, 1967, pp. 102–103; editorial: "Import Hearings: An Opportunity for Industry and Government," May 8, 1967, p. 47; "Independents Gear for Imports Battle," May 15, 1967; and *Oil Import Digest* vol. 1, p. A-37 (June 16, 1967); also the hearings cited in chapter 4, note 57.

    [4] "Interior Mulls Import Quota Bidding," *Oil and Gas Journal* March 25, 1968, p. 82. The quota-bidding program would have been the responsibility of the Treasury Department, and one of Udall's objectives in raising the issue at this time was to consolidate opinion in defense of his administration of the import program.

could best be done by the more neutral auction system, which would also capture for the government the rents going to refiners and other quota recipients.

Reaction to the auction proposal from the rest of the industry was uniformly negative. Existing producers and refiners were unwilling to give up the economic rents associated with historical allocations. Comments received by Interior totaled 100 against the proposal and 1 (i.e., TIPRO) in favor.[5] Spokesmen for the industry responded that the existing quota system was correct and appropriate, and that its only major defect was that it was poorly administered.[6] As a result, Interior cancelled further hearings on the proposal. Following hearings on the quota program, congressmen viewed as supporters of the industry submitted legislation to halt exceptions to the control program and called for investigations of its administration.[7] The political battle continued in the House Ways and Means and Interior committees. In August 1968 the latter committee approved a report denouncing the administration's handling of controls, charging that the program was no longer being administered in such a way as to maintain a healthy domestic industry.[8] As noted in chapter 5, there were efforts at this same time to obtain, and to resist, a number of measures to relax import controls. No final action was taken on these proposals, and the whole situation was in the usual pre- and postelection flux. With the election settled, however, it was possible again to give long-term attention to this matter.

In February 1969, shortly after he assumed office, Nixon reasserted presidential authority over oil import policy by moving it from the Department of the Interior to the White House.[9] On March 25 a number of other actions were taken. The Oil Import

[5] "Quota Bidding Swamped by Opponents," *Oil and Gas Journal* April 29, 1968, p. 42.

[6] "IPAA Lambastes Special Import Quotas," *Oil and Gas Journal* May 13, 1968, p. 46.

[7] House Interior Committee, Subcommittee on Mines and Mining, Hearings, "Mandatory Oil Import Program, Its Impact upon Domestic Minerals Industry and National Security," May 13–16, 1968, 90 Cong. 2 sess.; "Push to Curb Imports by Law Advances," *Oil and Gas Journal* May 20, 1968, p. 62.

[8] "Interior Hit on Import-Controls Handling," *Oil and Gas Journal* August 5, 1968, p. 89.

[9] "Memorandum to Secretary of the Interior," *Weekly Compilation of Presidential Documents* vol. 5, no. 8, p. 292. President Johnson had earlier removed this authority from the White House to avoid allegations or appearances of favoritism because of his presumed parochial interests in oil policy.

Administration in the Department of the Interior was (again) combined with the Office of Oil and Gas; it continued to handle the assignment of licenses, compliance efforts, and other administrative details of the program. In addition, a cabinet task force was created with the mission to rethink thoroughly all the issues surrounding oil import controls. Coincidentally, Nixon took these actions one month after an appeal by American Petroleum Institute President Frank N. Ikard to reevaluate the import program before "further changes or exceptions are made."[10]

Robert F. Ellsworth, an assistant to the president, was designated as coordinator of the policy review. Significantly, George P. Shultz, the new secretary of labor and a prominent economist and antitrust specialist, was selected to head the study group. He immediately announced plans to assemble a group of outside economists and a professional staff unconnected with the various special interest groups associated with the issues.[11] The task force group set about making perhaps the broadest and deepest study of the

[10] "API Leaders Ask White House for Imports Control Review," *Oil and Gas Journal* February 24, 1969, p. 42.

[11] *The Oil Import Question,* p. 1; see also *Oil and Gas Journal* April 14, 1969, p. 97. The president announced the study on March 25, 1969, with formation of the task force. The members of the task force included Secretary of State William P. Rogers, Secretary of the Treasury David M. Kennedy, Secretary of Defense Melvin R. Laird, Secretary of Interior Walter J. Hickel, Secretary of Commerce Maurice H. Stans, Director of Office of Emergency Preparedness George A. Lincoln, and Secretary of Labor George P. Shultz, Chairman. There were also six official observers: Director of the Bureau of the Budget Robert P. Mayo, Chairman of the Federal Power Commission John N. Nassikas, Assistant Attorney General Richard W. McLaren, Council of Economic Advisers Member Hendrik S. Houthakker, Special Representative for Trade Negotiations Carl J. Gilbert, and Office of Science and Technology Adviser S. David Freeman. The task force staff was headed by Phillip Areeda as executive director; James McKie served as chief economist; and Roland Homet, Jr., as chief counsel.

The task force issued a statement on its view of the issues on April 8, 1969 and on April 21 requested written comments on these issues. On May 22 it filed a formal notice which set forth its procedures and included a list of eighty-two questions on which responses were requested. Two rounds of submissions—allowing for rebuttal—were provided for, and in addition the staff consulted the literature, were supplied with special presentations, and participated in field trips and special seminars. Some outside studies were commissioned.

Secretary of Interior Hickel and Secretary of Commerce Stans did not associate themselves with the report, and Chairman Nassikas of the FPC joined them in a separate report, appended at pp. 343–393, along with the task force findings. *The Oil Import Question,* pp. iii–v; 1–2.

domestic oil situation up to that time, and certainly the first serious effort to relate oil imports to the national security.

The Cabinet Task Force Report

The findings of the report may be grouped under three categories: the effect of the quota program on prices, production, imports, and national security; the nature of the national security problem and the possible role of import controls in dealing with the problem; and the recommendations of the task force to deal with the national security problem.

With regard to the effect of the quota on prices as of 1969, the report concluded:

> Without import controls the domestic wellhead price would fall from $3.30 per barrel to about $2.00, which would correspond to the world price. Although we cannot exclude the possibility, we do not predict a substantial price rise in world oil markets over the coming decade.[12]

If the quota were removed, under conditions prevailing in 1969:

> American consumers would save about $5 billion annually now and over $8 billion annually by 1980. These savings would be about two-thirds as much if the domestic price was supported at a level of $2.50, and about one-fourth as much at a level of $3.00. These totals include the substantial savings that would be realized through the elimination of inefficiently utilized production and transportation resources.[13]

The short-term impact on domestic production would be:

> Texas and Louisiana "market demand prorationing" would become pointless if import controls were entirely abandoned or significantly relaxed, with the result that about 1.2 million barrels per day (MMb/d) of existing domestic capacity would come into use over about two years. This would more than offset the 0.5 MMb/d of high-cost "stripper well" production that would go out of production fairly rapidly after a drop in domestic prices to the world level. At a $2.50 price, about half as much of this high-cost production would be lost fairly rapidly.[14]

[12] *The Oil Import Question,* p. 124.
[13] Ibid.
[14] Ibid.

While for long-run supply:

> At world market prices total U.S. reserves, including those in
> Alaska, would decline slightly; outside Alaska we would expect
> additions to reserves to fall within six years to less than half their
> present rate. Nevertheless, anticipated 1980 production of 9.5
> MMb/d would still be only 1 MMb/d less than 1968 output,
> though about 4 MMb/d less than anticipated 1980 production at
> the present $3.30 price. If the domestic price were to be $2.50, an-
> ticipated production would be about 11 MMb/d or 2.5 MMb/d
> less than at $3.30; total U.S. reserves in this case would be about
> the same as or higher than they are today.[15]

The implications for imports:

> Because demand is growing faster than domestic supply, imports
> would have to expand by 1980 even at the present $3.30 price, and
> by then could amount to about 27% of our demand at that price.
> Imports would be about 42% of demand in 1980 at a $2.50 price,
> but it appears that appropriate trading policies could, if desired,
> insure that all these imports were from Western Hemisphere
> sources. At a $2.00 price, imports could amount to about 51%
> of domestic demand. Perhaps half of these imports would be from
> the Eastern Hemisphere; about 40% of all imports—or 20% of
> domestic demand—would be from Arab sources.[16]

The report acknowledges the potentially severe dislocations with
respect to employment and investment in the domestic oil industry, but concludes that the impact on the economy would be small
and would dissipate quickly.

As to the risk of import interruptions, the report discounts the
dangers associated with several U.S. war contingencies, but in any
event these dangers may be subsumed within the risks of politically
inspired export interruptions. In this case, the report concludes:

> Persian Gulf or North African oil might be denied at the source
> as a result of some kind of regional take-over. Or hostile govern-
> ments may arise in oil-producing states; but the simultaneous
> emergence in most exporting countries of such regimes willing to
> dispense with their oil revenues for a prolonged period is unlikely
> —at least in the absence of outside support or concerted activity.
> Such a "group boycott" directed against only one or two import-
> ing countries would not impair total free world supplies. Thus, a
> difficult world supply problem would arise only if all or most Mid-
> dle Eastern and North African supplies were to be cut off to all

15 Ibid.
16 Ibid., p. 125.

major markets. Although such a boycott would be difficult to sustain for a prolonged period, it is in light of present regional tensions the possibility most productive of concern.[17]

In the event of a one-year Arab oil boycott in 1980, at the prevailing price of $3.30 maintained by the quota, only 0.4 MMb/day of supply would be lost to the United States; in the free-trade case, with a $2 price, only 4.0 MMb/day would be lost.[18] If Iran joined the Arab boycott, the corresponding losses in U.S. supplies would rise to 0.5 MMb/day with the quota and to 4.8 MMb/day with free trade.[19] These estimates assume that supplies from all other sources continue at their pre-crisis rates. If the U.S. and Canadian oil markets are considered as an integrated unit, complete isolation of the North American continent for one year would not result in the loss of any oil supplies if the quota is continued and in only a 4.7 MMb/day loss in 1980 with the free trade scenario.[20] Combining the North and South American oil markets, complete hemispheric isolation for one year would result in no lost oil supplies with either the quota or free trade scenarios.

In view of these estimates, the report concluded that:

> The present import control program is not adequately responsive to present and future security considerations. The fixed quota limitations that have been in effect for the past ten years, and the system of implementation that has grown up around them, bear no reasonable relation to current requirements for protection either of the national economy or of essential oil consumption. The level of restriction is arbitrary and the treatment of secure foreign sources internally inconsistent. . . .
>
> We find that a phased-in liberalization of import controls would not so injure the domestic industry as to weaken the national economy to the extent of impairing our national security.[21]

But, the report stops short of recommending the free trade alternative:

> We are unable on present evidence to rule out the possibility that abandonment of all import controls would result in an inability to satisfy our essential oil requirements by acceptable emergency measures in response to certain conceivable supply

17 Ibid., p. 126.
18 Ibid., p. 127.
19 Ibid.
20 Ibid., p. 128.
21 Ibid., pp. 128–129.

interruptions. Whether such conceivable interruptions are "reasonably possible" is a matter on which judgments may vary. Our estimates indicate that a one-year supply crisis in 1980 would leave about 21% of the United States and Canadian demand unmet if North America received no Eastern Hemisphere or Latin American oil. Moreover, the likelihood of such an extreme interruption might be increased because the United States would not be in a position to offer a significant preference as an inducement to nondiversion of Latin American oil. In case of such an interruption, military and essential civilian demand could be met only by severe and perhaps intolerable rationing. Knowledge of this fact could encourage supplying countries to try to take advantage of it and might reduce our freedom of action in dealing with those countries. Although the probability of such an extreme interruption is small, these considerations and the uncertainty of our estimates render the Task Force unable to say that complete abandonment of import controls at this time would be consistent with the national security.[22]

Instead, the task force recommended that:

A tariff system, involving some relaxation of import restraints and accompanied by suitable preference and safeguard arrangements, would protect the United States from becoming so dependent on insecure foreign supplies as to impair our ability, in a "reasonably possible" oil supply interruption, to satisfy military and essential civilian oil requirements with acceptable emergency replacement measures.[23]

Specifically, the task force recommended a reduction in the domestic price (by elimination of the quota system and imposition of a tariff) in effect to $3 (from $3.30) and then to $2.50, after a review of the operation of the first reduction with regard to effects on domestic supply prospects. Finished and other unfinished oils were to be taxed at the crude oil rate plus 10 cents per barrel in order to encourage domestic refining. It was recommended that residual fuel oil imports from Western Hemisphere sources pay the same duty as crude oil, but an additional 30 cents per barrel was to be added for imports from other sources. In the transition period, oil imports from Western Hemisphere sources were to be exempted from other duties up to a specified quantity. Even in the longer run, imports from Western Hemisphere sources were to pay

[22] Ibid., p. 129.
[23] Ibid.

lower duties than those applied to oil from other geographical sources. As an additional security adjustment, if imports from Eastern Hemisphere sources were projected to exceed 10 percent of domestic demand, import licenses would be required, with the licenses to be auctioned. Such imports would be subject to the tariff as well as to the purchase cost of the special import license. For a transition period of three years, the group recommended a declining tariff-free quota for existing "specially favored beneficiaries of the quota system."[24]

The task force also recommended that consideration be given to developing additional oil security policies, such as strategic storage, subsidization of shale oil or coal oil capacity, and development of the Naval Petroleum Reserves. Finally, the task force recommended the creation of a Cabinet-level oil policy and administration committee, to be headed by the director of the Office of Emergency Preparedness.[25]

Reactions to the Report

While the task force study was not officially released until February 1970, preliminary findings of the study group and research reports commissioned for the study drew comments throughout the fall of 1969. Indeed, the nature and strength of preliminary comments may have been the cause for the delay in releasing the report and in Nixon's decision to delay any radical changes in the oil import control program. A study by Charles River Associates (CRA) drew particular attention from the oil industry and trade associations.[26] All industry groups disputed the main conclusion of the CRA report that national security could be assured more cheaply by ending barriers to imported foreign oil and by providing instead emergency storage to be used in the event of interruption.[27]

24 Ibid., pp. 134–138.

25 Ibid., pp. 138–139.

26 Charles River Associates Inc., *An Analytical Framework for Evaluating the Oil Import Quota*, prepared for the Energy Policy staff, Office of Science and Technology (Cambridge, Mass., July 15, 1969).

27 "Industry Blasts Charles River Report," *Oil and Gas Journal* August 25, 1969, pp. 58–59.

198 LIMITING OIL IMPORTS

Industry sources disputed estimates of the cost of the quota and of the storage alternative. Whereas the CRA report estimated the cost of the quota at $6.2 billion for 1969, Shell Oil estimated the cost at $0.6 billion, Standard of Indiana at $1.1 billion, and Standard of New Jersey at $0.8 billion.[28] Industry criticisms of the CRA estimate of storage costs centered on the amount of oil required for an emergency and on the costs of administering a storage and rationing program. Many of the criticisms turned out to be well taken. In particular, the CRA estimates of the long-run supply of oil, similar to those in the task force report, were said to be too high at a price of $3 per barrel or below. In addition, the critics charged that additional supplies from Canada and Venezuela could not be counted on to the extent expected in the CRA study (and later repeated in the task force report).

Months before the task force report was released, it became known that it would recommend a tariff system as a replacement for the quota. The industry responded with warnings that the domestic industry would be destroyed if the quota were abandoned. In part, the intense level of concern was due to the added rumor that the tariff rate would be set at a level which would lower the domestic price. In part, however, the opposition resulted from the expected change wrought by the tariff mechanism itself. Producing industry spokesmen realized that a tariff is less rigid in its quantitative effect than is a quota, and thus changes in underlying conditions would bring changes in import levels rather than in prices. The tariff also had the undesirable characteristic of making the cost of controls explicit. During this period there was also confusion and misunderstanding about the implications of the tariff control mechanism as an import-restricting device.

In December 1969 it was reported that the departments of Treasury, Labor, and State were in favor of the tariff alternative, that Commerce and Interior were opposed, and that Defense and OEP took a neutral position. One hundred congressmen signed a letter to the president warning against any action that would force a reduction in U.S. crude oil prices. Included in this group were eight House committee chairmen representing Ways and Means, Appropriations, Interior, Rules, Commerce, Education and Labor,

[28] Ibid.

Agriculture, and Foreign Affairs.[29] Spokesmen for, and supporters of, the industry were taking the fight directly to the White House.

Additional studies critical of the proposed tariff system were offered before the report was even released. New Jersey Standard presented an analysis that concluded that a tariff system would place the country at the mercy of Middle East oil and would prevent development of the North Slope.[30] A study by Walter Levy objected to tariffs in principle; he said there would be no way of predicting the effect of different tariff rates on the quantity of imports or on domestic prices. A complicated tariff system would be required, Levy argued, with respect to imports from different sources (particularly Western Hemisphere) and would require frequent adjustments in levels and exemptions to obtain the desired results.[31] In addition, a tariff would reveal to Middle Eastern producers that the U.S. government was earning more from imported oil than they were. A political reaction would be inevitable, with the most likely result that the exporting countries would coalesce and the posted price would be increased by the amount of the tariff. A study by Chase Manhattan Bank suggested that a drop in crude oil prices caused by the removal of the quota would eliminate marginal production, discourage exploration and drilling, and put small refiners and independent marketers out of business.[32] The output of natural gas would similarly decline. By 1980, the study estimated, the domestic industry would be able to satisfy no more than 32 percent of domestic consumption, with the remaining 68 percent to be imported at increasingly higher prices. Only 46 percent of natural gas consumption needs would be filled from domestic sources, 8 percent would be imported, and the remaining 46 percent would go unsatisfied or in search of alternatives.

[29] "Showdown Near on Imports Review," *Oil and Gas Journal* December 15, 1969, pp. 32–33.

[30] Standard Oil of New Jersey submitted several statements to the committee, the earliest dated July 14, 1969, the last December 12, 1969. See *Oil and Gas Journal* December 22, 1969, pp. 26–27.

[31] Walter Levy, statement before the Cabinet Task Force, December 12, 1969; also "Tariff Might Jar World Price Structure," *Oil and Gas Journal* January 19, 1970, pp. 24–25.

[32] Memo by John C. Winger, Chase Manhattan Bank, discussed in "What a 30-cent Crude Price Cut Would Do to the U.S.," *Oil and Gas Journal* January 5, 1970, pp. 70–71.

The one industry source lending support to a tariff was TIPRO, but only with the proviso that the tariff device not be used as a sub-terfuge—that is, that it not be substituted for the quota at a rate which would drive down the price of crude oil. If the appropriate level of protection were assured, TIPRO noted, the bulk of in-dustry criticism about a tariff would no longer apply.[33]

On February 20, 1970, President Nixon released the task force report with the announcement that any decision regarding the majority recommendations would be postponed until after congres-sional hearings and consultations with each of the foreign govern-ments affected by the proposal. Nixon did accept and act on one of its recommendations by creating a new Oil Policy Committee to fill the policy role formerly played by the secretary of interior. The designated head of the new committee was General George A. Lincoln, director of the Office of Emergency Preparedness, with the members including the secretaries of State, Treasury, Defense, Interior, and Commerce, the attorney general and the chairman of the Council of Economic Advisers. Significantly, the secretary of labor, George Shultz, was not included on the committee, and thus could remain the vocal supporter of the report's recom-mendations.[34] General Lincoln was a member of the protariff majority of the task force, but he did not share Shultz's goal of cutting U.S. prices beyond an initial 30 cents per barrel. In hear-ings before the House Interior Subcommittee on Mines and Min-ing on March 9, Lincoln testified that "I personally believe that a tariff system can be devised which is workable and will safeguard the national security as adequately as the quota system, at less cost to the consumer, with greater confidence on the part of the Amer-ican public, and with an increase in income to the Government, which is in the public interest."[35]

The subcommittee was hostile to the tariff proposal. In the sec-ond week of hearings, March 16–17, testimony was received from a large number of industry spokesmen, all of whom criticized vari-

33 "TIPRO Leans to Support of Tariff Import Program as Protective Tool," *Oil and Gas Journal* February 16, 1970, pp. 52–53.

34 A short time later, however, George Shultz became secretary of the treasury.

35 *Report on the Oil Import Question*, Committee Print no. 1, Subcommittee on Mines and Mining, House Committee on Interior and Insular Affairs, 91 Cong. 2 sess. (August 1970).

ous aspects of the task force report. The president of IPAA asserted, for example, that free imports would cost the United States $8.6 billion in lost income, so that the quota represented a net savings of over $3 billion to the United States, even on the terms assumed by the task force.[36] Meanwhile, the Senate Subcommittee on Antitrust and Monopoly began hearings on March 9 with George Schultz as the only witness.[37] Shultz repeated the task force case for tariffs aimed at reducing wellhead prices of crude in the United States from $3.30/bbl to $3 within three to five years, and his individual recommendation of reducing the price to $2.50. Shultz acknowledged the loss of marginal production, but noted that future supplies would depend on North Slope reserves. Landowners would be the major losers from lower prices through reduced royalties and bonuses, while consumers and the economy would gain, without imports rising so much as to jeopardize the national security.

Hearings by the subcommittee continued into April, with more industry spokesmen plus representatives from the coal industry, banking, and the United Mine Workers. All were critical of the task force report's analysis and recommendations. At the same time, the Senate Banking and Currency Subcommittee on Small Business heard from several northeastern congressmen criticizing the quota program and arguing for liberalizing import controls to limit price increases of petroleum products.[38]

The House Ways and Means Committee began hearings in June with industry representatives urging the committee to write into law the principles of the existing quota. On July 15, the committee voted to amend the Trade Expansion Act to specify that any restrictions on commodities under the national security clause shall be by quota.[39] The bill was opposed by the administration because of its lack of flexibility, and was subsequently defeated in the House.

---

[36] Ibid.

[37] "First Senate Hearing on Tariffs Mild," *Oil and Gas Journal* March 9, 1970, p. 24.

[38] *High Cost of No. 2 Home Heating Oil*, Hearings before the Subcommittee on Small Business of the Senate Committee on Banking and Currency, 91 Cong. 2 sess. (April 6–7, 1970).

[39] The Ways and Means Committee completed drafting its decision on current tariff proposals July 15; see *Congressional Record* of that date, vol. 116, p. D243, also vol. 116, part 14, p. 19387.

In late July the House Interior Subcommittee on Mines and Mining issued a report based on the hearings previously mentioned, in which it recommended a continuation of the existing quota system and denounced the findings of the task force report. The subcommittee reached several conclusions taking issue with the report, many of which are especially interesting in the light of subsequent events: (1) cost of the quotas is probably less than $1 billion, and when expected higher foreign crude prices are considered, there may actually be a net benefit from the quota; (2) imports currently amount to one-fifth of domestic demand, an already dangerous proportion; (3) the report overestimated supplies from Western Hemisphere sources and underestimated the probable need for Eastern Hemisphere oil in the future at lower prices; (4) the natural gas shortage will worsen and any cut in crude oil prices will further discourage the search for oil and gas; (5) hardest hit by the tariff proposal would be the small producers, refiners, and marketers; (6) the tariff proposal would cause a balance of payments outflow of at least $2.2 billion per year; (7) prorationing is a necessary conservation measure, the elimination of which would eventually mean a loss of production; (8) the shut-in capacity cushion is less than the task force estimated and could not be counted on in the future; (9) increasing dependence on foreign residual fuel oil at the expense of coal must be stopped; (10) research and development of synthetic fuels should be intensified; (11) increasing tension in the Middle East magnifies the danger of further reliance on oil from this source; and (12) it is necessary to limit imports to maintain a strong and healthy domestic petroleum industry. Five of the fifteen members of the subcommittee issued a dissenting statement calling for modifications of import controls to benefit consumers.

The opponents of the task force recommendations won the battle. During August 1970, General Lincoln sent a letter to President Nixon on behalf of the Oil Policy Committee recommending "that we discontinue consideration of moving to a tariff system of control."[40] Lincoln indicated that the advice was given at that time

[40] Reported in "Tariff Rejection Removes Uncertainty," *Oil and Gas Journal* August 24, 1970, pp. 30–31.

so that a final decision could be made in time for orderly planning of oil allocations for 1971. The basis for Lincoln's recommendation, which the president accepted, was twofold: that the quota program had been improved and that existing uncertainties made a policy shift unwise at that time. The changes he noted were: (1) elimination of historical quotas by the end of the year; (2) elimination of the Mexican turnaround; (3) institution of a formal system for controlling Canadian imports; (4) increasing No. 2 fuel oil imports into the East Coast and of residual fuel oil into the Midwest; and (5) additional relief for hardship cases by authorizing additional Canadian imports above the Canadian quota but within the overall quota. There were also plans to allow direct sale of import tickets. The uncertainties to which Lincoln referred had to do with changes in the world energy market, the uncertain timing of Alaskan supplies, the unknown effects of environmental programs, and the prospect of a rising proportion of supplies obtained from insecure sources. During a news conference on the subject, Lincoln denied that the Oil Policy Committee acted on direct orders from the White House or from pressure by any source.

The Task Force Estimates: Why So Wrong?

The task force report seriously overestimated the supply of domestically produced crude oil; overestimated the amount of other Western Hemisphere (especially Canadian) oil that would be available to the United States in the event of an embargo; and grossly underestimated the ability of certain members of the OPEC group to restrict supply and maintain the world price. These errors serve as a warning about the reliability of energy supply and demand forecasts, particularly in view of the resources and expertise used in preparing the report. The forecasts were not made in isolation or in ignorance; they were based on information provided by, among others, oil companies, the National Petroleum Council, and the Department of the Interior.

The significance of these forecast errors deserves some speculation as to what went wrong. First, and more specifically, why did the report forecast crude oil output for 1975 on the order of 9 MMb/day (excluding Alaskan production) at a $3 real price, while actually output was below 9 MMb/day at more than twice that real price?[41] One explanation would attribute the disparity to the abrupt structural change in the world market and to the domestic political response to the change. Because of the long lead time required for production to respond to a price change, actual output in 1975 was more closely related to the earlier $3 price, and expectations thereof, than the higher contemporaneous level. The discontinuous shift in the world price was followed by uncertainty about the ability of OPEC to maintain price stability and by uncertainty about oil price controls in the United States. The higher price encouraged producers to increase immediately the rate of output, but the greater risks discouraged investment in opportunities with long payoff periods. The industry was encouraged to invest in known prospects of smaller dimensions—with lower risks and shorter turnaround on their investment—in order to take advantage of high current prices. Long-term investments with potentially big payoffs became less attractive because their income streams extend far into the future and consequently the risks become inordinately great.

The response to the incentive structure just described would explain the combination of increased drilling activity in the United States after 1974, but with higher decline rates and lower output per well. An average of 1,660 drilling rigs were at work during 1975, compared with 1,471 in 1974 and 1,195 in 1973. The total number of wells completed in 1975 came to 39,097, the highest since 1965, while completions for the first half of 1976 show an increase of 14.5 percent above the same period in 1975. Despite the higher drilling rate, oil production declined from an average 9.2 MMb/day in 1973 to 8.7 MMb/day in 1974 and then to 8.4 MMb/day in 1975. Oil reserves reported by seventeen of the largest companies declined by 16.4 percent in 1975, while gas re-

---

[41] *The Oil Import Question*, pp. 228 ff. The $5.25 nominal price of old oil in 1975 has been estimated at closer to $2.65 in 1969 dollars when the combined impact of inflation and the elimination of the depletion allowance for large firms is figured in (see "U.S. Reserves Fall Despite Higher Prices, More Drilling," *Oil and Gas Journal* April 5, 1970, pp. 82–84). However, the relevant price is that for new reserves, which exceeded $11 in current dollars. Even with the same proportional adjustment as above, new production would be valued at approximately double the $3 price used in the report's estimates. See table 6-2 for the pattern of average real wellhead prices not taking tax changes into account.

serves declined by 14 percent.[42] The significant increase in drilling did not yield a net increase in reserves nor an increase in output. This combination has been cited as evidence of duplicity on the part of producers seeking higher prices, but it is more correctly viewed as the expected response to short-term profit incentives and long-term uncertainties, especially given the lags associated with the oil leasing, exploration, and development process.

It is also the case that the data on which the econometric studies in the report were based were difficult to interpret. There was no ready means to account for the effects of prorationing, for example, and the integrated nature of the industry meant that investment at the exploration and development stage responded to factors other than the regulated price. Additionally, expectations play an important role in determining the share of total revenue from oil production going to rents. For this reason, the price increases experienced after the OPEC price moves of the early 1970s may have been largely absorbed in nonresource payments because of expectations that the price would move higher still. If this indeed occurred, the effective price to which quantity supplied would respond did not move up with the wellhead price, but could well have fallen. The regime of price controls would have exacerbated this result. There are many reasons, then, why the anticipations of 1969 did not result in oil in 1975—but the fact remains that the task force overestimated domestic production.

The report's overestimate of supplies forthcoming from Canada is straightforward. The task force simply did not expect the self-sufficiency syndrome to arise in Canada; it also failed to anticipate the falloff in the rate of discovery there. The disruption of the world oil market in 1973 created a marked concern in Canada about the adequacy of its long-term energy supplies, particularly with a neighbor possessing an apparently insatiable oil appetite, and led the national government to impose price controls at home combined with large taxes on exported oil. Indeed, the price controls were so restrictive (and consequently the tax was so high at $4.50 per barrel) as to lower the real price at the wellhead and thus reduce previous incentives for exploration. Perhaps for this

[42] American Petroleum Institute, *Basic Petroleum Data Book*, tables III-13a, IV-5a.

reason, total wells drilled in Canada remained about constant throughout 1974 and 1975, but the number of wildcat wells declined 23.6 percent in 1975; total footage declined 4.4 percent and wildcat footage declined 28.1 percent in 1975.[43] The resulting decline in Canadian output exacerbated fears of inadequate energy supplies for domestic purposes and justified a continuation of the national policy to reduce and ultimately to eliminate exports.

The most disturbing prediction error contained in the report concerns the unexpected upheaval in the world oil market because this mistake was the source of errors elsewhere in the report. There was no expectation of this change even though its forerunner appeared within 6 months with the Libyan production cutbacks of May 1970. Indeed, all of the projections and much of the analysis in the report was rendered obsolete even before the embargo of October 1973.[44] Within four years the revolution was complete.

That the success of OPEC was unexpected may be explained in part by the view that it was a result of political actions (or inactions) on the part of the U.S. government and not the result of predictable economic and political trends in the oil market. This is the implication of the argument expounded by M. A. Adelman, which held that the U.S. government was so concerned with security of supply that to get it, it was willing to yield higher prices and increased producer–government control over the market.[45] The U.S. government insisted on collective negotiations that brought

[43] "Footage Falls 4.4% in Canada," *Oil and Gas Journal* May 10, 1976, p. 42.

[44] In remarks published in April 1973 and aimed primarily at the task force's projections, James E. Akins was led to observe that "Oil experts, economists, and government officials who have attempted in recent years to predict future demand and prices for oil have had only marginally better success than those who foretell the advent of earthquakes or the second coming of the Messiah," "The Oil Crisis: This Time the Wolf Is Here," *Foreign Affairs* vol. 51, no. 3 (April 1973) pp. 462–490. For developments that led up to OPEC and for an analysis of the reasons for its success, see Douglas R. Bohi, Milton Russell, and Nancy McCarthy Snyder, *Oil Imports and Energy Security: An Analysis of the Current Situation and Future Prospects*, Report of the Ad Hoc Committee on the Domestic and International Monetary Effect of Energy and Other Natural Resource Pricing of the Committee on Banking and Currency, House of Representatives, 93 Cong. 2 sess. (September 1974) chapter II, pp. 39 ff.

[45] M. A. Adelman, "Is the Oil Shortage Real? Oil Companies as OPEC Tax-Collectors," *Foreign Policy* (Winter, 1972/73) pp. 69–107. An opposing view is given by James E. Akins, "The Oil Crisis."

together all consuming countries, oil companies, and producing nations. There was no opportunity for market forces to develop and discipline individual producers. A negotiated settlement was reached that reinforced the position of the OPEC group as a cartel organization and encouraged monopoly price behavior. Writing in late 1972, Adelman prophetically stated that "The OPEC nations have had a great success with the threat of the embargo and will not put the weapon away. The turbulence will continue as taxes and prices are raised again and again."[46]

The oil companies were amenable to the tax increases, at least in the beginning, because "they used the occasion to increase their margins and return on investment in both crude and products."[47] Consequently, according to Adelman's thesis, the multinational companies acted as tax collectors for the producing nations. The oil companies remained essential to the producing nations for their dual role as crude oil marketers and tax collectors, but also because the intermediary role of the oil companies provided a means by which the price could be maintained. Because the taxes paid to host governments are public knowledge, the floor price of taxes-plus-cost for each member of OPEC is observable and any reduction is easily detected. Such openness reduces the temptation to cheat on the other members of the cartel and prevents an erosion of the price to the competitive level.

The OPEC development, whatever its cause and however difficult to forecast, dramatically altered supply–price relationships for oil and oil substitutes. Reservation prices for known reserves increased along with the expected return required for investment in new reserves. At the same time, oil prices became a political issue in both exporting and importing countries. Governments in exporting countries now talk of the "intrinsic" value of petroleum and emphasize the eventual exhaustion of their reserves. Governments in consuming countries are torn between resentment caused by a sense of exploitation by high foreign oil prices and resistance to providing the incentives necessary to encourage domestic energy production and conservation. In this milieu, the return to resource owners necessary to release their assets, an intangible concept that

[46] Ibid., p. 85.
[47] Ibid., p. 78.

even in stable periods is difficult to evaluate, becomes all the more confused.[48] The effect, however, is to further disturb the economic relationships between price and quantity. Unfortunately, this means that all supply forecasts made before 1973 are outdated, and all supply forecasts made since 1973 have very little history to go on.

The Price Control Program

The controversy over the task force report occurred during the early stages of a severe inflation. Government efforts to control inflation soon came in conflict with the purposes of the oil import control program, and forced the latter to give way. Interestingly enough, however, the price control program was administered in such a way as to take on the characteristics of a substitute oil import control program. This anomaly, as we shall see below, resulted from the fact that imported crude oil price increases could not, until phase 4 of the program, be passed along in higher consumer prices. Since the willingness of oil companies to sell imported oil at a loss was limited, imports were "voluntarily" restricted below the quota allotments.

Prelude to Controls

After 1965, general price inflation became a matter of national concern (see table 6-1). The upward drift in prices was ameliorated slightly and briefly during the mini-recession of 1967, but prices rose rapidly again in 1968, and more rapidly still in 1969. Early in 1969 the government responded with a combination of monetary and fiscal restraint that sharply reduced the growth of demand and forced the economy into another recession by the end of that year. The growth of real GNP fell from 5.8 percent between the last two quarters of 1968 to 3.8 percent during the first two quarters of 1969, and to a negative rate over the next five quarters. Unemployment rose from 3.3 percent in late 1969 to 4 percent by the

---

[48] See the discussion in Douglas R. Bohi and Milton Russell, *U.S. Energy Policy: Alternatives for Security* (Baltimore, Johns Hopkins University Press for Resources for the Future, 1975) chapter 3.

Table 6-1. Percent Changes in Selected Price Series, 1960–74 (Seasonally Adjusted Annual Rates)

Index	1960–65	1966–69	Dec. 68–Dec. 69	Dec. 69–Dec. 70	Dec. 70–Aug. 71	Phases 1 and 2 Aug. 71–Jan. 73	Phase 3 Jan. 73–June 73	Phase 3½ and 4 June 73–Apr. 74	Phase 4 Dec. 73–Apr. 74
Consumer price									
All items	1.3	5.4	6.1	5.5	3.8	3.3	8.3	10.7	12.2
Food	1.4	5.1	7.2	2.2	5.0	5.6	20.3	16.2	12.8
Nonfood	1.3	5.2	5.7	6.5	3.4	2.7	5.0	8.7	11.8
Commodities	0.5	4.4	4.5	4.8	2.9	2.0	5.2	9.2	14.9
Services	2.4	6.3	7.4	8.2	4.5	3.5	4.3	8.6	8.8
Wholesale price									
All items	0.3	3.9	4.8	2.2	5.2	5.7	24.4	15.2	21.9
Farm products	0.7	5.4	7.5	−1.4	6.5	13.3	49.8	6.3	0.4
Industrial commodities	0.2	3.4	3.9	3.6	4.7	2.9	14.4	19.6	33.9

Sources: Department of Labor, Bureau of Labor Statistics, and *Economic Report of the President*, 1973, 1974, 1975.
Note: December to December data are unadjusted.

beginning of 1970, and to 6 percent by the end of that year. Nevertheless, underlying trends in the economy raised doubts that the battle with inflation was over;[49] and closer examination of the price indexes indicated that inflation was more rapid than official figures revealed.[50]

Observers found it difficult to account for the persistence of inflation during the 1970–71 period in the face of declining demand and production.[51] What is important from the point of view of oil import controls, however, is that administration economists chose to explain the phenomenon as the result of inflationary expectations: past experience with price trends had led consumers, businessmen, union leaders, and others to expect these trends to continue, and thus caused them to behave in ways that would realize their expectations.[52] Given this explanation, deflationary monetary and fiscal policies could not stop inflation—or, more properly, would be too costly in other dimensions if carried to the point required to "break" expectations. Consequently, the administration decided to impose a 90-day freeze on prices and wages starting August 16, 1971, in an effort to end the inflationary mood which it thought was causing price increases.

Even earlier, however, it was becoming increasingly evident that the country was moving toward energy shortages at existing prices. On November 11, 1970 crude oil prices rose 15–25 cents per barrel at the wellhead, and the wholesale price of gasoline increased by 0.7 cents per gallon. In response to this development, the president announced a series of moves designed to relieve demand pressure on energy prices.[53] Increased imports from Canada would be permitted to ease immediate shortages. In addition, the president assailed state prorationing controls as holding down the supply of crude oil and ordered that conservation jurisdiction over all undisputed areas of the Outer Continental Shelf revert to the control of

[49] *Economic Report of the President* (Washington, GPO, 1972) pp. 40 ff.

[50] Barry Bosworth, "Phase II: The U.S. Experiment with an Incomes Policy," in Arthur M. Okun and George L. Perry, eds., *Brookings Papers on Economic Activity* vol. 2 (Washington, Brookings Institution, 1972) pp. 343–383.

[51] Ibid.

[52] *Economic Report of the President* (Washington, GPO, 1971) pp. 60–62; and the *Economic Report of the President*, 1972, *passim*, but especially p. 108.

[53] "Oil Added by Nixon Acts No Threat to Price Boosts," *Oil and Gas Journal* December 14, 1970, pp. 45–49.

Table 6-2. Average Wellhead Price of Crude Oil and Natural Gas (in Current and Constant 1967 Dollars[a]), 1947–75

	Crude (dollars per barrel)		Natural gas (cents per thousand cubic feet)	
	Current	1967	Current	1967
1947	$1.93	$2.52	6.0	7.8
1950	2.51	3.07	6.5	7.9
1955	2.77	3.15	10.4	11.8
1960	2.88	3.03	14.0	14.8
1965	2.86	2.96	15.6	16.1
1970	3.18	2.88	17.1	15.5
1971	3.39	2.98	18.2	16.0
1972	3.39	2.85	18.6	15.6
1973	3.89	2.90	21.6	16.1
1974	6.74	4.21	30.4	19.0
1975	7.56	4.32	44.5	25.4

Source: American Petroleum Institute, *Basic Petroleum Data Book* (Washington, 1976), sec. VI, tables 1 and 2.

[a] Deflated by wholesale price index.

the secretary of interior. In response to the pressure to roll back the November price increases, industry spokesmen argued that crude oil prices were rising much slower than the wholesale price index; while gasoline prices were only 14 percent above the 1957–59 base, consumer prices in general were 37.4 percent higher. The industry resented "being singled out for criticism and retaliation in spite of an inflation record that is better than business generally."[54] These spokesmen failed to mention, however, that throughout this period oil prices had been artificially maintained well above their world market levels through state conservation controls and oil import restrictions.

Table 6-2 shows the remarkable stability of crude oil and natural gas prices through the early 1970s. The wellhead price of crude oil did not increase significantly until after the October 1973 embargo; on an annual basis, its deflated price actually decreased until 1974. Increases in energy prices at the consumer level were less stable, however, as shown in table 6-3. Prior to 1973, most energy prices did not rise as fast as consumer prices in general, notable exceptions being electricity and natural gas. Dur-

54 Ibid.

Table 6-3. Changes in the Consumer Price Index and Indexes of
Selected Energy Prices, 1966–75 (Annual Percentage Rates)

Period	CPI all items	Energy index[a]	Electricity	Fuel oil[b]	Gasoline[c]	Natural gas
1966–69	4.1	2.1	1.2	2.8	2.6	0.9
1969–72	4.5	3.1	5.0	3.4	0.9	6.0
1972–73	6.2	8.0	5.0	15.4	9.8	4.6
1973–74	11.0	29.3	18.1	58.4	35.4	12.5
1974–75	9.1	10.6	13.2	8.3	6.8	19.9

Sources: Council of Economic Advisers, *Economic Report of the President, 1977,* pp. 94 and 246; *1976,* p. 86; and from data supplied by Dept. of Labor, Bureau of Labor Statistics.

[a] Also includes coal and motor oil, not shown separately.

[b] No. 2 fuel oil.

[c] Regular and premium pump prices.

ing 1973, however, energy prices increased significantly faster than the CPI, and during 1974 much faster still.

The impending shortages of energy products, or perhaps more appropriately, the prospect of ever-increasing prices of energy products, prompted President Nixon to give the first presidential address on energy to Congress on June 4, 1971.[55] The message noted that the economy had been built on the presumption of continuing supplies of energy at stable prices, but that brownouts, fuel shortages, and rising energy prices indicated that actions must be taken to increase energy supplies for the future. The message called for (1) increased federal support for energy research and development; (2) acceleration of OCS leasing; (3) expanded nuclear energy supply; (4) dissemination of information on energy conservation; and (5) creation of a department of natural resources to coordinate energy resource development programs. This program turned out to be too little and too late to alter developments which were then under way, as subsequent events were to show. Two months later the administration introduced price controls which would, contrary to the promises of the June message, exacerbate the energy supply situation.

[55] U.S. President, "A Program to Insure an Adequate Supply of Clean Energy in the Future," Message to the Congress, June 4, 1971. A convenient reference for this and other presidential statements on energy during the crucial 1973–75 period is *Executive Energy Messages,* Senate Committee on Interior and Insular Affairs, 94 Cong. 1 sess., Serial No. 94-22 (Washington, GPO, 1975).

Phase 1

Acting under authority of the Economic Stabilization Act of 1970, the president announced on August 15, 1971 an immediate 90-day freeze on prices and wages and the creation of a cabinet-level Cost of Living Council (CLC) to administer the freeze and to advise on further stabilization policies and actions.[56] Policy was implemented through an organizational system headed by the director of OEP; thus there was an overlap with administrative control over oil import policy. The basic principle of the freeze as applied to wages and prices was that the rate of payment during the freeze period— August 16 to November 13—could not exceed the rate during the base period—July 16 through August 14. Any contracts entered into before August 16 calling for increased payments during the freeze period were set aside.[57] Price increases on imports were allowed to be passed on to consumers if they were caused by dollar depreciation or price changes in world markets, so long as the imported good retained its original form. If an import was physically transformed, as in refining, the price increase had to be absorbed. This ruling had the effect of favoring imports of petroleum products over crude oil. But, to ensure that the higher prices were restricted to import costs, imported products had to be kept physically segregated from domestic products all the way to the ultimate consumer. This meant that duplicate transportation and storage facilities had to be maintained for imported and domestic petroleum products in order to qualify for the pass-through. Since the industry was not organized or equipped to comply with this ruling, imports of products were discouraged along with imports of crude oil.

Two immediate difficulties arose in the oil industry from Phase 1 controls. First, the independent marketers of gasoline and other re-

---

56 The CLC consisted of the secretaries of Treasury, Agriculture, Commerce, Labor, Housing and Urban Development, the director of the Office of Management and Budget, the chairman of the Council of Economic Advisers, the director of OEP, and the special assistant to the president for consumer affairs. The organization and procedures of the CLC are set out in Executive Order 11588, August 15, 1971, *Federal Register* vol. 36, pp. 15727–29 (August 17, 1971).

57 Difficulties were encountered with respect to new products and seasonal price adjustments, among others. Nearly 6,000 requests for exemptions were considered by the CLC, but only 5 exemptions were made (*Economic Report of the President, 1972*, pp. 77–79).

fined products experienced a profit squeeze because discounts traditionally provided by the majors to bulk purchasers were eliminated as sales contracts expired.[58] The resulting higher prices could not be passed along to their customers. The integrated oil companies had some flexibility to adjust to the freeze that the independent segment of the industry did not enjoy.

A second problem concerned the price of distillates, especially No. 2 fuel oil and diesel fuel.[59] Distillate stocks were unusually high during the summer—the base period of the freeze—owing to two previous warm winters. The combination of abundant stocks and the choice of the base period being the seasonal low meant that the price of distillates was frozen at a depressed level. This development, together with the elimination of discounts on refined products to independent marketers, exaggerated the profit differential between gasoline and distillates, and encouraged refiners to maximize gasoline production at the expense of distillates.

The effect of these distortions was evident by the fall of 1971. Independent marketers increased their demands for additional import allocations of distillates while northeastern congressmen renewed their attack on the import control program. The president responded in November by extending indefinitely the right of District I terminal operators to import No. 2 fuel oil to meet all obligations.[60] This was the first of many instances where the oil import control program was relaxed or otherwise altered because of the price control system.

Phase 1 was quite successful in stopping the rise in prices, as evidenced in table 6-1. Most of the increases shown there are attributable to exemptions, such as food and taxes. Moreover, the broad public support for and compliance with the freeze indicated a general willingness to support continued price control efforts. It was clear, however, that the freeze could not be extended indefinitely in a dynamic economy where changing demand and cost patterns require corresponding price changes.

---

[58] William A. Johnson, "The Impact of Price Controls on the Oil Industry: How to Worsen an Energy Crisis," in Gary Eppen, ed., *Energy: The Policy Issues* (Chicago, University of Chicago Press, 1975) pp. 99–121. Also, Charles Phelps and Rodney Smith, *Petroleum Regulation: The False Dilemma of Decontrol* (R–1951 RC) (Rand Corporation, January 1977).

[59] No. 2 fuel oil and diesel fuel are chemically equivalent.

[60] Proclamation 4092, November 5, 1971 (see *Federal Register* vol. 36, p. 21397, November 9, 1971).

Phase 2

On October 7 the president announced Phase 2 of the price control program, which lasted from November 15, 1971 to January 10, 1973.[61] The goal of the program was to limit the rate of inflation to 2 to 3 percent by the end of 1972, about half the prefreeze rate. The CLC was to continue overseeing the program and to establish goals and policy, but decisions on all price changes were to be handled by a price commission composed of seven public members. The basic approach adopted by the commission was to control prices indirectly by controlling profit margins on a firm-by-firm basis.[62]

This approach necessitated further rules to simplify the administration of controls. First, smaller firms were not required to report price increases which were consistent with the basic guidelines, intermediate firms were required to report any price changes, while the largest firms were required to obtain advance approval of the price commission for any changes.[63] Second, the price commission granted term limit pricing (TLP) arrangements to multiproduct firms for certain of their products. Under this arrangement, firms were permitted to spread their allowed average price increase over the TLP products in whatever manner they wished. In the oil industry, however, the TLP arrangements were not applied to gasoline, No. 2 fuel oil, and residual fuel oil, even though these products accounted for about three-fourths of domestic refinery yield. Politically, it was not feasible to allow the oil companies this pricing freedom. Thus a system which allowed considerable flexibility to most enterprises was denied to the petroleum industry.

The combination of the TLP system with firm-by-firm decisions caused difficulties for both the price commission and the oil com-

---

[61] Executive Order 11627, October 7, 1971 (see *Federal Register* vol. 36, p. 20139, October 16, 1971).

[62] The general rule was to maintain a profit margin per dollar of sales that was below the highest average of two of the three final years ending prior to the control program.

[63] Small firms were defined as those with sales less than $50 million per year (comprising about 10 million enterprises with 50 percent of all sales); intermediate firms were those with sales between $50 and $100 million (1,000 firms with 5 percent of sales); and large firms were those with sales above $100 million (1,500 firms with 45 percent of all sales) *Economic Report of the President* (1972) p. 87.

panies.[64] The overall allowed percentage price increase varied for
different companies and was applicable to a different bundle of
commodities. Thus, different companies were charging different
prices for the same products. This made the price control program
very confusing for firms and their customers, and very difficult for
the price commission to monitor and enforce. At the same time,
price adjustments for products excluded from TLP arrangements
were severely restricted. In effect, the prices for these products remained frozen during Phase 2. The serious distortion in the relative profitability of gasoline versus No. 2 fuel oil thus continued.
OEP urged the oil companies to increase fuel oil output against
their own best interests but, understandably, the response was not
sufficient to avoid shortages. In the meantime, gasoline production
was so great as to occasionally force the price below the ceiling.

The shortage of fuel oil was exacerbated by three additional developments. One was the unusually cold and wet weather during
the fall of 1972, which the price commission could not prevent but
for which it could have allowed adjustments, as the market would
have adjusted in the absence of controls. The second was the rule
applied to imports that allowed price pass-throughs of import costs
only if the foreign products were kept physically separate from
domestic products. This discouraged the import of No. 2 fuel oil
to fill the growing shortage. Finally, diesel fuel was included
among the TLP products and No. 2 fuel oil was not, even though
the two are chemically equivalent. Price increases allowed by the
TLP system thus ensured that diesel fuel was in good supply
throughout 1972 while fuel oil remained scarce. Eventually some
fuel oil customers started burning diesel fuel in spite of its higher
price and added highway taxes.

Most accounts of phases 1 and 2 regard the overall program as
highly successful because of the effect on price indexes. Consumer
prices for all items had been limited to a 3.3 percent rate of increase, with the nonfood sector limited to 2.7 percent (see table
6-1). The wage–price index increased by 5.7 percent, but industrial
commodities by only 2.9 percent. The target of reducing measured
inflation in the nonfood sectors below 3 percent had been achieved.
Price indexes do not tell the whole story, however; they give no

---

[64] See the discussion by Johnson, "The Impact of Price Controls," pp. 102–103.

indication of efficiency losses or of shifts in product mix or quality. Thus, "With excess capacity declining at the end of 1972, there was a clear possibility that continuation of the Phase 2 controls program would interfere increasingly with production, productivity, and investment decisions, and raise administrative costs, especially if the economy continued to expand as expected."[65] It was time to permit greater price flexibility.

Phase 3

Phase 3 lasted from January 11 to June 13, 1973. The price commission was eliminated, with its function absorbed by the CLC. The basic principles of price regulation developed during Phase 2 were to be extended in Phase 3, but were to be self-administered by firms. Price reports were to be filed only by firms with sales over $250 million. The profit margin limitation was changed to allow firms to choose the best two-year average between 1968 and 1972, with no limit if a firm's average price increase was less than 1.5 percent in a year.[66]

The self-administered program lasted only until March 6, 1973 for the major oil companies. Shortly after the program started, retail fuel oil prices jumped 7.4 percent.[67] The resulting criticism from Congress and the public forced the CLC to hold hearings investigating the oil price increases. The conclusion was that the price increases were consistent with Phase 3 guidelines. Nevertheless, on March 6, the CLC ruled that cost justification was required of the twenty-three major companies if they sought price increases adding more than 1 percent to their total revenues and that an increase yielding more than 1.5 percent was prohibited if the profit margin was above the base period average.

During early 1973, world oil prices were rising to and exceeding domestic levels, but the ruling by the Cost of Living Council prohibited the large oil companies from passing along the higher prices in the domestic market. With world prices above domestic prices, and the major importers unable to pass along the costs to

[65] *Economic Report of the President* (Washington, GPO, 1974) p. 89.
[66] Ibid., pp. 91, 94.
[67] Ibid., p. 94.

U.S. customers, the incentive to import was reduced. Correspondingly, the value of import licenses established by the quota system fell to zero. The quota was no longer an effective deterrent to imports; it had been supplanted by the price control program.

Conditions had been created wherein there was no market incentive to raise domestic production, no incentive to reduce consumption, and no incentive to increase imports. As these developments were coming together, President Nixon made his second address to Congress on the energy situation (April 18, 1973) in which he announced suspension of the mandatory quota program:[68]

> In order to correct a short-term fuel shortage and to keep fuel costs as low as possible, it will be necessary for us to increase fuel imports....
>
> The present quota system for oil imports ... was established at a time when we could produce more oil at home than we were using....
>
> Today, however, we are not producing as much oil as we are using, and we must import ever larger amounts to meet our needs.
>
> As a result, the current Mandatory Oil Import Program is of virtually no benefit any longer. Instead, it has the very real potential of aggravating our supply problems, and it denies us the flexibility we need to deal quickly and efficiently with our import requirements....
>
> Effective today, I am removing by proclamation all existing tariffs on imported crude oil and products. Holders of import licenses will be able to import petroleum duty free. This action will help hold down the cost of energy to the American consumer.
>
> Effective today, I am also suspending direct control over the quantity of crude oil and refined products which can be imported. In place of these controls, I am substituting a license-fee quota system.
>
> Under the new system, present holders of import licenses may import petroleum exempt from fees up to the level of their 1973 quota allocations. For imports in excess of the 1973 level, a fee must be paid by the importer.

We will return to a discussion of the April 18 energy message and the new license-fee system in the next section. For now it is suffi-

[68] Message to the Congress (April 18, 1973), and Proclamation 4210 (April 18, 1973) (*Federal Register* vol. 38, p. 9645, April 19, 1973); *Executive Energy Messages*, pp. 13–29.

cient to say that the elimination of the quota program had little effect on oil imports. After many years of debate and acrimony, after the volumes of study and testimony, the quota system ultimately passed quietly from the petroleum policy scene. The course of events, and particularly the Nixon administration's approach to the problem of inflation, had rendered the quota program ineffective before it was replaced.

The CLC ruling pertaining to the large oil companies had the effect of extending the Phase 1 and 2 distortions through Phase 3, and added some new problems as well. Under the control system in effect, price differences were not allowed to allocate petroleum products. Major integrated oil companies, for example, had no incentive to treat the wholesale market any differently than the retail market, and rationally chose to favor their own outlets over those of others. Indeed, Special Rule No. 1 (of March 6, 1973)[69] actually discouraged importers from swapping crude oil on a one-for-one basis with inland refiners because the importers had to charge crude price increases against the overall allowable price increases. Severe supply problems were created for independent marketers, fuel oil distributors, and other bulk customers of the integrated firms. The result was a deep public distrust of the major oil companies and pressure on the government to allocate product supplies.

Once the flexibility was gone from the crude oil market, the pressure for allocations was extended to crude. The elimination of import quotas (indeed, the earlier fall of the value of quota licenses to zero) removed a major benefit to inland independent refiners. Without the advantage from lower cost imports, tidewater companies would no longer swap domestic crude oil for the licenses allocated to inland refiners. The smaller refiners were thus forced into direct competition with the majors for domestic sources of crude. They could bid away raw material supplies from the majors because they, but not the majors, could pass along the costs in higher product prices. They were able to charge these higher prices in the final products market only because the overall product shortage left a market share for them even after the majors' lower priced supplies were fully exhausted. Thus, the combination

---

[69] *Federal Register* vol. 38, pp. 6283–84 (March 8, 1973).

of CLC rules left the independents with significantly higher product prices than the major integrated firms, reversing their traditional competitive roles in the market.

Phase 3½

Phase 3 did not go well for prices in general. Between January 1973 and June 1973, the CPI for all items rose at an 8.3 percent annual rate, with food rising by 20.3 percent and nonfood by 5 percent. The WPI was even more alarming: all commodities increased at a 24.4 percent rate, with farm products rising by 49.8 percent and industrial commodities by 14.4 percent. The disappointingly high rate of inflation in the first 5 months of 1973 aroused public dissatisfaction and added to pressure on the administration to take stronger actions. It was decided to freeze prices for 60 days (from June 13 to August 12, 1973) until a new set of Phase 4 controls could be implemented.[70]

For the oil industry, the 60-day freeze meant again that higher imported oil costs could not be passed through to consumers. Since the freeze applied to small firms as well as to large, the deterrent to imports was more widespread than with either the Phase 2 or Phase 3 controls. There were limited pass-through provisions for refined products, but only if the products were sold directly to consumers without refining and if the imported products were kept physically separate from domestic products. Nevertheless, this provision created a dilemma for oil companies with both domestic and foreign operations. "If they were to sell higher-priced imported products at the purchase price and lower-priced domestic oil at the freeze price, which customers would be penalized and which would be favored? The Cost of Living Council's regulations in effect forced these companies to violate the Robinson–Patman Act, which requires nondiscriminatory pricing among customers for the same class of product sold in the same marketplace."[71]

Accounts of price discrimination received widespread publicity and contributed to the growing distrust of the oil companies. Ob-

---

[70] *Economic Report of the President* (Washington, GPO, 1974) pp. 94 ff.
[71] Johnson, "The Impact of Price Controls," p. 108.

servers found it difficult to understand that the practice of charging different prices for the same good was being forced on the industry by the CLC's price control rulings. Inequities and inefficiencies were created, harming some sectors and helping others, but confusing all. The stage was set for the federal government to take a more active and broader role in controlling oil industry prices and in allocating crude oil and product supplies among refiners and marketers.

Phase 4 and More

Phase 4 lasted from August 12, 1973 to April 30, 1974, when the Economic Stabilization Act expired. The Phase 4 controls on oil prices did not end with the expiration of the Economic Stabilization Act, however, but continued with some modifications under the provisions of the Emergency Petroleum Allocation Act.[72] The responsibility for controls imposed on the oil industry was transferred from the CLC to the newly created Federal Energy Office (FEO).[73] The Emergency Petroleum Allocation Act was followed by the Energy Policy and Conservation Act of December 1975, which altered further and expanded the basic controls on the domestic oil market.[74]

The remainder of this section will outline the sequence of oil price control decisions following the introduction of Phase 4 in order that the reader can appreciate the continuity of oil pricing policy following the end of the quota program. The next section will discuss general energy policy developments following the termination of the mandatory quota program.

Returning to the Phase 4 controls, the CLC instituted a number of significant changes in the regulations before administrative responsibility shifted to FEO. With regard to imports, the new regulations permitted the pass-through of foreign crude oil and product costs without the provision requiring separation from domestic oil. Commingled foreign and domestic oil could be sold at a weighted

[72] Public Law 93-159, S. 1570, 93 Cong. 1 sess. (May 17, 1973).

[73] Executive Order 11748 of December 4, 1973 (*Federal Register* vol. 38, p. 33575, December 6, 1973) and *Executive Energy Messages*, p. 109.

[74] Public Law 94-516, S. 622, 94 Cong. 1 sess. (December 8, 1975).

average price reflecting higher import costs.[75] This change was absolutely necessary, in view of the rapid increases in world oil prices in late 1973, if the United States was to import sufficient oil to even approximately satisfy domestic consumption.

With regard to domestic crude oil, the CLC established a two-tier price system to encourage new domestic production. The wellhead price of oil obtained from existing wells continued at the frozen level, but the price of new crude oil was freed from control and permitted to rise to the higher world price level. New oil was defined as any increase in production from a leaseholding above the 1972 level (on a month-over-comparable-month basis).[76] For every barrel of new oil, the regulations permitted a barrel of old oil to be sold at the free market rate. In addition, in December 1973 the Emergency Petroleum Allocation Act required that all stripper-well production (i.e., oil from wells producing less than 10 bbl/day) be exempted from price controls.

The two-tier system produced difficulties for refiners and marketers. All refiners did not have equal access to cheaper old oil; many were largely or wholly dependent on unregulated domestic or imported crude. Consequently, there were significant differences in crude input prices, which under the cost pass-through rules in

[75] FEO announced in May 1974 that some importers were charging a higher weighted average price than justified by import costs and threatened additional restrictions (Johnson, "The Impact of Price Controls," p. 121).

[76] Misunderstanding of how the base period was designated caused confusion throughout the program. In early 1972, domestic production was restrained by market demand prorationing. Thus the early months in the 1974 calendar year showed *more* "new" oil than did the later months, giving the appearance that the higher price for new oil was not leading to more production. For an example of faulty conclusions based on the belief that the intrayear decline in "new" oil was the result of underlying physical or economic forces, rather than being an administrative anomaly, see Barry M. Blechman, Edward M. Gramlich, and Robert W. Hartman, *Setting National Priorities: The 1976 Budget* (Washington, Brookings Institution, 1975) p. 160. Additionally, the expected decrease in the proportion of "old" oil did not materialize, and thus prices expected by some analysts were wildly in error. A further source of confusion was the mistaken belief that $5.25 was the ceiling price for "old" oil. The ceiling was instead the actual price (on a lease-by-lease basis) as of the June 13, 1973 freeze, plus $1. The average price was estimated to be $5.25. This estimate turned out to be wrong—the actual price was somewhat lower. That error caused considerable difficulty—including poisonous suspicions of administration dissembling—when it was discovered in the final manuvering between the administration representatives and Congress at the time the Energy Policy and Conservation Act was being put together in late 1975.

effect, resulted in differences in allowed product prices by refiners (with prices in the Northeast the highest). Those refiners and marketers dependent on new and imported oil were able to pass along their full costs only if market conditions permitted—that is, only if those firms with lower costs could not satisfy the market. The firms with access to cheaper oil were able to pass along their full costs, obtain the full allowed mark-up and maintain high levels of utilization as well. Moreover, there were opportunities for extralegal gain because the system could not be effectively policed, and the market pressed toward a single selling price.

The basic philosophy of the Phase 4 regulations, as distinct from the earlier phases, was to impose ceilings on retail prices except where cost-justified. This approach was intended to work backward and restrict wholesale prices in the process. Instead, in the petroleum industry where crude costs were imposed from without, wholesale prices continued to rise, squeezing profit margins at the retail level. Consequently, the independent retailers were particularly unhappy with the Phase 4 regulations. On two successive days in September 1973, 1,000 heating-oil distributors and 2,000 gasoline dealers marched on Washington to press for changes in the regulations; four changes were made within a month, each progressively favoring the retail sector of the industry.[77] By the end of 1973 only the profit margin limitation and the one-price-increase-per-month rule remained as effective price control measures. These rules contributed to station closings, long lines, and periodic gasoline shortages in spite of increasing gasoline inventories.

The government was moving toward a system of mandatory allocations of petroleum products even before the oil embargo. In early October, mandatory allocations of propane began under legislative authority provided by the Eagleton Amendment of 1973 to the Economic Stabilization Act, with the top priority customers being agricultural production, food processing, residential heating, mass transit, health and public safety, and other users with no feasible alternatives.[78] Propane suppliers were required to satisfy the normal requirements of this priority list before making

[77] Ibid., p. 112.

[78] Public Law 93-28, 93 Cong., 2 sess., April 30, 1973; for propane regulations, see *Federal Register* vol. 38, p. 27397 (October 2, 1973); for middle distillate regulations, see *Federal Register* vol. 38, p. 28660 (October 16, 1973).

sales to other customers. On October 22, mandatory allocations of middle distillates began in a similar fashion.

Shortly after the embargo, on November 7, the president directed the Office of Petroleum Allocation to prepare a plan to allocate all crude oil and refined products; on November 8 he asked Congress for authority to implement the plan and for powers to ration gasoline and fuel oil to ultimate consumers.[79] On November 27, Congress passed the Emergency Petroleum Allocation Act (EPAA) (P.L. 93-159), directing the president to allocate crude oil and refined products. The regulations took effect at the beginning of 1974. In general the regulations under EPAA gave first priority to users involved in food production, fuel production, health and public safety, and mass transit. Specific regulations applied to separate fuels were vague and confusing, however, and underwent numerous changes throughout the year.[80] The regulations specified cutbacks on distillate supplies of 10 percent from 1972 levels for industrial users, 15 percent for homeowners, and 25 percent for commercial establishments. The earlier disincentive to produce this fuel continued to restrict its supplies relative to other fuels. Resid users were to be cut back 15 percent for space heating purposes, while utilities were to receive 100 percent of their 1972 base and other industrial users 110 percent. Gasoline production was to be reduced by limiting each refiner to 96 percent of the amount produced in 1972.

Similar controls extended back to the raw material stage. Crude oil suppliers were to be wedded to purchasers as of December 1, 1972 and could not sell their available output to new customers unless old buyers refused a bona fide offer at lawful prices. Moreover, crude oil supplies were to be reallocated among refiners in such a way that refiners with crude supplies above the industry average (first set at 76.31 percent of capacity) were required to

---

[79] "Address on the Energy Emergency," to the Nation on November 7, 1973, pp. 81–87 and Message to the Congress, November 8, 1973. *Executive Energy Messages,* pp. 81, 95–98.

[80] Proposed rule *Federal Register* vol. 38, p. 34414 (December 13, 1973), revised and then made effective in *Federal Register* vol. 39, p. 1924 (January 15, 1974); changes and determinations of detail were published irregularly thereafter. Refiners' buy-sell lists were first prescribed in *Federal Register* vol. 39, p. 2522 (January 22, 1974). Space-heating use was tied to specified 6–10° thermostat reduction. The FEA hearings preparatory to these latter rules were held September 24–25, 1974.

sell the excess to refiners whose supplies were more than 2 percent below the industry average. The selling price was the initial weighted average cost plus transport costs and a 6 percent fee for handling. In addition, the seller was permitted to raise his refined product prices by enough to recover 84 cents per barrel of crude sold—so that he would be partially compensated for his loss of output. In the initial allocation period—February through April 1974—Gulf Oil Corp. was forced to sell the most excess crude— 11,900,268 barrels.[81]

Two major objections to the crude oil allocation scheme were raised. The sellers, primarily the major oil companies, objected because the weighted average selling price plus the other payments did not approach the replacement cost of oil; that cost was about $12.50 per barrel, the approximate cost of imported oil. Court injunctions filed on behalf of the majors were not successful in blocking the program. Some independent refiners and major integrated firms, on the other hand, argued that the allocation program did not go far enough. It provided them with crude, but at a price which for other reasons made their products noncompetitive. Their feedstock costs rose because of a disproportionate dependence on uncontrolled domestic crude and imported oil.

Under the cost-based price control program, each firm was allowed to recover its total costs, more or less, though it was not assured of a market at its legal price. Thus there was little difficulty with unequal crude input prices under the shortage conditions that obtained from the fall of 1973 through mid-1974. When the last of the shortages disappeared, however, those firms with high crude input costs found that cost-covering prices were too high to be competitive with other firms. Hence capacity utilization rates for some firms fell to half of those for others, while the latter were obtaining the full legal price and the former were required to discount below costs to maintain their place in the market. The economic repercussions and the equity implications of a government program with this result demanded some action. That action could have been to decontrol crude oil prices. Instead, while declaring that decontrol was the ultimate objective, on October 24,

---

[81] "Gulf to Give Up Most Crude Under New Allocation Formula," *Oil and Gas Journal* January 28, 1974, pp. 82–83.

1974, the newly created cabinet-level Energy Resources Council, headed by Interior Secretary Rogers C. B. Morton, advised the president to develop a crude-oil cost equalization program. The "entitlements" program, as the new set of controls was to be called, was intended to equalize the crude oil acquisition cost of all refiners. It was expected to bring the prices of products from different firms closer together by forcing refiners with access to low-priced oil to subsidize the purchase of high-priced oil by other refiners.

According to the entitlements rules issued by FEA on December 4, 1974, each refiner would receive entitlements for old, price-controlled crude oil equal to the national average ratio of old crude to crude runs to stills. FEA would establish this ratio each month, beginning with 41.05 percent starting in January 1975. Refiners with less than 175,000 bbl/day runs would receive bonus entitlements on a sliding scale similar to that under the old import quota program.[82] Refiners with less than the national average of old oil would sell entitlements to refiners with more than the national average. The price of entitlements, fixed by FEA, was based on the spread between the estimated controlled ($5.25) and uncontrolled ($10.50 to $12) prices. The initial price was set at $5 per barrel, with $69,119,895 changing hands the first month.[83] In the second month the entitlements price went up to $6 per barrel, resulting in transfers of $80 million.

The entitlements program was thus a mirror image of the import quota. Under the quota program, a refiner gained access to imports of low-cost imported oil by refining high-cost domestic oil

---

[82] The bonus started at 12.38 percent of runs for refiners running up to 10,000 bbl/day. See *Federal Register* vol. 39, pp. 42249, 43103 (December 4, 1974); also *Oil and Gas Journal* December 9, 1974, p. 40.

[83] The figure would have been $21 million higher if refiners with less than 175,000 bbl/day capacity had not been exempt from purchase obligations for the first 30,000 bbl/day of their average volume of crude runs. In the first month there were 95 sellers of entitlements, consisting mainly of independents, but the largest were major integrated firms: Amerada Hess (2,656,513 barrels), Standard of California (2,025,243), Mobil (1,222,652), Atlantic Richfield (938,681), and Texaco (621,024). There were twenty-nine sellers, including some independents, but the majors accounted for the bulk of the obligations: Shell (2,977,721 barrels), Union of California (1,830,725), Amoco (1,368,413), Exxon (1,399,361), Sun (940,842), Gulf (775,693), and Marathon (721,622). See "Majors Are Largest Entitlements Sellers," *Oil and Gas Journal* January 20, 1975, pp. 52–53.

as well. With the entitlements program, utilizing high-cost imported oil purchased a "right" to cheaper domestic crude. In each
case the marginal cost of crude to the refiner became, thereby, its
average cost to the industry as a whole.[84] Special exceptions and
biases in the quota program were carried over into the entitlements program, including special treatment of resid. The major
difference in the two programs was in the determination of the
"price" of entitlements compared with the exchange "price" of import quota tickets. While the latter were determined by market
forces and exchanges arranged by private parties, the entitlement
value was set by the FEA, which also arranged buy-sell lists to
facilitate the transactions. The premises behind this further FEA
involvement were that private market action would not lead to
minimum transactions costs and that market power could be exerted by some to manipulate the price in their favor.[85] The entitlements program did not result in the exact equalization of product
prices because of differences in other costs carried forward and differences in allowed pass-throughs under the price control program.
It did, however, eliminate gross disparities in crude input costs.
The political effect of the entitlements program was to create
vested interests in controls where none existed before, and to eliminate some industry pressure for abandoning the Emergency
Petroleum Allocation Act, originally scheduled to expire in February 1975. Had it not been for the entitlements program, the real
economic dislocations occurring under EPAA would have been
more obvious to the public, and, in addition, the special interests
of many refiners and marketers would have been joined with those
of producers instead of in opposition to them.

Throughout the rest of 1975 Congress and the administration
set about coming to agreement on a comprehensive energy program. The result of that process, to be discussed in the next section, was the Energy Policy and Conservation Act, signed into law

---

[84] A contrary view is given by Phelps and Smith, *Petroleum Regulation*.

[85] There was bitter conflict within the administration over this issue. The pro-
involvement forces won out over those who argued that if there was to be an entitlements program, it could be administered most efficiently by allowing market forces to
work. The fear that the public would perceive market power working to the advantage
of the major oil companies, and that independents would allege discrimination, was
an important element in the final decision.

on December 22, 1975.[86] The principal feature of the act was the retention of at least standby price and allocation controls on the industry for five years and the broadening of the crude oil controls to include new oil, released oil, and stripper-well oil. At his discretion, the president was empowered to put the price controls on standby after 40 months. The act maintained the distinction between new and old oil begun in Phase 4 but, in addition, established control over the weighted average price. The initial weighted average price ceiling was set at $7.66 starting on February 1, 1976, a reduction of more than $1 per barrel from what was thought to be the prevailing $8.75 average level. With old oil still fixed at its earlier level on a lease-by-lease basis, the $7.66 ceiling meant that the price of previously unregulated oil was forced down to about $11.30 from approximately $14 per barrel.

The act permitted the president on the basis of a finding of need to increase the average price by up to 3 percent per year plus an inflation factor, with the total limited to 10 percent. He was also empowered, barring disapproval by a majority of either house of Congress, to add further price increases as an incentive to greater production. Congressional disapproval of such a price increase would impose a price freeze until the next presidential effort to seek another increase.[87]

In conjunction with the price control features, the act amended the Emergency Petroleum Allocation Act by (1) extending its life to September 30, 1981; (2) converting many mandatory allocation provisions to standby authority; (3) permitting exemptions from petroleum product price and allocation controls, barring disapproval by a majority of either house of Congress; (4) exempting small refiners from buying entitlements; (5) granting the president discretionary authority to have a federal agency become the sole importer and purchaser of foreign oil (upon submitting a procedure and an assurance that the move would reduce imported oil prices), barring disapproval by either house of Congress; (6) granting the president authority to directly control refining operations; (7) granting authority over petroleum inventories in the event of an existing or impending shortage of any fuel; (8) providing for development of a plan to deal with an energy supply interruption,

[86] Public Law 94-163, S. 622, 94 Cong. 1 sess. (December 22, 1975).

[87] The 10 percent limit could be exceeded to allow for new production from high-cost sources.

which plan is to be submitted to Congress for approval and is not to include price increases in any form as an element in rationing or allocating the available energy supply; (9) prohibiting hoarding of petroleum in excess of reasonable needs during an emergency; and (10) including asphalt as a product that could be allocated or price controlled.

Price controls were thus retained on petroleum products even after they were removed from the remainder of the economy, and on crude oil even after some products were decontrolled. Generalized shortages did not appear because imports of both crude and products were free and unrestricted, but the differences in prices for crude oil by production class in the United States (new, old, stripper, released, enhanced recovery, upper-tier, lower-tier, Alaska North Slope, etc.—the classifications changed with the legislation) and between the U.S. regulated price and the world price, gave rise to complex allocation and adjustment processes. These processes and accompanying administrative efforts were made more complex still by efforts to accommodate the previous extra-economic industry arrangements which were created in response to the incentives of the mandatory quota program. The very definition of oil by class was sometimes in dispute, but always essentially arbitrary. These crude oil pricing and entitlements provisions were superimposed over the already tortuous cost pass-through and allocation requirements on refineries. Confusion, misunderstanding, and multiple opportunities for chicanery were, of course, created throughout the industry. By late 1975 it was still no exaggeration to state that in large segments of the industry there was uncertainty as to actual current costs and legal prices, about possible retrospective gains or liabilities when regulations were sorted out and finally applied, and about whether or not operations were or were not in compliance with regulations as they eventually would be interpreted.[88]

[88] Among the major controversies, two multibillion dollar ones stand out: the timing and nature of allowed refinery cost pass-throughs were interpreted differently by different refiners due, apparently, to ambiguous wording of the regulations and different interpretations within FEA; the proper definition of a producing "property" which, because it was interpreted differently, led to greater higher-tier production relative to lower-tier for some firms than for others. The classic error, of course, arose over what the actual prices were at the time that EPCA was put into effect; the FEA had overestimated the existing average price, and thus the planned-for escalations had to be delayed to bring the actual average crude oil price into conformance with the legislated mandate.

The formal end of the mandatory quota program was thus preceded and then followed by pervasive government intervention in petroleum pricing and allocation decisions. That end came with the replacement of quotas with fees as the formal import control device.

Energy Policy After the Quota Program

The mandatory quota program was followed by a series of other initiatives, the first being the special import fee intended as its direct replacement. The nation was unable to meet its energy needs in the face of both price controls and the quota, so the quota was finally replaced in form as well as in fact. Energy policy must continue to follow energy developments, however, and these developments were both quick in coming and dramatic in size during the months after the mandatory quota program ended. The world price of crude oil rose at an unprecedented rate for any major commodity in world trade. The production cutbacks in the Arab countries and the efforts to embargo selected countries, including the United States, made energy insecurity an actual rather than potential threat to the well-being of the nation. The policy responses to these stimuli were first the replacement of the quota program and then various efforts to deal with newly felt energy insecurity. Energy policy had not reached an equilibrium after the developments of 1973–74 or even by late 1976, but the steps along the way are intriguing, in part because of the pervasive influences on seemingly unrelated policy decisions inherited from the mandatory quota program.

The License-Fee System

The license-fee system that replaced the mandatory quota program in 1973 did not represent a new departure in the taxation of oil imports. For the most part, it merely extended existing fees, with certain exemptions assigned to historical importers as established under the quota program, but with the fees and exemptions adjusted over time to become more restrictive and to provide greater protection for domestic production and refining. The continuity of oil duties as part of import policy can be traced at least to the Internal Revenue Act of 1932, which imposed the first import duty on crude oil and products.[89] The duty amounted to 21 cents a barrel for crude oil, resid, and some products; $1.05 per barrel for gasoline and distillates; and $1.68 per barrel for lubricating oil (see table 6-4). Duties at this level were truly restrictive; crude oil in the field was priced at less than $1 per barrel in the United States, and the tank-wagon price of gasoline was about 10 cents per gallon.[90] The United States was a net exporter of crude oil and of petroleum products. The Venezuelan Trade Agreement Act of 1938 reduced the duty on crude and resid to 10.5 cents per barrel when the volume of imports totaled less than 5 percent of the total quantity processed in U.S. refineries during the preceding year. Imports in excess of the 5 percent limit were subject to the previously established 21-cent fee.[91] The act also extended these conditions to topped crude, gas oil, and all grades of fuel oil.

The Mexican Trade Agreement Act of 1943 eliminated the 5 percent rule and reduced all duties to the lower 10.5 cent rate. The act expired on January 1, 1951, but all fees continued at the 10.5 cent level. In 1952, a supplementary Venezuelan agreement reduced the import fee on crude oil and products with less than 25° API gravity to 5.25 cents per barrel. Imports above 25° continued at the 10.5 cent rate established by the 1943 Mexican act.[92] The 1952 act was obviously designed to accommodate Venezuelan products since residual fuel oil generally tests below 25°, while most other crude and product imports have a higher gravity.

The Kennedy round of trade agreements resulted in the Trade Expansion Act of 1963. The Trade Expansion Act maintained the fee structure on crude oil and resid established by the Venezuelan agreement, but cut the fees on all other imported products by one half. This fee structure (table 6-4) remained in force until Proclamation 4210 of April 18, 1973 (as amended by Proclamation 4227 of June 19, 1973) eliminated all prevailing fees (and quotas) and substituted a more complex license-fee system.[93]

[89] Being part of the Internal Revenue Act, the duty is called a fee rather than a tariff.

[90] API, *Petroleum Facts and Figures, Centennial Edition* (1959) pp. 374, 379.

[91] *Oil Import Digest* p. A-28 (November 17, 1967).

[92] Ibid.

[93] The 10 percent surcharge imposed on imports for balance of payments reasons during the August 15–December 20, 1971 period did not apply to petroleum products (except mineral oil and paraffin), or other imports controlled under "national security" clauses (*Federal Register* vol. 38, p. 9645, April 19, 1973 and *Federal Register* vol. 38, p. 16195, June 21, 1973).

Table 6-4. Oil Import Fees, 1932, 1963, 1973, and Schedules for 1973 Forward

(cents per barrel)

| | Imported commodity | | | | | | | | Canadian imports | |
| | Crude oil | | Residual fuel oil | | | | | | | |
	Under 25° gravity	Over 25° gravity	Under 25° gravity	Over 25° gravity	Motor gasoline	Distillates	Lubricating oil	Other products[a]	Motor gasoline	Other products[a]
1932 Rates (Int. Revenue Act)	21	21	21	21	105	105	168	21	[b]	[b]
1963 Rates (Trade Exp. Act)	5.25	10.5	5.25	10.5	52.5	52.5	84	10.5	[b]	[b]
Rates established in 1973 as of:										
May 1, '73	10.5	10.5	15	15	52	15	15	15	0	0
Nov. 1, '73	13	13	20	20	54.5	20	20	20	0	0
May 1, '74	15.5	15.5	30	30	57.0	30	30	30	5.7	3.0
Nov. 1, '74	18	18	42	42	59.5	42	42	42	6.0	4.2
May 1, '75	21	21	52	52	63.0	52	52	52	12.6	10.4
Nov. 1, '75	21	21	63	63	63.0	63	63	63	12.6	12.6
May 1, '76	21	21	63	63	63.0	63	63	63	22.1	22.1
Nov. 1, '76	21	21	63	63	63.0	63	63	63	22.1	22.1
May 1, '77	21	21	63	63	63.0	63	63	63	31.5	31.5
Nov. 1, '77	21	21	63	63	63.0	63	63	63	31.5	31.5
May 1, '78	21	21	63	63	63.0	63	63	63	41.0	41.0
Nov. 1, '78	21	21	63	63	63.0	63	63	63	41.0	41.0
May 1, '79	21	21	63	63	63.0	63	63	63	50.4	50.4
Nov. 1, '79	21	21	63	63	63.0	63	63	63	50.4	50.4
May 1, '80	21	21	63	63	63.0	63	63	63	63.0	63.0

Source: National Petroleum Refiners Association, *Oil Import Digest*, vol. 1, p. A-28 (11-17-67) and p. A-22; A-22.1 (8-25-74). Some figures are interpolated from cited data.

a. Excludes ethane, propane, butanes, and asphalt beginning on May 1, 1973.

b. Same as imports from other sources.

Table 6-5. Percentage of Initial Allocation Exempt from License Fees

After April 30 of:	Percentage
1973	100
1974	90
1975	80
1976	65
1977	50
1978	35
1979	20
1980	0

Sources: *Oil Import Digest*, p. A-22.1 (8-25-74), and Proclamation 4210 (*Federal Register* vol. 38, pp. 9645–56) April 19, 1973.

The new license-fee system started by eliminating all import duties on existing quota allocations.[94] According to new regulations issued by the Department of the Interior for implementation on May 1, slightly over 7 million barrels per day of oil and products qualified for duty exemption for the rest of 1973. This included about 2 MM bbl/day of crude, unfinished oils, and finished products (other than residual fuel oil) for Districts I–IV from sources other than Mexico and Canada; 50,000 bbl/day of No. 2 fuel oil for District I for which the Western Hemisphere restriction had been suspended; 960,000 bbl/day of crude and products into Districts I–IV from Canada; 950,000 bbl/day of crude and products (except resid) into District V; 2,900,000 bbl/day of resid in District I, 42,000 bbl/day of resid in Districts II–IV, and 75,600 bbl/day of resid in District V; 32,500 bbl/day of oil from Mexico into all districts by qualified historical applicants; and 227,221 bbl/day of imports into Puerto Rico. The 7 MM bbl/day fee-free volume was about 1 MM bbl/day above actual import levels during the first quarter of 1973. It also amounted to over 40 percent of the rate of total U.S. oil consumption during 1973.

The fee-exempt status of existing allocations was scheduled to be phased out over seven years. The percentages of the initial allocations (listed above) to be exempt in the future are shown in table 6-5. Imports of asphalt, ethane, propane, and butane were to remain fee-free through this period.

[94] Because the duties were established by presidential proclamation, they continued to be called import fees rather than tariffs.

Imports by companies above their existing allocations were permissible and subject only to the new fee schedule that rose periodically after May 1, 1973 (see table 6-4). The fee on crude oil started at the then-existing level of 10.5 cents per barrel and rose to its limit of 21 cents by May 1, 1975. The fee on gasoline imports started at 52 cents (1/2 cent per barrel below the previous duty) and rose to 63 cents by the same time. Only the fee on residual fuel oil began at a higher rate than the previous schedule (15 cents per barrel compared with 5.25 cents or 10.5 cents, depending on gravity) and rose to 63 cents by November 1, 1975. All other products had the same schedule as resid. Imports from Canada were singled out for special treatment. There was no import duty until May 1, 1974, at which time gasoline was to be taxed 5.7 cents per barrel and other products at 3 cents per barrel. These fees were to be increased gradually to the same levels as those from other sources of imports, but not until May 1, 1980. Imports into Puerto Rico were to be subject to the same schedule as those to the mainland, and all refined products produced in Puerto Rico could be shipped to the mainland duty free. Imports of crude and products into the Virgin Islands and free-trade zones were exempted from fees after May 1, 1973, but subsequent reshipments to the mainland from these areas were subject to prevailing fees. Fee-free imports under existing quota allocations to the Defense Department (including that for Guam) were to be phased out along with other allocations.

Also effective May 1, 1973, any person or company could import crude or products by applying for an import license and paying the appropriate license fees. Companies building new refineries or petrochemical plants, or expanding existing facilities, were granted fee-exempt allocations amounting to 75 percent of their feedstock requirements for the first five years of operation. In addition, the regulations provided for a refund of license fees paid for unfinished feedstocks used for conversion into chemicals or finished products which were exported. Finally, the Oil Import Appeals Board was granted a fee-free allocation of 50,000 bbl/day to be distributed to hardship cases, with a special eye toward the problems of independent refiners and marketers.

Clearly, the new fee system represented a significant easing of controls on imports. Historical importers could get nearly all they needed duty-free for the first year or two, whereas previously a fee was required for imports permitted under quota allocations. In addition, importers could get additional supplies without the delays and administrative costs associated with the quota system. Finally, the eventual fee structure represented an increase of only 10.5 cents per barrel for both crude and products above the 1963 rate structure, which in turn was equal to or less than the pre-1963 structure. Compared with the increases in world oil prices during 1973 and afterward, the increased fees, even if they had applied fully and immediately, were trivial indeed. Thus, the system could not be regarded as a real substitute import control scheme, whatever the official intention. Of course, crude oil needed little additional protection, with foreign prices already as high as domestic prices. The fee system did provide a cost differential between crude and product fees to help encourage domestic refinery construction.

The special import duties imposed by President Ford early in 1975 were a different matter. They were substantially greater and imposed on top of the fee structure described above. However, they were designed more to motivate Congress to act on the president's comprehensive energy program than to limit imports. Nonetheless, the president's comprehensive energy program did include as one element a permanent $2 per barrel tariff; had this measure been accepted, along with decontrol of domestic energy prices, a substantial effect on imports would have been achieved through the combined restriction on demand and enhancement of domestic supply. These special duties were removed with the passage of the Energy Policy and Conservation Act in December 1975, however, and the tariff proposal was not included in the act.

The Project Independence Strategy

While one of the short-term policy problems facing the United States in 1973 was how to increase oil imports and reduce their price to restrain pressing inflation, the long-term strategy issue was energy security. Consequently, to the confusion of both public understanding of the issues and policy, the twin issues of energy pricing and energy security were addressed in the April 18 energy message that suspended the quota program. With reference to U.S.

reserves of conventional sources of energy, the president stated that "Properly managed, and with more attention on the part of consumers to the conservation of energy, these supplies can last for as long as our economy depends on conventional fuels."[95] In the long run, "America's vast capabilities in research and development can provide us with new, clean and virtually unlimited sources of power."[96]

To these ends, the president proposed:[97] (1) to deregulate the price of natural gas in new and expiring contracts and to permit the higher costs to be passed along to consumers; (2) to provide a tax credit for all exploratory drilling costs for new oil and gas fields, with a higher credit for successful wells than for unsuccessful ones; (3) to triple offshore lease offerings by 1979; (4) to seek a delay by states of implementation of secondary clean air standards; (5) to increase funds for energy research and development, starting with a 20 percent increase (to $771.8 million) for fiscal year 1974; (6) to speed up site approval for nuclear and other energy plants; (7) to obtain early approval of the Alaskan pipeline; (8) to authorize creation of a department of energy and natural resources to coordinate federal activities with respect to energy supplies; and (9) to create the Office of Energy Conservation in the Department of the Interior to coordinate federal efforts to promote energy conservation. It is worth noting that the president emphasized the importance of relying on the price mechanism to achieve the desired results for both domestic energy supply and energy conservation.

The president's proposals were not enthusiastically received by either the Congress or the oil industry. The IPAA, for example, concluded that the combination of freeing imports and controlling domestic prices, along with freeing new gas prices and a tax credit, would not spur domestic exploration enough to achieve the goals outlined.[98] With no congressional action in prospect, on June 29,

95 President of the United States, Message to the Congress (April 18, 1973), *Executive Energy Messages,* p. 13.

96 Ibid.

97 Ibid., pp. 16–29.

98 "IPAA: Nixon Policies Won't Do the Job," *Oil and Gas Journal* May 14, 1973, pp. 46–48.

1973, the president issued another statement supporting his legislative proposals.[99] In addition, he proposed the creation of the Energy Research and Development Administration (ERDA) to centralize and coordinate the government's research and development programs and to separate the promotional from the regulatory functions in nuclear affairs. A $10 billion effort over five years was the proposed funding level for energy research and development. Finally, in the same statement, he announced the abolishment of the three-man Special Energy Committee established on April 18 and its replacement with an Energy Policy Office within the Executive Office of the President. This office was given responsibility for formulating and coordinating energy policy at the presidential level.[100]

Shortly after the Arab oil embargo, on November 8, 1973, the president gave his third message on energy to Congress.[101] The bulk of the message dealt with short-term measures in response to the immediate shortages, including (1) restrictions on conversion from coal to oil by industries and utilities; (2) a 10 percent reduction in the allocations of jet fuel for aircraft; (3) a 15 percent reduction in the supply of distillate heating oil; and (4) a reduction in energy consumption by the federal government. In addition, he asked for legislation to: (1) restrict public and private energy consumption for nonessential purposes; (2) reduce highway speed limits to 50 miles per hour; (3) exempt or waive existing environmental regulations; (4) empower the Atomic Energy Commission to grant temporary operating licenses for nuclear power plants without holding public hearings; (5) authorize full production of Naval Petroleum Reserve 1 and exploration and development of Naval Petroleum Reserve 4; (6) permit daylight saving time on a year-round basis; (7) "authorize the President, where practicable, to order a power plant or other installation to convert from the use of a fuel such as oil to another fuel such as coal and to make such equipment conversions as are necessary"; and (8) "grant the

99 Statement of June 29, 1973, *Executive Energy Messages*, pp. 49–55.

100 The Special Energy Committee had included John D. Erlichman, Henry Kissinger, and George P. Shultz. The head of the new Energy Policy Office was John A. Love, former Governor of Colorado.

101 Message to the Congress (November 8, 1973), *Executive Energy Messages*, p. 95.

President additional authority to allocate or ration energy supplies."

The president also reiterated the energy proposals outlined above to meet long-range energy needs. This was the start of the effort to achieve energy self-sufficiency, known as "Project Independence." In a speech to the nation on November 25, the president said,[102]

> Let me conclude by restating our overall objective. It can be summed up in one word that best characterizes this Nation and its essential nature. That word is "independence." . . .
> What I have called Project Independence–1980 is a series of plans and goals set to insure that by the end of this decade Americans will not have to rely on any source of energy beyond our own.

On December 4, President Nixon asked Congress to authorize the creation of a Federal Energy Administration (FEA) to formulate and implement the Project Independence program.[103] For the interim, the president abolished the Energy Policy Office under John Love, and established, by executive order, the Federal Energy Office (FEO), first headed by William Simon, to be the forerunner of FEA.[104] At this time controls established for energy matters under the Economic Stabilization Act of 1970 were shifted from the CLC to FEO, together with the authority vested in the president by the Emergency Petroleum Allocation Act of 1973.

FEO began 1974 with two major tasks: to respond to the immediate problems of meeting the energy shortages and to develop a plan, with accompanying analysis, to achieve the long-term goal of energy independence. The short-term response centered around the problem of implementing the mandatory allocation program, rationing gasoline and fuel oil supplies, and using consumption taxes to dampen demand. In the development of a long-term energy strategy, FEO faced competition from the State Department. After the Arab embargo, Secretary Kissinger staked out a claim in developing energy policy because of the implications for overall foreign policy. The two agencies began to develop strategies that

[102] Address on the National Energy Policy, November 25, 1973, *Executive Energy Messages*, pp. 99–102.

[103] Remarks of the President upon Announcing Creation of the Federal Energy Office, December 4, 1973, *Executive Energy Messages*, p. 109.

[104] Executive Order, December 4, 1973, *Executive Energy Messages*, pp. 110–112.

were mutually inconsistent and were not independent of the short-term response to the energy crisis.

Kissinger's plan was based on the premise that world oil prices had to be reduced. He proceeded on the assumption that OPEC would be unable to restrict production to maintain high prices in the face of reduced demand. To reduce demand, his plan called for a unified consumer-nation block to undertake policies immediately to reduce imports and confront the producer nations at the conference table. The mechanism to achieve the price reduction, in other words, was negotiation. OPEC would be willing to negotiate if confronted with a united group and declining revenues. It was recognized, however, that the other consuming nations were not in the same bargaining position as the United States because they did not possess a similar domestic energy alternative. Consequently, an important ingredient in the State Department's unification effort was to guarantee a share of American oil to other consuming nations in the event of another oil supply reduction.

As early as the Washington Energy Conference in February 1974, it was evident that the Kissinger plan would not work. Delegates from Europe and Japan did not wish to antagonize the producer countries and did not receive the assurances they needed from the United States before they could afford to confront the producer group. FEO Administrator Simon refused to commit the United States to gasoline rationing in the event that such a policy were needed to implement a plan for sharing scarce oil with the consumer nations.[105] More important, the president's goal of energy independence was inconsistent with Kissinger's strategy of sharing oil with other importing countries. This inconsistency arose in two separate dimensions. First, the independence goal implied that the United States could not be committed, as perceived by the other consuming countries, to the plan to hold the consumer block together. Second, the independence strategy could not succeed if the Kissinger goal of reducing world oil prices was successful.

The Project Independence plan was premised on high energy prices in the future. This was reflected as early as January 23, 1974

---

[105] See Thomas H. Tietenberg, *Energy Planning and Policy* (Lexington, Mass., D. C. Heath, 1976) pp. 80–88 for a discussion of policy formulation during this period.

in Nixon's fourth energy message to Congress, in which the program for Project Independence was first laid out systematically:[106] "Project Independence entails three essential concurrent tasks. The first task is to rapidly increase energy supplies. . . . The second task is to conserve energy. . . . The third task is to develop new technologies." It was becoming increasingly evident that success in all three dimensions required high, not low energy prices, although the accompanying legislative proposals did not entirely reflect this realization. The president's position in this regard became clearer on March 6, 1974 when he vetoed the Energy Emergency Act, which called for a rollback of crude oil prices. In his veto message, Nixon noted that "If we are to achieve energy independence, hundreds of billions of private dollars will have to be invested in the development of energy from U.S. sources. This money will not be invested if investors do not have reasonable assurance of being able to earn a return in the marketplace. To make the price of oil a political football, as this act does, would be a serious setback for Project Independence."[107]

As the analysis of the Project Independence program proceeded, it became obvious among experts inside and outside the government that the goal of complete self-sufficiency was highly unreasonable and most likely unfeasible. Gradually, the goal of Project Independence evolved to one of "limited vulnerability" to interruption of foreign energy supplies. This change was enunciated as early as May 7, 1974 in a statement by Nixon on signing the Federal Energy Administration Act of 1974: "We must get on with the actions that are needed to meet the goals of Project Independence—to reduce the vulnerability of the United States to threats from other nations arising from our growing dependence upon foreign sources of energy." The first priority of FEA, the statement went on, would be "to prepare a comprehensive plan for achieving the goals of Project Independence. . . ."[108]

[106] "Proposals to Deal with the Energy Crisis," January 23, 1974, *Executive Energy Messages*, pp. 119–134.

[107] "Veto of the Energy Emergency Act, March 6, 1974," *Executive Energy Messages*, pp. 143–146.

[108] John Sawhill, Simon's deputy at FEO, was selected to head FEA. With the replacement of FEO, the new agency assumed the responsibilities of fuel allocation and petroleum pricing regulation, energy data collection and analysis, energy planning for Project Independence, and energy conservation. Operations transferred to FEA

For a short time after Gerald Ford assumed the presidency in August 1974, the goals of Project Independence became confused again. At first Ford relied on Kissinger's long-standing experience and prestige in the matter. In a speech to a World Energy Conference in September 1974 Ford reiterated the necessity for a reduction in the world price of oil.[109] In a subsequent address to Congress on energy and the economy on October 8, 1974, Ford committed the administration to the specific goal of reducing imports by 1 million barrels a day by the end of 1975. Moreover, he ruled out the possibility of using a gasoline tax to reach this goal, but suggested instead that it could be achieved by voluntary measures.

In a remarkably short time, however, the administration's position on the policies necessary to achieve independence changed dramatically. At the meetings at Camp David on December 14–15, 1974, with energy advisors from OMB, CEA, Treasury, and FEA prominent in the effort, it became clear that neither the short-term goal of reducing oil imports nor the long-term goal of energy independence could be won by half-hearted and voluntary measures.[110] The key conclusion reached was that however unpalatable the reality, it was very unlikely that the OPEC price would "break" and therefore that high world energy prices would prevail, though not necessarily at then-current real levels. While the rhetoric of not accepting the OPEC price action as irreversible continued, from that time on neither its expectation nor its achievement determined U.S. policy. After further meetings in Vail, Colorado, between the president and his chief advisors, the energy program was set and was outlined in the State of the Union Message on January 15, 1975.[111]

---

included the Energy Division of the CLC and the following offices from the Department of the Interior: Office of Petroleum Allocation, Office of Energy Data and Analysis, Office of Oil and Gas, and Office of Energy Conservation. Statement of the President on Signing of the Federal Energy Administration Act of 1974, *Executive Energy Messages*, pp. 149–151.

[109] Gerald Ford, "World Energy Conference: The President's Address to the Ninth Annual Conference in Detroit, Michigan, September 23, 1974," *Weekly Compilation of Presidential Documents* vol. 10, no. 39 (July–December 1974) pp. 1181–86.

[110] Tietenberg, *Energy Planning and Policy*, p. 88.

[111] State of the Union Message, January 15, 1975, *Executive Energy Messages*, pp. 175–187.

President Ford's program was similar to his predecessor's in its reliance on private incentives to encourage production and discourage consumption. The key to the program was the deregulation of oil and gas prices. Ford prepared to go even further in using the price mechanism by adding a permanent $2 per barrel tariff on crude and product imports, together with equivalent domestic oil and natural gas excise taxes. To encourage conservation, it was not thought enough to let domestic prices rise to world levels. Ford also made note of the necessity to maintain high domestic oil prices for the indefinite future: "To provide the critical stability for our domestic energy production in the face of world price uncertainty, I will request legislation to authorize and require tariffs, import quotas or price floors to protect our energy prices at levels which will achieve energy independence."[112] For energy security in the meantime, the president proposed the creation of a strategic petroleum storage reserve and standby authority to allocate crude and products, control prices, and ration supplies among users.

While these were the elements of the program that were expected to have substantial effects on energy security, a number of other proposals were forwarded to Congress as well. These included some proposals previously ignored and some efforts to widen the appeal of the energy policy package. There were thirteen titles in all, divided into those designed to increase domestic energy supply and availability, those designed directly to restrain demand, and those designed to provide standby authority in the event of an energy supply interruption. The proposed legislation was accompanied by proposals (but for reasons of tradition not by draft legislation) for tax changes which were designed to make the energy package as a whole distributionally neutral among income classes and major industry groups. Included in the proposed legislation were amendments to the Clean Air Act to make possible greater use of coal, actions to improve the financial condition and efficiency of electric utilities, to speed siting of important energy facilities, to mandate thermal efficiency standards in space heating and energy efficiency labeling of appliances and motor vehicles, and to subsidize energy-saving winterization of low-income resi-

112 Ibid., p. 183.

dences. The emergency standby provisions in the legislation were broad-gauged, and included authorizing legislation for U.S. participation in the International Energy Agency. To prompt Congress into action on these and the basic pricing proposals discussed above, President Ford announced he would impose by executive order a $1 per barrel special import duty to start on February 1, 1975 and to be increased to $3 per barrel over the following 2 months.[113]

Congress was reluctant to leave energy prices and output decisions to the private market. In particular, the overwhelming majority in Congress opposed using the price mechanism to encourage additional production and dampen energy consumption. There was an unwillingness to allow even a modest increase in gasoline taxes. When proposals were advanced to allow prices to rise (coupled with a windfall profits tax), and despite substantial rebates to minimize the effect on consumers, the initial meager support eroded away. By the summer of 1975 the administration abandoned the goal of immediate decontrol of petroleum prices and moved toward a program of phased decontrol. On July 14 the president announced a compromise oil decontrol plan to gradually decontrol the price of "old" oil over a 30-month period (by January 1978) and to place a ceiling on the price of uncontrolled oil at $13.50 during the same period.[114] The president also called for

[113] Proclamation 4341, January 23, 1975 (*Federal Register* vol. 40, pp. 3965–71, January 24, 1975). See also the Remarks of the President upon Signing a Proclamation on Oil Import Tariffs, January 22, 1975, *Executive Energy Messages*, p. 253. The special import fees prompted Congress to immediate action, not on an energy bill, but on a bill (H.R. 1767) to suspend for a 90-day period the authority of the president under section 232 of the Trade Expansion Act of 1962, or any other provision of law, to increase tariffs or to take any other import adjustment action with respect to petroleum and to negate any such action which may be taken by the president after January 15, 1975. Ford vetoed the bill and Congress did not override the veto. This action did lead the president to delay the second dollar increment to June 1, 1975 on the grounds of being "conciliatory" (Proclamation 4355, March 4, 1975, *Federal Register* vol. 40, pp. 10437–39). The third increment was never implemented.

The constitutionality of the fees was immediately challenged. An initial ruling by the U.S. Court of Appeals on February 21, 1975 found in favor of the president, but a second ruling on August 11, 1975 found that the president exceeded his authority. This decision was appealed to the Supreme Court, which ruled in 1976 that Congress had ceded to the Executive the power to impose fees on oil imports.

[114] Office of the White House Press Secretary, "Fact Sheet to Accompany the President's Compromise Oil Decontrol Plan," July 14, 1975, *Executive Energy Messages*, pp. 323–328.

enactment of energy taxes, including a windfall profits tax, and the other aspects of his January program.

The response to Ford's compromise decontrol package was the passage of the Petroleum Price Review Act, calling for a rollback of uncontrolled domestic prices, repeal of the "stripper well" exemption from price controls, and the establishment of a complex three-tier price system. Ford promptly vetoed this bill with the message that "it would increase petroleum consumption, cut domestic production, increase reliance on insecure petroleum imports and avoid the issue of phasing out unwieldy price controls."[115]

Unable to gain acceptance of his energy package, Ford finally, and reluctantly, accepted the Energy Policy and Conservation Act on December 22, 1975. At the same time, and as part of an agreement with the Congress, Ford removed the $2 per barrel special import fee imposed earlier in the year. As described above, the act established a weighted average price for crude oil produced domestically and left to the administration the determination of the ceiling price for each type of crude. Provision was made for possible periodic increases in the weighted price. The act also authorized planning for energy supply emergencies and mandated the creation of a strategic petroleum reserve within seven years, with a capacity equaling 3 months of imports. The new law provided a number of conservation measures, including a mandatory fuel-economy standard averaging 27.5 miles per gallon for new car fleets by 1985, conversion of some oil- and gas-fired utility and industrial plants to coal, and conditional federal assistance for state conservation programs.

The Quota and After: Concluding Comments

The mandatory quota program contributed to the confusion surrounding energy policy because it was perceived to have effects that were due instead to changes in underlying market forces and to price controls. The true conditions surrounding the nation's energy decisions became more visible with the end of the quota

---

[115] Message to the House of Representatives upon Vetoing H.R. 4035, July 21, 1975, *Executive Energy Messages*, p. 329.

and with the elimination of state prorationing restrictions on domestic production in 1973. These changes were accompanied, moreover, by changes in the tax system for petroleum and natural gas production, including the depletion allowance and income from foreign operations. As a result of all of these changes, by 1975 the preconditions were set for public policy toward energy to be formulated from a more nearly clean slate—no longer was it necessary for policy to take into account the many distortions created by other government actions.

Even in this context, however, decisions were taken which maintained special treatment of petroleum. Prices were controlled directly; domestic production and consumption were monitored and drew attention at the highest political levels; special programs were instituted to restrain consumption; its market structure was repeatedly examined, and its performance scrutinized. This special treatment reflected four partially contradictory concerns. The first was fear of the effects of future supply disruptions—the same energy security problem that had long motivated some strains of energy policy. The second was a combination of a fear of the economic and social effects of further energy price increases and the income distribution effects of these price increases. The third was the new importance attached to energy on the world political scene. The future of the developing countries, the evolving shifts in world power centers, and the foundations of U.S. foreign policy all became entwined in energy, especially oil, developments. Finally, there was a realization that a transition from a predominantly oil- and gas-based economic system was in some sense under way, accompanied by an only partially formed belief that this transition demanded public attention to its immense implications. Energy policy, then, became less parochial in the issues and interests addressed, and less susceptible to conceptual encapsulation. It also became more than ever before a topic of broad public concern. Arcane energy matters remained arcane, but were widely discussed. We shall return to these issues in chapter 10 where the mandatory quota program is considered in the context of the political milieu which formed it and which it in turn influenced.

In this context, the formal abandonment of the mandatory quota program signaled the end of treating energy security as an isolated issue. The effects of this program, however, continued to influence the industry and policy toward it. As we have noted above, some of the provisions of the mandatory quota program were carried forward directly into the succeeding license-fee scheme and were embodied later in the entitlements program and in EPCA. The quota program also affected the relations between the United States and the oil-exporting nations. The heritage of the mandatory quota program certainly raised questions about U.S. efforts to convince oil exporters that they should consider the effects of their actions on oil importers. The mandatory quota program had, and will continue to have, a major influence on energy policy even after its elimination.

7

Oil Import Controls and the Crude Oil Market: A Framework for Analysis

The economic effects of the mandatory quota program, and alternatives to it, have not always been clearly understood. As a consequence, the implications of decisions regarding import controls were not always appreciated by decision makers and observers. While disagreements regarding controls often turned on matters of special interest, they also, as the material presented in previous chapters demonstrates, sometimes reflected confusion about what alternatives to the quota implied in terms of other changes imposed upon the economy. Interpretation of the role of the mandatory quota program in the development of the U.S. energy situation must start, then, with an analysis of such controls in the petroleum market.[1]

An understanding of the effects of the mandatory quota program and its alternatives can be gained through recourse to a simple supply-and-demand model for petroleum in the United States. Such a model must, of course, be structured to take account

[1] See James C. Burrows and Thomas A. Domencich, *An Analysis of the United States Oil Import Quota* (Lexington, Mass., D. C. Heath, 1970) and Charles J. Cicchetti and William J. Gillen, "The Mandatory Oil Import Quota Program: A Consideration of Economic Efficiency and Equity," *Natural Resources Journal* vol. 13, no. 3 (July 1973) pp. 399–430. These works have addressed some of the same issues which we consider here.

of an institutional reality of overwhelming importance—the market demand prorationing system. Once this model is formulated, the similarities and differences of different forms of import controls can be identified and their economic effects ascertained. This chapter and the two which follow develop the analytical basis from which conclusions regarding the mandatory quota program can be drawn, and provide the understanding on which policy regarding energy security for the future can be based.

Government Controls and Crude Oil Supply and Demand

Our analysis of the economic effects of the mandatory quota program is based on a simple supply and demand model for crude oil in the United States. The usual place to begin such an analysis is with a discussion of industry market conditions to establish the relevance of the model, followed by a review of the assumptions and definitions underlying the model. Because of the enormous amount of work already published in this area, it is unnecessary to repeat these preliminaries. Instead, summarizing remarks should be sufficient.

To begin with, a number of studies concerned with market structure and performance in the petroleum industry have concluded that, in general, the industry appears no less competitive than industry in general, and in some respects more competitive.[2]

There are, however, aspects of the industry on which one may base a case for some sort of specific government action. These include concentration in the ownership of pipelines, along with their ownership by integrated companies, growing concentration in production and refining, the trend toward joint ventures, the increasing cost of developing oil resources in new provinces, and the diversification of petroleum companies into other energy sources.

[2] The most important earlier study is that by Melvin G. de Chazeau and Alfred E. Kahn, *Integration and Competition in the Petroleum Industry* (New Haven, Yale University Press, 1959). More recent studies include: William A. Johnson, Richard E. Messick, S. Van Vactor, and Frank R. Wyant, *Competition in the Oil Industry*, Occasional Papers on Energy Policy, vol. 1 (Washington, George Washington University, 1975) p. 101; and Thomas D. Duchesneau, *Competition in the U.S. Energy Industry* (Cambridge, Ballinger, 1975) pp. 115–157.

These are mostly, though, matters which are on the horizon; they do not affect our analysis of the industry during the period of the mandatory quota program. On the contrary, an earlier study by James McKie on the relationship between small and large firms engaged in the exploration for and development of crude oil reserves reveals a surprisingly strong degree of competition, at least at this stage of the industry and during the early years of the quota program.[3] He concludes that "the disadvantages of small size and obstacles to entry which prevent the independent and integrated enterprise from flourishing at other stages are apparently absent here."[4] Moreover, state conservation regulations have in the past ensured that, in the process of developing new fields and in obtaining access to markets generally, the independent would not be disadvantaged by major producers.[5]

On the basis of these studies, we proceed under what we believe is the thoroughly defensible assumption that the petroleum industry in general, and the crude oil production stage during the quota era especially, met the competitive standard necessary for effective use of simple supply and demand analysis.[6] This does not mean that prices and output were competitively determined. As we shall shortly describe, the influences of state prorationing controls, import controls and, more recently, price and allocation controls have determined these outcomes.

The supply-and-demand relationships used here are the so-called long-term relationships between price and quantity in the crude oil market. With respect to supply, long term refers to the length of time required to discover, develop, and bring new reserves into

---

[3] James W. McKie, "Market Structure and Uncertainty in Oil and Gas Exploration," *Quarterly Journal of Economics* vol. 74 (November 1960) pp. 543–570.

[4] Ibid.

[5] McKie, "Market Structure," and Stephen L. McDonald, "Petroleum Conservation in Theory and Practice," *Quarterly Journal of Economics* vol. 76 (February 1962) pp. 98–121.

[6] For more on supply and demand relationships in the petroleum market, see Stephen L. McDonald, *Petroleum Conservation in the United States: An Economic Analysis* (Baltimore, Johns Hopkins University Press for Resources for the Future, 1971), and M. A. Adelman, *The World Petroleum Market* (Baltimore, Johns Hopkins University Press for Resources for the Future, 1973). The limited effect of vertical integration on competition is illuminated in John S. McGee and Lowell R. Bassett, "Vertical Integration Revisited," *Journal of Law and Economics* vol. XIX, no. 1 (April 1976) pp. 17–38.

production. Demand refers to the derived demand of refineries, based on product demands by final consumers; and the long term means the length of time required to permit final consumers to switch from one energy source or pattern of use to another. Derived demand will be treated as the refiner's marginal revenue product for crude oil as an input into the production of final products. We shall refer to *the* price of crude oil, although we recognize there are many prices, depending on the variety and location of the oil. The supply-price relationship is assumed to be positive and the demand-price relationship is assumed to be negative, based on logic and the above-mentioned empirical evidence. The elasticities are more uncertain, although less so with respect to the period considered here than to the post-1973 era.

There is an additional complication with the use of the supply concept that will be abstracted from in this analysis. Because oil is an exhaustible resource, the supply curve may be thought of as shifting backward as the resource base is used up. Prices must rise with time, holding technology constant, in other words, to maintain the same rate of output. The extent of the shift depends on, among other things, the rate at which the resource base is used up and the extent to which discovery and exploitation of the reserve base proceeds systematically from less to more costly deposits. While it may be said with certainty that the resource base is finite, the total amount of oil available is nevertheless unknown. Given improving technology and uncertainty about the pattern of exploitation, we cannot say how much added production at one time reduces the possibility of producing later at the same cost.

Prorationing and the Price of Crude Oil

Major new oil discoveries and declining demand combined during the depression of the 1930s to depress oil prices and profits severely. Under the rule of capture, firms increased their production rate to the point where they could just recover their operating costs in order to obtain their share of the common resource. Industry efforts to restrict output and share the common resource for mutual benefit were unsuccessful, so oil operators pressed for government regulation of crude oil production. The result was a series of state conservation regulations controlling waste and inefficiency, and, not coincidentally, severely reducing crude oil production. In many states, waste was explicitly defined to include production in excess of "market demand."[7] The state regulatory agencies were empowered to prorate estimated demand for crude oil to all producing wells and fields. Demand was estimated on the basis of the current price, hence additional production was not allowed to undercut the existing price structure. The Connally Hot Oil Act added substance to the state conservation laws by prohibiting interstate sales of crude oil produced in violation of state restrictions.[8]

The effect of prorationing was to organize producers into a state-operated cartel, with output regulated to control the price. The cartel was open-ended, however, so new firms could enter or existing firms expand to share the overall production quota. The higher, stable price increased the present value of oil reserves, while the controls on output increased the time required for ultimate recovery of costs and for realization of the value of the resources discovered. Individual producers could increase allowable output only by drilling more wells. Consequently, there was an incentive for excess production capacity to rise. Through market demand prorationing, variations in the level of excess capacity became the means by which prices were stabilized: if prices threatened to rise, existing excess capacity would be brought into production; if prices threatened to fall, it could be withdrawn.

The effect of prorationing controls is illustrated in figure 7-1, where S_d and D are domestic supply and demand for crude oil. Without prorationing, the competitive market price and output would be established at the intersection of S_d and D. To obtain the target price P_d, total quantity is restricted to Q. The domestic supply relationship becomes distorted at Q, breaking the relationship between price and supply. As noted above, the higher price encourages investment in excess capacity, although not as much as the S_d relationship would imply at price P_d because of the disincentives created by production quotas. Capacity would be added until the average costs of production rose to the point where at the target price, excess returns would be eliminated from the industry and additional investment would no longer be attracted.

---

[7] For example, in Texas, Louisiana, Oklahoma, New Mexico, Kansas, and North Dakota.

[8] McDonald, *Petroleum Conservation*, p. 39.

Figure 7-1. Effect of production controls

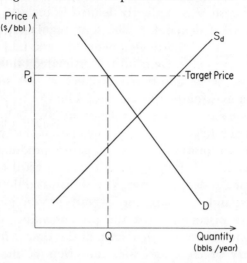

Unfortunately, the incentive to invest was biased in favor of less risky development wells compared with high risk but potentially higher yielding exploratory wells.[9] This bias resulted from, first, the incentive to obtain a greater quota in order to exploit existing reserves and, second, the disincentive to invest large sums in risky exploratory activity where the results might be great but production controls extended the time necessary to recoup investment expenses. Thus, the idle capacity generated by prorationing was of unusually short-term character; it merely enabled existing reserves to be drawn down faster than they could be replaced. Consequently, when called upon during the late 1960s and early 1970s (see chapter 6), excess capacity was quickly absorbed and production soon peaked.

The production control system also had the effect of insulating the market price from transitory changes in supply and demand. The result was a market price that remained virtually constant in nominal terms for twenty years before 1971. The stable price meant, however, that buyers and sellers would not receive price

[9] In addition to McDonald, *Petroleum Conservation,* see Walter J. Mead, "Petroleum: An Unregulated Industry?" in Robert J. Kalter and William A. Vogely (eds.), *Energy Supply and Government Policy* (Ithaca, Cornell University Press, 1976) pp. 130–160.

signals reflecting changes in market conditions—even secular changes such as began to occur in the late 1960s. Energy consumers became accustomed to a stable price, one even declining in real terms, and patterned their consumption accordingly. Oil producers in market demand prorationed states were somewhat less isolated from underlying conditions because variations in the allowed rate of production served as proxies for price changes.

State conservation regulations were necessary to stop physical waste, and production controls introduced a sense of security as well as market stability in an uncertain world. But this security and stability were not achieved without cost, as we shall see in the next section. The controls were not universally popular, even within the industry. Average costs were higher than necessary, capacity utilization too low, and from the point of view of the individual firm, revenues were constrained by production controls. The restrictions were regarded as a penalty to entrepreneurs who had invested their capital to develop oil-producing facilities but subsequently could not take full advantage of their efforts. Outside the industry, criticism of prorationing centered on the higher prices and production inefficiencies created by controls.

Prorationing and Import Controls

Before World War II, the controlled U.S. price also served as the base price for oil produced and sold elsewhere in world markets. After the war, with growing European consumption and with production coming on-stream from Middle Eastern sources, the focus for price determination in world markets moved from the United States to Europe.[10] Supported by unofficial sanctions and the restraint of the international oil companies who controlled most of the oil trade, a two-price system developed whereby the world price was only about two-thirds of the U.S. price. This differential was too great for an influx of imports to be held back by "voluntary" measures, as we have detailed in chapter 2. Ultimately the mandatory quota program was adopted.

Prior to the mandatory quota program, state conservation authorities had responded to the rise of imports by cutting back

[10] For a fuller discussion, see Peter R. Odell, *Oil and World Power* (London, Penguin Books, 1975).

production allowables in order to maintain the domestic price. In terms of figure 7-1, the quantity of domestic output shifted to the left to allow the gap between domestic supply and domestic demand to be filled by imports. In practice, to determine production allowables under the market demand prorationing authority, the Texas Railroad Commission estimated domestic demand net of imports.

The increasing flow of imports necessitated a continual decline in production allowables; in Texas they were as low as 33 percent by 1958. The mandatory quota program established a proportional relationship between imports and domestic production, with imports restricted to the ratio existing in 1957–58. Consequently, the quota had the effect of validating the price structure already established by the Texas Railroad Commission; it eliminated the need for further reduction of output-to-capacity ratios due to growing imports. The ratios continued to respond to transitory shocks and to changes in domestic supply and demand conditions. (See table 2-4.)

Import controls could have been imposed without production controls, though greater restriction of imports would have been required to maintain prices to producers at the level they reached through the combined policies. The existence of production controls, however, altered the relative effects on price and output among possible control measures. Production controls without import controls would have led to declines in allowed output which could not be sustained.

Three means of controlling imports could have been used—the fixed quota, the proportional quota, and the tariff. The proportional quota device was chosen. Here we analyze and compare the three methods, and remark upon their relative suitability given the existence of market demand prorationing and the twin goals of stimulating domestic production and minimizing effects on prices to consumers.

Refer to figure 7-2 where S_d is long-run domestic supply, D is long-run domestic demand, and P_w is the world price of oil, assumed to remain constant over the range of U.S. import demand considered here.[11] With free trade, domestic production would be

[11] An important question at this stage is whether a change in U.S. demand for foreign oil would affect the world price. It has been suggested that the world price would remain unchanged because the increment to foreign demand would be minor (cf. *The*

Figure 7-2. Comparison of a proportional quota with a conventional quota or tariff

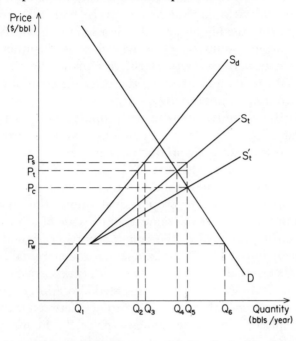

Q_1 and domestic consumption would be Q_6, with the difference filled by imports. A tariff could be applied to imports, raising the domestic price to P_t with the effect of encouraging domestic supply to increase to Q_2 and reducing domestic consumption to Q_4. The gap $(Q_4 - Q_2)$ would again be filled by imports. Alternatively, a quota could be applied limiting imports to $(Q_4 - Q_2)$, which in

---

Oil Import Question, appendix B). Certainly the increment was small historically; whether it would have been small enough not to make a difference under free trade conditions is unknown. The absence of a foreign supply relationship makes it impossible to answer this question on *a priori* grounds. The most that can be argued is that foreign production and transport conditions were such that a higher price was not a necessary prerequisite for additional capacity to supply imports. Marginal costs of production outside the United States were stable for many years and small relative to taxes and royalties. With reference to transportation cost, for most of the period up to the late 1960s, tanker capacity was large enough to handle additional U.S. import requirements at little additional cost (Adelman, *The World Petroleum Market,* pp. 103–130). Tanker transport, moreover, appears to be a constant cost industry in the long run (ibid.). We conclude that for the period covered by this study, it is realistic to assume a world price invariant to U.S. demand changes of the magnitude implied. For analytical purposes, of course, this assumption is unnecessary. It does, however, simplify the presentation.

turn would force the domestic price to P_t. Thus, for given supply–demand conditions in a competitive market, a conventional tariff or quota would yield equivalent results. In both cases consumers would be paying the higher price P_t for a smaller quantity Q_4, and domestic output would be Q_2. The value of the quota to importers, or alternatively of the tariff receipts to the government, would equal the amount given by the price differential $(P_t - P_w)$ times the volume of imports $(Q_4 - Q_2)$.

To compare these results with the proportional quota, suppose that the ratio $(Q_4 - Q_2)/Q_2$ is set equal to k, as the desired proportion of imports to domestic production necessary to satisfy national security considerations. The curve S_t $[= S_d (1 + k)]$ shows the total supply of oil to the domestic market, that is, domestic supply plus allowed imports. With the proportional quota, the equilibrium price and output are not the same as in the case of a conventional quota or tariff which led to the same proportion of total demand being met by imports.[12] The reason is that the marginal cost of oil to refiners is less than the domestic price P_t (in contrast to the conventional quota), because of the associated allocation to the refiner of k import licenses valued at the difference between the domestic and world prices. That is, at domestic price P_t, the marginal cost is $P_t - k (P_t - P_w)$. The value of oil to refiners at the margin, in contrast, is P_t, remembering that the derived demand for oil is the marginal revenue product of oil as an input. This inequality is unstable; refiners are inclined to bid the price of domestic oil above P_t to obtain additional supplies and also additional import licenses. As total supply increases, the marginal revenue product will fall. This process will continue until the supply price of domestic oil rises to a point P_s where it exceeds the average price P_c by the value of import licenses, $k(P_c - P_w)$;[13] that is,

$$P_s = P_c + k (P_c - P_w)$$

[12] This distinction was demonstrated by Rachel McCulloch and Harry G. Johnson, "A Note on Proportionally Distributed Quotas," *The American Economic Review* vol. 63, no. 4 (September 1973) pp. 726–732.

[13] The average price of oil to refiners is given by

$$P_c = \frac{P_s + k P_w}{1 + k}$$

This follows by noting that refiners would purchase $k/ (1 + k)$ at the world price P_w and the difference $[1 - k/(1 + k)]$ at the domestic price P_s. Multiplying each proportion by its respective price and summing yields the average price.

The total supply of oil with the proportional quota is thus given by S'_t, which lies to the right of S_t because of the incentive to obtain additional import licenses. In effect, refiners are encouraged by the proportional quota to pass on to consumers part of the reduced cost of imported oil; i.e., pass on to consumers part of the scarcity rent of import licenses.

Compared with the conventional quota or tariff, the proportional quota achieves the objective of maintaining the same fixed ratio of imports to domestic production,[14] but at a higher supply price to domestic producers (P_s) and a lower input price for domestic consumers (P_c). Both producers and consumers are better off with the proportional quota. Domestic production is increased to Q_3 and total consumption is increased to Q_5. Thus, compared with conventional import controls, the proportional quota scheme is relatively more efficient in stimulating domestic production with a smaller impact on consumer prices.[15]

The advantages described above were *not*, however, obtained with the mandatory quota program, which did impose a proportional quota, because of the influence of state production controls. The condition described by figure 7-2 was not achieved because domestic supply was restricted (as described in figure 7-1) to maintain a higher target price P_d. This is illustrated in figure 7-3 (the mandatory quota program case) where domestic production is limited to Q_7 to allow for imports of $(Q_8 - Q_7)$. Total supply is thus distorted to S''_t and the advantages of the proportional quota are lost. Marginal cost is fixed at P_d and is equal to marginal revenue product. With the supply price Q equal to the demand price, refiners are not inclined to increase purchases of domestic oil. With the fixed domestic price, there is no incentive to base feedstock costs on the weighted average of domestic and imported oil. There is, therefore, no longer the incentive for refiners to pass along to consumers any of the rents associated with the quota.

---

[14] That is, $(Q_5 - Q_3)/Q_3 = (Q_4 - Q_2)/Q_2$, because both quantities are determined by the distance from S_d to S_t, which is equal to the desired ratio of imports to domestic production.

[15] The combination of domestic price controls and the entitlements program encourages an analogous but inverse result. Imports are, in effect, subsidized by the entitlements program, encouraging a higher volume and producing a higher average price as a result.

Figure 7-3. Combined quota plus production
controls

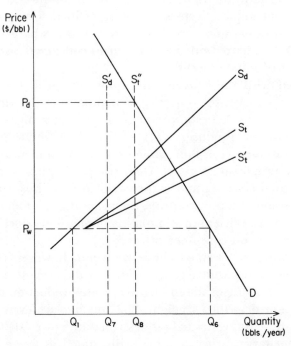

The higher domestic oil price imposed by controls raised consumer prices and misallocated resources within the U.S. economy.
Referring to figure 7-3, the difference between the domestic price
(P_d) and the world price (P_w) times the quantity consumed (Q_8)
represents the additional payments by consumers for crude oil. In
addition to the excess payment on the actual amount consumed,
consumers lose because they are prevented by the higher price
from purchasing the additional amount (measured by the distance
from Q_8 to Q_6) that would have been purchased at the lower world
price. The loss of "consumer surplus" (measured by the area of the
triangle formed by the demand curve D and the price line P_w, over
the quantity in question) is what consumers would have been willing to pay to obtain the additional quantity ($Q_6 - Q_8$) over and
above the payment actually required at the single world market
price P_w.

The import quota created a resource cost for the domestic
economy by supporting relatively inefficient domestic production.

Domestic output with the quota is at Q_7, but would fall to Q_1 with free trade. The area of the triangle formed by the supply curve S_d and the price line P_w over the quantity from Q_1 to Q_7 represents the additional cost of supporting relatively inefficient domestic production rather than importing cheaper foreign oil. In addition, the higher price P_d encourages more domestic production capacity than that necessary to support the rate of output at Q_7. The cost of the investment in additional idle capacity, not determinable from the graph, but represented by the distortion of S_d to S_d', may also be charged against the quota.

The situation illustrated in figure 7-3 existed from 1959 through 1970. The domestic and world prices remained almost constant over this period, but the quantities of oil consumed from both sources changed because of changes in supply and demand conditions. By 1971 demand had increased and domestic supply had decreased to the point where all excess capacity was absorbed at the market price. A decision was necessary to let the price move upward or to increase the proportion of oil that could be imported. The latter option was taken. After 1971, the world price increased to and surpassed the domestic price (which was being controlled—see chapter 6), removing altogether the scarcity value of imports. The quota program became superfluous, but nevertheless remained on the books until May 1, 1973.

The transition to no restrictions on domestic output and the removal of quantitative restrictions on imports dramatically altered the conditions under which the domestic crude-producing industry operated. The absence of the quota removed the possibility of a reintroduction of effective market demand prorationing. The power to establish market prices and industry-wide output had been placed in abeyance. While the state laws remained on the books, their only effect was anticipatory in the sense that conditions might some day permit or require their revival.

Quotas versus Tariffs: Other Considerations

Recurrent proposals to use a tariff rather than a quota to control imports (e.g., the Ford administration proposal of January 1975) prompt further comparisons of the analytical similarities and differences between these two devices. The equivalence between conventional quotas and tariffs (and the relationship between proportional quotas and conventional quotas or tariffs) as described above assumes a static situation where supply and demand conditions are known with certainty. When uncertainty is introduced and supply and demand conditions are permitted to change, a number of important differences arise that may establish a preference for one or another as policy instruments. In addition, there are other distinguishing characteristics of tariffs and quotas that should be considered, including (1) how the right to import is determined, (2) the ease with which the controls may be administered, and (3) the distribution of the scarcity value of imports. These are discussed in turn below.

Price versus Quantity Control

A quota system clearly establishes the maximum quantity of imports that will be allowed into the country.[16] Competing domestic producers need not fear additional imports if domestic prices rise. This quantitative certainty makes quotas very appealing to existing domestic producers. Restricting imports requires the domestic price to rise enough to generate additional output and discourage consumption to make up for the decline in imports. How much the price must rise is uncertain, even if producers and consumers could react immediately to any price change.[17] Thus quantitative certainty is matched by price uncertainty. Consequently, a quota restriction is usually set at the existing level of imports to avoid the difficult question of gauging its prospective price effect. This approach is obviously inadequate if the existing level or proportion of imports is judged too high for national security.

---

[16] The quantity may be actually less than the maximum in the event that the foreign price is so high that the demand for imports is less than the quota allocation, or in the event the market is not allowed to otherwise work freely, as was the case under the price controls of the early 1970s.

In this section we consider the case which includes domestic production restraint. This simplifies the analysis and, moreover, is realistic in light of post-1973 conditions.

[17] The actual time lag in output and consumption changes adds to price uncertainty. There is also less urgency for producers to adjust production to a price increase. Since foreign encroachment in domestic markets is prohibited, there is less competitive pressure to force producers to react to the change.

Tariffs, on the other hand, provide relatively greater certainty about the resulting domestic price but less certainty about the quantity of imports. The new price is simply the world price plus the tariff. The tariff rate may be chosen with the intention of increasing the prevailing price to a specific target level. This approach may be appealing if the goal is to induce added domestic production from heretofore uneconomic sources.[18] For production using new technology, the expected price is more important than the amount of oil that will be imported, because the price determines whether the firm can enter the market in the first place.

As demand and supply conditions change over time, the price/quantity distinction between tariffs and quotas becomes even more important. The differences may be illustrated through figure 7-4. Starting with demand D and supply S_d, the domestic price P_d is raised above the world price P_w with a tariff or by a quota restricting imports to $Q_3 - Q_2$. The areas given by Roman numerals represent the cost of controls to consumers: area (I + II + III) gives the additional oil bill and area IV the loss of consumer surplus. Area I represents transfers from consumers to producers in the form of rents, area II represents the extra resource cost of additional domestic production, and area III represents rents accruing to importers (in the case of a quota, where import rights are granted without cost) or revenues accruing to the government (in the case of the tariff, or where quotas are auctioned).

Now suppose demand increases to D'. With the tariff system, the domestic price remains unchanged at P_d as long as the import price does not change. The increase in demand is accommodated by an increase in imports from the original amount $Q_3 - Q_2$ to the new amount $Q_5 - Q_2$. Total domestic consumption increases to Q_5, but domestic production remains unchanged at Q_2. There is no additional incentive to domestic production without an increase in the price. As a result, the areas given by I, II, and IV remain unchanged. That is, there is no additional transfer of income from consumers to domestic producers, no change in domestic resource costs, and no change in the amount of consumption lost to consumers. Only area III, tariff revenues to the govern-

---

[18] For example, the target price may be set to yield an attractive rate of return on the production of synthetic crude oil and gas from coal or oil shale.

Figure 7-4. Comparing a tariff and a quota

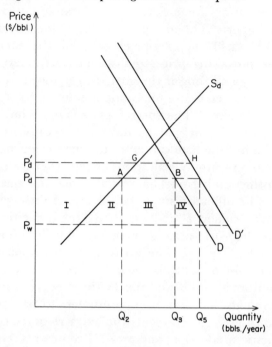

ment, increases to include the additional revenues from the increase in imports. Per unit consumer opportunity costs do not change; the total amount of consumer opportunity costs increases only with the larger tariff revenues received by the government. This, of course, constitutes a transfer of income from petroleum consumers as a group to taxpayers as a group.

If a quota system is used instead, the quantity of imports must remain at $Q_3 - Q_2$ after the increase in demand. The resulting adjustment is shown in the figure as an increase of the domestic price from P_d to P_d', where the difference between the quantity of oil produced and consumed in the United States remains the same as before (i.e., the distance from point A to point B equals the distance from point G to point H). In other words, if the quantity of imports is fixed, the increase in demand must be met through domestic sources, and this requires an increase in the domestic price. The price must rise enough to generate additional supply or to reduce the quantity demanded until the market is cleared. Both per unit and total opportunity costs to consumers increase with the quota. Resource costs (area II) must increase to generate additional domestic supplies; and this means that the income received by existing production (area I) must increase as well. The scarcity value of imports (area III) increases as the gap between the domestic price and the import price widens (the per unit consumer opportunity cost rises) for the same amount of imports. Area IV increases as domestic consumers are forced to reduce the quantity of purchases relative to the amount desired at the free trade price.

A similar set of conclusions follows if the import price should fall. With a tariff, the domestic price would fall by the same amount, leaving per unit opportunity costs unchanged. With a quota, the domestic price remains unchanged and the opportunity costs increase in all four categories. In other words, the tariff instrument permits the domestic economy to take advantage of a reduction of the price of foreign oil, while the quota device does not. For domestic producers, the quota eliminates any risk of having the domestic price fall if the world price should decline. The tariff, in contrast, retains this element of risk. If the import price should rise, however, the domestic price rises with the tariff but not with the quota.

Thus, an important distinction between tariffs and quotas develops, depending on whether one expects the import price to rise over time, fall, or simply fluctuate a great deal. If the world price simply fluctuates, the quota would be the best device to protect the domestic market from disruption. If the world price is expected to rise over time, the quota will create smaller opportunity costs. If the world price is expected to fall, the tariff permits the domestic economy to take advantage of cheaper imports, but jeopardizes marginal domestic production. A variable tariff is sometimes suggested to handle the risk to domestic producers from fluctuating or declining prices. This form of tariff simply approximates the effects of a quota, but a quota is easier to apply.

Discrimination

Quotas are inherently discriminatory. The criteria by which the government allocates import licenses are not based on impersonal market forces (unless the licenses are auctioned); licenses are allocated subjectively in a way that is usually influenced by political considerations and the fact that allocation necessarily benefits some and harms others. Typically, licenses are distributed on the basis of previous patterns. Those importing in the past are allocated licenses for importing in the future. This does not necessarily lead to an efficient distribution of future import shares because it discourages competition by limiting the entry of newcomers, but it is easy to apply and appears fair. Any nonmarket allocation system creates a potential monopoly position that could be exploited at the expense of consumers. The tariff system, in contrast, operates through the market system. Anyone wanting to import from wherever he chooses may do so. The only limitation is the impersonal criterion of the ability to find a market at the higher price.

Both tariffs and quotas may be designed to discriminate according to the source of imports. With a quota, licenses may be based on country of origin. Similarly, the tariff schedule may incorporate a factor that varies according to source. In the oil import restriction case, for example, Western Hemisphere exporters might receive unlimited licenses or pay no duty, while Arab exporters might be limited in the amount they could ship or be required to pay the highest duty.[19] However, it is difficult for the United States to limit the sources of its imports, just as it was for exporters to limit the ultimate destination of their exports during the recent embargo. Substantial leakage may be expected in both cases due to the fungibility of oil in world markets. Similarly, a price difference due to differential tariffs is unlikely to last indefinitely. Actions of buyers and sellers, and the difficulty in policing them, eventually force such differences to converge.

Administrative Flexibility

Under existing law, quotas are in general easier to implement and change than are tariffs because quotas may be altered by executive action without formal procedures or legislation. Changes in tariff rates, on the other hand, require both legislative and executive approval. This general statement requires modification in the case

---

[19] This approach violates the most-favored-nation clause of several U.S. trade agreements, but such violations are usually permitted under accompanying national security clauses.

of oil because in 1976 the Supreme Court ruled that the Congress had ceded to the Executive Branch the power to impose license fees on oil imports. This power may be withdrawn by the Congress whenever it chooses, however, so that tariffs still require implicit consent by the legislative branch. Greater flexibility is advantageous if changes in market conditions warrant changes in the restrictions placed on imports. However, there is much to be said for maintaining public debate and representation, which means legislative involvement, even at the expense of flexibility.

The costs of administering quotas are said to be higher than those of tariffs. A larger administrative apparatus is required to control the trading pattern and volume and to issue and review the forms traders are required to fill out. Certainly, the record of the mandatory quota program bears witness to this observation. The administrative cost to private industry is similarly higher with quotas than tariffs. Tariffs are a straightforward accounting matter, while quotas involve application forms, processing delays, and assuring regulatory compliance.

Scarcity Value of Imports

As discussed above, the difference between the import price and the domestic price constitutes a scarcity rent that may accrue to the government, the importer, or the exporter. This differential is called a "scarcity rent" accruing to the right to import because it results from an increase in the value of imported oil artificially produced by import restrictions; it is not a necessary payment to attract imports. This difference would be the per unit import duty if a tariff system were used, or the license fee if quotas were auctioned to importers. If quota licenses were not auctioned—and they have never been so far in U.S. experience—then these rents might accrue either to importers or to exporters, depending on market conditions and on how the licenses are allocated. If the importer has the opportunity to fill his quota from any exporting country, and if exporting countries bid competitively for the sale, then the importer will receive the scarcity rent. If an effective oil cartel is maintained, exporters may require the full domestic price from importers, in which case the exporter receives the scarcity

Figure 7-5. Relative effect of tariffs and quotas
on import demand

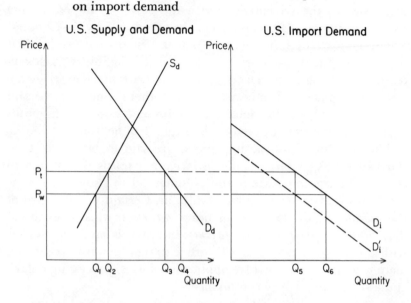

rents.[20] Alternatively, if the import licenses are allocated according to country of origin, the exporting country has the bargaining power and will to set the price to importers at the U.S. domestic level and capture all of the scarcity rents.

Although tariffs and quotas may be initially set to achieve equivalent results, the two will establish different price-setting incentives for an exporter-cartel. To illustrate, the left side of figure 7-5 gives U.S. domestic supply and demand while the right side translates excess domestic demand into the demand for imports, D_i. Starting with a domestic and world price at P_w, import demand would be the quantity $Q_4 - Q_1$ on the left, equal to quantity Q_6 on the right. A tariff or quota may be used to raise the domestic price to P_t and reduce import demand to $Q_3 - Q_2 = Q_5$. But, once established, the two control devices imply different import demand schedules.

If the exporter cartel chooses to raise or lower the world price, the tariff-inclusive domestic price rises or falls accordingly and the

20 M. A. Adelman has proposed that a quota auction system be used in an effort to absorb some of the monopoly rent otherwise going to OPEC. "Politics, Economics and World Oil," *American Economic Review* vol. 4, no. 2, pp. 58–67.

quantity of imports demanded decreases or increases. But, for each world price, the quantity of import demand is smaller with a tariff than without. The demand for imports shifts to the left of its original position, as shown by the broken line D_i' in the figure. With the quota, an increase in the world price will not affect import demand until it rises above the domestic price P_t, after which the quota is not constraining and import demand follows the original schedule. For all world prices below P_t, the quota is constraining and the demand for imports remains unchanged at Q_5. The demand for imports is therefore quite different between the two cases: with the tariff it shifts to the left; with the quota it remains unchanged above P_t and is completely inelastic below P_t.

Some implications for cartel pricing may be drawn, insofar as those decisions are influenced by U.S. import demand. With the quota, the cartel can gain nothing by lowering the price, but has everything to gain by raising the price at least to the U.S. level. The gain from further price increases depends on the elasticity of demand. With the tariff, the cartel may gain from a price increase or decrease, depending on demand elasticity. However, the potential profit-maximizing price is lower with a tariff than a quota because of the leftward shift in the demand curve.

.   .   .

This chapter has analyzed past developments in the domestic crude oil industry in terms of a simple supply–demand model and compared the characteristics of tariffs and quotas as they affect producers and consumers. With respect to the mandatory quota program, the model identifies the categories of costs of restrictions to consumers and the gains for producers. This analysis will be used as a basis for measurement in the next chapter. The model also provides guidance for estimating what may have taken place in the absence of a quota. The results from the theoretical comparison of tariffs and quotas will be used in the next chapter in comparing the estimated cost of a conventional tariff/quota with that of the mandatory quota program, and in the discussion of alternative policies for future energy security.

8

The Economic Effects of the
Mandatory Quota Program

The economic effects of the mandatory quota program were pervasive, though significant only for some segments of the economy. While all of these effects cannot be traced, the analytical framework set out in chapter 7 makes it possible to indicate the qualitative nature of the most important of them. In addition, somewhat crude quantitative estimates are feasible for some of these effects.

Isolation and explication of the economic effects of the mandatory quota program are essential if its development is to be understood. As discussed in the preceding chapters, the program was adopted and then altered in response to expectations that it would serve the wishes of parties at interest. As we note in this chapter, in some respects the effects of the program were consistent with those expectations and in others they were not. Further, the national willingness to sustain this program perhaps depended upon its perceived benefits and its costs. Better understanding of the actual costs and benefits, and of why they were sometimes perceived differently, will be useful in consideration of future import policy.

The first section of this chapter estimates the protective effect of the mandatory quota program over the period from 1960 through 1970. We end with 1970 because, after that year, rising world prices and general relaxation of controls progressively eliminated the protective effect of the quota. This effect is measured in terms of the amount of domestic production protected by the quota, the

268

conservation effects imposed on consumption, the reduction in imports, and the reduction in balance of payments deficit and embargo risks. These may be regarded as the "benefits" attributable to the quota.

In the second section, the protective effect is translated into the additional costs imposed on consumers by the quota. These estimates are confined to the direct costs associated with higher oil prices. The third section provides an indication of the distribution of these costs among recipients. The final section discusses some of the broader and less direct structural effects of the quota upon the petroleum industry and relates the quota with other energy sectors.

Estimating the Protective Effect of the Quota: 1960–70

Measuring the protective effect of the quota requires an estimate of what would have taken place in the alternative scenario of free trade. Figure 7-3 illustrates the comparison. Quantities Q_7 and Q_8 represent actual domestic production and consumption at the target price P_d. These may be compared with quantities Q_1 and Q_6 at the free trade price of P_w. Tracing the implications of the free trade alternative after 1959, in turn, requires consideration of the adjustments necessary to reach long-run equilibrium. Two major influences must be comprehended: the effects of eliminating market demand prorationing at the beginning of the period, and the transition from controlled output and consumption as U.S. prices tracked the world market. The first adjustment follows from the assumption that market demand prorationing would have been eliminated shortly after a decision was made to permit free imports. If the ineffectiveness of voluntary controls had resulted in the abandonment of import restraint rather than in the creation of the mandatory quota program in 1959, market demand prorationing would have fallen of its own weight by the beginning of 1960.[1]

---

[1] See chapter 2 for a discussion of the forces operating to disrupt voluntary import controls and for the pressures then existing on the market demand prorationing system.

The world price is assumed to follow the same course in this hypothetical exercise as it did in actual experience. That is, the world price is assumed to remain stable at $2.10/bbl until 1970, in spite of increased U.S. imports.[2] This assumption is based on the observation that non-U.S. production is based less on cost factors than on other determinants.[3] Although U.S. imports could be accommodated at the $2.10/bbl price, the post-1970 price changes may have occurred earlier as a result of the increased political importance of U.S. dependence even if strictly economic factors would not explain the change. Nevertheless, we adopt the assumption that price would not change for the period we consider here; it is at least as plausible as the alternative assumption, and no less arbitrary. As to the other issue, the domestic price is assumed to have reached the free trade equilibrium of $2.10/bbl by the beginning of 1960.

Under these assumptions, domestic production would increase at first as prorationing controls on existing wells were removed and flush wells were produced more rapidly.[4] Production would decline over time, of course, as existing reserves became exhausted and fewer prospects were drilled at the lower expected price. Consumption would increase, slowly at first, and then faster until a new equilibrium path was reached. Later, as the world price increased, the rate of domestic production would rise and the rate of domestic consumption would slow down. Thus, looking back to 1960, imports would be smaller than those actually observed in the early years and would increase rapidly during the latter half of the 1960s in response to long-run supply and demand conditions. We now attempt to assign quantitative estimates to these expected changes.

----

[2] The assumption of $2.10 as the delivered price of foreign oil abstracts from the many problems of estimating such a price. See M. A. Adelman, *The World Petroleum Market* (Baltimore, Johns Hopkins University Press for Resources for the Future, 1972), chapter 6 and appendixes.

[3] See footnote 11, chapter 7, for further discussion.

[4] Existing wells would continue to operate as long as the free trade price covered operating costs. The original fixed costs associated with finding and developing existing wells are already sunk as far as the short-run decision is concerned. These costs bulk large relative to operating costs, but the decision to shut down is based upon sales revenues relative to salvage value of equipment and variable operating costs, not including a user cost for oil reserves.

Starting with the production side, consider first the short-run response of output to the lower price and removal of production restrictions. Henry Steele has estimated the short-run marginal costs of U.S. crude oil production in 1965, including in his work a measure of the impact of prorationing controls on the rate of output.[5] Output of crude oil in 1965 was 2.7 billion barrels, while total productive capacity amounted to nearly 3.7 billion barrels. Including natural gas liquids (NGL), output amounted to about 3.0 billion barrels and capacity was about 4.3 billion barrels. Steele's estimates indicate that variable costs of production would have been covered at a $2.10/bbl price for nearly all production capacity in existence in 1965. We assume that the same relationship held for existing capacity as of 1959–60, when the prorationing controls are presumed to have been lifted in this exercise. Capacity at that time amounted to 3.9 billion barrels of crude oil, condensate, and NGL.[6]

All available capacity may not be produced even if operating costs are covered. First, there are the technical limitations of normal downtime due to equipment problems, well and reservoir characteristics, and so on. Second, there is the economic question of expected price changes in the future and their impact on current production. Owners expecting prices to rise in the future may choose not to deplete their asset today, but to hold it for future exploitation in anticipation of returns higher than those from the best alternative investment. (Alternatively, submarginal properties may be retained in production so that future profitable operation would not be precluded by the costs of reopening reservoirs.) Withholding of this type could apply only to cases where the concept of user cost is relevant, such as where single ownership of the reservoir or a unitized arrangement prevails, not where owners are motivated by the "rule of capture." In view of the limited applicability of user costs, and indeed of the probable expectation of stable or declining prices rather than rising prices, holding back production for economic reasons would probably have been of

5 "Statement of Henry Steele, Professor of Economics at the University of Houston," *Governmental Intervention in the Market Mechanism*, Part 1, Hearings before the Senate Committee on the Judiciary, 91 Cong. 1 sess. (March 26, 1969), pp. 208–222.

6 Production capacity and output figures are given in American Petroleum Institute, *Petroleum Facts and Figures*, 1971 ed., pp. 67, 101.

very little importance. Taking together these two factors limiting production, we assume that only 10 percent of capacity would not have been produced. Thus, we estimate that total output beginning in 1960 would have been approximately 3.5 billion barrels. This compares to an actual output of 2.7 billion barrels.

The long-run response to the fall in price would be a reduction in total productive capacity. The free trade price would not be sufficient to cover the exploration and development costs required for the replacement of the level of capacity which was induced by the higher protected price. Existing wells would be exhausted and not replaced by new discoveries as the range of potentially lucrative prospects was reduced at the lower price. Two important questions must therefore be addressed to ascertain the free trade output path: what is the equilibrium rate of output at the free trade price, and how long would it take to work off existing capacity to reach that equilibrium rate?

The long-run equilibrium rate of output depends, in the first instance, on the rate of exploration for and development of new reserves. Franklin Fisher has suggested that total discoveries in any given period are a function of the number of wildcat wells drilled, the success ratio, and the average size of each discovery, and that all three are a function of the price incentive as well as physical conditions.[7] Fisher's statistical results confirm his hypothesis, but need not be reported because they have since been revised and updated by Erickson and Spann.[8] Using data for the period from 1946 to 1959, Erickson and Spann estimate a price elasticity for new discoveries of +0.93. This is obtained from the sum of the elasticity of wildcat drilling (+1.48), the elasticity of the success ratio (−0.13), and the elasticity of discovery size (−0.42). These results imply that oil prospectors will expand their operations in response to an increase in the price by including prospects with

[7] Franklin M. Fisher, *Supply and Costs in the U.S. Petroleum Industry: Two Econometric Studies* (Baltimore, Johns Hopkins University Press for Resources for the Future, 1964). The implicit assumption is that technological progress offsets any decline in the quality of the resource base, leaving the real cost of exploration and development unchanged.

[8] Edward W. Erickson and Robert M. Spann, "Price, Regulation, and the Supply of Natural Gas in the United States," in Keith C. Brown, ed., *Regulation of the Natural Gas Producing Industry* (Washington, Resources for the Future, 1972).

higher risk and lower payoff than those projects justified at a lower price.

The price elasticity for additions to reserves may be translated into a price elasticity of long-run supply by noting that any difference between the rate of output and the rate of discoveries will in the long run adjust incentives so as to bring the two together. If production ran ahead of new discoveries, the rental value of reserves would rise and thus induce additional new discoveries. If the rate of production were lower than the rate of new discoveries, rents would fall until consumption increased and the rate of new discoveries declined enough to bring the two into equilibrium. Thus, a 1 percent decline in discoveries implies in the long run a 1 percent decline in the rate of output.

The sample period for these estimates lies before 1959. For future projections this might be a shortcoming, but for the purposes of this analysis it is desirable.[9] The data precede the imposition of import controls, so the estimates may provide a truer picture of the incentive structure that would have existed had the quota not been imposed. On the other hand, the estimates are probably understated because of the influence of market demand prorationing. Fisher found that the effect of an increase in Texas shut-down days (used as a measure correlated with overall restrictions) is to shift wildcat drilling to other parts of the country with less severe restrictions than Texas and to somewhat reduce overall exploratory activity. Generally, then, ". . . when crude price is maintained by production restrictions, not only is the geographical pattern of exploration slightly distorted, but the procedure is less efficient than direct subsidy as an incentive to exploration, because the positive effects of a high crude price are partly offset by the negative effects of the restrictions themselves."[10] Unfortunately, Fisher's study provides no guidance for adjusting the price elasticity of new reserves to a removal of prorationing controls. To correct for this bias, to avoid implications of unjustified precision,

---

[9] An important question is whether free trade would have rendered the historical elasticity estimates obsolete as, for example, the 1973 price increases rendered the task force supply projections obsolete (see chapter 6). We proceed on the assumption that the estimates remain valid.

[10] Fisher, *Supply and Costs*, p. 4.

and for convenience, the 0.93 supply elasticity is rounded to 1.0 in subsequent calculations.

Given the indicated 1.0 supply elasticity, the usual procedure would be to calculate the percentage reduction in the domestic price represented by the $2.10 free trade price and then to reduce 1959 output by the same percentage. In order that the calculated output level might be regarded as an equilibrium rate, however, the base output from which it was calculated must have been in equilibrium as well. It was not, again because of the distortions arising from prorationing controls.[11]

To find a more appropriate base period, note that during 1951 domestic output was considerably less constrained by production controls, with Texas wells producing 76 percent of the time (see table 2-4). The average wellhead price was stable at $2.53 per barrel for two consecutive years, and national output remained steady at about 2.5 billion barrels per year, including NGL. Assuming the price dropped from $2.53 to $2.10, a 17 percent decline, the implied decline in the rate of output would have been 0.4 billion barrels, using the 1.0 supply elasticity. The resulting 2.1 billion barrel base period estimate may be a little low after adjustments for general (though minor) inflationary expectations and therefore we adopt 2.2 billion barrels as the long-run equilibrium production rate at $2.10 per barrel.

It is useful, however, to compare this estimate with those obtained in other studies. The Cabinet Task Force study concluded that long-run equilibrium output of petroleum liquids (i.e., including NGL) would be 2.7 billion barrels per year (not including the Alaskan North Slope production) at a price around $2 per barrel.[12] This estimate was based on the Fisher–Erickson supply elasticity estimate and on submissions from industry sources.[13]

In another study, Richard Mancke, while on the staff of the Cabinet Task Force, estimated that the long-run equilibrium rate

[11] At the $2.88 price then current, Texas wells were operating on a 34 percent schedule.

[12] *The Oil Import Question,* A Report on the Relationship of Oil Imports to the National Security by the Cabinet Task Force on Oil Import Control (Washington, GPO, 1970) p. 236.

[13] Ibid., p. 225 ff. To obtain industry-based estimates, the task force applied its elasticity estimate to the average amount of output that industry sources estimated would be forthcoming at prevailing prices.

of crude oil output in the "lower 48" would range between 1.3 and 2.0 billion barrels of crude oil per year at a $2.10 price.[14] His conclusion was based on a supply elasticity derived from the volume of rents generated by crude oil production, rather than on the basis of costs of production. Mancke's estimate implies a much higher supply elasticity than does that of Fisher and Erickson. However, Mancke's estimate of long-run output was probably too low because he failed to take into account the distortions in rents created by market demand prorationing restrictions.[15] His estimate would be slightly larger, also, had natural gas liquids been included. Finally, the procedure used by Mancke is suspect because it presumes that the elasticity of supply is constant down to a zero price.

A study by Thomas Stauffer sought to "estimate the economic costs of finding and producing U.S. crude oil for the base year 1965, excluding any transfer payments such as royalties or lease bonuses and omitting all income tax effects. . . ."[16] In effect, he sought the mirror image of the supply relationship considered by Mancke. Stauffer's results are based on a cross-sectional analysis of U.S. crude oil production by well depth and flow rates. Cost factors are then applied to obtain finding, development, and lifting costs, deflated by a credit for the production of associated natural gas and natural gas liquids. Stauffer concludes that 76 percent of U.S. crude oil output in 1965 was produced at a long-run economic cost of less than $2 per barrel. Total production of crude oil and NGL was 3.2 billion barrels in 1965; thus, Stauffer's results imply that 2.5 billion barrels could have been produced at a price of $2.

The results from these independent approaches suggest strongly that a reasonable estimate of the equilibrium rate of output lies somewhere between 2.0 and 2.5 billion barrels per year at the $2.10 price. The 2.2 billion barrel figure adopted here therefore seems to be a reasonable "point" estimate. As for the length of

[14] Richard Mancke, "The Longrun Supply Curve of Crude Oil Produced in the United States," *The AntiTrust Bulletin* (Winter, 1970) pp. 727–756.

[15] Rents are inversely related to costs of production. Hence, given prorationing, the estimate using Mancke's method would be too low because it is based on rents, for reasons converse to those that lead to the conclusion that estimates based on costs may be too high.

[16] Thomas R. Stauffer, "Economic Cost of U.S. Crude Oil Production," *Journal of Petroleum Technology* (June 1973) pp. 643–657.

time required to reach the new equilibrium, it seems advisable to accept the conclusion of the Cabinet Task Force that excess capacity would be absorbed within five years.[17] In other words, it is assumed that equilibrium would be reached within the same five-year period that excess capacity would be absorbed.

On the other side of the market, there is very little evidence on the price elasticity of the demand for crude oil. The demand for crude oil is, of course, derived from the demand for petroleum products. What little evidence there is suggests a long-run price elasticity on the order of −0.5.[18] The length of the adjustment period required to reach the long run is unknown. For simplicity in presentation, and on the grounds that the bulk of the adjustment would at least be under way, we assume that the new consumption equilibrium will be achieved over the same five-year period that it takes supply to adjust to the lower price. The annual response to the price change is calculated on the basis of assuming a gradual acceleration in the response which leads to the equilibrium path in five years.

All of the essential elements are now available to construct a set of estimates of domestic oil consumption, domestic production, and crude oil imports in the free trade case so that a comparison with the results under the quota system is possible. These estimates and the actual data observed are given in table 8-1. The figures include crude oil, NGL, and imported products (except residual fuel oil), with product imports converted to crude oil on a barrel-for-barrel basis.

Columns (1)–(3) of table 8-1 show actual domestic consumption, production, and imports. Column (5) gives the estimated amount of consumption assuming the U.S. price fell to $2.10 per barrel.

---

[17] *The Oil Import Question*, appendix D, p. 218.

[18] A justification for the −0.5 elasticity estimate may be found in James C. Burrows and Thomas A. Domencich, *An Analysis of the United States Oil Import Quota* (Lexington, Mass., D. C. Heath, 1970). More recent elasticity estimates for final products imply the price elasticity of crude oil is above −0.5; see Michael Kennedy, "An Economic Model of the World Oil Market," *Bell Journal of Economics and Management Science* vol. 5, no. 2 (Autumn, 1974) pp. 540–579, especially pp. 555–559. Another recent study estimates the derived demand for energy on the basis of its direct and indirect uses, and yields an own-price elasticity of −0.47; see Ernest R. Berndt and David O. Wood, "Technology, Prices and the Derived Demand for Energy," *The Review of Economics and Statistics* vol. LVII (August 1975) pp. 259–268. We would expect total energy demand to be less elastic than that for each energy component.

Table 8-1. U.S. Oil Consumption, Production, and Imports: Actual versus Estimated with No Import Restrictions, 1960–70

(billion bbls/year)

Year	Actual figures				Estimated at free trade prices			
	Consumption (1)	Production (2)	Imports (3)	Imports as percent of consumption (4)	Consumption (5)	Production (6)	Imports (7)	Imports as percent of consumption (8)
1960	3.3	2.9	0.4	12.1	3.4	3.5	0.0	0.0
1961	3.4	3.0	0.4	11.8	3.6	3.2	0.4	11.1
1962	3.6	3.1	0.5	13.9	3.8	3.0	0.8	21.0
1963	3.6	3.2	0.5	13.9	4.0	2.7	1.3	32.5
1964	3.7	3.2	0.5	13.5	4.3	2.5	1.8	41.9
1965	3.9	3.2	0.6	15.4	4.6	2.2	2.4	52.2
1966	4.1	3.8	0.6	14.6	4.8	2.2	2.6	54.2
1967	4.2	3.7	0.5	11.9	5.0	2.2	2.8	56.0
1968	4.5	3.9	0.6	13.3	5.3	2.2	3.1	58.5
1969	4.6	3.9	0.7	15.2	5.5	2.2	3.3	60.0
1970	4.8	4.1	0.7	14.6	5.7	2.2	3.5	61.4

Source: Actual figures are from U.S. Bureau of Mines, *Minerals Yearbook*; estimates are derived as discussed in the text.

The long-run response to the price decline is an increase of 18 percent in the quantity of crude oil demanded, applying the assumed —0.5 price elasticity. This is applied to the actual consumption figures for 1965 and beyond to obtain the long-run price effect on consumption. Estimated data for the transition period from 1960 through 1964 were derived by applying a straight-line interpolation to reach the 1965 equilibrium consumption level consistent with the lower price. Column (6) gives estimated production using the procedure and assumptions discussed above. Estimated imports, column (7), are the difference between estimated consumption and estimated production.

If the figures reported in table 8-1 are reasonably credible, the implications for national security are striking. By 1970 over 61 percent of total U.S. consumption of petroleum would have been imported under this free trade scenario. This compares with imports of 36 percent of consumption during the 1973 embargo. Estimated imports, at 3.5 billion barrels, are five times larger than actual imports in 1970, and nearly 40 percent larger than the volume reported during 1973. Thus, while the quota imposed large costs on consumers and interfered with the market adjustment mechanism, on the basis of this analysis it also reduced the amount of adjustment required as a result of the 1973 embargo and the accompanying increase in the price of oil.[19]

Another perspective on the implications of these estimates for national security may be obtained by considering the probable sources of the additional imports. In determining the sources of such a large volume of imports, security of supply must be expected to play a dominant role. Consistent with the view of the Cabinet Task Force, and with the administration of the mandatory quota program, it can be assumed that first priority for U.S. requirements would have been given to Western Hemisphere sources. Moreover, this preference can be assumed to have been exercised without significant constraints imposed by regionally dominated crude oil characteristics because, without import controls, appropriate refinery capacity would have been constructed.

[19] The quota may also be said to have prevented the development of storage capacity and alternative strategies to deal with an embargo. One cannot assume that only the levels of domestic production and consumption would have changed.

Table 8-2. Sources of U.S. Crude Oil Imports, 1950–70

(million bbl/year)

Year	Total U.S. imports	Canada	Venezuela	Other non-Arab	Arab
1950	174	10	108	26	40
1955	294	16	149	31	98
1960	401	41	200	58	101
1961	472	66	180	66	100
1962	411	85	169	56	101
1963	413	90	174	58	90
1964	439	102	174	60	102
1965	452	108	158	74	113
1966	447	127	147	69	104
1967	412	150	131	68	62
1968	472	169	126	72	106
1969	514	203	112	89	110
1970	483	245	98	63	77

Source: U.S. Department of the Interior, Bureau of Mines, *Minerals Yearbook*, annual.

Table 8-2 provides a breakdown of the actual sources of U.S. crude oil imports by area during the period in question, while table 8-3 shows estimated additional imports without the quota, by source. As the discussion below explains, the major share of the extra imports would have come from the Eastern Hemisphere, meaning predominantly Arab sources. The Cabinet Task Force study was overly optimistic in assuming that major increases in Canadian imports would be forthcoming even at a $2 price.[20] The task force study noted that some excess capacity existed in Canada during the early 1960s so that imports could have been larger, with unlimited access to the American market, if distribution bottlenecks had been removed. With the benefit of hindsight, however, we conclude that free access to the United States would have simply advanced the date when Canadian proved reserves leveled off, so that total imports from Canada would not have varied much from the actual volume.[21]

U.S. crude oil imports from Venezuela, the predominant Latin American producer, declined steadily throughout the 1960s. With

[20] The report assumed they would rise from 0.5 MMb/day to 1.5 MMb/day between 1968 and 1980 (*The Oil Import Question*, p. 48).

[21] Canadian reserves declined because of government policies affecting the industry, not because of limitations of the resource base. The assumption regarding Canadian exports therefore implies the same though, perhaps earlier, policy response.

Table 8-3. Expected Sources of Additional U.S. Imports

(million bbl/year)

Year	Total additional U.S. imports with no quota	Additional imports from Latin America	Additional imports from Eastern Hemisphere
1960	(−400)	0	0
1961	0	0	0
1962	300	100	200
1963	800	500	300
1964	1,300	500	800
1965	1,800	500	1,300
1966	2,000	600	1,400
1967	2,300	600	1,700
1968	2,500	600	1,900
1969	2,600	700	1,900
1970	2,800	800	2,000

Source: The first column is calculated from table 8-1: (7)–(3). The second is based on the difference between U.S. imports from Latin America and potential total Latin American exports. The third column is the difference between estimated total U.S. import requirements and the amount available from Latin America.

residual fuel oil included, the decline is less marked, but it still persists from 1965 to 1972. During 1968, total Latin American production came to 1.8 billion barrels, of which 1.2 billion barrels were exported (including residual fuel oil). Only 0.8 billion barrels were exported to North America.[22] The United States did not absorb more of the total because of the preference for lighter and sweeter crudes. This bias would have been less pronounced if refinery capacity had been developed to handle sour crude. With the expanded U.S. import requirements in the case of free trade, it will be assumed that all of the Latin American export capacity would be absorbed by the United States, leading to receipt of an additional 0.5 billion barrels per year. With the increase in demand for Latin American crude, total export capacity is assumed to have increased by 5 percent per year, matching the overall growth rate in Latin American production capacity during this period.

The remainder of U.S. import demand is assumed to be supplied from Eastern Hemisphere sources (see table 8-3), about 2.0 billion barrels in 1970. Estimated Eastern Hemisphere imports

[22] British Petroleum Co. Ltd., *BP Statistical Review of the World Oil Industry* (London, 1969) p. 11.

come to 39 percent of estimated domestic consumption, or over eight times the actual percentage reached in 1970. This volume of imports almost matches total U.S. imports from all sources during the 1973 embargo, and is nearly three times the 1973 percentage imported from the Eastern Hemisphere. It is difficult to say how much of the 2 billion barrels would come from Arab sources, because a preference for non-Arab oil might have been exercised, but it would seem likely that over half would be so required.

Based on these estimates, it may be said that the import quota reduced U.S. oil imports substantially, and reduced imports from the Eastern Hemisphere more than proportionately. Had nothing else changed, the 1973 embargo would have been more severe in its disruption of industry and transportation. Consumption would have been reduced more drastically; domestic production would have had an operating capacity only 60 percent of the actual 1973 level. Of course, had imports actually reached these estimated levels, there would have been more attention paid to the potential problems from an oil supply interruption. Countervailing policies, such as strategic storage, may well have been adopted by the United States and other consuming governments. Additionally, the private sector would likely have adjusted to this situation as well—perhaps by adopting different inventory policies or by altering the regional allocation of exploration and development expenditures.[23] Finally, the oil-exporting nations may also have behaved differently because they would have faced a different incentive structure. Nonetheless, while the increased level and different source of imports cannot be translated directly into increased vulnerability to supply interruption, they can be interpreted as exacerbating the problem that did exist. Consequently, the mandatory quota program contributed something to oil supply security.

In addition to reducing the security risk associated with the volume of imports, the quota also prevented an increase in the balance of payments cost of oil imports. Following the approach used in the Cabinet Task Force study, the balance of payments outflows associated with oil imports consist of retained earnings

[23] If, on the other hand, private industry learns from experience that price increases resulting from an embargo will be regarded as unfair profits and taxed away, there would be no point in investing in greater inventories.

282   LIMITING OIL IMPORTS

Table 8-4. Balance of Payments Cost Factors per Barrel of U.S. Imports
(dollars)

Cost factors	Latin America	Eastern Hemisphere
Retained value[a]	1.137	0.946
Transportation[b]		
1961–64	0.25	0.65
1965–69	0.15	0.40
Capital stock[c]	2.48	0.50
Respending in U.S.[d]	0.514	0.219

[a] The figure for Latin America corresponds to the average during 1962–67 calculated for Venezuela in *The Oil Import Question*, appendix H. The figure for the Eastern
Hemisphere is obtained by a weighted average of the figure for Libya ($0.885), Kuwait
($0.864), Iran ($0.962), and Saudi Arabia ($1.00), with twice the weight assigned
to the last two to reflect their relative importance.

[b] Estimates for 1961–64 reflect costs using 70,000 dwt tankers; those for 1965–69
assume the use of 200,000 dwt tankers (*The Oil Import Question*, appendix H). It is
assumed that larger import volumes with free trade would have induced necessary
port improvements to handle the large tankers after 1964.

[c] Based on estimates provided in *The Oil Import Question*, appendix H. See footnote a
regarding weighting the Eastern average.

[d] Based on estimates in ibid. The estimates are limited to respending that would
occur within one year. See footnote a regarding weighting the Eastern Hemisphere
average.

in the country of origin (taxes, royalties, and factor payments),
transportation charges, and additional capital investment abroad to
expand capacity.[24] Netted against these gross outflows are U.S.
exports sold to these countries as a result of their additional dollar
earnings (including American-made oil field equipment) and the
repatriation of company profits earned abroad. Estimates of the
effects of each of these components on the balance of payments
for each barrel imported are provided in table 8-4.[25] Applying these
cost factors to the incremental import volumes in table 8-3 pro-
duces the estimated additional balance of payments outflows shown
in table 8-5.

The estimates imply that the negative impact on the balance of
payments with no import controls is not of major importance.
Gross incremental outflows are less than $4 billion by 1970, and

[24] *The Oil Import Question,* appendix H.

[25] The balance of payments cost estimate for the Eastern Hemisphere includes the
outflow arising from investment required to produce an additional 500 million barrels
to replace Venezuelan exports assumed to be diverted from Europe to the United
States.

Table 8-5. Balance of Payments Cost of Additional U.S. Imports
Without Quota

($ billions)

Year	Latin America		Eastern Hemisphere		Totals	
	Gross outflows	Net outflows	Gross outflows	Net outflows	Gross outflows	Net outflows
1961	0	0	0	0	0	0
1962	0.140	0.068	0.470	0.367	0.610	0.435
1963	0.695	0.338	0.730	0.570	1.425	0.908
1964	0.695	0.338	1.530	1.195	2.225	1.533
1965	0.645	0.314	2.005	1.566	2.650	1.880
1966	1.022	0.497	1.940	1.515	2.962	2.012
1967	0.774	0.376	2.445	1.910	3.219	2.286
1968	0.774	0.376	2.665	2.081	3.439	2.457
1969	1.151	0.559	2.565	2.003	3.716	2.562
1970	1.280	0.622	2.700	2.109	3.980	2.731

Source: Based on the cost factors in table 8-4 and the import volumes in table 8-3. Gross outflows are obtained by multiplying the retained value and transportation cost factors times the import figures. Spending on capital stock is included only when an increase in annual import flows occurs. For Latin America, such spending occurs after imports increase beyond 500 million barrels, this base volume being diverted from destinations in Europe and replaced by exports from the Eastern Hemisphere, where capital spending must increase as a consequence. For example, there is no capital spending in Latin America associated with the 100 million barrels of additional imports in 1962 from that region, but it is necessary to add $50 million to gross outflows to the Eastern Hemisphere to replace European imports from Latin America that are diverted to the United States.

net outflows are less than $3 billion. These compare with actual imports of goods and services of $59.3 billion, and net exports of $3.5 billion, in 1970. The estimates of outflows are probably overstated. In the first place, the calculations do not reflect the adjustments that would occur in the U.S. economy as a result of cheaper fuel. Increased productivity in the United States, and increased competitiveness of U.S. energy-intensive industries could result in an expansion of exports that would swamp the cost of oil imports. Other adjustments may also occur in the oil-exporting countries. Additional revenues may result in import demands above those implied by historical respending patterns, particularly in direct trade with the United States. Finally, the gross outflow estimate is adjusted by respending that would occur within one year. This is an arbitrary time period chosen only because the balance of payments accounts are recorded on an annual basis. Eventually, nearly all dollar expenditures abroad would return to the United States as payments for U.S. exports, and the corresponding net balance of payments cost would fall to zero. This reflects the fact that the real cost of additional oil purchases is not found in the figures recorded in balance of payments accounts, but in the export of American goods and services in exchange for the oil.

Cost of the Quota to Consumers

The preceding section provides much of the information necessary to estimate the cost of the quota to oil consumers over the period 1960 through 1970. Recalling the discussion from the previous chapter, consumer costs are composed of two elements: the additional payment for actual consumption above the free trade price and the loss of consumer surplus resulting from the higher price. The first element may be estimated by multiplying the differential between domestic and world prices by the quantity consumed. The second element is estimated by multiplying the price differential by the additional quantity that would be purchased at the free trade price, times one-half.[26] The appropriate quantities are given in table 8-1.

The price differential is another matter. The Cabinet Task Force report chose to estimate the price differential on the basis of the value of import tickets, calculated at $1.174 per barrel for 1969.[27] Unfortunately, it is difficult to obtain similar estimates for the rest of the period. An approximation may be obtained, however, by subtracting the world price ($2.10) from the average domestic wellhead price[28] plus transport costs to the East Coast. Average transport costs are set at $0.18 per barrel, a figure consistent with costs reported elsewhere[29] and which achieves agree-

[26] This is a linear approximation of the area under the demand curve and above the world price for the additional quantity.

[27] *The Oil Import Question*, pp. 260–261. The estimate is based on the average value of import tickets in each PAD district, weighted by the percent of oil consumed in each district. The differences in the value of import tickets arise largely because of different transportation costs to the East Coast.

[28] Reported in U.S. Bureau of Mines, *Minerals Yearbook*, annual.

[29] For example, Mancke, "Longrun Supply Curve." See also Adelman, *The World Petroleum Market*, on transportation charges over this period.

Table 8-6. Estimated Direct Cost of the Quota to Consumers

($ billions)

Year	Price differential (1)	Additional cost of crude oil (2)	Loss of consumer surplus (3)	Total direct cost (4)
1960	0.96	3.2	0.05	3.2
1961	0.97	3.3	0.1	3.4
1962	0.98	3.5	0.1	3.6
1963	0.97	3.5	0.2	3.7
1964	0.96	3.6	0.3	3.9
1965	0.94	3.7	0.3	4.0
1966	0.96	3.9	0.3	4.2
1967	1.00	4.2	0.4	4.6
1968	1.04	4.7	0.4	5.1
1969	1.17	5.4	0.5	5.9
1970	1.26	6.0	0.6	6.6

Source: The factors of column (1) are derived from *The Oil Import Question* as described in the text. (2) = (1) × table 8-1, col. (1). (3) = (1) × ½ × table 8-1, col. (5) − col. (1).

ment with the 1969 price differential based on the value of import tickets.[30]

The resulting costs are reported in table 8-6. The additional cost of oil to consumers increases steadily from \$3.2 billion in 1960 to \$6.0 billion in 1970, and the loss of consumer surplus increases from \$0.05 billion to \$0.6 billion over the same period.[31] After 1970, as noted before, these costs quickly fell to zero, as the protective effect was eliminated by the easing of import restrictions.

The Cabinet Task Force report argues that the additional cost of oil should be adjusted downward because part of the savings accruing to refiners from cheaper imports would be passed along to consumers in the form of lower product prices.[32] This would be appropriate if refiners had been inclined to base feedstock costs on the weighted average of domestic and import prices. However, as argued in the last chapter, the combination of prorationing

[30] The 1969 average wellhead price at \$3.09 per barrel, plus \$0.18 transportation costs, less the \$2.10 world price, yields \$1.17 as the differential.

[31] Residual fuel is excluded from these calculations since it was imported at world prices. The task force estimate for 1969 was \$5.14 billion, based on a preliminary consumption figure of 4.379 billion barrels.

[32] *The Oil Import Question*, p. 261.

with the proportional quota destroys this incentive and removes the basis for making the adjustment.

Distribution of Consumer Costs

It is of interest to allocate the consumer costs calculated above among the various recipients. The loss of consumer surplus is not included because it involves the loss of welfare without a transfer payment. We shall distribute only the costs arising in 1969 ($5.4 billion) because of the availability of information. However, the results for 1969 will provide a rough breakdown that will be indicative of the division for the other years.

As noted in the previous chapter, part of the total will be used to employ resources in support of larger domestic crude oil production, part will be required to support the cost of maintaining excess crude oil production capacity, and part will become transfer payments in the form of extra profits, rents, lease bonuses, and royalties.[33] An estimate of the portion of consumer costs that covered the resource cost of inefficient domestic production protected by the quota is not provided by the Cabinet Task Force study. Instead, the study reported industry estimates of efficiency losses that may occur in the future, assuming the 1969 price differential remained constant.[34] The costs range from $1.0 to $1.5 billion for 1975 and $1.5 to $2.0 billion for 1980. Because of

---

[33] A fraction of the profits, lease payments, and royalties will accrue to federal and state governments and thereby act to reduce the burden on taxpayers. In the case of revenue to the state governments, only the transfer from oil consumers who are also taxpayers in the oil-producing states should be considered as offsetting. Information is not available to permit an estimate of this amount. Federal revenues from lease bonuses and royalties amounted to $650 million in 1969, a part of which results from the quota-supported price. If we suppose that these payments would fall in the same proportion as the drop in price, revenues would fall by as much as $215 million without the quota. Again, there is still the problem of matching payments by oil consumers with individuals receiving tax relief. Corporation profits taxes might work in the opposite direction, moreover, since the transfer payments to the oil industry as a result of the quota would be channeled to other sectors of the economy which, in general, experience a higher effective rate of taxation than the oil industry. See *The Oil Import Question*, p. 24. The issue of transfers to state governments from higher prices of a depletable resource, in this case natural gas, is analyzed in Milton Russell and Laurence Toenjes, *Natural Gas Producer Regulation and Taxation* (East Lansing, The Institute of Public Utilities, Michigan State University, 1971).

[34] *The Oil Import Question*, p. 29.

smaller quantities in 1969, one might infer from these estimates that 1969 efficiency costs would be slightly less than $1.0 billion.

Referring to figure 7-3, the cost of inefficient domestic production is the area under the long-run supply curve and above the world price for the quantity of domestic output that would be displaced by imports with free trade $(Q_1 - Q_7)$. At the world price of $2.10 per barrel, it was estimated earlier that domestic output would fall to a long-run equilibrium of 2.2 billion barrels per year (compared to 3.9 billion barrels) in 1969. If the industry were actually operating along its long-run supply curve in 1969, it would be possible to estimate resource costs directly from these two quantities and an assumed supply elasticity. (For example, assuming an elasticity of 1.0, such an estimate would be $1.4 billion.) This is not appropriate, however, because the effect of prorationing (as described in the previous chapter) was to force the industry off its long-run supply curve. The result was investment in considerable excess capacity. Thus the long-run supply concept may not be used to obtain a credible estimate of the cost of inefficient domestic production induced by the quota. The cost of inefficient domestic production includes the higher cost domestic capacity engaged in production and the cost of excess capacity as well. To proceed, we shall accept $0.9 billion as the industry estimate of the resource cost of capacity engaged in production, and estimate separately the cost of excess capacity following a procedure suggested by Wallace F. Lovejoy.[35]

Lovejoy estimated the cost of excess capacity as of the beginning of 1969, using capacity measures provided by the American Petroleum Institute.[36] Lovejoy's approach was to "estimate the amount of investment in unused oil-producing capacity and related facilities and then to apply an expected normal rate of return on investment for the oil industry in order to come up with the opportunity

[35] Wallace F. Lovejoy, "Oil Conservation, Producing Capacity, and National Security," in Albert E. Utton, ed., *National Petroleum Policy: A Critical Review* (Albuquerque, University of New Mexico Press, 1970) pp. 68–102.

[36] Note that in the special case of the oil industry under market demand prorationing, excess productive capacity is shared among all producing units. Thus producing facilities are not idled; they are operated at reduced output rates. Administrative and operating costs are mostly invariant with the rate of outputs; they are instead proportional to the number of wells operating, and hence these costs are magnified directly by the existence of excess capacity.

Table 8-7. Investment in Unused Oil-Producing Capacity in the United
States as of January 1969

($ billions)

Drilling and equipping excess producing wells	$4.6
Drilling excess dry wells	2.3
Excess artificial lift equipment	0.4
Excess lease equipment	2.0
	$9.3
Cost of excess investment with:	
10% discount rate	0.930
15% discount rate	1.395
Operating expense plus overhead	0.200
Total annual cost	$1.130 to 1.595

Source: Wallace F. Lovejoy, "Oil Conservation, Producing Capacity, and National
Security," in Albert E. Utton, ed., National Petroleum Policy: A Critical Review (Albuquerque, University of New Mexico Press, 1970) pp. 98, 100, 101.

cost for the unused resources in the oil industry which could have
been profitably employed in alternative investment opportunities.
This can be viewed as the annual cost of unused producing capacity."[37] Included in the cost of investment are drilling costs (adjusted to include dry wells), surface equipment, and certain operating costs that maintain idle capacity in a state of readiness. Not
included are the various downstream costs such as gathering, storage, and terminal facilities. Lovejoy's cost estimates are provided
in table 8-7. The $4.6 billion estimate of the cost of drilling and
equipping excess producing wells was derived by dividing the
average capacity per well into the total amount of idle capacity in
each region of the country, multiplying by the average cost per
well in each region, and summing over all regions. This procedure
spreads the cost of idle capacity over all existing wells. Converting
the amount of excess capacity into average well equivalents, Lovejoy calculates a total of 66,477 excess producing wells at the end of
1968. Use of the industry average of one dry well for every 2.97
producing oil wells implies that about 22,000 dry holes were
drilled to obtain excess producing wells.[38] Multiplying the esti-

[37] Lovejoy, "Oil Conservation," p. 90.

[38] Lovejoy argues that this is an overly conservative estimate, since it is based on
development wells only and does not include any exploratory wells. For comparison,
over four out of five exploratory wells are dusters. However, these wells are often
drilled to obtain information rather than add to production capacity.

mated number of dry holes by the overall average cost yields a total investment cost of $2.3 billion for excess dry holes.

Approximately 90 percent of the excess producing wells would require artificial lift equipment (applying the industry-wide average to this subset of wells). This means that about 59,829 wells required an expenditure of at least $6,000 per well, the minimum calculated by Lovejoy for lift equipment. Additional lease equipment was estimated to amount to $30,000 per well, bringing the total for lifting and lease equipment to about $2.0 billion.

Summing these separate items brings the investment in excess well capacity to $9.3 billion. An annual "opportunity cost" figure is obtained by applying an appropriate rate of return. Lovejoy suggests a figure in the 10 to 15 percent range as appropriate for the oil industry. This range yields an annual excess capacity cost of $0.93 billion to $1.395 billion. Added to this capital cost are operating expenses and administrative overhead charges, conservatively estimated at 10 percent of the amount of lifting and lease equipment, or $0.2 billion per year, bringing the total cost of excess capacity up to $1.130 to $1.595 billion per year.

These figures do not make any allowance for the normal level of idle capacity that the industry would require (even in the absence of the quota and prorationing) to provide for operational flexibility. How much idle capacity may be regarded as normal is unknown and cannot be inferred from historical statistics. Instead of making such an estimate, we shall assume that the average of the upper and lower estimates provided by Lovejoy ($1.4 billion) will be taken as the annual cost of excess capacity in the abnormal sense. Implicitly, we attribute the difference between that and the upper limit as the cost of idle capacity required for normal flexibility. This assumes that about 15 percent of actual excess capacity is necessary.

Summing the estimates of excess resources engaged in production and unnecessary idle capacity brings the estimate of the resource cost of the quota plus prorationing to $2.3 billion ($0.60 per barrel of output in 1969, on average). The difference between the consumer transfer ($5.4 billion) and resource cost ($2.3 billion) is an estimate of the income transferred from consumers to the petroleum industry and to owners of oil resources ($3.1 billion) as a result of the quota program. These transfers may be estimated independently in order to provide a check on the estimated resource cost.

The most straightforward component of rents is the scarcity value of imports accruing to refiners. This is equal to the price differential times the amount of imports (i.e., $1.17 × 0.7 billion barrels = $819 million). The remaining rents take the form of profits, royalties, lease bonuses, and severance taxes transferred to owners or leaseholders of oil resources and to oil-producing states. They are termed rents because they are not payments for productive services, but result from the higher value of oil in the ground. Following the procedure suggested by Richard Mancke,[39] the incremental rent generated by the quota will be estimated by calculating the actual amount of rents paid in 1969 and subtracting from it the amount that is estimated to have accrued at the lower price and production rate anticipated with unrestricted imports. With total domestic crude oil production of 3.9 billion barrels in 1969, valued at an average price of $3.09 at the wellhead, revenues accruing to the crude oil industry totaled approximately $12.1 billion.

Royalties and severance taxes are most often determined explicitly as a percentage of crude oil sales revenues. Royalties are usually set in the range from 12.5 to 16.7 percent of the wellhead price, while state severance taxes averaged from 2 to 4 percent in the major producing states in 1969.[40] Applying simple averages of 14.5 percent and 3 percent, respectively, to the total value of production yields total royalties of $1.753 billion and severance taxes of $363 million.

There is less institutional rigidity with regard to lease bonuses to holders of underground mineral rights, based as they are on the difference between expected production costs (including royalties and severance taxes) and the expected revenue from the lease. The common method of estimating lease payments is to relate them to current and past production data and then to extrapolate trends into the future. Richard Mancke calculated the ratio of a moving average of lease payments to the wellhead price (net of royalties and severance taxes), adjusted for the "decline rate" of production,

[39] Richard Mancke, "The Longrun Supply Curve," p. 751.
[40] Ibid.

and argued that this ratio is "a reasonably accurate estimate of what is at any specified time the expected share of 'lower 48' crude oil's net total costs accounted for by lease bonuses."[41] Mancke finds that the ratio is fairly stable at 16.4 percent of the net price, or 13.3 percent of the 1969 average wellhead price.[42] Accepting this methodology and Mancke's results, we obtain $1.069 billion as the estimate of lease payments.

The estimates made above of royalties, severance taxes, and lease bonuses total $3.7 billion for 1969. The amount of rents that would have been forthcoming in the absence of the quota can be obtained by applying the same percentages used above to the lower amount of domestic crude oil revenues. With the free trade price at $2.10 and the volume of output at 2.2 billion barrels, sales revenues would have come to $4.6 billion. Using this methodology, we estimate that rents would have been reduced to $1.4 billion without the quota. The estimated amount of rents attributable to the quota is therefore $2.3 billion. This procedure assumes that the average percentage of oil revenues going to rents would not change as a result of the displacement of domestic production and the decline in its price. This assumption is consistent with the notion of a unit elastic long-run supply curve, but one might nevertheless expect rents to be somewhat compressed under competitive pressure from cheaper imported oils and with the different expectations that would exist under the regime of free imports. The increment of rent generated by the quota would in that case be greater than the $2.3 billion estimate, implying that this figure may be conservative.

The sum of resource costs ($2.3 billion), rents accruing to refiners ($0.8 billion), and the rents transferred to resource owners and producers ($2.3 billion) completely accounts for the $5.4 billion independent estimate of the cost of the quota to consumers. The agreement between the estimates obtained from several different procedures, crude as they may be and based upon fragmentary information, provides some reassurance as to the appropriate magnitudes. These results supply a useful perspective on the distribution of income transfer created by the quota program.

[41] Ibid., p. 746.
[42] Ibid., p. 747.

Indirect Effects of the Mandatory Quota Program

The discussion to this point has focused on the direct effects of the quota on oil production, imports, and consumption. The program also produced a number of indirect effects, many of which were unintended and unexpected. In general, they resulted from the interdependence of different economic activities and the fact that the quota program interfered with market incentives in allocating resources over time and among different uses.

Oil Production and Consumption

We have already described in detail how the quota program, combined with prorationing, created the incentive to invest in excess oil production capacity. More specifically, we have described the incentive to invest in low risk and low production fields relative to high risk and potentially high yield prospects. Producers were more encouraged to develop known reserves intensively rather than to find new reserves. Consequently, known reserves were depleted faster, and replacement reserves were coming on-stream more slowly than they would have had the price been the same but without market demand prorationing. Given the long lead time in bringing new reserves to production, the responsiveness of domestic output to a change in price was reduced. Partly for these reasons, the amount of idle capacity that appeared to exist was not indicative of the ability of the industry to expand output in a time of need; it certainly led to overestimates of the ability to sustain higher levels of output. The misestimation of idle capacity was compounded by public misunderstanding of the application of market demand prorationing. Low productivity (stripper) wells were not restricted. The restriction of others to an "allowable" which was not frequently adjusted meant that, given the natural productive decline in reservoirs, relaxation of restrictions would not lead to a proportionate increase in output. The mandatory quota program, along with market demand prorationing, led observers to an unwarranted and exaggerated view of the extent of U.S. oil consumption security.

An unwarranted sense of security was also created by the long period of price stability resulting from the application of these controls. The domestic price remained almost constant in nominal terms from 1959 through 1972, and declined in real terms, despite the decline in reserve coverage of domestic consumption. Excess capacity changed in response to levels of demand for domestic oil rather than to price. Of course, for those reservoirs which were allowed to produce more as the consumption of domestic oil increased, there was an increase in revenues, but this incentive did not pervade the industry, and had no effect on the demand side. Price changes are necessary to help producers and consumers anticipate and react to changing supply and demand conditions, but they did not occur. If such signals do not work (or if they are perceived to be unreliable indicators of market conditions) and if response lags are long, an imbalance between quantities demanded and supplied at a given price can arrive with little warning, and discontinuous shifts in price would be required to equate them. This imbalance in fact occurred in the domestic oil industry during 1960–70, but its implications were hidden by expanding imports—setting the conditions for the economic shock of 1973–74.

There is, however, another side to the picture. The maintenance of artificially high and stable prices in the United States prevented the shifts in production and consumption that would have resulted had domestic prices followed world prices: first down, and then up. The estimates presented in the last section indicate that the quota program may have played a major role in ameliorating the impact of the 1973–74 oil price increase. Less oil was being consumed and thus consumption was less disrupted by the reduction in oil supply, and more domestic capacity was on-stream than would have been the case without the mandatory quota program. In addition, smaller resource reallocation costs were imposed on the economy because the price change was smaller than it otherwise would have been. These benefits must, of course, be balanced against the cost of the decade of resource misallocation due to U.S. prices being held above the world level.

It may be argued, however, that the consumer costs imposed by the mandatory quota program were appropriate because the additional charge was to account for the insecurity of imported oil. In this context, petroleum supply insecurity imposes a social cost that should be borne by consumers. The proceeds from the higher price were then transferred to domestic industry to subsidize secure output. The quota thus served to bring the private cost of oil consumption closer to its social cost.

Oil Substitutes

Because of substitution possibilities between oil and other fuels, the quota tended to raise other energy prices, lower total energy consumption, and increase total domestic energy production relative to the free trade alternative. The demand for specific oil substitutes was greater with the higher oil prices than without. Higher oil prices, for example, encouraged increased use of natural gas, causing the equilibrium price of natural gas to rise. To the extent the price of natural gas was permitted to rise, additional supply was encouraged. Due to controls on interstate natural gas prices, however, the price effect was transformed into a reduction in the reserve coverage for natural gas sales. The mandatory quota program, in the context of the controlled price of natural gas, thus contributed on the demand side to the shortage of natural gas which arose in the late 1960s. On the other hand, quota-protected oil production also increased natural gas production because natural gas reserves are sometimes found in the course of the search for oil.

The oil import quota produced only small support for the domestic coal industry because the major substitute for coal, residual fuel oil, was exempted from control in District I early in the program. In this market, the coal industry had to compete with free market oil prices, with the consequence that East Coast utilities became increasingly dependent on low-cost imported fuel oil. Still, however, some other coal markets were promoted by quota-supported oil prices. Thus, somewhat greater coal displacement would have occurred with free trade in oil, and the coal industry would have deteriorated further in its long period of decline starting in the late 1940s. Consequently, the industry would perhaps have been even less capable of meeting the growing increases in consumption that have occurred in the past few years.

Refining

Important distortions were imposed on the refining segment of the petroleum industry by the quota system. The quota discouraged the expansion of domestic refinery capacity, altered refinery location within the United States, altered the mix of final products, encouraged investment in cracking capacity, and discouraged investment in capacity to handle high-sulfur feedstocks. In part these distortions resulted from the general effects of import controls and in part from the specific provisions of the mandatory quota program.

The general effects of the quota resulted from price rigidities, from limited access to high-sulfur foreign feedstocks, and from uncertainties about adequate supplies of domestic feedstocks. Refinery capacity was not built to handle additional domestic crude because it became increasingly evident that additional supplies would not be forthcoming. Refineries were not built in adequate amounts to handle foreign feedstocks either. Import controls and expectations of such controls appeared to limit access to necessary feedstocks, and given the uncertainties involved, it appeared wiser to many firms to build refineries offshore. The offshore location provided flexibility in the face of regulatory uncertainties. As we note in chapter 5, some of these facilities were given access to U.S. markets. Consequently, domestic refinery capacity began to lag behind final product demand. To meet demand, importers increasingly sought to switch away from crude oil and toward finished products, and this switch was approved by import control authorities who foresaw domestic shortages if it was not allowed. The result was that the mandatory quota program discouraged investment in domestic refining and encouraged investment in foreign refining.[43]

The lack of domestic capacity to process high-sulfur (sour) foreign feedstocks created special problems after 1973. The bulk of domestic crude oil is low in sulfur content, while the most abundant foreign crude oil is high in sulfur content. Refineries built to handle low-sulfur crude must be reequipped to process sour crude. Thus, when some oil supplies were restricted, sour varieties of foreign oil could not be substituted for scarcer low-sulfur oil, and the shortages of feedstock for U.S. refineries were greater than the world reduction in supply alone necessitated.

[43] For more on the export of refinery capacity abroad, see Glenn P. Jenkins and Brian D. Wright, "Taxation of Income of Multinational Corporations: The Case of the United States Petroleum Industry," *The Review of Economics and Statistics* vol. LVII, no. 1 (February 1975) pp. 1–11.

Table 8-8. U.S. Refinery Capacity and Petroleum Product
Consumption, 1930–70

(million bbl/day)

Year	Operating refinery capacity (1)	Domestic petroleum consumption (2)	Ratio (1) ÷ (2) (3)
1930	3.7	2.5	1.48
1935	3.7	2.7	1.37
1940	4.2	3.6	1.17
1945	5.1	4.9	1.04
1950	6.7	6.5	1.03
1952	7.5	7.3	1.03
1954	8.1	7.8	1.04
1956	8.8	8.8	1.00
1958	9.4	9.1	1.03
1960	9.5	9.7	0.98
1962	9.8	10.2	0.96
1964	10.1	10.8	0.94
1966	10.2	11.8	0.86
1968	11.2	13.1	0.83
1970	11.9	14.7	0.81

Sources: American Petroleum Institute, *Petroleum Facts and Figures*, 1971 edition, pp.
140 and 283–284; and U.S. Bureau of Mines, *Minerals Yearbook*, 1972, p. 910.

The relationship between U.S. refinery capacity and domestic
petroleum product consumption for the period from 1930 to 1970
is shown in table 8-8. In the years up to 1960, refinery capacity exceeded domestic product consumption, with the excess available
to process crude oil for export. After 1960, the deficit in refinery
capacity steadily widened. From 1960 to 1970, refinery capacity increased a total of 25.2 percent while domestic product consumption grew by 52 percent, or more than twice as fast. Thus, the
United States became increasingly dependent on product imports.
When U.S. crude production declined after 1970, and high-sulfur
foreign crude could not be used, the dependence on product imports was exacerbated.

The conclusion that the quota protected domestic oil production thus cannot be extended to cover protection of domestic refinery capacity. Freer access to foreign crude would have reduced
the incentive to export refinery capacity and would have promoted
investment in high-sulfur crude oil processing facilities. Moreover,
to the extent that higher prices resulting from the quota discouraged final consumption, another damper was placed on refinery investment. Free trade would have reduced domestic oil

Table 8-9. Operating Refinery Capacity of Four Northern States, 1930–70
(thousand bbl/day)

Year	Minnesota	Montana	North Dakota	Wisconsin	Total
1930	—ᵃ	19.6	—	—	19.6
1935	—	21.6	—	—	21.6
1940	2.4	32.1	—	5.0	39.5
1945	8.0	35.8	—	5.0	48.8
1950	8.0	52.5	—	6.0	66.5
1955	50.2	65.6	35.6	6.0	157.4
1960	67.8	83.4	42.9	20.0	214.1
1965	104.8	111.2	46.7	25.0	287.7
1970	138.3	125.1	53.0	29.0	345.4

Source: American Petroleum Institute, Petroleum Facts and Figures (1971) pp. 139–140.
ᵃ — indicates no commercial refining capacity.

production, but not oil processing. Refinery capacity appears to be more dependent on the location of the market than the location of crude oil production.[44]

Special provisions in the quota program also created incentives affecting the location of refineries and the refinery output mix that proved troublesome later on. The special treatment of imports of Canadian crude oil, starting with the voluntary program in 1957, encouraged the location of refineries along the U.S. northern border. The increase in refinery capacity in Minnesota, Montana, North Dakota, and Wisconsin is shown in table 8-9. With the end of the quota program and the general increase in crude prices, these refineries could not compete with other domestic refineries better located to receive U.S. crude oil or imported feedstocks. Then, with the reduction and prospective elimination of Canadian crude oil exports, these refineries, and the markets they served, faced especially severe problems. Special allocation programs were required to keep them in business and, as of 1976, extraordinary efforts were being considered to move Alaskan oil into these markets.

Imports of products from Puerto Rico and the Virgin Islands received special treatment under the quota system. Consequently, refineries were encouraged to locate in these islands for reasons other than those the free market would dictate.

[44] Note, for example, the existence of a large refinery industry in several European countries and the location of U.S. East Coast refineries.

Table 8-10. U.S. Residual Fuel Oil Production and Imports, 1935–71
(million barrels)

Year	U.S. production	U.S. imports	Year	U.S. production	U.S. imports
1935	259.8	16.1	1964	266.8	295.8
1940	316.2	29.4	1965	268.6	345.2
1945	469.5	31.6	1966	263.9	376.8
1950	425.2	120.0	1967	275.9	395.9
1955	420.3	152.0	1968	275.8	409.9
1960	332.2	233.2	1969	265.9	461.6
1961	315.6	243.3	1970	257.5	557.8
1962	295.7	264.3	1971	274.7	557.7
1963	275.9	272.8			

Sources: American Petroleum Institute, Petroleum Facts and Figures (1971) p. 176; and Bureau of Mines, Minerals Yearbook, various dates.

The exemption of residual fuel oil imports from control altered the product mix capability of domestic refineries and created a special dependence on imports of heavy fuels. The drop in U.S. production of resid after 1955, and the increase in resid imports, is shown in table 8-10. A downward trend in residual fuel as a proportion of total output was evident before the import control program, as shown in table 8-11. From 1955 to 1965 the percent yield of resid per barrel of crude input was halved. This shift was partially explained by other factors, as we note in chapter 5.

When world oil prices began to rise after 1970, resid prices rose in response to the market, while other domestic prices increased only after the world price exceeded the domestic price. Consequently, compared with others, resid users experienced more rapid price increases between 1969 and 1974, due in part to the delayed effects of oil import policy. The years of virtually uncontrolled imports of resid, based on the world crude oil price, had so reduced domestic residual fuel oil production capacity that oil price controls following the expiration of the Economic Stabilization Act in 1974 had to be applied differently to this product than to others. While for most other products the allowed price charged by refineries was based on blended crude costs plus some markup, for residual fuel oil, the refiners were allowed to charge a virtually unregulated price, except that resid revenues were counted in the overall revenue constraint faced by firms. It was understood that the residual fuel oil price was set by the world market and that the

Table 8-11. Average Percentage Yield of U.S. Refineries, 1930–70

Year	Gasoline	Kerosine	Distillates	Residual	Others
1930	42.1	5.3	8.8	31.5	12.3
1935	44.2	5.8	10.4	26.8	12.8
1940	43.1	5.7	14.1	24.4	12.7
1945	40.5	4.7	14.5	27.2	13.1
1950	43.0	5.6	19.0	20.2	12.2
1955	44.0	4.3	22.0	15.3	14.4
1960	45.2	4.6	22.4	11.2	16.6
1961	44.7	4.7	23.2	10.5	16.9
1962	44.8	5.1	23.2	9.6	17.3
1963	44.1	5.1	23.9	8.6	18.3
1964	44.1	2.9	22.8	8.2	22.0
1965	44.0	2.8	23.0	8.0	22.2
1966	44.4	2.9	22.5	7.6	22.6
1967	44.0	2.7	22.2	7.7	23.4
1968	43.9	2.7	22.1	7.2	24.1
1969	44.8	2.6	21.7	6.8	24.1
1970	45.3	2.3	22.4	6.4	23.6

Sources: American Petroleum Institute, *Petroleum Facts and Figures* (1971) p. 203, and U.S. Bureau of Mines, *Minerals Yearbook*, various dates.

U.S. price could not be held down as it could be for other products. In summary, the quota program had encouraged, through relatively cheap imports, northeastern utilities and other consumers to favor heavy fuel oil and encouraged domestic refineries to alter their output mix toward the lighter products. When the special incentives ended, and all petroleum products became much more expensive, residual fuel oil consumers had to adjust more than did the rest of the economy. And they could not be protected by price controls. Those regions which developed exaggerated dependencies on this fuel thus found themselves more severely affected than were others after 1973 because residual fuel oil prices rose relative to other fuel prices. It should be remembered, however, that these same regions had benefited from preferential access to low-cost fuel during the preceding decade.

Concluding Remarks

The mandatory quota program distorted the allocation of resources and led to the development of a different energy sector in the United States than would otherwise have occurred. In some ways these differences proved beneficial in adjusting to the energy problems imposed in 1973, and in other ways they proved harmful.

On a different plane, the quota induced a quicker drawdown of the U.S. resource base, raising the question whether short-run energy security was achieved only at the cost of long-run security. Certainly each barrel left in the ground would still be there, but whether it would be equally available is more complex. For example, some wells abandoned because of free trade prices may not be reentered, for physical and economic reasons, so that oil left in the ground would not be equally available later. In addition, the quota coupled with production controls reduced the willingness of firms to explore for "bonanza" fields; they preferred instead to develop known and marginal reserves more intensely. This distortion may have resulted in a saving of some resources for the future.

In addition to these economic distortions, the quota system established vested interests that continued to influence energy policy after 1973. Property rights created by the quota system, sometimes in the form of support for uneconomic facilities and inefficient operations, were continued after the quota ended. The system disadvantaged some firms and consumers while benefiting others. The distortions may have been small and sometimes unidentifiable in the data. However, the strength of the feelings of special interests reported in chapter 5 attests to the importance of the incentives created. In some cases precedents were established that continued after the mandatory quota program ended. In other cases the removal of special treatment would have severely affected recipients.

Alternative measures to improve energy security would have had different effects. Even though it is difficult to strike the balance between social benefits and costs of the mandatory quota program, it is possible to compare its results with those of alternatives which would have had similar security-enhancing effects. This question is addressed in the next chapter.

9

Alternatives to the Quota

The effects of the mandatory quota program, as noted in the preceding chapters, were to impose higher energy costs on the American public, encourage depletion of American energy resources, maintain a larger oil production industry, reduce oil imports during 1959–73, and lessen the impact of the 1973 embargo and corresponding world price increases. These same policy goals could have been achieved in other ways; an important question is whether some of these alternatives may have been more attractive than the course selected. This issue is not of historical interest alone because petroleum policy in the foreseeable future may be forced to address again the direct limitation of oil imports, or other measures to enhance security of energy supplies.

While analysis of the mandatory quota program and alternatives to it provides some insights into energy security policy, no unambiguous recommendations can evolve from this exercise because any conclusions depend upon specific goals and criteria selected. The policy process did not provide any clear definition of the goals and criteria for performance of the mandatory quota program, nor is the political process likely to do so in the future. In the analysis that follows we proceed on the assumption that the true goals of the program may be inferred from its results in enhancing energy security, and endeavor to compare the cost of the quota with that of alternatives implemented to achieve a similar effect. There are problems in this approach because the quota program had secondary effects, many of which may be regarded as positive. These give rise to competing criteria for measuring success. In addition,

301

the quota program created a number of unintended results that may be regarded as undesirable, but which, like the indirect effects of alternatives, are impossible to weigh objectively in seeking the best option. Such comparisons can be made only on subjective grounds, if at all, and cannot be factored into any formal cost–benefit calculations.

Nevertheless, it is useful and interesting to compare some essential features of different policy tools that might be applied to limit either the amount of, or the risk associated with, oil imports. The mandatory quota program provides a unique experiment in the implementation of an important public policy, and timely lessons for the future may be acquired in viewing it in the context of alternative policies forgone. The alternatives compared here include tariffs, subsidies, consumption taxes, storage, and standby capacity. Before making the comparisons, however, we must digress to consider in greater detail the problems of policy choices in general, and of those surrounding the attainment of energy security in particular.

The Mandatory Quota Program and the National Security Objective

The relationship between U.S. oil imports and energy security and, in turn, between energy security and national security, is complex. These relationships depend only superficially on the percentage of oil consumption satisfied by imports. There is, first, the general question of whether less imports are always better than more imports. If this simple rule held, then the security goal would be successfully and unambiguously achieved when imports were reduced to zero. This rule does not hold, however, because not all imports pose a threat to national security, and because the elimination of all imports could impose costs on the economy that would so weaken it as to adversely affect national security. A less simple and more difficult approach to the national security question must be followed.

The relation between oil imports and national security encompasses a number of factors. First of all, national security includes many things in addition to energy security; for example, the economic cost of any program and its international implications must be considered. Further, even energy security itself is dependent on more than the simple proportion of oil consumption that is imported. Briefly, and partially, before this relationship can be judged relative to security levels attained, the capability to convert petroleum-using facilities to other fuels, to reduce consumption by taxation or end-use controls in an emergency, and to substitute other factors for energy must be taken into account. In addition, some consideration must be given to how much domestic production can be increased and to how much stocks can be drawn down during an emergency. Finally, the risk of import disruption must be factored in; imports from different foreign sources must be assigned different risk levels, and those risk levels in turn adjusted by the potential diversion of U.S. supplies to other consuming nations during periods of world supply disruptions.

Public statements and discussions during the period leading up to the mandatory quota program did not provide a clear indication of objectives, nor did they indicate an awareness of the complexities involved. The program was based upon an explicit statement that imports must be restricted in the interests of national security, and that the program was designed to support a "healthy" industry which would provide "ample" reserves and producing capacity for some undefined period into the future.[1] But there was no attempt to define what was meant by national security, by a healthy industry, or what were ample reserves. No scales of performance were provided for what might be expected of the industry under various hypothetical situations, present and future. Furthermore, no attempt was made to relate the volume of imports to other factors affecting the future supply of domestic oil or, for that matter, to the wider complex of energy industries.

The absence of any official analysis of the security problem posed by oil imports, at least prior to the Cabinet Task Force report, is perhaps not surprising when one reflects upon the circumstances under which the program was adopted. The origins of the program may be regarded as "political," in the narrow sense of responding to the protectionist efforts of the domestic oil producers. From such evidence as is available, it appears almost certain that, during the rising tempo of these efforts from 1950

[1] Refer to Proclamation 3279 in the appendix to chapter 3.

to 1955, the officials responsible for security planning were not much interested in the oil import question. The 1959 invocation of the security clause in the Trade Agreement Extension Act of 1955 took on the character of a tactical move to head off the drive for protectionist legislation by the Congress, rather than of a measured response to a perceived threat to national security. Protective legislation would have cut right across the declared policy of the American government to promote freer trade, as expressed in the General Agreement on Tariffs and Trade (GATT). By retaining discretionary action in its own hands, the Executive Branch could at least explain any action in the most favorable light, and thus minimize both hard feelings and harsh counter moves on the part of affected countries. This was important in the postwar American effort to keep countries aligned with the United States in order to ward off the penetration of communist influences. Collective security based on common economic interest was one of the cornerstones of the broader American security policy.

As circumstances developed, however, the purely tactical goal of warding off congressional action appears to have given way to real concern over the prospective flood of foreign oil. It really did appear that a substantial portion of the domestic industry faced imminent ruin. It could therefore be reasonably held that, on grounds of security, the potential flood of foreign oil should be dammed. Implementation of this general policy required that the appropriate level of imports be specified. As is usually the case in such matters, the easiest solution was to adopt the status quo as the standard and to relate the allowed level of imports to it. This is the substance of import policy from 1957 to 1970. A proportional relationship was established which was only slightly modified in principle until complete removal of controls. Import control has been, therefore, a holding operation behind which the domestic producing industry might operate with whatever "vigor" it was capable of displaying. Given this essentially passive character of import policy, it is understandable that the responsible authorities never felt it necessary to elaborate their views on the contribution of the domestic crude oil industry to national security. Under the circumstances, it is also not surprising that formal policy discussions did not elaborate on the program's role in various emergencies that could be hypothesized and that might have to be faced.

The circumstances facing the oil industry in the late 1950s were serious and the intensity of the drive for protection reflected this condition. The issue facing the producers was the impending destruction of large segments of an industry upon which other elements depended. Thousands of small producers were dependent upon market demand prorationing to assure them a share of the refinery market, and that system was threatened by an import flow which would cause an intolerable restriction of production. Back of these primary producers lay the interests of an array of auxiliary enterprises—independent refiners, drilling firms, equipment suppliers, service contractors, and the like: and back of them the livelihoods of numerous local communities. Still further back, the economic and fiscal structures of the main oil-producing states were at hazard. It was not doubted that the vast supply of cheap foreign oil that was developing would, in the absence of restrictive measures, have flowed into American markets, with devastating effects upon some segments of the domestic producing industry. The magnitudes involved are indicated in our analysis in chapter 8, where we conclude that domestic output would have fallen by almost one half and price by one third. The issues which led to the protectionist demands for restriction were not trivial. A potentially serious problem existed.

Accepting or understanding this view does not, however, provide any answer concerning the type and degree of import restriction to be applied. Policy would have to fall between one or the other of two antithetical goals—protection of domestic vested interests and enterprises or greater freedom of foreign trade. The whole controversy over import control would have been much more clear-cut if it could have been conducted in these terms, following the lines of the historic arguments over import controls. The exigencies of the situation, however, did not permit the debate to follow these lines. The national government was committed to a policy of promoting freer trade, as expressed in its subscription to the principles of GATT. Effective action to protect the oil industry could be taken as a measure to promote national security, permitted by GATT. Therefore, the argument for protection was forced into the mold of concern for national security.

Since national security and not trade policy provided the rationale for import controls, every discussion has been centered around national security. The heart of the argument is that imports should be so restricted that the incentives to search for new oil would keep reserves and producing capacity at some chosen level in relation to the requirements for domestic oil. As noted by the Cabinet Task Force, "This will require us to consider what portion of domestic (and perhaps allied) oil demand is essential; what interruptions from what sources and to what extent are 'reasonably possible'; and what alternative supplies are or might be available from ordinary and emergency sources."[2] Nevertheless, the report provided no systematic analysis relating dependence on oil imports to the degree of risk to national security. On one hand, the report concluded that "a phased-in liberalization of import controls would not so injure the domestic industry as to weaken the national economy to the extent of impairing our national security,"[3] but, on the other hand, "We are unable to present evidence to rule out the possibility that abandonment of all import controls would result in an inability to satisfy our essential oil requirements by acceptable emergency measures in response to certain conceivable supply interruptions."[4] The report does not provide any indication of a "threatening" level of imports, but does suggest the rule of thumb that dependence upon Eastern Hemisphere oil for more than 10 percent of domestic consumption would constitute a threat to national security.[5] The report codified the strategic argument that had been made by protectionists over the life of the efforts to limit imports. Chapter 4 described the controversy over the salient issue—the criteria for the level of imports. The "tactical" efforts to sustain the prescribed criteria were found in the battles against various special exemptions which would weaken the program—described in chapter 5.

On the basis of the criteria we infer were selected, the mandatory quota program must be regarded a success: domestic production was higher and imports lower relative to the free market alternative. The short-run national security was, in the crude definition of the day, enhanced. As of 1969, according to our esti-

<hr />

[2] *The Oil Import Question*, A Report on the Relationship of Oil Imports to the National Security, prepared by the Cabinet Task Force on Oil Import Control (Washington, GPO, 1970) p. 8.

[3] Ibid., p. 129.

[4] Ibid.

[5] Ibid., p. 98.

mates, the quota prevented the displacement of nearly 4 MM bbl/ day of domestic production by imports. Without the quota, and had nothing else changed, imports would have amounted to half of domestic demand by 1969; perhaps more importantly, 40 percent of consumption would have been supplied by Eastern Hemisphere sources. The program thus benefited the nation by reducing many adjustment costs that would have been required after the 1973 price increase. Certainly the mandatory quota program placed the United States in a position where it could pursue a much more flexible foreign policy than would have been the case with free trade. Had the United States been faced with the 1973 Arab–Israeli war under circumstances where a substantial part of U.S. oil was imported from Arab sources, it could not have acted as it did. The enlarged economic cost of a petroleum supply disruption might have led to reduced concern for Israel or to a less passive response to the Arab nations; the higher level of domestic energy supply made a more flexible response possible and provided time for a measured consideration of alternatives. In essence, the effects of the mandatory quota program made it possible to loosen the otherwise confining link between oil supply and foreign policy.

In achieving these results, the program increased the direct fuel bill of consumers in excess of $5 billion a year. The program encouraged a more rapid depletion of the U.S. resource base and created distortions in the industry, primarily in refining, that reduced the industry's capacity to adjust to events after the change in world oil market conditions. The issue remains as to whether the valuable national security gains could have been won at lower cost by use of programs other than the one adopted.

Problems of Comparing Policy Alternatives

The previous section has noted that the public policy goal of the mandatory quota program was to enhance national security, and that in gross terms this goal was promoted by the program. It is also clear, however, that the means by which national security was served by the program can only be inferred—they were not specified. There are many possible linkages between goals and instruments and the linkages are neither exclusive nor totally complementary. Consequently, an alternative instrument may achieve the same goal through a different mechanism, with different costs and subsidiary effects, and thus not be strictly comparable with the mandatory quota program. Unless tradeoffs are quantified, comparisons are at best imperfect, and at worst impossible. Seven proximate goals, or linkages between policy instruments and the national security goal, may be identified:

1. maintaining a fixed ratio of imports to domestic production;
2. maintaining a given amount of domestic production;
3. reducing the volume of imports;
4. reducing domestic consumption of oil;
5. reducing the volume of imports by a given amount with the least impact on domestic consumption;
6. reducing the long-run depletion of the U.S. oil reserve base;
7. providing capability for covering an interruption of imports.

Most of these proximate goals may be achieved by the mandatory quota program, and some or all of them by alternative instruments. With each mechanism, however, different costs and subsidiary effects are incurred, and these must be appropriately weighted and compared in selecting the package of policy instruments applied. Only in this way can a standard for an optimal policy evolve.

On the basis of the discussion in chapter 7, it may be argued that the proportional quota system (i.e., limiting imports to a proportion of domestic production) used in the mandatory quota program is superior to a tariff or conventional quota used alone if the objective is (1) to maintain a fixed ratio of imports to domestic production or (2) to maintain domestic production when superiority is defined to mean that the same results are achieved at less cost to consumers. On the other hand, judged on the same criterion, the tariff or conventional quota is preferable to a proportional quota if the proximate goal is (3) to reduce the volume of imports or (4) to reduce domestic consumption.

In another respect, a tariff is superior to a quota of either type because, to a greater degree, the price system continues to serve its resource allocation function. However, changes in foreign prices would be transferred to the domestic market and might affect one's preference for a quota or tariff, depending on the behavior pattern world prices are expected to follow. If the world price is expected to be unstable, the quota provides better protection to domestic production by insulating the market from erratic price changes. If the world price is expected to move upward, the tariff maintains the protective effect for producers (at the expense of consumers) while a fixed quota becomes less protective. If the world price is expected to move downward, the quota becomes increasingly protective relative to the tariff, but with the tariff consumers would benefit from a falling price. Other reasons for preferring either a tariff or a quota were discussed in chapter 7.

A subsidy to domestic producers may be preferred to either tariffs or quotas if the objective is to maintain domestic production while permitting consumption consistent with the world price. Conversely, the consumption tax may be the preferred approach if the objective is to reduce domestic consumption, and thereby imports, and yet force domestic production to compete at the free market price. However, as discussed further below, if a combination of the production and consumption effects is desired, a tariff or quota may be preferred to a subsidy and consumption tax. Subsidies or taxes aimed at specific segments of the industry, or at specific kinds of consumption, may also be used in conjunction with other policies.

Finally, use of strategic storage of oil and shut-in reserve capacity may be preferred to the other policies when the goal is protection against short-run supply interruptions and minimum interference with the market is desired. Storage and shut-in capacity provide passive protection against an interruption of imports. They allow market forces to allocate resources, permit the conservation of the domestic resource base, and reduce the probability of an embargo by increasing the cost of an embargo to the exporting country while reducing its cost to the importer. The important considerations here are the costs of storing or shutting in sufficient supplies to cover prospective import interruptions, and the manner in which those costs are covered.

Comparing the Policy Instruments

The procedure followed below in comparing the tariff, subsidy, consumption tax, storage, and standby reserve instruments with the mandatory quota program is to assume that the estimates in chapter 8 are correct in determining what would have happened from 1960 to 1970 without the program, and then to estimate the cost of obtaining a similar protective effect, defined in various ways, with each alternative instrument used alone. Other ancillary features of each device will be discussed as well.

Tariffs

The conceptual differences and similarities between tariffs and quota have already been discussed in detail in chapter 7 and need not be repeated here. It is important to emphasize, however, that a tariff could have reduced imports by the same extent as the quota without many of the side effects that resulted from interference with the price mechanism. The resource cost of the quota program was far higher than its gross, directly observable, effects indicate. In addition to these costs, the program also eroded confidence in the objectivity and responsiveness of government. Essentially arbitrary decisions, however innocently and honorably reached, inevitably caused suspicion of the decision process itself. Further, the differential effects of the program resulted in market responses which were transformed into an industry configuration which was in numerous respects uneconomic. The fact that this configuration was induced by government-created property rights has served as a justification for its continuation. When the mandatory quota program is compared with a price-oriented alternative such as the tariff, the proper measures on the quota side should therefore include the value of the wasted resources resulting from the distortions which are handed down—not just the losses from the misallocation of resources during the life of the program.

As for the direct effects on the crude oil market, three essential differences between a tariff and a quota were demonstrated in chapter 7: a tariff would lower the price paid to domestic producers, raise the average price paid by refiners, and transfer the scarcity value of imports from refiners to the government in the form of tax revenues. Figure 7-2 (page 255) provides a guide in measuring these differences, assuming the objective is to achieve the same ratio of imports to domestic production under a tariff as under the mandatory quota program. In this case, the tariff rate added to the import price P_w must be sufficient to raise the domestic price to P_t. Domestic production would be Q_2, consumption would be Q_4, imports would be $(Q_4 - Q_2)$, and the ratio of imports to domestic products would be $(Q_4 - Q_2)/Q_2$. Tariff revenues would be the amount $(P_t - P_w)(Q_4 - Q_2)$. Relative to the tariff, the proportional quota would boost the price to domestic producers to P_s, lower the average price to refiners to P_c, increase domestic production to Q_3, increase consumption to Q_5, and still result in the equal ratio of imports to domestic production $(Q_5 - Q_3)/Q_3$.[6] Rents accruing to refiners with the proportional quota would be equal to the difference between the marginal cost of oil and the import price, times the amount of imports, i.e., $(Q_5 - Q_3)(P_c - P_w)$.

Using the figures derived in chapter 8, these expressions may be quantified. The average 1969 domestic price was $3.27 per barrel, the import price was $2.10, so the average price to refiners was $3.14.[7] Rents accruing to refiners that would be lost with the tariff would be ($3.14 − $2.10) × 0.7 billion barrels/year = $728 million per year at the 1969 rate of crude oil imports.

By comparison, the tariff-included price would fall somewhere between $3.27 and $3.14 (i.e., between P_s and P_c). The differential is not very large, so it would not be far wrong to take the intermediate point of $3.20 as the tariff-included price, with the implied tariff rate equal to $1.10 per barrel. The slight reduction in the price of domestic oil to producers and the slight increase in the average price to refiners would not create measurable changes in production, consumption, or imports. The effect of prorationing would be the transfer of rents to the federal government as tariff revenues, including refiner's rents as calculated above plus a slight reduction in rents to domestic producers, totaling approximately $770 million (equal to $1.10 × 0.7 billion barrels). This figure is the amount of revenue that is lost to government through adoption of a proportional quota program rather than a tariff.

In summary, a tariff designed to limit imports to the same percentage of domestic production as the mandatory quota program would not significantly affect production, consumption, or imports, but would transfer rents from producers and refiners to the

---

[6] Equality of these two ratios is demonstrated in chapter 7.

[7] This is given by $[3.27 + (0.122) 2.10]/1.22 = (P_s + kP_w)/(k/1 + k)$ where k is the ratio of imports to domestic production (0.122).

federal government. The tariff rate would have to be periodically adjusted upward to maintain a fixed import ratio as domestic demand and foreign prices increase, but this constitutes a desirable feature of tariffs in that market changes are reflected in price changes.

Subsidies

As an alternative to import controls, the federal government could provide subsidies to domestic production in order to increase domestic output and limit the volume of imports. An estimate of the amount of the subsidy required to limit imports to the same ratio to domestic production that they had during the mandatory quota program is obtained below using the assumptions and data provided in chapter 8. A discussion of the advantages and disadvantages of the subsidy alternative follows.

While import controls combine the effects of subsidies and consumption taxes, a subsidy alone increases the price received by sellers without increasing the price paid by buyers (except indirectly as consumers are also taxpayers). Consumers pay the world price of oil, while producers receive an additional per barrel payment from the government. It was estimated in chapter 8 that U.S. consumption would have been 5.5 billion barrels per year by 1969 at the free trade price of $2.10/bbl, domestic production would have been 2.2 billion barrels, and imports would have been 3.3 billion barrels.

In order to achieve the same ratio of imports to domestic production as existed under the program in 1969 (17.9 percent), a subsidy must encourage enough additional production to replace all but 840 million barrels of consumption per year, i.e., must increase production from 2.2 billion barrels to 4.66 billion barrels. Using the long-run supply elasticity estimate of 1.0, this would be achieved if the price received by producers were increased from $2.10/bbl to $4.45/bbl, implying a subsidy of $2.35/bbl.[8] On these assumptions, total government subsidy payments to industry would have amounted to $10.95 billion per year at the 1969 rate.

---

[8] These and other estimates could be rounded to avoid the impression of undue precision, but that would make it difficult for the reader to duplicate the calculations.

The subsidy must be established several years in advance to achieve the desired level of domestic production by 1969 because of production lags. For earlier years, the lower volume of production would, of course, require smaller government subsidy payments. But as consumption continued to expand beyond the 1969 rate, the required subsidy would have to be adjusted upward to maintain a fixed ratio of imports to production. The magnitude of the estimate for 1969 suggests that the costs would have been unacceptable had sole reliance been placed on this device. Nevertheless, because of their ancillary effects, a limited use of subsidies might in some respects have been attractive as part of a national security package.

The general attributes of a subsidy are modified by the precise instrument utilized. Possibilities include both direct payments from the Treasury and indirect subsidies such as support of research and development programs or sharing of risks associated with energy production.[9] The cost effectiveness of indirect versus direct subsidies varies with the inefficiencies forced into the decision mechanism by their implementation. While the indirect-direct distinction need not be considered further here, when energy security is in question, there are important differences between subsidies based on increased energy supply *capacity* and those based on energy *output*. Greater capacity would be implanted with a direct capital subsidy than with an equivalent subsidy for production. The public infusion of resources is direct and immediate with a capital subsidy; no uncertainty exists. Note, however, that a capital subsidy leaves a firm dependent on market price and unit variable factor costs for its output decision. The firm has no choice

---

[9] Firms could be rewarded for units of energy produced and sold, with direct payment from the government upon proof of fuel transfer to a consuming party. Indirect subsidies could take such forms as the below-cost provision of goods and services to energy producers and reduced tax obligations. Research and development, subsidized transportation services, subsidized credit, free use of the environment for waste disposal, access to public mineral resources and water come immediately to mind as transfers of public assets to the energy sector. Tax subsidy devices are numerous: rapid tax writeoffs, investment tax credits, and depletion deductions beyond the level required to compensate for the wastage of the capital asset are among those which have been used. The discussion in the remainder of this section follows that found in Douglas R. Bohi and Milton Russell, *U.S. Energy Policy: Alternatives for Security* (Baltimore, Johns Hopkins University Press for Resources for the Future, 1975) chapter 5.

but to operate so long as its variable costs are covered by the market price. Because variable costs are controllable by the ultimate stratagem of varying the rate of production, capital subsidies lead to greater fluctuations in output than do equivalent production subsidies. Capacity exists to respond to emergencies without concomitant depletion of the domestic resource base. With production subsidies, on the other hand, output will not be restricted so long as variable costs are covered by the sum of market price and the unit subsidy. Thus fluctuations in output will be dampened with a per unit subsidy, though total capacity would be smaller. If the goal is to provide energy security, a subsidy on capacity can be presumed to be more cost effective.

There are other, more general reasons, to favor a capital subsidy over a production subsidy. After the original infusion of capital, no interference with the market mechanism is required. Individual consumers and producers act in a fashion that allocates resources efficiently. Further, capital subsidies reduce one barrier to entry in the energy industry. More competition is encouraged than if output were subsidized. Finally, the capital subsidy mechanism provides an opportunity to consider social costs and benefits beyond the nexus of the market decision. Superior overall allocation can result from capital subsidies where externalities are important, as they often are in energy supply. Though the subsidy process itself may be questionable as an effective or desirable government policy, if subsidies nonetheless are chosen as policy instruments, they should be placed on capital, not on output.

Perhaps the strongest case for government subsidies may be made for using the medium of government-sponsored energy research and development, including activities devoted to reducing energy consumption. The government could assist in the funding and dissemination of geological knowledge with reference to petroleum production or in funding research and capital costs for new energy technologies. In the latter case, an agency of the government could catalog unproven prospective energy supply techniques, array them in terms of their probable cost effectiveness, and fund those necessary to meet the appropriate quantitative energy goals. Each prospective technique could be pursued until it is proven to be technically and economically feasible or infeasible; abandoned if infeasible; released for commercial exploitation if feasible. With reference to energy consumption, a similar course could be followed with regard to technical "fixes" which reduce energy use in fulfilling consumer wants. The resulting information and patents would be in the public domain. The increased domestic energy production and reduced consumption induced by such measures to some extent would come at the expense of private sector activity. The net gains thus would be smaller—in some cases substantially smaller or even negative—than the apparent results such programs indicate.

Going beyond research and development efforts, the government could absorb the risk of producing additional domestic energy by direct involvement in production.[10] Extensive discussion of government production lies beyond the scope of this work, but it should be noted that government production would lower real energy costs only to the extent that economies of scale were exploited or other private-sector inefficiencies eliminated. Hence taxpayer support would be substituted for consumer support, and the cost would approximate that of the pure subsidy. Whatever the method of the subsidy, the result is the same: taxpayers by class are made worse off, and consumers better off, than through alternative mechanisms.

Consumption Tax

Energy security of a sort could also have been achieved by imposing a consumption tax which would have held petroleum use to a sufficiently low level that the ratio of imports to domestic production would have been no larger than under the mandatory quota program. In terms of the estimates in chapter 8 for 1969, the required consumption tax would have to be high enough to reduce consumption from the free trade level of 5.5 billion barrels per year to 2.6 billion barrels, leaving imports at 400 million barrels (recalling that free trade domestic production was estimated at 2.2 billion barrels). For long-run equilibrium to have been established, this tax would have had to have been in place for a number of years. On this basis, and assuming a long-run elasticity of

---

[10] The institutional device selected for this function is immaterial. For example, cost-plus contracts would have the same economic implications as would a government corporation.

demand over the relevant price range of —0.5, a price of $4.31/bbl would have held imports to 400 million barrels in 1969. The consumption tax would therefore have been $2.21/bbl, or over 100 percent, and total revenues would amount to $5.75 billion per year.

While a tax of this magnitude is clearly unpalatable in its implications for the domestic economy, there is substantial European experience with petroleum product taxes in this range, and the implied 100 percent levy can be compared to the approximately 50 percent "tax" imposed by the mandatory quota program. Sole reliance upon a consumption tax to restrict imports is unpalatable primarily because overall production in the economy would be reduced to meet the import objective. That is, only imperfect substitutes exist for oil.[11] With use of a consumption tax for energy security purposes, no part of the burden of restricting imports is absorbed by domestic supply enhancement, as it is with use of a quota or a tariff. Nonetheless, at least partial reliance on an energy consumption tax was a policy option—and one not taken.

Two major issues are involved in selection of an energy consumption tax instrument. First, should the tax be placed on the energy-consuming device (a capital tax) or on energy consumption itself? Second, should the tax be placed on all energy consumption (on grounds that the marginal energy input is imported oil) or only on the consumption of that energy in part obtained from insecure sources? The capital tax versus consumption tax issue has been addressed before by inference in connection with subsidies, and given the goal of energy security, the answer is the mirror image of that provided there. A capital tax would leave the energy price at the margin unchanged from the world price. Alternately, a consumption-based tax would require each use of energy to stand on a comparison between its benefits and its (tax-increased) price. On efficiency grounds, and in terms of tax effectiveness, the basis for levying the tax should be consumption. With reference to the

---

[11] A substantial body of literature, both analytical and empirical, is developing on the relationship between energy (and by inference, oil) consumption and the productive capacity of the economy. It is not necessary to cite this literature here, but it is useful to note that *ceteris paribus*, an increase in petroleum prices will reduce both productive capacity and consumer satisfaction. The question at issue revolves around how much.

second issue, a tax on insecure fuels alone may be warranted to encourage substitution of secure fuels. In this case a tax on all petroleum would be implied. Total energy consumed would be reduced, but the proportion produced domestically (of oil and other energy sources as well) would be increased.

Two final points should be made about the income distribution effects of an energy consumption tax. First, it is consistent with national tradition that those who benefit from a service should pay for it. The cost of energy security is real. That it should be borne by energy consumers in proportion to their benefit from energy security seems fair. In the absence of a better method of allocating energy insecurity costs among consumers, a unit tax on insecure fuels seems reasonable. The second point concerns the effect of an energy consumption tax on income distribution. While the regional concerns are serious enough, the effect on distribution by income class presents an even more potent political and economic issue. Any such tax will be borne in part by the poor. Few, if any, systematic and thorough studies of the distributional effects of energy taxes have been made.[12] Even if energy taxes should prove to be regressive, however, and even if the effect should prove substantial, that does not imply that the consumption tax need be abandoned. Devices exist to neutralize the distributional effects of a consumption tax if it were otherwise deemed desirable.

Storage for Emergencies

An emergency supply of oil kept in storage to be used in the event of a supply interruption is an alternative to limiting insecure imports. The problem of supply interruption is bounded by the likelihood of such an event and the quantity of supply that would be affected. Reduction in supply by the oil-exporting nations is essentially an economic weapon used for political ends. The many polit-

---

[12] On a slightly different topic, an unpublished dissertation in progress by Nancy McCarthy Snyder has shown that the total effects of the 1973–74 energy price increase were roughly proportional ("Income Distribution Effects of Increasing Energy Prices," Southern Illinois University). See also Robert A. Herendeen and Jerry Tanaka, *Energy Cost of Living*, CAC document 171 (University of Illinois at Urbana, Champaign Center for Advanced Computation, 1975). These authors found that purchases of energy, including energy embedded in capital and services, rise only slightly less than proportionately with income until rather high income levels are reached.

ical differences among OPEC members all but preclude their finding a common rallying cause to coincidentally reduce supply, and the fungibility of oil makes it extremely difficult to target an embargo.[13] Moreover, the costs of an overall OPEC embargo against the United States would be borne unequally. Venezuela, for example, exports nearly two-thirds of its output to this country. Some OPEC nations export little, if any. Action to minimize the damage from the complete OPEC embargo or supply disruption is thus not required for effective energy security because its likelihood is so small. Also, loss of a portion of imports would not be disruptive because adjustment at low cost would be possible; hence a potential loss of a limited quantity of imports need not be a matter for policy attention, either. Embargo by a group of OPEC nations, or a substantial reduction of supply, is a different matter, as history shows. The Arab countries have attempted to disrupt oil supplies to the United States before, and the geopolitics of the Middle East make future use of the "oil weapon" a continuing possibility. As noted in chapter 8, U.S. dependence on Eastern Hemisphere imports in 1969 would have been as much as 68 percent of total imports, or 40 percent of consumption, if the quota had not been imposed. Most Eastern Hemisphere imports would have come from Arab sources. Interruption of imports of even much smaller volumes would have had serious effects on the U.S. economy.

Of the estimated 2.2 billion barrels which would have been imported from the Eastern Hemisphere in 1969 without the mandatory quota program, perhaps as much as 1.5 billion barrels would have come from Arab sources; this is the quantity we accept as most insecure. It is difficult to anticipate how long an embargo would last. It has been suggested in the context of pre-1973, that a period of 6 months is an upper limit.[14] On these grounds, adequate protection against the worst results of an embargo would be

[13] This statement is perhaps more appropriate for the past than the future. For example, the International Energy Agency oil sharing plan might help producing countries to focus an embargo on participants, although the members account for such a high proportion of demand that the focus is very broad. Also, the prospective reduction in the importance of international oil companies as distributors of OPEC oil, and the trend of producing countries to move into downstream activities, tend to reduce the fungibility of oil in the future.

[14] M. A. Adelman, *The World Petroleum Market* (Baltimore, Johns Hopkins University Press for Resources for the Future, 1972) p. 271.

Table 9-1. Storage Cost Estimates with 1969 Estimated Volumes
($ millions/year)

Six months:	Low estimate[a]	High estimate[b]
Arab imports:		
750 million barrels	338	548
Eastern Hemisphere imports:		
1.100 billion barrels	495	803
Total imports:		
1.650 billion barrels	742	1,204

[a] Using the $0.45/bbl cost estimate; see text.
[b] Using the $0.73/bbl cost estimate; see text.

provided by capacity to replace Arab imports for approximately 180 days. Immediate action to reduce consumption and to increase both domestic output and imports from other sources would stretch 180 days of storage to something like one year's embargo protection.

At an oil price of $2.10 per barrel, the annual cost of oil storage in steel tanks would range between 45 and 73 cents per barrel (at 1969 cost levels), depending on whether the costs were spread over twenty-five years or ten years, respectively, and on whether the discount rates were calculated at 5 percent or 10 percent, respectively.[15] Using these estimates, storage of 180 days of estimated Arab imports in 1969 would have ranged from $338 million to $548 million per year. Annual storage cost of 180 days of total estimated imports would have ranged from $742 million to $1.204 billion (see table 9-1).

Standby Capacity

Standby capacity is an alternative to storage for protection against supply interruption. Such capacity could be developed by prorationing existing private production, by developing new reservoirs, or by using the Naval Petroleum Reserves. The cost of inducing private holders to delay production of their reserves would be equal to the net revenues they forgo. The opportunity cost of

[15] Assuming capital costs composed of tankage costs at $2.50 per barrel; salvage at $0.30; land costs at $0.25; and annual management, repair, maintenance, and evaporation loss of $0.12 per barrel. See *The Oil Import Question,* pp. 301–302.

government-owned capacity would be the same, even though accounting costs might differ. We estimate the cost of reserves used as standby capacity on the presumption that they are in addition to reserves maintained for production and that they therefore bear a higher cost. This perhaps exaggerates the cost because it assumes reserves taken out of production and replaced by imports would not contribute to security. However, the U.S. resource base would be conserved for future use.

The production rate of most reservoirs allows no more than one-tenth of the proved reserves to be produced in the first year. Hence, to have had 4.0 MMb/day shut-in capacity (the estimated rate of Arab imports in 1969) would have implied an increase in reserves of 14.6 billion barrels. To have had 9.0 MM b/day (the estimated 1969 rate of total imports) would have required an incremental 28.8 billion barrels. Proved oil reserves in the United States in 1969 were approximately 30 billion barrels, so these figures imply a 50–100 percent increase in reserves. The exploration effort and annual capital cost required to use shut-in capacity as a primary defense against import interruptions would have been staggering, but certainly smaller than the effort to create continuing self-sufficiency. To place this requirement in perspective, moreover, it is recalled that 1969 idle productive capacity in the United States was estimated at 3.2 MMb/day.[16]

Reserves held on standby need be discovered only once; reserves that are used must be continually replaced. A buildup of standby capacity would have occurred along with the rise in Eastern Hemisphere imports had this policy rather than an import restraint program been adopted. This gradual requirement likely could have been met without increasing factor costs—other, perhaps, than for oil in the ground. Those reservoirs capable of most rapid production could have been dedicated to the standby program, and thus the resource cost per barrel for this capacity could have been below the average cost for produced reservoirs.

To calculate the cost of shut-in capacity, let Q be the quantity of first-year production to be shut in, k the maximum decline

16 Wallace F. Lovejoy, "Oil Conservation, Producing Capacity, and National Security," in A. E. Utton, ed., *National Petroleum Policy: A Critical Review* (Albuquerque, University of New Mexico Press, 1970) p. 84. This figure should be discounted, however, for the reasons given in chapter 7.

rate over the life of the reservoir, r the interest rate, and P the price of crude oil. Then V, the present value of the oil asset, is given by

$$V = \int_{0}^{\infty} PQ \, e^{-(r+k)t} \, dt = \frac{PQ}{(r + k)}$$

for given values of P, Q, r, and k. The present value of this stream of revenues delayed one year is $V/(1 + r)$, so the revenue lost per year by delaying production is

$$V - \frac{V}{1 + r} = V\left(\frac{r}{1 + r}\right)$$

The price required to stimulate exploration and development for additional reserves would have to be above the world price of \$2.10/bbl. To stimulate an additional 4 MMb/day capacity would have required a price of about \$3.50/bbl, using the elasticity assumption of chapter 8, −0.5. This is slightly above the actual 1969 price in order to induce an expansion of capacity from the actual 3.2 MMb/day to 4 MMb/day. Stimulation of an additional 9 MMb/day of production capacity would have required a price of about \$5.25/bbl.

At these prices, and assuming an interest rate of 10 percent and a decline rate of 10 percent, the payment to resource owners for 4 MMb/day of shut-in capacity would amount to \$2.323 billion per year. For 9 MMb/day, the annual payment to resource owners would be \$7.840 billion. These payments must be made for each year that it is desired to have the capacity held back from the market. The payments would have to increase if the market price of oil rose above that used to value shut-in reserves. At higher prices, resource owners would experience opportunity losses and would prefer to bring their shut-in capacity into production. This, of course, would have happened in 1973, or perhaps before, had the annual payment been retained at the 1969 levels hypothesized above. In an emergency, therefore, the government could act to retain the standby capacity by raising the payment or else let the reserve fulfill its function of flowing to market when external supplies were reduced.

Standby capacity would have had a number of advantages over alternative measures. First, compared with the quota, it would have preserved the ability of U.S. consumers to take advantage of lower world prices. The issue of energy security would not have prejudiced the efficient allocation of resources. Additionally, it would have retained for this nation unutilized petroleum reserves until the dimensions of replacement technology became clearer. If instead of following the "drain America first" policy implied by the quota, we had retained a portion of our oil reserves and used those of other countries, the current uncertainty in the development of new energy technology would have been lessened for this country. Compared with strategic storage, there are clear environmental benefits in retaining unproduced reserves underground. While environmental costs are included in the costs of storage, the possibility of an unanticipated cataclysmic disruption, or of unacknowledged marginal but cumulative environmental degradation is eliminated. Further, again compared with storage, there is some reason to believe that existence of standby capacity would have reduced the probability that oil exporters would have used supply disruption for political ends. The fact that standby capacity has no certain time limit, as has storage, means that an embargo implies a commitment to a virtually open-ended revenue drain for the exporting countries. They would have been unable to predict the point at which the United States would be forced to retreat from its position, and hence they might have been less inclined to initiate an embargo in the first instance.

The higher costs and inflexibility of standby capacity probably made it unacceptable as a sole source of energy security. The benefits described above may, however, make standby capacity attractive as an adjunct to any security program.

Comparing Alternative Programs

We have considered individual elements of alternatives to the generalized protective devices—some form of quota or tariff. It is now appropriate to consider policy bundles which may have been more attractive than the program chosen or than any of the single alternatives to it. Reconstruction of plausible policy bundles in this fashion does not imply that they would have been politically feasible during the period in question. But they may be feasible in the post-1973 world.

The mandatory quota program is the basis for comparing policy alternatives to achieve the levels of energy security chosen. The ramifications of this program were complex; they have been explored in great detail previously and cannot be adequately summarized here. The direct resource costs of the program in 1969 approximated $2.3 billion, with an additional transfer from consumers to producing interests and refiners of about $3.1 billion. As viewed by consumers of petroleum products, therefore, the cost of the program was about $5.4 billion. This cost can be compared with the estimated costs for alternative "bundles" of policy instruments which would provide a degree of energy security commensurate with that resulting from the program. These comparisons are incomplete because they do not include ancillary effects which by their nature are not quantifiable. They do, however, provide useful information for selecting from among possible approaches to future policy those which deserve more study.

Combined Storage and Standby Capacity

A program that combined storage and standby capacity would have been better than one that utilized either instrument alone as a means of dealing with the uncertainty of foreign energy supply. Standby capacity, even in the most favorable of circumstances, cannot be made available immediately. Moreover, the process of activating fields for temporary production is expensive. There remains, too, the political difficulty of actually retaining large installations that are not being used; that difficulty escalates as the cost of the installation increases. Storage combined with standby capacity would have significantly lowered these costs in 1969, the year selected for the comparison.

One possible mixture of storage and standby capacity would be a coverage of three-quarters of Arab imports, with one-quarter in storage and one-half held in standby capacity.[17] If Arab oil were

---

[17] This program is a "best estimate" of the level of protection commensurate with that provided by the mandatory quota program.

being imported at the 4 MMb/day level, standby capacity of 2 MMb/day might be adequate if accompanied by 90-day storage. The average daily available crude over one year would be 3 MMb/day, including drawdown of the stored oil. The annual storage cost for 90-day storage would be $281 million per year (with oil priced at $2.10 and using the higher storage cost estimate). The implicit price necessary to attract an additional 2 MMb/day of shut-in capacity would about equal the $3.27 actual price prevailing in 1969. At this price, the cost of 2 MMb/day standby capacity would be about $1.085 billion per year, using the other assumptions discussed above. The total cost of a policy combining standby capacity and storage geared toward the 4 MMb/day Arab import level in 1969 would thus approach $1.366 billion per year. These expenditures represent resources consumed, and thus may be compared to the estimated $2.3 billion resource cost of the mandatory quota program in 1969.

If a higher level of protection were chosen—one which considered the entire 9 MMb/day of estimated imports—the cost of storage and standby capacity would be substantially larger. Storage equal to imports for 90 days would cost $619 million. Standby capacity to cover insecure imports of 9 MMb/day could be reduced to 5 MMb/day if there were 90 days of storage. This would give an annual combined drawdown averaging 7.2 MM b/day, more than enough to cover any likely embargo. The implicit price of this much shut-in capacity would be $3.84 per barrel and would require an annual payment of $3.187 billion. The cost of this package of protection would thus be $3.806 billion. Again, this entire cost would represent resource use.

Consumption Tax Plus Storage and Standby Capacity

The increased consumption associated with the lower free trade price of oil greatly increases the cost of any security alternative because it increases the amount of insecure imports. For 1969, for example, consumption is estimated to increase from the actual 4.6 billion barrels to 5.5 billion barrels at the lower price. The associated increase in imports is nearly 2.5 MMb/day. An alternative policy package which would limit supply vulnerability could combine free imports—which would mean that domestic

Table 9-2. Constrained Consumption and Free Imports

(billion bbl/year)

Year	Consumption	Production	Imports	Eastern Hemisphere imports
1960	3.3	3.5	0.0	0.0
1961	3.4	3.2	0.2	0.0
1962	3.6	3.0	0.6	0.1
1963	3.6	2.7	0.9	0.4
1964	3.7	2.5	1.2	0.6
1965	3.9	2.2	1.7	0.9
1966	4.1	2.2	1.9	1.0
1967	4.2	2.2	2.0	1.0
1968	4.5	2.2	2.3	1.2
1969	4.6	2.2	2.4	1.3
1970	4.8	2.2	2.6	1.5

Source: From table 8-1, juxtaposing actual consumption and estimated "free trade" production: Eastern Hemisphere imports supply the remainder of consumption after all available Latin American production has been appropriated by the United States.

production would be based on the world price—with a consumption tax on all oil (foreign and domestic) to constrain the quantity demanded. The remaining vulnerability would then be countered with storage and standby capacity.

Specifically, let us consider a policy package in which a consumption tax was imposed so that the price to consumers would remain at the actual level in the United States over the decade of the 1960s (e.g., in 1969 the tax would have been $1.17/bbl). Total consumption would have remained at actual levels experienced during this period, but domestic production would have been replaced by imports to the extent estimated in chapter 8. Revised consumption, production, and import estimates are given in table 9-2. By 1969, production would have fallen to 2.2 billion barrels per year and required imports would have been 2.4 billion barrels (compared with 3.3 billion barrels). Required Eastern Hemisphere imports would have been no more than 1.3 billion barrels (down from 2.2 billion barrels), of which less than 1 billion need have come from Arab sources.

The revenue generated from the consumption tax, under this policy, could be used to pay for emergency storage and standby capacity, with any surplus returned to taxpayers. With a tax of $1.17 per barrel, total proceeds would amount to $5.4 billion per year at the 1969 consumption rate. This is, of course, the same transfer experienced by consumers under the mandatory quota program.

Storage costs for 250 million barrels (90 days' storage of Arab imports) would come to no more than $190 million per year (at the upper cost estimates provided above). In addition, 500 million barrels of standby annual production capacity would be required to meet the security levels identified above. Along with drawdown of storage, this level of standby capacity would provide three-fourths of the insecure imports for one year. Using the same procedure discussed in the standby capacity section above, and an implicit price of $2.58 per shut-in barrel, the cost would be $586 million per year. Total resource cost of the passive security portion of this program would thus be $776 million per year at the reconstructed 1969 level of imports with a tax that left consumer prices at their actual levels. Given that consumers would have suffered the same welfare loss as under the mandatory quota program (the price was the same), this $809 million can be compared directly to the estimated $2.3 billion resource cost of the mandatory quota program actually implemented.

Using this same policy structure and procedure, we may estimate the cost of the greater level of security implied by maintaining the ability to cover for one year three-fourths of all imports. The storage requirement for 90 days' supply (600 million barrels) would have cost $450 million per year using the estimates developed above. Standby capacity of 1.2 billion barrels per year (at an implicit supply price of $3.25 per barrel) would have cost $1.772 billion, for a total resource cost of $2.222 billion, or approximately the same resource cost as entailed by the mandatory quota program.

Tariff Plus Storage and Standby Capacity

Another alternative to the mandatory quota program could have been a tariff associated with storage and standby capacity. A tariff would increase the price of all oil to consumers, lowering consumption; it would increase the price to domestic producers, raising output. A reasonable program to protect against the interruption of estimated Arab imports would have imposed a tariff of 40 cents per barrel. At the resulting $2.50 price, consumption in 1969 would have reached 5.2 billion barrels (rather than the actual 4.6

billion), production 2.7 billion barrels (rather than 3.9), and imports 2.5 billion barrels (rather than 0.7). Under this scenario, we hypothesize Eastern Hemisphere imports would have reached 1.5 billion barrels in 1969, and oil from Arab sources would have been approximately 1 billion barrels. Import vulnerability would have been smaller than the face trade alternative (3.3 billion barrels total, with 2.2 billion from the Eastern Hemisphere and 1.5 billion from Arab countries), and consumers would have generated the funds directly and indirectly to pay its cost. The total transfer from consumers would have been $2.08 billion, of which $1.08 billion would have flowed directly to producers ($0.40 times 2.7 billion barrels) and $1 billion ($0.40 times 2.5 billion barrels) to the government as tariff receipts.

The cost of passive protection against insecurity again would have been made up of the annualized costs of storage and standby capacity. Storage of 250 million barrels, 90 days' supply, would have cost $190 million. Required standby annual production capacity of 500 million barrels would have been higher than under the consumption tax alternative discussed above because the industry, due to the higher target price ($2.50 rather than $2.10) would have already been producing further out on its supply schedule. Following the procedure discussed above, the implicit supply price of 500 million barrels of additional shut-in capacity would have been $2.96 per barrel, and the annual payment would have been $673 million. Total resource cost of the passive protection portion of this alternative would thus have been $863 million, a sum easily covered by the $1 billion government tariff receipts.

In comparing the total resource cost of this policy package with that of the mandatory quota program, account must be taken of the extra resources used in producing the additional domestic oil (500 million barrels) induced by the higher domestic price. The extra resources consumed per barrel would be the difference between the domestic price with a tariff ($2.50) and the world price ($2.10), less the extra domestic rent transferred to producers. Given the assumed supply elasticity of 1.0, one-half (20 cents) of the per barrel extra payments to domestic producers would represent resource costs.[18] Multiplied by 500 million barrels per year, the

---

[18] The remaining 20 cents per barrel is already included in consumer cost.

annual charge is $100 million. Added to the costs of storage and standby capacity, this leaves $965 million as the resource costs which would have been incurred had this security policy been adopted to guard against interruption of Arab imports.

Conclusions

The mandatory quota program was only one of many alternatives which could have been chosen to enhance U.S. energy security. As we suggest elsewhere, it was selected because it met important political goals in addition to its contributions to energy security.

The mandatory quota program was costly. In 1969 we estimate that the program resulted in direct transfers from consumers on the order of $5 billion, and in resource costs it represented a drain upon the economy of approximately $2.3 billion. It appears that a commensurate level of security could have been provided with less substantial direct effects had any one of a number of alternative programs been pursued instead. The comparisons involved are, of course, imprecise; we indicate in some detail that the imprecision results from difficulty in ascertaining the objective function to be achieved by the policy as well as from measurement and estimation problems. The magnitudes of the differences found, however, sufficiently dwarf the analytical and estimation problems to suggest that the mandatory quota program was not the optimal instrument to achieve the public policy goal of enhancing security.

Approaches to energy security may be characterized by whether they achieve their end by reducing imports (active policies), or whether they provide security through minimizing the effect of supply interruptions (passive policies). The active policies considered include the mandatory quota program itself and a protective tariff designed to accomplish the same end. While the direct effects of a tariff are similar to those of a quota, the indirect effects are substantially different. Use of the tariff instrument would have avoided much of the bureaucratic machinery made necessary to allocate quota licenses. Moreover, the arbitrary decisions described in chapters 3 through 6 would have been unnecessary and their detrimental effects upon the process of government avoided. Similarly, the tariff instrument would not have induced the waste and inefficiency, the distortions of market incentives, and the creation of special interests which plagued the petroleum industry and petroleum policy even after the end of the mandatory quota program. In short, given the decision to meet the needs of energy security by restricting imports through greater domestic production and lower consumption, the tariff instrument had substantial advantages which were surrendered when the mandatory quota program was implemented.

Subsidies and consumption taxes could also have been used to promote energy security through continuous reduction of imports. The direct and indirect effects of these instruments are largely the same as those of a tariff. A tariff, however, is more general in its effects, and less capable of being targeted on particular aspects of energy supply and demand. While there are some advantages with a "targetable" instrument, specificity of impact also gives rise to the discriminatory potential that was so detrimental to both economic efficiency and the perceived equity and legitimacy of government action under the program actually used. In addition, sole reliance on either consumption taxes or subsidies alone would have been more disruptive than use of a tariff. Distortions and inefficiencies increase more than proportionally with the depth to which a policy must cut, so that constraining either energy supply or demand would have been less satisfactory than operating on both together. We conclude that, had an active energy security policy been indicated, a general protective tariff, perhaps including some discrimination in favor of imports judged more secure, would have been the policy of choice.

Policies designed to protect against the more serious consequences of petroleum supply interruptions could also have been used. As the estimates for 1969 indicate, however, such programs as emergency storage and standby capacity, taken alone, would have been demonstrably less satisfactory than in combination with actions that increased domestic production and reduced consumption. The estimates above indicate that substantial benefits could have been captured had such combination programs been implemented. These alternatives were not considered seriously in the period leading up to implementation of the quota program. This omission may be explained by the novelty of these approaches, by the institutional rigidities of decision making, by the special interests that the alternative chosen served, and by the fact that the program evolved from a series of incremental changes that never offered a real opportunity for review of the options available. It can also be explained, however, by the fact that the security problem was never taken really seriously, and by the fact that implementation of the mandatory quota program itself did not represent a substantial drain on national resources in the context of the world oil market in which it was operating.

The Arab embargo of 1973 awakened national attention to the dangers of energy insecurity. A national will has developed to respond to the dangers posed by it. Changes in the world oil market and in the domestic supply–demand balance at world prices at the same time have made approaches such as the mandatory quota program obsolete; the costs of attaining energy security in the future through a similar program would be prohibitive.

10

The Quota Program and
Subsequent Energy Policy

We have indicated throughout this study that institutional factors affected each aspect of the implementation and administration of the mandatory quota program. Not surprisingly, these factors, not economic efficiency requirements, dominated decisions on energy policy during the 1959–73 period. The arguments for import controls may have been couched in national security terms, but it was political forces that led to the decision to adopt them. The quota instrument was selected to implement these controls because it could be adapted to diverse ends and to meet political goals. The economic ramifications of the quota program were discussed in chapters 6 and 8. This chapter examines some of the political influences that derive from the quota program, and that affected energy policymaking after it ended. It also suggests implications for the direction of energy policy in the future and notes that while the thrust of policy may be already determined, some freedom remains to select among instruments to implement it.

Energy Policy After the Quota

The same factors that influenced the development of the quota program continued to affect energy policy development after direct import controls were abandoned. They were intensified and made more complex by the special interests created by the controls themselves. The embargo and OPEC price increase of 1973 increased suspicion and hostility against oil-exporting governments, enhanced anxiety about energy supplies, and elicited a mood of further withdrawal into autarky. The international oil companies who served as intermediaries between oil exporters and consumers also lost favor with the general public. Consequently, efforts to achieve agreement on an energy policy strained the political system and did not produce results completely satisfactory to any party.

The major matters requiring a policy response after the effective demise of the quota program were the market pressures created by price controls; the disruption resulting from the October 1973 embargo and long-term energy insecurity; the increased relative price of energy; and the prospective difficulty of the transition to more abundant or inexhaustible energy supplies. The ultimate response to each of these issues, through 1975, was to reject a market solution and to impose more and more centralized decision making. In substance, the response was to downplay economic efficiency in favor of policies which met political, including distributional, goals. The pattern that began with state demand prorationing continued with the decision to restrict oil imports and to adopt the quota system, and was reinforced in a series of decisions between 1973 and 1976.

Response to the Market Strains from Oil Price Controls

Price controls associated with the Economic Stabilization Act created the first test of energy policy direction after the effective end of the quota program. Market-clearing prices were precluded, and, as noted in chapter 6, imports were effectively constrained. Scattered shortages of petroleum products occurred. While controls were a major cause of the shortages, the public placed the blame on the oil industry, and especially on the major integrated oil companies. The shortages became politically impossible to ignore, and the response then was to add more controls, not to eliminate those which were causing the problem. President Nixon in his June 1973 energy message had emphasized the desirability of freeing energy prices, but nonetheless he instituted allocations of propane and middle distillate fuels. Fuel allocation was thus adopted before the substantial price increases of 1973 occurred, and before the embargo. Its continuation was inevitable with the added strains that followed.

The effect of adding the allocation system to price controls was to lower still further the incentive of oil companies to increase supplies. Before allocation was in effect, increased supplies could be used to assure, and perhaps expand, market shares, even if their incremental cost was greater than their controlled selling price. When allocation led to transfers of such supplies to competitors, however, that incentive disappeared entirely. Hence, the controls designed to "manage" the control-created shortage increased the shortage itself.

The attitudes reinforced in the quota period were instrumental in the adoption of ever-tightening controls. There was hostility and suspicion of the major oil companies. Actions consistent with market incentives were seen as an exercise of inordinate market power. Energy was considered a commodity over which price and allocation controls were required, even though the rest of the economy might be free. Income distribution effects were given precedence over efficiency results, and protecting consumers against price increases and protecting the small and nonintegrated sectors of the industry were chosen over efficient allocation of resources. In short, attitudes were such that when strains arose, the special interests created by the quota program were sustained despite changes in objective conditions.

Response to the Embargo and Energy Insecurity

The oil embargo of 1973 thus occurred in a context in which a market solution had lost legitimacy as the fundamental guide for energy activity.[1] Partly because the problem was imposed from

[1] We pointed out earlier that the "embargo" was made effective by an overall reduction in world oil production, not by the effort to target U.S. consumption by the Arab producers. What occurred was a temporary reduction in oil supply which led to a substantial price increase to consumers. The Arab oil exporters, for their own internal reasons, chose to garb this reduction in political terms as aimed against the United States. The United States, in turn, chose to respond to it in like manner. There was surely a political component in the oil supply reduction, but it should be recognized for what it was: an economic action aimed against all oil-consuming nations to induce them to alter their behavior toward Israel. No "embargo" can be targeted toward a single consumer unless all major OPEC nations join in the effort and unless post-shipment transportation and distribution links are controlled by OPEC. For

abroad, an effective economic response to the oil supply reduction and associated price increases was subordinated to a political reaction. It was hard for most politicians to conceive, much less choose, a market solution to the decline in energy supply. The passage of the Emergency Petroleum Allocation Act in the fall of 1973 provided the statutory basis for the allocation program, and though its short-term focus was indicated by its scheduled expiration (February 15, 1975), it implemented far-reaching controls which affected the way energy would be supplied and consumed. Under this act, crude oil buy–sell requirements were established, user priorities were authorized, the refinery output mix could be modified, and price controls were made both more binding and more detailed. The status quo, including the distortions arising from the quota program, was largely written into the regulations.

The embargo of 1973–74 thus was "managed," to the extent it was handled at all, largely through central allocation. Both the Democratic Congress and the Republican administration joined in this decision. In his November 7, 1973 speech, President Nixon called for voluntary reductions in energy use, downward adjustments in fuel allocations to certain users and industries, reduced federal energy consumption, and most importantly, he ordered that contingency plans be prepared for formal rationing to consumers and for special taxation of oil products.[2] In his follow-up address of November 25, 1973, the president announced further measures to restrict energy use in order to protect fuel supplies for industry and home heating.[3] In his January 19, 1974 address, the president explicitly rejected a price-based allocation of fuel supplies during the embargo.[4] Nonetheless, the Nixon administration continued to call for a market approach to the long-run energy security problem. Higher prices, supplemented by federal

reasons given previously, the preconditions for such an embargo did not exist in 1973 and are unlikely to exist in the foreseeable future. We continue to use the term "embargo," however, because the 1973–74 situation was viewed that way by participants.

[2] Richard M. Nixon, Address, November 7, 1973, *Executive Energy Messages*, U.S. Senate, Committee on Interior and Insular Affairs, Serial No. 94-22 (92-112), 1975, pp. 81–87.

[3] Richard M. Nixon, Address, November 25, 1973, *Executive Energy Messages*, pp. 99–102.

[4] Richard M. Nixon, Address, January 19, 1974, *Executive Energy Messages*, pp. 116–117.

R and D and other activities, would lead the nation closer to energy independence, which in turn would make it invulnerable to foreign disruption. But this approach was relegated to the future; for the period of emergency, not only did governmental action restrict a market-oriented response, but the rhetoric of even a Republican president rejected such a response *in principle*.

The end of the embargo found little policy in place to deal specifically with future embargos. However, a pattern had developed. The supply reduction was handled as a political problem involving economic effects, not as an economic problem with political repercussions. This response created expectations of what would be done in the event of future oil supply disruptions: the federal government would "nationalize" the available oil supply and allocate it on the basis of government-chosen criteria as to need. Such expectations discouraged efforts by the private sector to prepare for an uncertain future. It became clear that the cost of such preparations would be borne individually, but that benefits would be shared collectively.[5]

The energy security program adopted by President Ford in the fall and winter of 1974–75 exhibited some of the ambivalence of early Nixon efforts: it retained elements of a market approach to the long-term problem but added an administered dimension for energy disruptions during the interim.[6] Embargo protection prior to energy independence was to be provided by a strategic petroleum storage program and various standby and planning authorities. Congress, however, was unwilling to accede to a program relying primarily upon private market forces, while the Ford administration stood ready to block a complete government takeover of the energy market, even if Congress could have agreed on such a course. The Energy Policy and Conservation Act of 1975, when it came in late December, was the product of this stalemate.

The political (rather than economic) approach to energy security as an international issue was initiated formally when the United

[5] It should be noted, however, that private oil storage did rise sharply between the end of the embargo and early 1976, according to an American Petroleum Institute survey. "Private Oil-Storage Capacity Up 300 Million bbl Since Embargo," *Oil and Gas Journal* May 24, 1976, pp. 36–37.

[6] Executive Office of the President, Energy Independence Act of 1975, Submission to the Congress (The White House, mimeo, January 30, 1975).

States, led by Henry Kissinger as secretary of state, convened the Consumer Energy Conference in Washington in February 1974. It was designed to weld together an alliance of consumer countries that could bargain with the OPEC nations on more equal terms than could individual consuming countries. This effort culminated in the organization of the International Energy Agency and in associated agreements to share supplies in the event of an embargo, to share energy technologies, and, most relevant for oil import controls (at least in principle), to hold domestic oil prices *up*.

The latter device, which was promoted under the title "minimum safeguard price" (MSP), was predicated on the fear that a precipitous price break could restrict efforts contributing to energy independence.[7] With an MSP, it was argued, producers of substitutes for OPEC oil would be encouraged to expand investment because the risk of an energy price below the MSP would be eliminated. Consumers of energy also would be induced to develop and install additional energy-saving processes. They could be more confident conservation investments would pay off because the energy price to consumers would not be allowed to fall below MSP, whatever happened to the OPEC price.

The national and international conflict over the MSP was, predictably, very intense; substantial leverage was required, and used, to obtain the assent of those consuming nations without substantial energy production prospects. Domestically, the proposition was finally accepted more as a means to show that something was being "done" than with any view that substantial benefits would accrue. Indeed, the policy debate had an Alice-in-Wonderland quality in which MSP was depicted internally as necessary to bring the consuming nations together, while abroad those same consuming nations were being told that they must agree to MSP in order to obtain other benefits the United States was willing to bestow.[8] The

---

[7] Curiously, advocates of the MSP had conflicting views of the resiliency and cohesiveness of the OPEC cartel. Some felt that the cartel was so strong that it could manipulate prices, first down and then up, and thus preclude an effective non-OPEC supply response. Others felt that with an MSP the non-OPEC supply could be so great as to "break" OPEC, and perhaps OPEC would break anyway. Clearly, while substantial energy producers could thus support an MSP on either ground, those without domestic production would find little advantage in doing so if OPEC were indeed vulnerable to disarray.

[8] It is intriguing to note that the administration agreed to put a *floor* under the price of imported oil at roughly the same level that it agreed to put a *ceiling* over domestic oil.

MSP agreement did not dictate what method of price support was to be used by each member nation, but discussion within U.S. government circles revolved around possible use of a tariff or of the quota instrument; the latter had the advantage because it could be implemented quickly and was well understood.

With IEA and MSP in place, the consuming countries thought themselves prepared to negotiate with OPEC. There were two goals of these negotiations: assured supplies and lower prices. Neither were realized. Assuring continued supplies was consistent with the economic interest of OPEC nations, but credible agreements could not be reached. Overriding political goals of some OPEC members were inconsistent with a promise to be reliable suppliers, and in any event, there was no mechanism to guarantee performance. The price of oil, in turn, was found to be a direct distributional issue not subject to a negotiated settlement that would improve the position of both parties. It could be demonstrated that high oil prices harmed the world economy, lowered the welfare of the nonoil LDCs, and heightened international instability, but it could not be demonstrated that OPEC as a whole could be compensated for lowering the oil price.

The danger to the U.S. position was that once oil price and availability were accepted as fit subjects for negotiation among countries, then those matters lost their market orientation. They could be affected more easily than before by other political issues and the United States could in some ways be left in a more vulnerable position than it was before. For example, the OPEC countries sought to protect the price of oil against depreciation through inflation. For the United States to accept "indexation" to prevent the relative price of oil from falling would strengthen OPEC pricing power because it might enlist the U.S. government in policing price shavers. Or again, once the international price of oil was set in diplomatic forums rather than in the marketplace, the demand for similar treatment of other commodities produced by less developed countries could prove irresistible. Moreover, once the United States stated that another nation had no right to interrupt oil supplies, this nation's freedom to restrict food exports in time of agricultural emergency was lessened. Having originally responded to the energy security issue as an international political problem, the United States was ultimately forced to scramble to avoid the unpleasant consequences of its original action.

The policy record regarding supply security was thus of the same order as the response to the strains created by price controls: sufficient increases in government intervention in the domestic and international energy markets to preclude an adequate private response, but not enough to achieve the ends sought. Though the private market alternative was enunciated, and though it conformed to the ideological predilections of the Nixon and Ford administrations, it was not pursued with sufficient vigor and commitment to achieve success. Indeed, the domestic actions taken by the Nixon administration during the 1973–74 embargo restricted the nation's ability to adopt a market orientation later, just as the early diplomatic efforts marked commodity prices as fit subjects for intergovernmental attention rather than leaving them to economic forces. With the weakened presidency during 1973–75, the administration was unable or unwilling to undertake a campaign to change public attitudes in the face of a hostile Congress. But it was also unable to face up to the implications of this decision. Thus it did not embrace the pervasive controls and broad-scale nationalization that would have been required if energy security were to be provided by fiat.

Response to Higher World Energy Prices

After the embargo was over, and the emergency mood dissipated, the issue became how to adjust to higher world energy prices. The availability of unlimited quantities of foreign oil at the world price meant that ceilings on domestic prices could be sustained without creating shortages—the result would instead be that imports would rise, both relatively and absolutely. Consequently, the choice between the two basic alternatives—restricting the domestic price or allowing it to go to world levels—had direct implications for energy security.

A two-tier crude oil pricing system, under which "new" and imported oil was removed from controls, had been established before the late-1973 price increase. The expectation was that the ceiling price on "old" oil would be allowed to rise. The rapid rise in imported oil prices in late 1973, however, and the failure of Congress to enact a windfall profits tax, meant that one increase for "old" oil—from roughly $4.25/bbl to approximately $5.25/bbl—in the fall of 1973 was all that was politically feasible. When in late 1974 petroleum product shortages disappeared, refiners with relatively high-cost crude supplies lost their markets and faced bankruptcy. Rather than decontrol all prices, the policy response was to equalize the cost of crude to different refiners by requiring those with price-controlled supplies to subsidize competitors who purchased a disproportionate amount of high-cost foreign and domestic crude, just as tidewater refiners were required to share with all refiners the benefits of low-cost imported oil at an earlier period. All consumers were thus faced with product prices based on the average, not the incremental, price of oil. The political effect of this decision was to create vested interests in controls where none existed before, and to eliminate some industry pressure for abandoning controls. Its economic effect was to increase energy consumption and imports and to lower allocational efficiency.

The instrument used to implement this program was a lineal descendant of the mandatory quota program. The "entitlements" system, as it was called, continued many of the same provisions and exceptions of that program, but substituted government decree for market transactions in determining the charge for the entitlements (quota tickets). A quota program allocating the right to process cheap foreign oil was thus transmuted into a program allocating the right to process cheap domestic crude.

The Ford administration proposal with regard to energy prices (described in chapter 6) was that the economy be required to adjust to the levels established by OPEC. Congress did not accept the president's pricing program, and as 1975 dragged on, the country became more confused, divided, and bored with energy policy. As energy supplies became adequate, as the sense of urgency declined, and as the 1976 elections drew nearer, there was less and less willingness to make the hard decisions that were required, and more and more temptation to temporize. After a number of last-minute extensions of controls and a presidental effort to put a phased decontrol program into place, Congress passed the Energy Policy and Conservation Act of 1975 (EPCA), which reduced domestic oil prices from what they were, and perpetuated controls on them.

EPCA represented a reversal of the principles originally supported by the Ford administration. While under the EPCA the president was empowered to remove price controls after 40 months, it was clear that the price of domestic oil then might not be much closer to the world price than it was in 1975 and that pressure to retain controls would consequently be great. Special interests in regulation would be well established, onerous and even silly regulations would have lost some of their capacity to shock, and adjustments to resource misallocation would be well underway.

The conflict over how to respond to the changed relative price of energy was thus settled by choosing to minimize the observed change and by accepting the costs of higher world oil prices in other forms. These costs include losses from inefficient resource allocation; a higher level of imports; public expenditures to increase energy supplies, to reduce energy demand, and to prepare for supply disruptions; and the loss of flexibility and responsiveness in the economy. In the political milieu of 1975 these costs were either ignored or considered acceptable when the alternative was a free market in oil. Thus, as with the two previous issues we considered, the microeconomically efficient policy choice was rejected in favor of a politically more expedient path; that path was made easier to choose because of the precedents set and special interests created by the mandatory quota program.

The Transition Away from Oil and Gas

The final policy issue addressed in the post-1973 period was the process by which the nation would move from primary reliance on oil and gas to reliance on more abundant or inexhaustible energy sources. Once an oil price policy had been adopted which, by holding prices down, increased consumption and lowered the private incentive to find and utilize substitutes, it became more necessary for government to consider alternative means to make energy supplies available. The Ford administration proposed specific legislation to support creation of private nuclear fuel enrichment facilities and to promote development of synthetic liquid and gaseous fuels. It also proposed, but did not support intensively, a comprehensive financial program (the Energy Independence Authority) to benefit a wide spectrum of energy-related activities. In these efforts the Ford administration sought to redress the distortion it had in part created. In a reversal of form, these initiatives represented a political response to an economic problem that did *not* get support from the Congress. However, Congress and the administration did agree in principle that research and development activities for future energy production and conservation should be sponsored by the federal government.

Energy Policy for the Future

Passage of EPCA in late 1975 did not resolve the policy issues. The combination of market forces and legislation then in force left three interdependent energy concerns pending. Policy was left to deal with (1) the rising cost of energy, (2) the increasing vulnerability to import disruption, and (3) the timely transition in the long run from primary dependence on oil and gas toward reliance on more abundant or renewable energy sources.

The real cost of energy, its replacement cost, was determined by the cost of imported oil; that cost was expected to rise in the foreseeable future. Since 1973, U.S. energy prices to consumers and producers had been held below the replacement cost of energy. To continue this policy would have meant a subsidy to energy consumption and a tax on domestic production, results which would have further increased real energy costs to the economy. But it would have had other effects beyond those which influenced the ratio between domestic consumption and production. For example, an increase in the price of energy would have affected such aspects of the nation's well-being as environmental amenities, income distribution, the level of economic activity, and future productivity. The issue was further complicated because the real cost of energy may be dependent upon U.S. policy. A policy to reduce imports through government intervention, for example, would have raised the effective cost of energy to Americans above the world level. Alternatively, a policy of broader and more productive economic ties between oil-producing and oil-consuming nations might have reduced pressure within OPEC for rising prices.[9]

Dependence on imported energy supplies was the basic reason for special concern about energy relative to other commodities.

[9] See the authors' *U.S. Energy Policy: Alternatives for Security* (Baltimore, Johns Hopkins University Press for Resources for the Future, 1975) chapter 6.

The risk associated with imports had been the basis for energy policy in the past, just as it is likely in the future to be the driving force behind policy. The temptation to respond as before with quantitative controls ran up against the plain fact that conditions had changed. In short, the United States had less capacity than before to satisfy petroleum demands domestically, and no monopsonistic power to exert in holding import prices down. Hence, to adopt quantitative controls would conflict even more seriously than before with the aims fulfilled by lower energy costs. Nonetheless, as we point out below, their imposition remains a distinct possibility.

Both rising energy costs and continued vulnerability affected possible approaches to the third policy problem: achieving, on a timely basis, a nondisruptive shift from primary dependence on oil and natural gas to reliance on more abundant domestic energy sources, particularly coal. This transition could have been speeded by measures that raised the cost of using oil and natural gas, measures that lowered the price of using alternatives, or by direct regulation. However, taxes, subsidies, and regulations were all politically sensitive, and the speed of the transition was known to affect potential tradeoffs in such areas as environmental quality and the production growth rate of goods and services. The broader question, of course, was whether any such policy was required; whether, that is, market forces, as constrained by other energy policies, would not yield a satisfactory rate of growth in alternatives.

The crucial question in 1976 was how the nation would respond to these problems, and that question remained open at the time of this writing. The record of the past offers some guidance on what to expect—broader government control—and also suggests the requirements for exercising it effectively.

The Prospective Role of Government

The role of government in the energy sector is now large and will likely grow larger. Alternative paths emphasizing economic criteria and utilizing market institutions may be (and, in our view, are) preferable, but, given the record of the past two decades, and particularly the legacy of the mandatory control program, they are not likely to be chosen. While market forces continue to dominate decisions in some phases of the energy industry, a market system does not exist. That is to say, the quantities of energy that will be consumed, produced, and imported are not determined by a multitude of interlocking but independent private decisions based on economic interest. The quantities of resources that will be devoted to investment in energy production and consumption for the future are not the result of self-adjusting individual responses to the alternatives available. Those private decisions which remain are largely limited to reactions to the incentives created by the government and by the OPEC cartel. For example, private parties continue to decide to drill for oil in particular areas, but the price incentive to which they respond is imposed from without; it does not evolve from the aggregated activities of prospective consumers and producers of petroleum. Or again, energy research and development continues to be performed mostly by the private sector, but mainly in response to the decisions and expenditures of government, based on judgments as to the socially optimal level and direction of such activity.

Substantial changes would be required in strongly held beliefs and in increasingly pervasive and powerful institutions to reverse the drift toward centralized decision making in energy matters. Such a reversal failed during the Nixon and Ford years and is unlikely to be more successful in the future. It is feasible that if the existing arrangement does not bring satisfactory results, such a restructuring of the energy sector could take place. It is more likely, however, that failure would be ascribed to the private sector and broader government responsibility would follow. In that case, it is critical that government be able to act effectively.

The absence of a private energy decision system places substantial responsibility upon government. For the medium term, that responsibility will likely be driven by the effort to limit the level of oil imports and to restrict importers to more "secure" suppliers. Import levels, and through them the source of imports, derive from the level of energy consumption and domestic energy supply. If it is to control import levels, then, government must also have some control over the amount and kind of energy demanded and supplied. In achieving this control, government may be forced to modify lifestyles to achieve its goals. It must establish mechanisms to determine an appropriate consumption mix among fuels, and do so without the guidance provided by consumer decisions among products with variable relative prices. It must determine appropriate levels for research and development on energy consumption and production and be prepared to achieve those levels either directly or by motivating the private sector. It must also determine the investment levels needed to meet the established supply goals and see that this investment is made. These tasks must be carried out with appropriate consideration of alternative uses of capital, within acceptable bounds of environmental quality, and without the guidance of responsive relative prices. Clearly, this set of tasks requires a massive undertaking and an unprecedented level of detailed intervention in consumer and producer decisions.

The U.S. government was without either the authority or the instruments to make and implement decisions required of a centralized system, even after passage of the energy legislation of 1973–75. Four additional institutions or arrangements were required to fulfill the energy responsibilities left to government by the attenuation of the market system; energy policy will be affected by the way they evolve.

The first of these is an administrative apparatus and set of mechanisms through which decisions could be transmitted to the private sector. The requisite authorities to some extent have been available on a standby basis, but permanent and active instruments are required to allocate energy among competing uses, to induce production of certain energy sources, to motivate minimum energy efficiencies in consumption and to decide upon energy-environment tradeoffs. The lesson of the mandatory quota program is that quantitative regulations are less flexible and responsive to change than are economic incentives which induce voluntary responses from the private sector. Being more explicit and visible, economic incentives are also less likely to be the vehicles by which special interests are served to the detriment, and against the wishes, of the majority. Consequently, the experience with the quota program suggests that in implementing policy, taxes and subsidies which shift relative prices would be preferable to instruments which attempt to dictate desired outcomes directly.

The second element necessary for a centrally controlled energy sector is a decision framework capable of meshing the interacting subsectors involved in producing, consuming, and importing energy. The essence of that framework is a monitoring system capable of signaling when adjustments are required so that substantial dislocations can be avoided. If a market system does not exist, an administrative substitute to perform its information and coordination function is required.

Beyond the operational elements suggested above, consensus is required about the basic energy–economy–environmental goals of society and about the process by which they are to be sought. The consensus on national defense might serve as an example of the level of agreement required. There are disagreements over more bombers or fewer nuclear submarines, but not over the basic military mission. Military action to repulse armed aggression is a policy which has legitimacy, and the Executive Branch has the authority to carry it out. Analogously, political conflicts over energy are tolerable at the margin—somewhat more or less production, consumption, or imports—but not over positions as fundamental as negative energy growth versus unlimited stripmining of coal, or over the free market versus government control. Achieving this consensus will be extremely difficult; its absence marked the period of conflict and confusion following the embargo.

Finally, principles of separation between the centrally controlled energy sector and the self-regulating private sector are required. Such boundaries are necessarily fuzzy, but they must be drawn with maximum precision and rigor if energy controls are not to beget other controls. Even so, there remains a question of how satisfactorily an economy can function when parts that respond to market forces must be integrated with others where political decisions rule.

It is clear that as of 1976 the trio of concerns regarding energy price, reliability of supply, and future energy availability retained their importance as objects of policy analysis and debate. The energy and related sectors of the U.S. economy were directed by an unsatisfactory and unstable melange of market and political forces. In area after area, the conditions resulting from application of the existing combination of policies were found unsatisfactory— so unsatisfactory as to suggest the necessity for their modification or replacement. Energy security was of particular importance.

Import Controls in the Future

The level and perceived reliability of oil imports likely to be engendered by policies in place at the end of 1975 was widely thought to leave the United States excessively vulnerable to foreign disruption. We conclude that strong action, such as imposition of quantitative import controls, will commend itself to those who view energy security as a primary goal of policy and price responses as unsatisfactory means to achieve it. The implications of such controls should be understood before they are imposed, and the record of the mandatory quota program yields some insights as to those implications.

Once quantitative import controls are instituted, the import safety valve which makes domestic price controls possible without rationing will be closed, and the nation will be forced to choose an even more fully planned energy sector or else make a break with the previous quarter-century and attempt to institute a market system. Given the political forces described earlier in the work, including the legacy of the mandatory quota program, such a break with the past is highly unlikely.

The choice between quotas and other instruments such as tariffs bears careful examination because the mechanism chosen can have an important bearing on the ability of the economy to meet other goals. For example, the record of the mandatory quota program suggests that the rigidities imposed by quantitative controls would be difficult to remove if objective conditions changed in the future so as to make them unnecessary. Beyond the question of instrument, moreover, there remains the more basic question of whether quantitative import controls are desirable even within a centralized energy decision system.

Quantitative import controls, whether they result in higher prices or in rationing, impose costs on the economy. The issue is what and how much may be gained in exchange for these expenditures. Possible gains may arise from two effects. First, the lower level of imports would reduce the demand for OPEC oil and might therefore lead to lower oil prices, but that conclusion rests on the assumption that the OPEC cartel works in a specified way, and other assumptions are perhaps equally plausible. Moreover, it implies that lower imports can be best achieved through a quota, though this same end might instead be better reached indirectly through higher domestic energy supply or lower oil consumption. If lower world oil prices did result, however, they would benefit all oil consumers, not just the United States; the benefits from imposing import controls would be shared internationally, while the costs would rest solely on the United States.

Second, import controls would lessen the amount of oil that others could deny the United States. Import controls represent a boycott—a self-imposed embargo—which can be implemented at the rate and level chosen by the importer to minimize disruption, rather than on terms of the exporter's choosing. As to the resulting embargo "protection," then, the choice between import controls and free trade (from the import security aspect) involves a trade-off between two sets of economic costs: the present value of the *uncertain* future costs of an embargo that would be prevented by import limitations, versus the present value of *certain* current and future costs imposed by the import controls themselves. Import controls involve, in other words, certain present costs that will continue indefinitely, while embargo costs are uncertain, in the future, and, if they occur, may not last forever. Viewed in this way, the probability of an embargo must be very high, and its future costs must be substantially larger than those of a boycott, if import controls are to be justified on economic grounds. The political and international repercussions of an embargo are largely dependent upon the economic costs it imposes, not on denial of oil *per se,* and hence even these factors, when considered carefully, resolve into a comparison between prospective economic outcomes.

Import controls on oil during the mandatory control program served as an instrument to achieve goals other than energy security in itself. Energy security in the context of a broad government energy policy, however, need not bear the same extraneous burdens. It can be implemented by measures judged solely by their efficiency in achieving that single goal. Once other energy-related goals are approached as fit matters for political decision and government intervention, it will be unnecessary to use energy security as a subterfuge. Consequently, a more centralized and political energy decision structure, paradoxically, may make it possible to choose more efficient import control instruments, or to conclude that, despite their simplistic appeal, quantitative import controls of any sort are unwieldy means of achieving desired ends.

A nationalized or centralized energy production and consumption system means that the costs of energy security will be internalized to the decision makers. The system will bring with it a price tag composed of some combination of explicit economic costs and explicit consumer–citizen dissatisfaction. It will also bring levels of energy security that are easier to measure and to evaluate than in the mixed public–private system which existed during the mandatory quota program.

Conditions changed dramatically during the existence of the Mandatory Oil Import Program, and changed even more after the embargo of 1973–74. Nonetheless, it remains true that both the economic effects of that program and the institutional and political forces it brought in its train demonstrate that what are thought to be circumscribed efforts to respond in a limited way to particular problems sometimes have far-reaching effects. The ultimate lesson for policy to be drawn from this analysis is that great care should be taken to understand what those effects may be before instituting any such program. And beyond that, it is also imperative to build in a mechanism through which policy can be reversed in case unforeseen effects prove deleterious.

Index

Library of Congress Cataloging in Publication Data

Bohi, Douglas R
 Limiting oil imports.

 Includes index.
 1. Petroleum industry and trade—United States. 2. Import quotas—United States.
3. Energy policy—United States—History. I. Russell, Milton, 1933–joint author.
II. Resources for the Future. III. Title.

HD9566.B59   382′.42′2820973   77-18881
ISBN 0-8018-2106-1